ESSENTIALS OF
ORGANIZATIONAL BEHAVIOR

ESSENTIALS OF ORGANIZATIONAL BEHAVIOR

tenth edition

Stephen P. Robbins

San Diego State University

Timothy A. Judge

University of Florida

Prentice Hall

Upper Saddle River, NJ 07458

Library of Congress Cataloging-in-Publication Data

Robbins, Stephen P.
  Essentials of organizational behavior/Stephen P. Robbins, Timothy A. Judge.—10th ed.
  p. cm.
  Includes bibliographical references and index.
  ISBN 0-13-607761-7
  1. Organizational behavior.   I. Judge, Tim.   II. Title.
  HD58.7.R6 2009
  658.3—dc22   2008055739

Acquisitions Editor: Jennifer M. Collins
Editorial Director: Sally Yagan
Product Development Manager: Ashley Santora
Editorial Assistant: Elizabeth Davis
Editorial Project Manager: Claudia Fernandes
Director of Marketing: Patrice Lumumba Jones
Marketing Manager: Nikki Jones
Marketing Assistant: Ian Gold
Permissions Project Manager: Charles Morris
Senior Managing Editor: Judy Leale
Production Project Manager: Kelly Warsak

Senior Operations Specialist: Arnold Vila
Operations Specialist: Benjamin Smith
Senior Art Director: Janet Slowik
Designer: Steve Frim
Interior Design: Janet Slowik/Steve Frim
Cover Designer: Ray Cruz
Composition: GGS Publishing Services
Full-Service Project Management: Ann Courtney/GGS Higher Education Resources, A Divison of Premedia Global, Inc.
Cover Printer: Lehigh-Phoenix Color/Hagerstown
Printer/Binder: Edwards Brothers
Typeface: 10/12 Janson Text

Credits and acknowledgments borrowed from other sources and reproduced, with permission, in this textbook appear on appropriate page within text.

Pearson Education Ltd., London
Pearson Education Singapore, Pte. Ltd
Pearson Education, Canada, Inc.
Pearson Education–Japan
Pearson Education Upper Saddle River, New Jersey

Pearson Education Australia PTY, Limited
Pearson Education North Asia, Ltd., Hong Kong
Pearson Educación de Mexico, S.A. de C.V.
Pearson Education Malaysia, Pte. Ltd

Prentice Hall
is an imprint of

www.pearsonhighered.com

10 9 8 7 6 5 4 3 2 1
ISBN-13: 978-0-13-607761-9
ISBN-10: 0-13-607761-7

This book is dedicated to our friends and colleagues in

The Organizational Behavior Teaching Society,

who, through their teaching research and commitment

to the learning process, have significantly

improved the ability of students

to understand and apply OB concepts.

Brief Contents

Contents

ix

Preface

This book was created as an alternative to the 600- or 700-page comprehensive text-book in organizational behavior (OB). It attempts to provide balanced coverage of all the key elements comprising the discipline of OB, in a style that readers will find both informative and interesting. We're pleased to say that this text has achieved a wide following in short courses and executive programs, as well as in traditional courses as a companion volume with experiential, skill development, case, and readings books. It is currently used at more than 500 colleges and universities in the United States, Canada, Latin America, Europe, Australia, and Asia. It's also been translated into Spanish, Portuguese, Japanese, Chinese, Dutch, Polish, Turkish, Danish, and Bahasa Indonesian.

RETAINED FROM THE PREVIOUS EDITION

What do people like about this book? Surveys of users have found general agreement about the following features. Needless to say, they've all been retained in this edition.

- *Length.* Since its inception in 1984, we've tried diligently to keep this book in the range of 325–350 pages. Users tell us this length allows them considerable flexibility in assigning supporting materials and projects.

- *Balanced topic coverage.* Although short in length, this book continues to provide balanced coverage of all the key concepts in OB. This includes not only traditional topics, such as personality, motivation, and leadership, but also cutting-edge issues such as emotions, negotiation, and teamwork.

- *Writing style.* This book is frequently singled out for its fluid writing style and extensive use of examples. Users regularly tell us that they find this book "conversational," "interesting," "student friendly," and "very clear and understandable."

- *Practicality.* This book has never been solely about theory. It's about *using* theory to better explain and predict the behavior of people in organizations. In each edition of this book, we have focused on making sure that readers see the link between OB theories, research, and implications for practice.

- *Absence of pedagogy.* Part of the reason we've been able to keep this book short in length is that it doesn't include review questions, cases, exercises, or similar teaching/learning aids. It continues to provide only the basic core of OB knowledge, allowing instructors the maximum flexibility in designing and shaping their courses.

- *Integration of globalization, diversity, and ethics.* The topics of globalization and cross-cultural differences, diversity, and ethics are discussed throughout this book. Rather than being presented in stand-alone chapters, these topics have been woven into the context of relevant issues. Users tell us they find that this integrative approach makes these topics more fully part of OB and reinforces their importance.

- *Comprehensive supplements.* Although this book may be short in length, it's not short on supplements. It comes with a complete, high-tech support package for both faculty and students. This includes a comprehensive Instructor's Manual and Test Item File; a dedicated Web site (www.prenhall.com/robbins); PowerPoint slides; and the Self-Assessment Library, which provides students with insights into their skills, abilities, and interests. These supplements are described in detail later in this preface.

NEW TO THE TENTH EDITION

This tenth edition has been updated in terms of research, examples, and topic coverage. New material in this edition includes:

- *New chapter on attitudes*, which considers the latest research and applications on work attitudes, and introduces new concepts such as employee engagement (Chapter 4)

- *New* **Global Implications** *section* in each chapter; more than ever, OB is becoming a global concept, and we've kept pace by devoting a new section of each chapter to global issues (every chapter)

- New material on *evidence-based management* (Chapter 1)

- New section on *creating a positive work environment* and discussion of positive organizational scholarship (Chapter 1)

- Updated and revised material on *ethics and decision making* (Chapter 3)

- New material on *commitment* and *employee engagement* (Chapter 4)

- New material on *intrinsic motivation* (Chapter 5) and *alternative work arrangements* (Chapter 6)

- New section on *emotional intelligence* (Chapter 7)

- New material on *virtual teams* (Chapter 9)

- Updated material on *diversity effects on team performance* (Chapter 9)

- Revised and updated coverage of *electronic communication*, including new sections on networking software and Internet logs (blogs) (Chapter 10)

- Updated material on *authentic and ethical leadership* (Chapter 11)

- Revised recommendations for effective use of *distributive bargaining tactics* (Chapter 13)

- Revised and updated treatment of the *virtual organization* (Chapter 14)
- New section on creating a *positive organizational culture* (Chapter 15)
- Substantially revised and updated treatment of *organizational change* and work *stress* (Chapter 16)

SUPPLEMENTS PACKAGE

Essentials of Organizational Behavior continues to be supported with an extensive supplement package for both students and faculty.

FACULTY RESOURCES

Instructor's Resource Center

Register.Redeem.Log in.

www.pearsonhighered.com/educator is where instructors can access a variety of print, media, and presentation resources available with this text in downloadable, digital format.

It gets better.   Once you register, you will not have additional forms to fill out, or multiple usernames and passwords to remember to access new titles and/or editions. As a registered faculty member, you can log in directly to download resource files, and receive immediate access and instructions for installing Course Management content to your campus server.

Need help?   Our dedicated Technical Support team is ready to assist instructors with questions about the media supplements that accompany this text. Visit http://247pearsoned.custhelp.com for answers to frequently asked questions and toll-free user support phone numbers. The following supplements are available to adopting instructors.

> **For detailed descriptions of all of the supplements listed below, please visit:**
> www.pearsonhighered.com/educator
> Instructor's Manual with Test Item File
> TestGen test generating software
> PowerPoints
> Videos on DVD—ISBN: 0136077676

STUDENT RESOURCES

Prentice Hall's Self-Assessment Library (S.A.L.)

The Self-Assessment Library is available with this text in print, CD-ROM, and online. It contains more than sixty self-scoring exercises that provide insights into your skills, abilities, and interests. To order *Essentials of Organizational Behavior* with the Self-Assessment Library, please use ISBN # 0138152977.

Companion Website

www.prenhall.com/robbins contains valuable resources for both students and professors, including an online study guide with multiple-choice, true/false, and short-answer questions.

CourseSmart eTextbooks

CourseSmart is an exciting new choice for students looking to save money. As an alternative to purchasing the print textbook, students can purchase an electronic version of the same content and save up to 50 percent off the suggested list price of the print text. With a CourseSmart eTextbook, students can search the text, make notes online, print out reading assignments that incorporate lecture notes, and bookmark important passages for later review. For more information, or to purchase access to the CourseSmart eTextbook, visit www.coursesmart.com.

FEEDBACK

The author and product team would appreciate hearing from you! Let us know what you think about this textbook by writing to college_marketing@prenhall.com. Please include "Feedback about Robbins/Judge 10e" in the subject line.

ACKNOWLEDGEMENTS

We owe a debt of gratitude to all those at Prentice Hall who have supported this text over the last 25 years and who have worked so hard on the development of this latest edition. On the editorial side, we want to thank Editor Jennifer M. Collins, Project Manager Claudia Fernandes, Editorial Assistant Elizabeth Davis, and Editorial Director Sally Yagan. On the production side, Project Manager Kelly Warsak did an outstanding job. Last but not least, we would like to thank Marketing Manager Nikki Jones and Director of Marketing Patrice Lumumba Jones and their sales staff who have been selling this book over its many editions. Thank you for the attention you've given this book.

About the Authors

Stephen P. Robbins
Ph.D. University of Arizona

Stephen P. Robbins is professor emeritus of management at San Diego State University and the world's best-selling textbook author in the areas of both management and organizational behavior. His books are used at more than a thousand U.S. colleges and universities, have been translated into nineteen languages, and have adapted editions for Canada, Australia, South Africa, and India. Dr. Robbins is also the author of the best-selling books *The Truth About Managing People*, 2nd ed. (Financial Times/Prentice Hall, 2008) and *Decide & Conquer* (Financial Times/Prentice Hall, 2004).

In his "other life," Dr. Robbins actively participates in masters' track competitions. Since turning 50 in 1993, he's won 18 national championships; 12 world titles; and set numerous U.S. and world age-group records at 60, 100, 200, and 400 meters. In 2005, Dr. Robbins was elected into the USA Masters' Track & Field Hall of Fame.

Timothy A. Judge
Ph.D. University of Illinois at Urbana-Champaign

Timothy A. Judge is currently the Matherly-McKethan Eminent Scholar in Management at the Warrington College of Business Administration at the University of Florida. He has held academic positions at the University of Iowa, Cornell University, Charles University in the Czech Republic, Comenius University in Slovakia, and University of Illinois at Urbana-Champaign. Dr. Judge's primary research interests are in (1) personality, moods, and emotions; (2) job attitudes; (3) leadership and influence behaviors; and (4) careers (person-organization fit, career success). Dr. Judge published more than 90 articles in these and other major topics in journals such as the *Academy of Management Journal* and the *Journal of Applied Psychology*. He is a fellow of several organizations, including the American Psychological Association and the Academy of Management. In 1995, Dr. Judge received the Distinguished Early Career Contributions Award from the Society for Industrial and Organizational Psychology, and in 2001, he received the Larry L. Cummings Award for midcareer contributions from the *Organizational Behavior* Division of the Academy of Management. He is a co-author of *Organizational Behavior*, 12th ed. with Stephen P. Robbins and *Staffing Organizations*, 5th ed. with Herbert G. Heneman III. He is married and has three children, who range in age from an 18-year-old daughter who is a freshman at Florida State University to a 4-year-old son.

CHAPTER 1

Introduction to Organizational Behavior

After studying this chapter, you should be able to:

1. Define organizational behavior (OB).
2. Explain the value of the systematic study of OB.
3. Identify the contributions made to OB by major behavioral science disciplines.
4. Describe how OB concepts can help make organizations more productive.
5. List the major challenges and opportunities for managers to use OB concepts.
6. Identify the three levels of analysis in OB.

If you ask managers to describe their most frequent or troublesome problems, the answers you get tend to exhibit a common theme. The managers most often describe *people* problems. They talk about their bosses' poor communication skills, employees' lack of motivation, conflicts between team members, overcoming employee resistance to a company reorganization, and similar concerns. It may surprise you to learn, therefore, that it's only recently that courses in *people skills* have become an important part of business school programs.

Although practicing managers have long understood the importance of interpersonal skills to managerial effectiveness, business schools have been slower to get the message. Until the late 1980s, business school curricula emphasized the technical aspects of management, specifically focusing on economics, accounting, finance, and quantitative techniques. Coursework in human behavior and people skills received minimal attention relative to the technical aspects of management. Over the past two decades, however, business faculty have come to realize the importance that an understanding of human behavior plays in determining a manager's effectiveness, and required courses on people skills have been added to many curricula. As the director of leadership at the Massachusetts Institute of Technology (MIT) Sloan School of Management recently put it, "M.B.A. students may get by on their technical and quantitative skills the first couple of years out of school. But soon, leadership and communication skills come to the fore in distinguishing the managers whose careers really take off."[1]

To get and keep high-performing employees, organizations recognize the importance of developing managers' interpersonal skills. Regardless of labor market conditions, outstanding employees are always in short supply. Companies with reputations as good places to work—such as Starbucks, Adobe Systems, Cisco, Whole Foods, American Express, Amgen, Goldman Sachs, Pfizer, and Marriott—have a big advantage. So having managers with good interpersonal skills is likely to make the workplace more pleasant, which, in turn, makes it easier to hire and keep qualified people. In addition, creating a pleasant workplace appears to make good economic sense. For instance, companies with reputations as good places to work (such as the companies that are included among the "100 Best Companies to Work for in America") can generate superior financial performance.[2]

Technical skills are necessary, but they are not enough to succeed in management. In today's increasingly competitive and demanding workplace, managers can't succeed on their technical skills alone. They also have to have good people skills. This book has been written to help both managers and potential managers develop those people skills.

THE FIELD OF ORGANIZATIONAL BEHAVIOR

The study of people at work is generally referred to as the study of organizational behavior. Let's begin, then, by defining the term *organizational behavior* and briefly reviewing its origins.

Organizational behavior (often abbreviated as OB) studies the influence that individuals, groups, and organizational structure have on behavior within organizations. The chief goal of OB is to apply that knowledge toward improving an organization's effectiveness. And because OB is concerned specifically with employment-related situations, it emphasizes behavior related to jobs, work, absenteeism, employment turnover, productivity, human performance, and management.

OB focuses on the three determinants of behavior in organizations: individuals, groups, and organizational structure. Although scholars increasingly agree on what topics constitute the subject area of OB, they continue to debate the relative importance of each. In this book, we focus on the following core topics:

- Motivation
- Leader behavior and power
- Interpersonal communication
- Group structure and processes
- Perceptions and attitudes
- Personality, emotions, and values

- Change processes
- Conflict and negotiation
- Work design[3]

COMPLEMENTING INTUITION WITH SYSTEMATIC STUDY

Each of us is a student of behavior. Since our earliest years, we've watched the actions of others and have attempted to interpret what we see. Whether or not you've explicitly thought about it before, you've been *reading* people almost all your life. You watch what others do, trying to understand why they engage in their behavior and perhaps attempting to predict what they might do under different sets of conditions. Unfortunately, a casual or commonsense approach to reading others often leads to erroneous predictions. To improve your predictive ability, you can supplement your intuitive opinions with a more systematic approach, as informed by the study of OB.

—OB's goal is to understand and predict human behavior in an organization; the complexities of human behavior are not easy to predict, but neither are they random—certain fundamental consistencies underlie the behavior of all individuals.

Using the systematic approach in this book, we will uncover important facts and relationships that will enable you to make more accurate predictions of behavior. Underlying this systematic approach is the belief that behavior is not random. Rather, certain fundamental consistencies underlie the behavior of all individuals, and these fundamental consistencies can be identified and then modified to reflect individual differences.

Without these fundamental consistencies, we would have great difficulty predicting behavior. For example, when you get into your car, you make some definite and, usually, highly accurate predictions about how other people will behave. In North America, you would predict that other drivers will stop at stop signs and red lights, drive on the right side of the road, and pass on your left. Can you imagine what would happen if driving behaviors were unpredictable?

Obviously, the rules of driving make predictions about driving behavior fairly easy. What may be less obvious are the rules (written and unwritten) that exist in almost every setting. For instance, do you turn around and face the doors when you get into an elevator? Almost everyone does. But did you ever read that you're supposed to do this? Probably not! We would argue that it's possible to predict behavior (undoubtedly, not always with 100 percent accuracy) in supermarkets, classrooms, doctors' offices, elevators, and in most structured situations. Just as we make predictions about automobile drivers (for which there are definite rules), we can make predictions about the behavior of people in elevators (for which there are few written rules).

In short, behavior is generally predictable, and the *systematic study* of behavior is a means to making reasonably accurate predictions. By **systematic study**, we mean the following:

- Examining relationships.
- Attempting to attribute causes and effects.
- Basing our conclusions on scientific evidence—that is, on data gathered under controlled conditions and measured and interpreted in a reasonably rigorous manner.

An approach that complements systematic study is evidence-based management. **Evidence-based management (EBM)** involves basing managerial decisions on the best available scientific evidence. We'd want doctors to make decisions about patient care based on the latest available evidence, and EBM argues that we want managers to do the same. That means managers must become more scientific in how they think about management problems. For example, a manager might pose a managerial question, search for the best available evidence, and apply the relevant information to the question or case at hand. You might think it is difficult to argue against this (what manager would argue that decisions shouldn't be based on evidence?), but the vast majority of management decisions are still made "on the fly," with little or no systematic study of available evidence.[4]

Systematic study and EBM augment **intuition**, those "gut feelings" about "what makes others tick." Of course, a systematic approach does not disprove things you have come to believe in an unsystematic way. Some of the conclusions we make in this text, based on reasonably substantive research findings, will only support what you already considered true, but some research evidence may run counter to what you thought was common sense. We hope that you can enhance your intuitive views of behavior and improve your accuracy in explaining and predicting behavior by practicing systematic analysis.

CONTRIBUTING DISCIPLINES TO THE OB FIELD

OB is an applied behavioral science built on contributions from a number of behavioral-based disciplines, including psychology and social psychology, sociology, and anthropology. Psychology's contributions have informed analysis mainly at the individual level (micro level), whereas the other disciplines have contributed to our understanding of group processes and organizations (macro levels), as illustrated in Exhibit 1-1.

Psychology

Psychology is the science that seeks to measure, explain, and sometimes change the behavior of humans and other animals. Psychologists concern themselves with studying and attempting to understand individual behavior. Those who have contributed and continue to add to the knowledge of OB are learning theorists, personality theorists, counseling psychologists, and, most important, industrial and organizational psychologists.

Early industrial/organizational psychologists concerned themselves with the problems of fatigue, boredom, and other factors relevant to working conditions that could impede efficient work performance. More recently, psychologists' contributions have expanded to include learning, perception, personality, emotions, training, leadership effectiveness, needs and motivational forces, job satisfaction, decision-making processes, performance appraisals, attitude measurement, employee-selection techniques, work design, and job stress.

Social Psychology

Social psychology blends concepts from both psychology and sociology, though it is generally considered a branch of psychology. It focuses on people's influences on one another. One major area receiving considerable investigation from social psychologists has been *change*—how to implement it and how to reduce barriers to its acceptance. In addition, we find social psychologists making significant contributions in the areas of measuring, understanding, and changing attitudes; communication patterns; and negotiation. Social psychologists also have made important contributions to our study of group behavior, power, and conflict.

EXHIBIT 1-1   Toward an OB Discipline

Sociology

Although psychology focuses on the individual, **sociology** is the study of people in relation to their social environment or culture. Sociologists have contributed to OB through their study of group behavior in organizations, particularly formal and complex organizations. Perhaps most importantly, sociologists have contributed to research on organizational culture, formal organization theory and structure, organizational technology, communications, power, and conflict.

—*There are several social science disciplines that contribute to OB, but none are more important than psychology.*

Anthropology

Anthropology is the study of societies for the purpose of learning about human beings and their activities. Anthropologists' work on cultures and environments has helped us understand differences in fundamental values, attitudes, and behavior among people in different countries and within different organizations. Much of our current understanding of organizational culture, organizational environments, and differences among national cultures comes from the work of anthropologists or those using their methods.

FEW ABSOLUTES IN OB

Few, if any, simple and universal principles explain OB. The physical sciences—chemistry, astronomy, physics—have laws that are consistent and apply in a wide range of situations. They allow scientists to generalize about the pull of gravity or to be confident about sending astronauts into space to repair satellites. But as a noted behavioral researcher aptly concluded, "God gave all the easy problems to the physicists." Human beings are complex and diverse, limiting our ability to make simple, accurate, and sweeping generalizations. Two people often act very differently in the same situation, and one person's behavior changes in different situations, say at church on Sunday and at a party that night.

That doesn't mean, of course, that we can't offer reasonably accurate explanations of human behavior or make valid predictions. However, it does mean that OB concepts must reflect situational, or contingency, conditions. We can say that x leads to y, but only under conditions specified in z—the **contingency variables**. The science of OB was developed by taking general concepts and applying them to a particular situation, person, or group. For example, OB scholars avoid stating that everyone likes complex and challenging work (the general concept) because not everyone wants a challenging job and some people prefer the simple over the complex. In other words, a job that is appealing to one person may not appeal to another, so the attraction of the job is contingent on the person who holds it.

As you proceed through this book, you'll encounter a wealth of research-based theories about how people behave in organizations. But don't expect to find a lot of straightforward cause-and-effect relationships. There aren't many! OB theories mirror the subject matter they address. People are complex and complicated, and so too must be the theories developed to explain their actions.

CHALLENGES AND OPPORTUNITIES FOR OB

Understanding OB has never been more important for managers. Consider some of the dramatic changes now taking place in organizations:

- Workers represent a large range of cultures, races, and ethnic groups.
- The typical employee is older.
- More women are in the workplace.
- Global competition requires employees to become more flexible and to learn to cope with rapid change.
- Corporate downsizing and the heavy use of temporary workers are severing the bonds of loyalty that historically tied many employees to their employers.

In short, today's challenges offer managers many opportunities to use OB concepts. Let's review some of the more critical issues confronting managers for which OB offers solutions—or at least some meaningful insights toward solutions.

Responding to Globalization

Organizations are no longer constrained by national borders. A British firm owns Burger King, and McDonald's sells hamburgers in Moscow. ExxonMobil, a so-called U.S. company, receives almost 75 percent of its revenues from sales outside the United States. New employees at Finland-based phone maker Nokia are increasingly being recruited from India, China, and other developing countries—with non-Finns now outnumbering Finns at Nokia's renowned research center in Helsinki. And all major automobile manufacturers now build cars outside their home country's borders— Honda in Ohio, Ford in Brazil, Volkswagen in Mexico, and both Mercedes and BMW in South Africa.

As the world becomes a global village, the manager's job is changing.

Increased Foreign Assignments If you're a manager, you are increasingly likely to find yourself in a foreign assignment—transferred to your employer's operating division or subsidiary in another country. Once there, you'll have to manage a workforce that is likely to be very different in needs, aspirations, and attitudes from those you were used to back home.

—There are many reasons why it is more important than ever to learn OB concepts.

Working with People from Different Cultures Even in your own country, you're going to find yourself working with bosses, peers, and other employees who were born and raised in different cultures. What motivates you may not motivate them. To work effectively with people from different cultures, you will have to understand how their culture, geography, and religion have shaped them and how to adapt your management style to their differences.

Overseeing Movement of Jobs to Countries with Low-Cost Labor It's increasingly difficult for managers in advanced nations, where minimum wages are typically $6 or more an hour, to compete against firms relying on workers from China and other developing nations where labor is available for $.30 an hour. The exportation of jobs, however, often comes with strong criticism from labor groups, politicians, local community leaders, and others who see such practices as undermining the job markets in developed countries. Managers must deal with the difficult task of balancing the interests of their organizations with their responsibilities to the communities in which they operate.

Managing Workforce Diversity

One of the most important and broad-based challenges currently facing organizations is adapting to people who are different. The term we use for describing this challenge is *workforce diversity*. Whereas globalization focuses on differences among people *from* different countries, workforce diversity addresses differences among people *within* given countries.

Workforce diversity means that organizations are becoming a more heterogeneous mix of people in terms of gender, age, race, ethnicity, and sexual orientation.

A diverse workforce, for instance, includes women, people of color, the physically disabled, senior citizens, and gays and lesbians (see Exhibit 1-2). Managing this diversity has become a global concern. It's an issue not just in the United States but also in Canada, Australia, South Africa, Japan, and Europe. For instance, managers in Canada and Australia are finding it necessary to adjust to large influxes of Asian workers. The "new" South Africa is increasingly characterized by blacks who are holding important technical and managerial jobs. Women in Japan, long confined to low-paying temporary jobs, are moving into managerial positions. And the European Union cooperative trade arrangement, which opened up borders throughout much of Western Europe, has increased workforce diversity in organizations that operate in countries such as Germany, Portugal, Italy, and France.

Workforce diversity has important implications for management practice. Managers have to shift their philosophy from treating everyone alike to recognizing differences and responding to those differences in ways that ensure employee retention and greater productivity while, at the same time, not discriminating. This shift includes, for instance, providing diversity training and revamping benefits programs to accommodate the different needs of different employees. Diversity, if positively managed, can increase creativity and innovation in organizations and improve decision making by providing different perspectives on problems.[5] When diversity is not

EXHIBIT 1-2   Major Workforce Diversity Categories

Gender
Nearly half of the U.S. workforce is now made up of women, and women are a growing percentage of the workforce in most countries throughout the world. Organizations need to ensure that hiring and employment policies create equal access and opportunities to individuals, regardless of gender.

Race
The percentage of Hispanics, blacks, and Asians in the U.S. workforce continues to increase. Organizations need to ensure that policies provide equal access and opportunities, regardless of race.

National Origin
A growing percentage of U.S. workers are immigrants or come from homes where English is not the primary language spoken. Because employers in the United States have the right to demand that English be spoken at the workplace during job-related activities, communication problems can occur when employees' English-language skills are weak.

Age
The U.S. workforce is aging, and recent polls indicate that an increasing percentage of employees expect to work past the traditional retirement age of 65. Organizations cannot discriminate on the basis of age and need to make accommodations to the needs of older workers.

Disability
Organizations need to ensure that jobs and workplaces are accessible to the mentally, physically, and health challenged.

Domestic Partners
An increasing number of gay and lesbian employees, as well as employees with live-in partners of the opposite sex, are demanding the same rights and benefits for their partners that organizations have provided for traditional married couples.

Religion
Organizations need to be sensitive to the customs, rituals, and holidays, as well as the appearance and attire, of individuals of non-Christian faiths such as Judaism, Islam, Hinduism, Buddhism, and Sikhism, and ensure that these individuals suffer no adverse impact as a result of their appearance or practices.

managed properly, the potential for higher turnover, more difficult communication, and more interpersonal conflicts increases.

Improving Quality and Productivity

Today's managers understand that the success of any effort made to improve quality and productivity must include their employees. These employees not only will be a major force in carrying out changes but increasingly will actively participate in planning those changes. OB offers important insights into helping managers work through these changes.

Improving Customer Service

Today, the majority of employees in developed countries work in service jobs. For instance, 80 percent of the U.S. labor force is employed in service industries. In the United Kingdom, Germany, and Japan the percentages are 69, 68, and 65, respectively. Examples of these service jobs include technical support representatives, fast-food counter workers, sales clerks, waiters or waitresses, nurses, automobile repair technicians, consultants, credit representatives, financial planners, and flight attendants. The common characteristic of these jobs is that they require substantial interaction with an organization's customers. Many an organization has failed because its employees failed to please the customer. Thus, management must create a customer-responsive culture. OB can provide considerable guidance in helping managers create such cultures— cultures in which employees exhibit these qualities:

- Friendly and courteous
- Accessible
- Knowledgeable
- Prompt in responding to customers' needs
- Willing to do what's necessary to please the customer[6]

Improving People Skills

We opened this chapter by demonstrating how important people skills are to managerial effectiveness. We said that "this book has been written to help both managers and potential managers develop those people skills."

As you proceed through the chapters, you'll find relevant concepts and theories that can help you explain and predict the behavior of people at work. In addition, you'll gain insights into specific people skills that you can use on the job. Specifically, you'll learn ways to design motivating jobs, techniques for improving your listening skills, and ideas about how to create more effective teams.

Stimulating Innovation and Change

Whatever happened to Montgomery Ward, Woolworth, Smith Corona, Eastern Airlines, Enron, Bear Stearns, Bethlehem Steel, and WorldCom? All these giants went bust. Why have other giants, such as Sears, Boeing, and Lucent Technologies, implemented huge cost-cutting programs and eliminated thousands of jobs? To avoid going broke. Even media darling Starbucks has been forced to lay off employees.

Today's successful organizations must foster innovation and master the art of change or they'll become candidates for extinction. Victory will go to the organizations that maintain their flexibility, continually improve their quality, and beat their competition to the marketplace with a constant stream of innovative products and services. Domino's single-handedly brought on the demise of thousands of small pizza parlors whose managers thought they could continue doing what they had been doing for years. Amazon.com is putting a lot of independent bookstores out of business as it proves you can successfully sell books from an Internet Web site. Dell has become the world's largest seller of computers by continually reinventing itself and outsmarting its competition.

An organization's employees can be the impetus for innovation and change or they can be a major stumbling block. The challenge for managers is to stimulate their employees' creativity and encourage their tolerance for change. The field of OB provides a wealth of ideas and techniques to aid in realizing these goals.

Coping with Temporariness

With change comes temporariness. Globalization, expanded capacity, and advances in technology have combined in recent years to make it imperative that organizations be fast and flexible if they are to survive. The result is that most managers and employees today work in a climate best characterized as *temporary*.

Evidence of temporariness is everywhere in organizations. Jobs are continually being redesigned; tasks are increasingly being done by flexible teams rather than individuals; companies are relying more on temporary workers; jobs are being subcontracted out to other firms; and pensions are being redesigned to move with people as they change jobs.

Workers must continually update their knowledge and skills to perform new job requirements. For example, production employees at companies such as Caterpillar, Ford, and Alcoa now need to know how to operate computerized production equipment. That was not part of their job descriptions 20 years ago. Work groups are also increasingly in a state of flux. In the past, each employee was assigned to a specific work group, and that assignment was relatively permanent. Employees enjoyed a considerable amount of security in working with the same people day in and day out. That predictability has been replaced by temporary work groups, teams that include members from different departments and whose members change all the time, and the increased use of employee rotation to fill constantly changing work assignments. In addition, organizations themselves are in a state of flux. They continually reorganize their various divisions, sell off poorly performing businesses, downsize operations, subcontract noncritical services and operations to other organizations, and replace permanent employees with temporary workers.

Today's managers and employees must learn to cope with temporariness. They must learn to live with flexibility, spontaneity, and unpredictability. The study of OB can provide important insights into helping you better understand a work world of continual change, how to overcome resistance to change, and how best to create an organizational culture that thrives on change.

Helping Employees Balance Work–Life Conflicts

In the 1960s and 1970s, employees typically showed up at the workplace Monday through Friday and did their job in eight- or nine-hour chunks of time. The workplace and hours were clearly specified. That's no longer true for a large segment of today's workforce. Employees are increasingly complaining that the line between work and nonwork time has become blurred, creating personal conflicts and stress.[7] At the same time, however, today's workplace presents opportunities for workers to create and structure their work roles.

The field of OB offers a number of suggestions to guide managers in designing workplaces and jobs that can help employees deal with work–life conflicts.

Improving Ethical Behavior

In an organizational world characterized by cutbacks, expectations of increasing worker productivity, and tough competition in the marketplace, it's not altogether surprising that many employees feel pressured to cut corners, break rules, and engage in other forms of questionable practices.

Members of organizations increasingly find themselves facing ethical dilemmas, situations in which they are required to define right and wrong conduct. For example, should they "blow the whistle" if they uncover illegal activities taking place in their company? Should they follow orders with which they don't personally agree? Do they give an inflated performance evaluation to an employee they like, knowing that such an evaluation could save that employee's job? Do they allow themselves to play politics in the organization if it will help their career advancement?

What constitutes good ethical behavior has never been clearly defined, and, in recent years, the line differentiating right from wrong has become even more blurred. Employees see people all around them engaging in unethical practices: elected officials are indicted for padding their expense accounts or taking bribes; corporate executives inflate their companies' profits so they can cash in lucrative stock options; and university administrators "look the other way" when winning coaches encourage scholarship athletes to stay eligible by taking easy courses in place of those needed for graduation. When caught, these people may give excuses such as "Everyone does it" or "You have to seize every advantage nowadays." Is it any wonder that employees are expressing decreased confidence and trust in management and that they're increasingly uncertain about what constitutes appropriate ethical behavior in their organizations?[8]

Today's manager needs to create an ethically healthy climate for his or her employees, in which employees can work productively and confront a minimal degree of ambiguity regarding what constitutes right and wrong behaviors. In upcoming chapters, we'll often bring ethical issues into our topical discussions, reflecting that most decisions about how to manage people involve ethically ambiguous situations.

Creating a Positive Work Environment

Although competitive pressures on most organizations are stronger than ever, we've noticed an interesting turn in both OB research and management practice, at least in some organizations. Instead of responding to competitive pressures by "turning up the heat," some organizations are trying to realize a competitive advantage by fostering a positive work environment. For example, Jeff Immelt (CEO of GE) and Jim McNerney (President and CEO of Boeing), both disciples of Jack Welch (former CEO of GE), have tried to maintain high performance expectations (a characteristic of GE's culture) while also fostering a positive work environment in their organizations (GE and Boeing). "In this time of turmoil and cynicism about business, you need to be passionate, positive leaders," Mr. Immelt recently told his top managers.

At the same time, a real growth area in OB research has been **positive organizational scholarship** (also called *positive organizational behavior*), which concerns how organizations develop human strengths, foster vitality and resilience, and unlock potential. Researchers in this area argue that too much of OB research and management practice has been targeted toward identifying what's wrong with organizations and their employees. In response, these researchers try to study what's *good* about organizations.[9]

For example, positive organizational scholars have studied a concept called "reflected best-self"—asking employees to think about situations in which they were at their "personal best" in order to understand how to exploit their strengths. These researchers argue that we all have things at which we are unusually good, yet too often we focus on addressing our limitations and too rarely think about how to exploit our strengths.[10]

Although positive organizational scholarship does not deny the presence (or even the value) of the negative (such as critical feedback), it does challenge researchers to look at OB through a new lens. It also challenges organizations to think about how to exploit their employees' strengths rather than dwell on their limitations.

THE PLAN OF THIS BOOK

How is this book going to help you better explain, predict, and control behavior? Our approach uses a building-block process. As illustrated in Exhibit 1-3, OB is characterized by three levels of analysis. As we move from the individual level to the organization system level, we increase in an additive fashion our understanding of behavior in organizations.

Chapters 2 through 7 deal with the individual in the organization. We begin by looking at such foundations of individual behavior as personality and values. Then we consider perceptions, decision making, and attitudes. Next, we focus on the fundamental role of motivational states on individual behavior. We conclude this section with a discussion of moods and emotions.

The behavior of people in groups is something more than the sum total of each individual acting in his or her own way. People's behavior in groups is different from their behavior when they are alone. Chapters 8 through 13 address group behavior. We introduce basic group concepts, discuss ways to make teams more effective,

EXHIBIT 1-3   Levels of OB Analysis

consider communication issues and group decision making, and then investigate the important topics of leadership, power, politics, conflict, and negotiation.

OB reaches its highest level of sophistication when we add the formal organization system to our knowledge of individual and group behavior. Just as groups are more than the sum of their individual members, organizations are not necessarily merely the summation of the behavior of a number of groups. In Chapters 14 through 16, we discuss how an organization's structure affects behavior, how each organization has its own culture that acts to shape the behavior of its members, and the various organizational change and development techniques that managers can use to affect behavior for the organization's benefit.

IMPLICATIONS FOR MANAGERS

Managers need to develop their interpersonal or people skills if they are going to be effective in their jobs. OB is a field of study that investigates the impact that individuals, groups, and organizational structure have on behavior within organizations, for the purpose of applying such knowledge toward improving an organization's effectiveness.

We all hold generalizations about the behavior of people. Some of our generalizations may provide valid insights into human behavior, but many are erroneous. OB uses systematic study to improve predictions of behavior that would be made from intuition alone. You can achieve your potential as a manager by enhancing your intuitive views of behavior with systematic analysis, in the belief that such analysis will improve your accuracy in explaining and predicting behavior.

OB offers both challenges and opportunities for managers:

- It offers specific insights to improve a manager's people skills.

- It recognizes differences and helps managers to see the value of workforce diversity and practices that may need to be changed when managing in different countries.

- It can improve quality and employee productivity by showing managers how to empower their people, design and implement change programs, improve customer service, and help employees balance work–life conflicts.

- It can help managers to cope in a world of temporariness and to learn ways to stimulate innovation.

- It can offer managers guidance in creating an ethically healthy work climate.

C H A P T E R   2

Personality and Values

O ur personalities shape our behaviors. So if we want to better understand the behavior of someone in an organization, it helps if we know something about his or her personality. In the first half of this chapter, we review the research on personality and its relationship to behavior. In the latter half, we look at how values shape many of our work-related behaviors.

PERSONALITY

Why are some people quiet and passive, while others are loud and aggressive? Are certain personality types better adapted than others for certain job types? Before we can answer these questions, we need to address a more basic one: What is personality?

What Is Personality?

When we talk of personality, we don't mean that a person has charm, a positive attitude toward life, a smiling face, or a place as a finalist for "Happiest and Friendliest" in this year's Miss America contest. When psychologists talk of personality, they mean a dynamic concept describing the growth and development of a person's whole psychological system. Rather than looking at parts of the person, personality looks at some aggregate whole that is greater than the sum of the parts.

—Personality—the sum total of ways in which an individual reacts to and interacts with others—is partly genetic in origins; yet, personality can be easily measured by various methods, including self-report surveys.

Defining *Personality*   The definition of *personality* we most frequently use was produced by Gordon Allport nearly 70 years ago. He said personality is "the dynamic organization within the individual of those psychophysical systems that determine his unique adjustments to his environment."[1] For our purposes, you should think of **personality** as the sum total of ways in which an individual reacts to and interacts with others. We most often describe it in terms of the measurable traits a person exhibits.

Measuring Personality   The most important reason managers need to know how to measure personality is that research has shown that personality tests are useful in hiring decisions. Scores on personality tests help managers forecast who is the best bet for a job.[2] And some managers want to know how people score on personality tests to better understand and more effectively manage the people who work for them. Far and away the most common means of measuring personality is through self-report surveys, with which individuals evaluate themselves by rating themselves on a series of factors such as "I worry a lot about the future." Though self-report measures work well when well constructed, one weakness of these measures is that the respondent might lie or practice impression management—that is, the person could "fake good" on the test to create a good impression. This is especially a concern when the survey is the basis for employment. Another problem is accuracy. In other words, a perfectly good candidate could have just been in a bad mood when the survey was taken.

Observer-ratings surveys provide an independent assessment of personality. Instead of self-reporting, a coworker or another observer does the rating (sometimes with the subject's knowledge and sometimes not). Even though the results of self-report surveys and observer-ratings surveys are strongly correlated, research suggests that observer-ratings surveys are a better predictor of success on the job.[3] However, each can tell us something unique about an individual's behavior in the workplace.

Personality Determinants   An early debate in personality research centered on whether an individual's personality was the result of heredity or of environment. Was the personality predetermined at birth, or was it the result of the individual's interaction with his or her surroundings? Clearly, there's no simple black-and-white answer. Personality appears to be a result of both hereditary and environmental factors. However, it might surprise you that research in personality development has tended to better support the importance of heredity over the environment.

Heredity refers to factors determined at conception. Physical stature, facial attractiveness, gender, temperament, muscle composition and reflexes, energy level, and biological rhythms are generally considered to be either completely or substantially influenced by who your parents are—that is, by their biological, physiological, and inherent psychological makeup. The heredity approach argues that the ultimate explanation of an individual's personality is the molecular structure of the genes, located in the chromosomes.

Studies of young children lend strong support to the power of heredity.[4] Evidence demonstrates that traits such as shyness, fear, and aggression can be traced to inherited genetic characteristics. This finding suggests that some personality traits may be built into the same genetic code that affects factors such as height and hair color.

Researchers in many different countries have studied thousands of sets of identical twins who were separated at birth and raised separately.[5] If heredity played little or no part in determining personality, you would expect to find few similarities between the separated twins. But the researchers found a lot in common. For almost every behavioral trait, a significant part of the variation between the twins turned out to be associated with genetic factors. For instance, one set of twins who had been separated for 39 years and raised 45 miles apart were found to drive the same model and color car. They chain-smoked the same brand of cigarette, owned dogs with the same name, and regularly vacationed within three blocks of each other in a beach community 1,500 miles away. Researchers have found that genetics accounts for about 50 percent of the personality differences and more than 30 percent of the variation in occupational and leisure interests.

Interestingly, the twin studies have suggested the parental environment doesn't add much to our personality development. In other words, the personalities of identical twins raised in different households are more similar to each other than to the personalities of the siblings they were actually raised with. Ironically, the most important contribution our parents may have made to our personalities is giving us their genes!

This is not to suggest that a person's personality never changes. Over periods of time, people's personalities do change. Most research in this area suggests that while some aspects of our personalities do change over time, the rank orderings do not change very much. For example, people's scores on measures of dependability tend to increase over time. However, there are still strong individual differences in dependability, and despite the fact that most of us become more responsible over time, people tend to change by about the same amount so that the rank order stays roughly the same.[6] An analogy to intelligence may make this clearer. Children become smarter as they age so that nearly everyone is smarter at age 20 than they were at age 10. Still, if Madison is smarter than Blake at age 10, she is likely to be so at age 20, too. The same holds true with personality: If you are more dependable than your sibling now, that is likely to be true in 20 years, even though you both should become more dependable over time.

Early work on the structure of personality tried to identify and label enduring characteristics that describe an individual's behavior. Popular characteristics include shy, aggressive, submissive, lazy, ambitious, loyal, and timid. When someone exhibits these characteristics in a large number of situations, we call them **personality traits**. The more consistent the characteristic and the more frequently a trait occurs in diverse situations, the more important that trait is in describing the individual.

A number of early efforts tried to identify the primary traits that govern behavior.[7] However, for the most part, they resulted in long lists of traits that were difficult to generalize from and provided little practical guidance to organizational decision makers. Two exceptions are the Myers-Briggs Type Indicator and the Big Five Model. Over the past 20 years, these two approaches have become the dominant frameworks for identifying and classifying traits.

The Myers-Briggs Type Indicator

The **Myers-Briggs Type Indicator (MBTI)** is the most widely used personality-assessment instrument in the world.[8] It's a 100-question personality test that asks people how they usually feel or act in particular situations. On the basis of their answers, individuals are classified as extraverted or introverted (E or I), sensing or intuitive (S or N), thinking or feeling (T or F), and judging or perceiving (J or P). These terms are defined as follows:

- *Extraverted versus introverted.* Extraverted individuals are outgoing, sociable, and assertive. Introverts are quiet and shy.
- *Sensing versus intuitive.* Sensing types are practical and prefer routine and order. They focus on details. Intuitives rely on unconscious processes and look at the "big picture."
- *Thinking versus feeling.* Thinking types use reason and logic to handle problems. Feeling types rely on their personal values and emotions.
- *Judging versus perceiving.* Judging types want control and prefer their world to be ordered and structured. Perceiving types are flexible and spontaneous.

These classifications together describe 16 personality types. To illustrate, let's take several examples. INTJs are visionaries. They usually have original minds and great drive for their own ideas and purposes. They are skeptical, critical, independent, determined, and often stubborn. ESTJs are organizers. They are realistic, logical, analytical, and decisive and have a natural head for business or mechanics. They like to organize and run activities. The ENTP type is a conceptualizer. He or she is innovative, individualistic, versatile, and attracted to entrepreneurial ideas. This person tends to be resourceful in solving challenging problems but may neglect routine assignments.

The MBTI is widely used in practice by organizations including Apple Computer, AT&T, Citigroup, GE, 3M Co., many hospitals and educational institutions, and even the U.S. Armed Forces. In spite of its popularity, the evidence is mixed as to whether the MBTI is a valid measure of personality—with most of the evidence suggesting that it isn't.[9] One problem is that it forces a person into either one type or another (that is, you're either introverted or extraverted). There is no in-between, though people can be both extraverted and introverted to some degree. The best we can say is that the MBTI can be a valuable tool for increasing self-awareness and providing career guidance. But because results tend to be unrelated to job performance, managers probably shouldn't use it as a selection test for job candidates.

The Big Five Personality Model

The MBTI may lack for strong supporting evidence, but the same can't be said for the five-factor model of personality typically called the **Big Five Model**, or the "Big Five." An impressive body of research supports its thesis that five basic dimensions underlie all others and encompass most of the significant variation in human personality.[10] The Big Five factors are:

- *Extraversion.* The **extraversion** dimension captures one's comfort level with relationships. Extraverts tend to be gregarious, assertive, and sociable. Introverts tend to be reserved, timid, and quiet.

- *Agreeableness.* The **agreeableness** dimension refers to an individual's propensity to defer to others. Highly agreeable people are cooperative, warm, and trusting. People who score low on agreeableness are cold, disagreeable, and antagonistic.

- *Conscientiousness.* The **conscientiousness** dimension is a measure of reliability. A highly conscientious person is responsible, organized, dependable, and persistent. Those who score low on this dimension are easily distracted, disorganized, and unreliable.

- *Emotional stability.* The **emotional stability** dimension—often labeled by its converse, neuroticism—taps a person's ability to withstand stress. People with positive emotional stability tend to be calm, self-confident, and secure. Those with high negative scores tend to be nervous, anxious, depressed, and insecure.

- *Openness to experience.* The **openness to experience** dimension addresses one's range of interests and fascination with novelty. Extremely open people are creative, curious, and artistically sensitive. Those at the other end of the openness category are conventional and find comfort in the familiar.

—The Big Five personality traits are related to many OB criteria; each of the five traits has proven its usefulness to understanding individual behavior in organizations.

How Do the Big Five Traits Predict Behavior at Work?   Research on the Big Five has found relationships between these personality dimensions and job performance.[11] As the authors of the most-cited review put it: "The preponderance of evidence shows that individuals who are dependable, reliable, careful, thorough, able to plan, organized, hardworking, persistent, and achievement-oriented tend to have higher job performance in most if not all occupations."[12] In addition, employees who score higher in conscientiousness develop higher levels of job knowledge, probably because highly conscientious people exert greater levels of effort on their jobs. The higher levels of job knowledge then contribute to higher levels of job performance.

Although conscientiousness is the Big Five trait most consistently related to job performance, the other traits are related to aspects of performance in some situations. All five traits also have other implications for work and for life. Let's look at the implications of these traits one at a time. Exhibit 2-1 summarizes the discussion.

People who score high on emotional stability are happier than those who score low. Of the Big Five traits, emotional stability is most strongly related to life satisfaction, job satisfaction, and low stress levels. This is probably true because high scorers are more likely to be positive and optimistic in their thinking and experience fewer negative emotions. People low on emotional stability are hyper-vigilant (looking for problems or impending signs of danger), and high scores are associated with fewer health complaints. One upside of low emotional stability, however, is that when in a bad mood, such people make faster and better decisions than emotionally stable people in bad moods.[13]

Compared to introverts, extraverts tend to be happier in their jobs and in their lives as a whole. They experience more positive emotions than do introverts, and they more freely express these feelings. They also tend to perform better in jobs that require significant interpersonal interaction, perhaps because they have more social skills—they usually have more friends and spend more time in social situations than introverts. Finally, extraversion is a relatively strong predictor of leadership emergence in groups; extraverts are more socially dominant, "take charge" sorts of people, and they are generally are more assertive than introverts.[14] One downside of extraversion is that extraverts are more impulsive than introverts; they are more likely to be

EXHIBIT 2-1   Model of How Big Five Traits Influence OB Criteria

BIG FIVE TRAIT	WHY IT IS RELEVANT?	WHAT DOES IT AFFECT?
Emotional stability	• Less negative thinking and fewer negative emotions • Less hyper-vigilant	• Higher job & life satisfaction • Lower stress levels
Extraversion	• Better interpersonal skills • Greater social dominance • More emotionally expressive	• Higher performance* • Enhanced leadership • Higher job & life satisfaction
Openness	• Increased learning • More creative • More flexible & autonomous	• Training performance • Enhanced leadership • More adaptable to change
Agreeableness	• Better liked • More compliant and conforming	• Higher performance* • Lower levels of deviant behavior
Conscientiousness	• Greater effort & persistence • More drive and discipline • Better organized & planning	• Higher performance • Enhanced leadership • Greater longevity

*In jobs requiring teamwork or frequent interpersonal interactions.

absent from work and engage in risky behavior such as unprotected sex, drinking, and other impulsive or sensation-seeking acts.[15]

Individuals who score high on openness to experience are more creative in science and in art than those who score low. Because creativity is important to leadership, open people are more likely to be effective leaders. Also, open individuals are more comfortable with ambiguity and change than are those who score lower on this trait. As a result, open people cope better with organizational change and are more adaptable in changing contexts.[16]

You might expect agreeable people to be happier than disagreeable people, and they are, but only slightly. When people choose romantic partners, friends, or organizational team members, agreeable individuals are usually their first choice. Thus, agreeable individuals are better liked than disagreeable people, which explains why they tend to do better in interpersonally oriented jobs such as customer service. Agreeable people also are more compliant and rule abiding. Agreeable children do better in school and as adults are less likely to get involved in drugs or excessive drinking.[17] Thus, agreeable individuals are less likely to engage in organizational deviance. One downside of agreeableness is that it is associated with lower levels of career success (especially earnings). This may occur because agreeable individuals are poorer negotiators; they are so concerned with pleasing others that they often don't negotiate as much for themselves as do others.[18]

Interestingly, conscientious people live longer than less conscientious people because they tend to take better care of themselves (eat better, exercise more) and engage in fewer risky behaviors (smoking, drinking/drugs, risky sexual or driving behavior).[19] Still, there are downsides to conscientiousness. It appears that conscientious people, probably because they're so organized and structured, don't adapt as well to changing contexts. Conscientious people are generally performance oriented. They have more trouble than less conscientious people learning complex skills early in the training process because their focus is on performing well rather than on learning. Finally, conscientious people are often less creative than less conscientious people, especially artistically.[20]

Other Personality Traits Relevant to OB

Although the Big Five traits have proven to be highly relevant to OB, they don't exhaust the range of traits we can use to describe someone's personality. Below is a partial list of other personality traits that are relevant to OB:

- **Core Self-Evaluation**   People differ in the degree to which they like or dislike themselves and whether they see themselves as capable and effective. This self-perspective is the concept of **core self-evaluation**. People who have positive core self-evaluations like themselves and see themselves as effective, capable, and in control of their environment. Those with negative core self-evaluations tend to dislike themselves, question their capabilities, and view themselves as powerless over their environment. People with positive core self-evaluations perform better than others because they set more ambitious goals, are more committed to their goals, and persist longer at attempting to reach these goals. For example, one study of life insurance agents found that core self-evaluations were critical predictors of performance. In life insurance sales, 90 percent of sales calls end in rejection, so an agent has to believe in him- or herself to persist. In fact, this study showed that the majority of successful salespersons had positive core self-evaluations.[21]

    You might wonder whether someone can be *too* positive. In other words, what happens when someone thinks he is capable, but he is actually incompetent? One study of *Fortune 500* CEOs, for example, showed that many are overconfident, and their perceived infallibility often causes them to make bad decisions.[22] Teddy Forstmann, chairman of the sports marketing giant IMG, said of himself, "I know God gave me an unusual brain. I can't deny that. I have a God-given talent for seeing potential."[23] One might say that people like Forstmann are over-confident, but very often we humans sell ourselves short and are less happy and effective than we could be because of it. If we decide we can't do something, for example, we won't try, and not doing it only reinforces our self-doubts.

- **Self-Monitoring**   Refers to an individual's ability to adjust his or her behavior to external, situational factors.[24] Individuals high in self-monitoring show considerable adaptability in adjusting their behavior to external situational factors. They are highly sensitive to external cues and can behave differently in different situations. High self-monitors are capable of presenting striking contradictions between their public persona and their private self. Low self-monitors can't disguise themselves in that way. They tend to display their true dispositions and attitudes in every situation; hence, there is high behavioral consistency between who they are and what they do.

The evidence indicates that high self-monitors tend to pay closer attention to the behavior of others and are more capable of conforming than are low self-monitors.[25] They also receive better performance ratings, are more likely to emerge as leaders, and show less commitment to their organizations.[26] In addition, high self-monitoring managers tend to be more mobile in their careers, receive more promotions (both internal and cross-organizational), and are more likely to occupy central positions in an organization.[27]

■ **Type A Personality**   Do you know people who are excessively competitive and always seem to be experiencing a sense of time urgency? If you do, it's a good bet those people have **Type A personalities**. A person with a Type A personality is "aggressively involved in a chronic, incessant struggle to achieve more and more in less and less time, and, if required to do so, against the opposing efforts of other things or other persons."[28] In the North American culture, such characteristics tend to be highly prized and positively associated with ambition and the successful acquisition of material goods. Type A's are always moving, walking, and eating rapidly, tend to feel impatient with the rate at which most events take place, and strive to think or do two or more things at once. Type B's, conversely, are "rarely harried by the desire to obtain a wildly increasing number of things or participate in an endless growing series of events in an ever-decreasing amount of time."[29] Type B's never suffer from a sense of time urgency with its accompanying impatience, can relax without guilt, and so on.

Type A's operate under moderate to high levels of stress. They subject themselves to more or less continuous time pressure, creating for themselves a life of deadlines. These characteristics result in some rather specific behavioral outcomes. For example, Type A's are fast workers because they emphasize quantity over quality. In managerial positions, Type A's demonstrate their competitiveness by working long hours and, not infrequently, making poor decisions to new problems. This constant level of stress takes a toll on the health of Type A individuals, which is why those with strong Type A personalities are at risk for cardiovascular disease.

■ **Proactive Personality**   Did you ever notice that some people actively take the initiative to improve their current circumstances or create new ones while others sit by passively reacting to situations? The former individuals have been described as having **proactive personalities**. Proactives identify opportunities, show initiative, take action, and persevere until meaningful change occurs. They create positive change in their environment, regardless of or even in spite of constraints or obstacles.[30]

Not surprisingly, proactives have many desirable behaviors that organizations covet. For instance, evidence indicates that proactives are more likely than others to be seen as leaders and more likely to act as change agents within an organization.[31] Other actions of proactives can be positive or negative, depending on the organization and the situation. For example, proactives are more likely to challenge the status quo or voice their displeasure when situations aren't to their liking. As individuals, proactives are more likely than others to achieve career success.[32] They select, create, and influence work situations in their favor. Proactives are more likely than others to seek out job and organizational information, develop contacts in high places, engage in career planning, and demonstrate persistence in the face of career obstacles.

Having discussed personality traits—the enduring characteristics that describe a person's behavior—we now turn to values. Although personality and values are related, they're not the same. Values are often very specific and describe belief systems rather than behavioral tendencies. Some beliefs or values don't say much about a person's personality, and we don't always act in ways that are consistent with our values.

VALUES

Is capital punishment right or wrong? If a person likes power, is that good or bad? The answers to these questions are value laden. Some might argue, for example, that capital punishment is right because it is an appropriate retribution for crimes such as murder and treason. Others might argue, just as strongly, that no government has the right to take anyone's life.

Values represent basic convictions that "a specific mode of conduct or end-state of existence is personally or socially preferable to an opposite or converse mode of conduct or end-state of existence."[33] They contain a judgmental element in that they carry an individual's ideas as to what is right, good, or desirable. Values have both content and intensity attributes. The content attribute says that a mode of conduct or an end-state of existence is *important*. The intensity attribute specifies *how important* it is. When we rank an individual's values in terms of their intensity, we obtain that person's **value system**. All of us have a hierarchy of values that forms our value system. This system is identified by the relative importance we assign to values such as freedom, pleasure, self-respect, honesty, obedience, and equality.

Are values fluid and flexible? Generally speaking, no. They tend to be relatively stable and enduring.[34] A significant portion of the values we hold is established in our early years—from parents, teachers, friends, and others. As children, we are told that certain behaviors or outcomes are *always* desirable or *always* undesirable, with few gray areas. You were told, for example, that you should be honest and responsible. You were never taught to be just a little bit honest or a little bit responsible. It is this absolute, or "black-or-white," learning of values that more or less ensures their stability and endurance. The process of questioning our values, of course, may result in a change. More often, our questioning merely acts to reinforce the values we hold.

The Importance of Values

Values are important to the study of organizational behavior because they lay the foundation for our understanding of people's attitudes and motivation and because they influence our perceptions. Individuals enter an organization with preconceived notions of what "ought" and "ought not" to be. Of course, these notions are not value free. On the contrary, they contain interpretations of right and wrong. Furthermore, they imply that certain behaviors or outcomes are preferred over others. As a result, values cloud objectivity and rationality.

Values generally influence attitudes and behavior. Suppose you enter an organization with the view that allocating pay on the basis of performance is right, while allocating pay on the basis of seniority is wrong. How are you going to react if you find that the organization you've just joined rewards seniority and not performance? You're likely to be disappointed—and this can lead to job dissatisfaction and a decision not to exert a high level of effort because "it's probably not going to lead to more money anyway." Would your attitudes and behavior be different if your values aligned with the organization's pay policies? Most likely.

Terminal Versus Instrumental Values

Can we classify values? Yes. In this section, we review two approaches to developing value typologies.

Rokeach Value Survey   Milton Rokeach created the Rokeach Value Survey (RVS).[35] It consists of two sets of values, each containing 18 individual value items. One set, called **terminal values**, refers to desirable end-states. These are the goals a person would like to achieve during his or her lifetime. The other set, called **instrumental values**, refers to preferable modes of behavior, or means of achieving the terminal values. Exhibit 2-2 gives common examples for each of these sets.

Several studies confirm that RVS values vary among groups.[36] People in the same occupations or categories (for example, corporate managers, union members, parents, students) tend to hold similar values. For instance, one study compared corporate executives, members of the steelworkers' union, and members of a community activist group. Although there was a good deal of overlap among the three groups,[37] there were also some very significant differences. The activists had value preferences that were quite different from those of the other two groups. They ranked "equality" as their most important terminal value; executives and union members ranked this value 12 and 13, respectively. These differences are important, because executives, union members, and activists all have a vested interest in what corporations do. These differences make things difficult for groups that have to negotiate with each other and can create serious conflicts when they contend with each other over an organization's economic and social policies.

EXHIBIT 2-2   Terminal and Instrumental Values in the Rokeach Value Survey

Terminal Values	Instrumental Values
A comfortable life (a prosperous life)	Ambitious (hardworking, aspiring)
An exciting life (a stimulating, active life)	Broad-minded (open-minded)
A sense of accomplishment (lasting contribution)	Capable (competent, efficient)
A world at peace (free of war and conflict)	Cheerful (lighthearted, joyful)
A world of beauty (beauty of nature and the arts)	Clean (neat, tidy)
Equality (brotherhood, equal opportunity for all)	Courageous (standing up for your beliefs)
Family security (taking care of loved ones)	Forgiving (willing to pardon others)
Freedom (independence, free choice)	Helpful (working for the welfare of others)
Happiness (contentedness)	Honest (sincere, truthful)
Inner harmony (freedom from inner conflict)	Imaginative (daring, creative)
Mature love (sexual and spiritual intimacy)	Independent (self-reliant, self-sufficient)
National security (protection from attack)	Intellectual (intelligent, reflective)
Pleasure (an enjoyable, leisurely life)	Logical (consistent, rational)
Salvation (saved, eternal life)	Loving (affectionate, tender)
Self-respect (self-esteem)	Obedient (dutiful, respectful)
Social recognition (respect, admiration)	Polite (courteous, well-mannered)
True friendship (close companionship)	Responsible (dependable, reliable)
Wisdom (a mature understanding of life)	Self-controlled (restrained, self-disciplined)

Source: Reprinted with the permission of The Free Press, a Division of Simon & Schuster Adult Publishing Group, from *The Nature of Human Values* by Milton Rokeach. Copyright © 1973 by The Free Press. Copyright renewed © 2001 by Sandra J. Ball-Rokeach. All rights reserved.

Generational Values

Contemporary Work Cohorts   Researchers have integrated several recent analyses of work values into four groups that attempt to capture the unique values of different cohorts or generations in the U.S. workforce.[38] Exhibit 2-3 proposes that employees can be segmented by the era in which they entered the workforce. Because most people start work between the ages of 18 and 23, the eras also correlate closely with the chronological age of employees.

Before going any further, let's look at some limitations of this analysis. First, we make no assumption that the framework would apply universally across all cultures. Second, although there is a steady stream of press coverage, there is very little rigorous research on generational values, so we have to rely on an intuitive framework. Finally, these are imprecise categories. There is no law that someone born in 1985 can't have similar values to someone born in 1955. You may see your values better reflected in other generations than in your own. Despite these limitations, values do change over generations,[39] and we can gain some useful insights from analyzing values this way.

Workers who grew up influenced by the Great Depression, World War II, the Andrews Sisters, and the Berlin Blockade entered the workforce through the 1950s and early 1960s, believing in hard work, the status quo, and authority figures. We call them *Veterans* (some use the label *Traditionalists*). Once hired, Veterans tended to be loyal to their employer and respectful of authority, hardworking, and practical. These are the people Tom Brokaw wrote about in his book *The Greatest Generation*. In terms of terminal values on the RVS, these employees are likely to place the greatest importance on a comfortable life and family security.

Boomers (*Baby Boomers*) are a large cohort born after World War II, when veterans returned to their families and times were good. Boomers entered the workforce from the mid-1960s through the mid-1980s. This cohort was influenced heavily by the civil rights movement, the women's movement, the Beatles, the Vietnam War, and baby boom competition. They brought with them a large measure of the "hippie ethic" and distrust of authority. However, they place a great deal of emphasis on achievement and material success. They work hard and want to enjoy the fruits of their labors. They're pragmatists who believe that ends can justify means. Boomers see the organizations that employ them merely as vehicles for their careers. Terminal values, such as a sense of accomplishment and social recognition, rank high with them.

EXHIBIT 2-3   Dominant Work Values in Today's Workforce

Cohort	Entered the Workforce	Approximate Current Age	Dominant Work Values
Veterans	1950s or early 1960s	65+	Hardworking, conservative, conforming; loyalty to the organization
Boomers	1965–1985	Mid-40s to mid-60s	Success, achievement, ambition, dislike of authority; loyalty to career
Xers	1985–2000	Late 20s to early 40s	Work/life balance, team oriented, dislike of rules; loyalty to relationships
Nexters	2000 to present	Under 30	Confident, financial success, self-reliant but team oriented; loyalty to both self and relationships

The lives of *Xers* (*Generation Xers*) have been shaped by globalization, two-career parents, MTV, AIDS, and computers. They value flexibility, life options, and the achievement of job satisfaction. Family and relationships are very important to this cohort. Unlike Veterans, Xers are skeptical, particularly of authority. They also enjoy team-oriented work. Money is important as an indicator of career performance, but Xers are willing to trade off salary increases, titles, security, and promotions for increased leisure time and expanded lifestyle options. In search of balance in their lives, Xers are less willing to make personal sacrifices for the sake of their employer than previous generations. On the RVS, they rate high on true friendship, happiness, and pleasure.

The most recent entrants to the workforce, the *Nexters* (also called *Netters*, *Millennials*, *Generation Yers*, and *Generation Nexters*) grew up during prosperous times. They have high expectations and seek meaning in their work. Nexters have life goals more oriented toward becoming rich (81 percent) and famous (51 percent) than do Generation Xers (62 percent and 29 percent, respectively). Nexters are at ease with diversity and are the first generation to take technology for granted. They've lived much of their lives with ATMs, DVDs, cellphones, laptops, and the Internet. More than other generations, they tend to be questioning, socially conscious, and entrepreneurial. At the same time, some have described Nexters as needy. One employer said, "This is the most high-maintenance workforce in the history of the world. The good news is they're also going to be the most high-performing."[40]

An understanding that individuals' values differ but tend to reflect the societal values of the period in which they grew up can be a valuable aid in explaining and predicting behavior. Employees in their late 60s, for instance, are more likely to accept authority than their coworkers who are 10 or 15 years younger. And workers in their 30s are more likely than their parents to balk at having to work weekends and more prone to leave a job in mid-career to pursue another that provides more leisure time.

LINKING AN INDIVIDUAL'S PERSONALITY AND VALUES TO THE WORKPLACE

Thirty years ago, organizations were concerned only with personality because their primary focus was to match individuals to specific jobs. That concern still exists. But, in recent years, that interest has expanded to include how well the individual's personality *and* values match the *organization*. Why? Because managers today are less interested in an applicant's ability to perform a *specific* job than with the *flexibility* to meet changing situations and commitment to the organization.

We'll now discuss person–job fit and person–organization fit in more detail.

Person–Job Fit

The effort to match job requirements with personality characteristics is best articulated in John Holland's **personality–job fit theory**.[41] Holland presents six personality types and proposes that job satisfaction and the propensity to leave a position depend on the degree to which individuals successfully match their personalities to a job. Each one of the six personality types has several congruent occupations. Exhibit 2-4 describes the six types and their personality characteristics and gives examples of congruent occupations.

EXHIBIT 2-4 Holland's Typology of Personality and Congruent Occupations

Type	Personality Characteristics	Congruent Occupations
Realistic: Prefers physical activities that require skill, strength, and coordination	Shy, genuine, persistent, stable, conforming, practical	Mechanic, drill press operator, assembly-line worker, farmer
Investigative: Prefers activities that involve thinking, organizing, and understanding	Analytical, original, curious, independent	Biologist, economist, mathematician, news reporter
Social: Prefers activities that involve helping and developing others	Sociable, friendly, cooperative, understanding	Social worker, teacher, counselor, clinical psychologist
Conventional: Prefers rule-regulated, orderly, and unambiguous activities	Conforming, efficient, practical, unimaginative, inflexible	Accountant, corporate manager, bank teller, file clerk
Enterprising: Prefers verbal activities in which there are opportunities to influence others and attain power	Self-confident, ambitious, energetic, domineering	Lawyer, real estate agent, public relations specialist, small business manager
Artistic: Prefers ambiguous and unsystematic activities that allow creative expression	Imaginative, disorderly, idealistic, emotional, impractical	Painter, musician, writer, interior decorator

Holland developed the Vocational Preference Inventory questionnaire, which contains 160 occupational titles. Respondents indicate which of these occupations they like or dislike, and their answers form personality profiles. Research strongly supports the resulting hexagonal diagram shown in Exhibit 2-5.[42] The closer two fields or orientations are in the hexagon, the more compatible they are. Adjacent categories are quite similar, whereas diagonally opposite ones are highly dissimilar.

EXHIBIT 2-5 Relationships among Occupational Personality Types

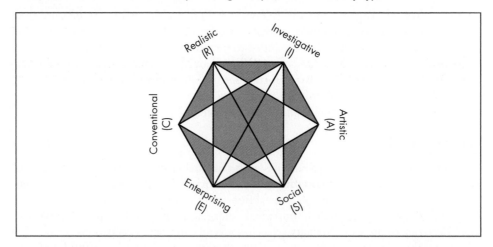

What does all this mean? The theory argues that satisfaction is highest and turnover is lowest when personality and occupation are in agreement. Social individuals should be in social jobs, conventional people in conventional jobs, and so forth. A realistic person in a realistic job is in a more congruent situation than a realistic person in an investigative job. A realistic person in a social job is in the most incongruent situation possible. The key points of this model are that (1) there do appear to be intrinsic differences in personality among individuals, (2) there are different types of jobs, and (3) people in jobs congruent with their personality should be more satisfied and less likely to voluntarily resign than people in incongruent jobs.

Person–Organization Fit

We've noted that researchers in recent years have looked at matching people to *organizations* as well as to jobs. If an organization faces a dynamic and changing environment and requires employees who are able to readily change tasks and move easily between teams, it's more important that employees' personalities fit with the overall organization's culture than with the characteristics of any specific job.

The person–organization fit essentially argues that people are attracted to and selected by organizations that match their personalities, and they leave organizations that are not compatible with their personalities.[43] Using the Big Five terminology, for instance, we could expect that people high on extraversion fit well with aggressive and team-oriented cultures, that people high on agreeableness match up better with a supportive organizational climate than one that focuses on aggressiveness, and that people high on openness to experience fit better into organizations that emphasize innovation rather than standardization.[44] Following these guidelines at the time of hiring should lead to selecting new employees who fit better with the organization's culture, which should, in turn, result in higher employee satisfaction and reduced turnover. Research on person–organization fit has also looked at people's values and whether they match the organization's culture. The fit of employees' values with the culture of their organization predicts job satisfaction, commitment to the organization, and turnover.[45]

> —Values do appear to vary across cultures, meaning that, on average, people's values in one nation tend to differ from those in another; however, there is substantial variability in values within a culture.

GLOBAL IMPLICATIONS

Personality

Do personality frameworks, such as the Big Five Model, transfer across cultures? Are dimensions such as the Type A personality relevant in all cultures? Let's try to answer these questions.

The five personality factors identified in the Big Five Model appear in almost all cross-cultural studies.[46] These studies have included a wide variety of diverse cultures—such as China, Israel, Germany, Japan, Spain, Nigeria, Norway, Pakistan, and the United States. Differences tend to be in the emphasis on dimensions and whether countries are predominantly individualistic or collectivistic. For example, Chinese managers use the category of conscientiousness more often and the category of agreeableness less often than do U.S. managers. And the Big Five appear to predict a bit better in individualistic than in collectivist cultures.[47] But there is a surprisingly high amount of agreement, especially among individuals from developed countries. As a case in point, a comprehensive review of studies covering people from the 15-nation European Community found that conscientiousness was a valid predictor of performance across jobs and occupational groups.[48] This is exactly what U.S. studies have found.

Values

Because values differ across cultures, an understanding of these differences should be helpful in explaining and predicting the behavior of employees from different countries.

Hofstede's Framework for Assessing Cultures   One of the most widely referenced approaches for analyzing variations among cultures was done in the late 1970s by Geert Hofstede.[49] He surveyed more than 116,000 IBM employees in 40 countries about their work-related values and found that managers and employees vary on five value dimensions of national culture:

- *Power distance.* **Power distance** describes the degree to which people in a country accept that power in institutions and organizations is distributed unequally. A high rating on power distance means that large inequalities of power and wealth exist and are tolerated in the culture, as in a class or caste system that discourages upward mobility of its citizens. A low power distance rating characterizes societies that stress equality and opportunity.

- *Individualism versus collectivism.* **Individualism** is the degree to which people prefer to act as individuals rather than as members of groups and believe in individual rights above all else. **Collectivism** emphasizes a tight social framework in which people expect others in groups of which they are a part to look after them and protect them.

- *Masculinity versus femininity.* Hofstede's construct of **masculinity** is the degree to which the culture favors traditional masculine roles, such as achievement, power, and control, as opposed to viewing men and women as equals. A high masculinity rating indicates the culture has separate roles for men and women, with men dominating the society. A high **femininity** rating means the culture sees little differentiation between male and female roles and treats women as the equals of men in all respects.

- *Uncertainty avoidance.* The degree to which people in a country prefer structured over unstructured situations defines their uncertainty avoidance. In cultures that score high on uncertainty avoidance, people have an increased level of anxiety about uncertainty and ambiguity and use laws and controls to reduce uncertainty. Cultures low on **uncertainty avoidance** are more accepting of ambiguity and are less rule oriented, take more risks, and more readily accept change.

- *Long-term versus short-term orientation.* This is the newest addition to Hofstede's typology. It focuses on the degree of a society's long-term devotion to traditional values. People in a culture with **long-term orientation** look to the future and value thrift, persistence, and tradition. In a **short-term orientation**, people value the here and now; they accept change more readily and don't see commitments as impediments to change.

How do different countries score on Hofstede's dimensions? Exhibit 2-6 shows the ratings for the countries for which data are available. For example, power distance is higher in Malaysia than in any other country. The United States is very individualistic. In fact, it's the most individualistic nation of all (closely followed by Australia and Great Britain). The United States also tends to be

EXHIBIT 2-6   Hofstede's Cultural Values by Nation

Country	Power Distance Index	Rank	Individualism Versus Collectivism Index	Rank	Masculinity Versus Femininity Index	Rank	Uncertainty Avoidance Index	Rank	Long-Versus Short-Term Orientation Index	Rank
Argentina	49	35–36	46	22–23	56	20–21	86	10–15		
Australia	36	41	90	2	61	16	51	37	31	22–24
Austria	11	53	55	18	79	2	70	24–25	31	22–24
Belgium	65	20	75	8	54	22	94	5–6	38	18
Brazil	69	14	38	26–27	49	27	76	21–22	65	6
Canada	39	39	80	4–5	52	24	48	41–42	23	30
Chile	63	24–25	23	38	28	46	86	10–15		
Colombia	67	17	13	49	64	11–12	80	20		
Costa Rica	35	42–44	15	46	21	48–49	86	10–15		
Denmark	18	51	74	9	16	50	23	51	46	10
Ecuador	78	8–9	8	52	63	13–14	67	28		
El Salvador	66	18–19	19	42	40	40	94	5–6		
Finland	33	46	63	17	26	47	59	31–32	41	14
France	68	15–16	71	10–11	43	35–36	86	10–15	39	17
Germany	35	42–44	67	15	66	9–10	65	29	31	22–24
Great Britain	35	42–44	89	3	66	9–10	35	47–48	25	28–29
Greece	60	27–28	35	30	57	18–19	112	1		
Guatemala	95	2–3	6	53	37	43	101	3		
Hong Kong	68	15–16	25	37	57	18–19	29	49–50	96	2
India	77	10–11	48	21	56	20–21	40	45	61	7
Indonesia	78	8–9	14	47–48	46	30–31	48	41–42		
Iran	58	29–30	41	24	43	35–36	59	31–32		
Ireland	28	49	70	12	68	7–8	35	47–48	43	13
Israel	13	52	54	19	47	29	81	19		
Italy	50	34	76	7	70	4–5	75	23	34	19
Jamaica	45	37	39	25	68	7–8	13	52		
Japan	54	33	46	22–23	95	1	92	7	80	4
Korea (South)	60	27–28	18	43	39	41	85	16–17	75	5
Malaysia	104	1	26	36	50	25–26	36	46		
Mexico	81	5–6	30	32	69	6	82	18		
The Netherlands	38	40	80	4–5	14	51	53	35	44	11–12
New Zealand	22	50	79	6	58	17	49	39–40	30	25–26
Norway	31	47–48	69	13	8	52	50	38	44	11–12
Pakistan	55	32	14	47–48	50	25–26	70	24–25	0	34
Panama	95	2–3	11	51	44	34	86	10–15		
Peru	64	21–23	16	45	42	37–38	87	9		
Philippines	94	4	32	31	64	11–12	44	44	19	31–32
Portugal	63	24–25	27	33–35	31	45	104	2	30	25–26
Singapore	74	13	20	39–41	48	28	8	53	48	9
South Africa	49	35–36	65	16	63	13–14	49	39–40		
Spain	57	31	51	20	42	37–38	86	10–15	19	31–32
Sweden	31	47–48	71	10–11	5	53	29	49–50	33	20
Switzerland	34	45	68	14	70	4–5	58	33	40	15–16
Taiwan	58	29–30	17	44	45	32–33	69	26	87	3
Thailand	64	21–23	20	39–41	34	44	64	30	56	8
Turkey	66	18–19	37	28	45	32–33	85	16–17		
United States	40	38	91	1	62	15	46	43	29	27
Uruguay	61	26	36	29	38	42	100	4		
Venezuela	81	5–6	12	50	73	3	76	21–22		
Yugoslavia	76	12	27	33–35	21	48–49	88	8		
Regions:										
Arab countries	80	7	38	26–27	53	23	68	27		
East Africa	64	21–23	27	33–35	41	39	52	36	25	28–29
West Africa	77	10–11	20	39–41	46	30–31	54	34	16	33

Scores range from 0 = extremely low on dimension to 100 = extremely high.

Note; 1 = highest rank. LTO ranks: 1 = China; 15–16 = Bangladesh; 21 = Poland; 34 = lowest.

Source: Copyright Geert Hofstede BV, hofstede@abovt.nl. Reprinted with permission.

short term in orientation and is low in power distance (people in the United States tend not to accept built-in class differences between people). The United States is also relatively low on uncertainty avoidance, meaning that most adults are relatively tolerant of uncertainty and ambiguity. The United States scores relatively high on masculinity, meaning that most people emphasize traditional gender roles (at least relative to countries such as Denmark, Finland, Norway, and Sweden).

You'll notice regional differences. Western and Northern nations such as Canada and the Netherlands tend to be more individualistic. Compared with other countries, poorer countries such as Mexico and the Philippines tend to be higher on power distance. South American nations tend to be higher than other countries on uncertainty avoidance, and Asian countries tend to have a long-term orientation.

Hofstede's cultural dimensions have been enormously influential on OB researchers and managers. Nevertheless, his research has been criticized. First, although the data have since been updated, the original work is more than 30 years old and was based on a single company (IBM). A lot has happened on the world scene since then. Some of the most obvious changes include the fall of the Soviet Union, the transformation of Central and Eastern Europe, the end of apartheid in South Africa, the spread of Islam throughout the world today, and the rise of China as a global power. Second, few researchers have read the details of Hofstede's methodology closely and are therefore unaware of the many decisions and judgment calls he had to make (for example, reducing the number of cultural values to just five). Some results are unexpected. For example, Japan, which is often considered a highly collectivist nation, is considered only average on collectivism under Hofstede's dimensions.[50] Despite these concerns, Hofstede has been one of the most widely cited social scientists ever, and his framework has left a lasting mark on OB.

The GLOBE Framework for Assessing Cultures   Begun in 1993, the Global Leadership and Organizational Behavior Effectiveness (GLOBE) research program is an ongoing cross-cultural investigation of leadership and national culture. Using data from 825 organizations in 62 countries, the GLOBE team identified nine dimensions on which national cultures differ.[51] Some of these—such as power distance, individualism/collectivism, uncertainty avoidance, gender differentiation (similar to masculinity versus femininity), and future orientation (similar to long-term versus short-term orientation)—resemble the Hofstede dimensions. The main difference in the GLOBE framework is that it added dimensions, such as humane orientation (the degree to which a society rewards individuals for being altruistic, generous, and kind to others) and performance orientation (the degree to which a society encourages and rewards group members for performance improvement and excellence).

Which framework is better? That's hard to say, and each has its adherents. We give more emphasis to Hofstede's dimensions here because they have stood the test of time and the GLOBE study confirmed them. However, researchers continue to debate the differences between these frameworks, and future studies may, in time, favor the more nuanced perspective of the GLOBE study.[52]

IMPLICATIONS FOR MANAGERS

Personality   What value, if any, does the Big Five Model provide to managers? From the early 1900s through the mid-1980s, researchers sought to find a link between personality and job performance. "The outcome of those 80-plus years of research was that personality and job performance were not meaningfully related across traits or situations."[53] However, the past 20 years have been more promising, largely due to the findings surrounding the Big

Five. Screening candidates for jobs who score high on conscientiousness—as well as the other Big Five traits, depending on the criteria an organization finds most important—should pay dividends. Each of the Big Five traits has numerous implications for important OB criteria. Of course, managers still need to take situational factors into consideration.[54] Factors such as job demands, the degree of required interaction with others, and the organization's culture are examples of situational variables that moderate the personality–job performance relationship. You need to evaluate the job, the work group, and the organization to determine the optimal personality fit. Other traits, such as core self-evaluation or self-monitoring may be relevant in certain situations, too.

Although the MBTI has been widely criticized, it may have a place in organizations. In training and development, it can help employees to better understand themselves, and it can help team members to better understand each other. And it can open up communication in work groups and possibly reduce conflicts.

Values   Why is it important to know an individual's values? Values often underlie and explain attitudes, behaviors, and perceptions. So knowledge of an individual's value system can provide insight into what "makes the person tick."

Employees' performance and satisfaction are likely to be higher if their values fit well with the organization. For instance, the person who places great importance on imagination, independence, and freedom is likely to be poorly matched with an organization that seeks conformity from its employees. Managers are more likely to appreciate, evaluate positively, and allocate rewards to employees who "fit in," and employees are more likely to be satisfied if they perceive that they do fit in. This argues for management to strive during the selection of new employees to find job candidates who have not only the ability, experience, and motivation to perform but also a value system that is compatible with the organization's.

CHAPTER 3

Perception and Individual Decision Making

WHAT IS PERCEPTION?

Perception is a process by which individuals organize and interpret their sensory impressions in order to give meaning to their environment. However, what we perceive can be substantially different from objective reality. For example, all employees in a firm may view it as a great place to work—favorable working conditions, interesting job assignments, good pay, excellent benefits, understanding and responsible management—but, as most of us know, it's very unusual to find such agreement.

—People have inherent biases in how they see others (perception) and in how they make decisions (decision making). We can better understand people by understanding these biases.

Why is perception important in the study of OB? Simply because people's behavior is based on their perception of what reality is, not on reality itself. *The world as it is perceived is the world that is behaviorally important.*

Factors That Influence Perception

How do we explain the fact that individuals may look at the same thing yet perceive it differently? A number of factors operate to shape and sometimes distort perception:

- *Perceiver.* When an individual looks at a target and attempts to interpret what he or she sees, that interpretation is heavily influenced by the personal characteristics of the individual perceiver. For instance, if you expect police officers to be authoritative, young people to be lazy, or individuals holding public office to be unscrupulous, you may perceive them as such, regardless of their actual traits.

- *Target.* Characteristics of the target we observe can affect what we perceive. Loud people are more likely to be noticed in a group than quiet ones. So, too, are extremely attractive or unattractive individuals. Because we don't look at targets in isolation, the relationship of a target to its background also influences perception, as does our tendency to group close things and similar things together.

- *Situation.* The context in which we see objects or events is also important. The time at which we see an object or event can influence attention, as can location, light, or any number of situational factors. For example, at a nightclub on Saturday night, you may not notice a young guest "dressed to the nines." Yet that same person so attired for your Monday morning management class would certainly catch your attention (and that of the rest of the class). Neither the perceiver nor the target changed between Saturday night and Monday morning, but the situation is different.

PERSON PERCEPTION: MAKING JUDGMENTS ABOUT OTHERS

Now we turn to the most relevant application of perception concepts to OB. This is the issue of *person perception*, or the perceptions people form about each other.

When making judgments about people, what factors drive that judgment? One framework that seeks to answer this question is attribution theory. Because of its importance to person perception, we spend a fair amount of time reviewing the theory and its relevance to perception.

Attribution Theory   Kelly (1972)

Our perceptions of people differ from our perceptions of inanimate objects such as desks, machines, or buildings because we make inferences about the actions of people that we don't make about inanimate objects. Nonliving objects are subject to the laws of nature, but—unlike people—they have no beliefs, motives, or intentions. The result is that when we observe people, we attempt to develop explanations of why they behave in certain ways. Our perceptions and judgments of people's actions, therefore, will be significantly influenced by the assumptions we make about their internal states.

Attribution theory suggests that when we observe an individual's behavior, we attempt to determine whether it was internally or externally caused.[1] *Internally* caused behaviors are those that are believed to be under the personal control of the individual. *Externally* caused behaviors are seen as resulting from outside causes; that is, the person is seen as having been forced into the behavior by the situation. For example, if one of your employees is late for work, you might attribute his lateness to his partying into the wee hours of the morning and then oversleeping; this would be an internal attribution. If you attribute his arriving late to an automobile accident that tied up traffic on the road that this employee regularly uses, this would be an external attribution.

Our determination of internally and externally caused behavior depends largely on three factors:

1. *Distinctiveness.* Distinctiveness refers to whether an individual displays different behaviors in different situations. Is the employee who arrives late today also the source of complaints by coworkers for being someone who regularly blows off commitments? We want to know whether this behavior is unusual. If it is, the observer is likely to give the behavior an external attribution. If this action is not unusual, it will probably be judged as internal.

2. *Consensus.* If everyone who faces a similar situation responds in the same way, we can say the behavior shows consensus. The behavior of the tardy employee would meet this criterion if all employees who took the same route to work were also late. From an attribution perspective, if consensus is high, you would be expected to give an external attribution to the employee's tardiness, whereas if other employees who took the same route made it to work on time, your conclusion as to causation would be internal.

3. *Consistency.* Does the person respond the same way over time? Coming in 10 minutes late for work is not perceived in the same way for the employee for whom it is an unusual case (she hasn't been late for several months) as it is for the employee for whom it is part of a routine pattern (she is late two or three times a week). The more consistent the behavior, the more the observer is inclined to attribute it to internal causes.

Exhibit 3-1 summarizes the key elements in attribution theory.

One of the more interesting findings from attribution theory is that errors or biases distort attributions. Substantial evidence suggests that when we make judgments about the behavior of other people, we have a tendency to underestimate the

EXHIBIT 3-1   Attribution Theory

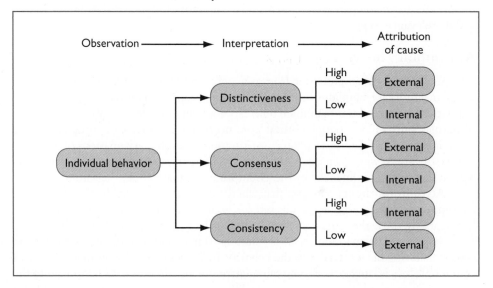

influence of external factors and overestimate the influence of internal or personal factors.[2] This is called the **fundamental attribution error** and can explain why a sales manager is prone to attribute the poor performance of her sales agents to laziness rather than to the innovative product line introduced by a competitor. Also, individuals and organizations have a tendency to attribute their own successes to internal factors such as ability or effort while putting the blame for failure on external factors such as bad luck or unproductive coworkers; this is called the **self-serving bias**.[3]

Frequently Used Shortcuts in Judging Others

We use a number of shortcuts when we judge others. These techniques are frequently valuable: They allow us to make accurate perceptions rapidly and provide valid data for making predictions. However, they are not foolproof. They can and do get us into trouble. Understanding these shortcuts can help you recognize when they can result in significant distortions.

Selective Perception   Any characteristic that makes a person, an object, or an event stand out will increase the probability that we will perceive it. Why? Because it is impossible for us to assimilate everything we see; we can take in only certain stimuli. This tendency explains why you're more likely to notice cars like your own or why a boss may reprimand some people and not others who are doing the same thing. Because we can't observe everything going on about us, we engage in **selective perception**. Selective perception allows us to "speed-read" others, but not without the risk of drawing an inaccurate picture. Because we see what we want to see, we can draw unwarranted conclusions from an ambiguous situation.

Halo Effect   When we draw a general impression about an individual on the basis of a single characteristic, such as intelligence, sociability, or appearance, a **halo effect** is operating. Consider former HP CEO Carly Fiorina. Early in her tenure, she was lauded as articulate, decisive, charismatic, savvy, and visionary. At the time of her appointment, *BusinessWeek* said, "She has it all." After Fiorina was fired, though, she was described as unproven, egotistical, inflexible, and uncompromising. The very same periodical—*BusinessWeek*—that hailed Fiorina before now faulted her for her unwillingness to delegate and inability to execute.[4] So, when Fiorina was deemed effective, everything about her was good. But when she was fired for supposed ineffectiveness, the same people who lauded her before now saw few if any redeeming features. That's both sides of the halo (halo or horns, you might say).

Contrast Effects   An old adage among entertainers says, "Never follow an act that has kids or animals in it." Why? Audiences love children and animals so much that you'll look bad in comparison. This example demonstrates how **contrast effects** can distort perceptions. We don't evaluate a person in isolation. Our reaction to a person is influenced by other persons we have recently encountered.

In a series of job interviews, for instance, interviewers can make distortions in any given candidate's evaluation as a result of his place in the interview schedule. A candidate is likely to receive a more favorable evaluation if preceded by mediocre applicants and a less favorable evaluation if preceded by strong applicants.

Stereotyping   When we judge someone on the basis of our perception of the group to which he or she belongs, we are using the shortcut called **stereotyping**.[5]

We rely on generalizations every day because they help us make decisions quickly. They are a means of simplifying a complex world. It's less difficult to deal with an unmanageable number of stimuli if we use heuristics or stereotypes. The problem occurs, of course, when we generalize inaccurately or too much. In organizations, we frequently hear comments that represent stereotypes based on gender, age, race, religion, ethnicity, and even weight:[6] "Women won't relocate for a promotion," "men aren't interested in child care," "older workers can't learn new skills," "Asian immigrants are hardworking and conscientious," "overweight people lack discipline." Stereotypes can be so deeply ingrained and powerful that they influence life-and-death decisions. One study showed that, controlling for a wide array of factors (such as aggravating or mitigating circumstances), the degree to which black defendants in murder trails looked stereotypically black essentially doubled their odds of receiving a death sentence if convicted.[7]

One of the problems of stereotypes is that they *are* widespread and often *useful* generalizations, despite the fact that they may not contain a shred of truth when applied to a particular person or situation. So we constantly have to check ourselves to make sure we're not unfairly or inaccurately applying a stereotype in our evaluations and decisions. Stereotypes are an example of the warning, "The more useful, the more danger from misuse."

THE LINK BETWEEN PERCEPTION AND INDIVIDUAL DECISION MAKING

Individuals in organizations make **decisions**. That is, they make choices from among two or more alternatives. Top managers, for instance, determine their organization's goals, what products or services to offer, how best to finance operations, or where to locate a new manufacturing plant. Middle- and lower-level managers determine production schedules, select new employees, and decide how pay raises are to be allocated. Of course, making decisions is not the sole province of managers. Nonmanagerial employees also make decisions that affect their jobs and the organizations for which they work. Individual decision making, therefore, is an important part of organizational behavior. But how individuals in organizations make decisions and the quality of their final choices are largely influenced by their perceptions.

Decision making occurs as a reaction to a **problem**; that is, a discrepancy exists between the current state of affairs and some desired state, requiring us to consider alternative courses of action. For example, if your car breaks down and you rely on it to get to work, you have a problem that requires a decision on your part. Unfortunately, most problems don't come neatly packaged and labeled "problem." One person's *problem* is another person's *satisfactory state of affairs*. One manager may view her division's 2 percent decline in quarterly sales to be a serious problem requiring immediate action on her part. In contrast, her counterpart in another division of the same company, who also had a 2 percent sales decrease, might consider that percentage quite acceptable. So the awareness that a problem exists and whether a decision needs to be made is a perceptual issue.

—Perceptual and decision-making biases and heuristics are not necessarily bad. They allow us to process information more quickly and efficiently. The key is to be self-aware enough to see when a bias or shortcut may be counterproductive.

Moreover, every decision requires us to interpret and evaluate information. We typically receive data from multiple sources and need to screen, process, and interpret it. Which data, for instance, are relevant to the decision and which are not? The perceptions of the decision maker will answer that question. We also need to develop alternatives and evaluate the strengths and weaknesses of each. Again, because alternatives don't come with their strengths and weaknesses clearly marked, an individual decision maker's perceptual process will have a large bearing on the final outcome. Finally, throughout the entire decision-making process, perceptual distortions often surface that can bias analysis and conclusions.

DECISION MAKING IN ORGANIZATIONS

Business schools generally train students to follow rational decision-making models. Although these models have considerable merit, they don't always describe how people actually make decisions. This is where OB enters the picture: If we are to improve how we make decisions in organizations, we need to understand the decision-making errors that people commit (in addition to the perception errors just discussed). In the sections that follow, we describe these errors, and we begin with a brief overview of the rational decision-making model.

The Rational Model, Bounded Rationality, and Intuition

Rational Decision Making   We often think the best decision maker is **rational** and makes consistent, value-maximizing choices within specified constraints.[8] These decisions follow a six-step **rational decision-making model**. The six steps are listed in Exhibit 3-2.

The rational decision-making model relies on a number of assumptions, including that the decision maker has complete information, is able to identify all the relevant options in an unbiased manner, and chooses the option with the highest utility. As you might imagine, most decisions in the real world don't follow the rational model. For instance, people are usually content to find an acceptable or reasonable solution to a problem rather than an optimal one. People tend to consider a few options, and then chose the first one that appears satisfactory. As one expert in decision making put it, "Most significant decisions are made by judgment, rather than by a defined prescriptive model."[9] What's more, people are remarkably unaware of making suboptimal decisions.[10] If the rational model does not accurately describe most decision making, how are decisions really made? One answer is provided by the concept of bounded rationality.

Bounded Rationality   Most people respond to a complex problem by reducing it to a level at which they can readily understand it. The limited information-processing capability of human beings makes it impossible to assimilate and understand all the

EXHIBIT 3-2   Steps in the Rational Decision-Making Model

1. Define the problem.
2. Identify the decision criteria.
3. Allocate weights to the criteria.
4. Develop the alternatives.
5. Evaluate the alternatives.
6. Select the best alternative.

information necessary to optimize.[11] So people *satisfice*; that is, they seek solutions that are satisfactory and sufficient.

When you considered which college to attend, did you look at every viable alternative? Did you carefully identify all the criteria that were important in your decision? Did you evaluate each alternative against the criteria in order to find the optimal college? The answers are probably "no." Well, don't feel bad. Few people made their college choice this way. Instead of optimizing, you probably satisficed.

Because the human mind cannot formulate and solve complex problems with full rationality, we operate within the confines of **bounded rationality**. We construct simplified models that extract the essential features from problems without capturing all their complexity.[12] We can then behave rationally within the limits of the simple model.

How does bounded rationality work for the typical individual? Once we've identified a problem, we begin to search for criteria and alternatives. But the list of criteria is likely to be far from exhaustive. We identify a limited list of the most conspicuous choices, both easy to find and highly visible, that usually represent familiar criteria and tried-and-true solutions. Next, we begin reviewing them, but our review will not be comprehensive. Instead, we focus on alternatives that differ only in a relatively small degree from the choice currently in effect. Following familiar and well-worn paths, we review alternatives only until we identify one that is "good enough"—that meets an acceptable level of performance. That ends our search. So the solution represents a satisficing choice—the first *acceptable* one we encounter—rather than an optimal one.

Intuition   Perhaps the least rational way of making decisions is to rely on intuition. **Intuitive decision making** is a nonconscious process created from distilled experience.[13] Its defining qualities are that it occurs outside conscious thought; it relies on holistic associations, or links between disparate pieces of information; it's fast; and it's affectively charged, meaning that it usually engages the emotions.[14]

Intuition is not rational, but that doesn't necessarily make it wrong. Intuition doesn't necessarily operate in opposition to rational analysis; rather, the two can complement each other. And intuition can be a powerful force in decision making. For most of the twentieth century, experts believed that decision makers' use of intuition was irrational or ineffective. That's no longer the case. There is growing recognition that rational analysis has been overemphasized and that, in certain instances, relying on intuition can improve decision making.[15] Although intuition can be invaluable in making good decisions, we can't rely on it too much. Because it is so unquantifiable, it's hard to know when our hunches are right or wrong. The key is not to either abandon or rely solely on intuition but to supplement it with evidence and good judgment.

Common Biases and Errors in Decision Making

Decision makers engage in bounded rationality, but an accumulating body of research tells us that decision makers also allow systematic biases and errors to creep into their judgments.[16] These come from attempts to shortcut the decision process. To minimize effort and avoid difficult trade-offs, people tend to rely too heavily on experience, impulses, gut feelings, and convenient rules of thumb. In many instances, these shortcuts are helpful. However, just as perceptual biases can distort our impressions of reality, decision-making biases can lead to severe distortions of rationality. Following are the most common biases in decision making.

Overconfidence Bias   It's been said that "no problem in judgment and decision making is more prevalent and more potentially catastrophic than overconfidence."[17] When we're given factual questions and asked to judge the probability that our answers are correct, we tend to be far too optimistic. For instance, studies have found that, when people say they're 65 to 70 percent confident that they're right, they are actually correct only about 50 percent of the time. And when they say they're 100 percent sure, they tend to be 70 to 85 percent correct.[18]

From an organizational standpoint, one of the most interesting findings related to overconfidence is that those individuals whose intellectual and interpersonal abilities are *weakest* are most likely to overestimate their performance and ability. So as managers and employees become more knowledgeable about an issue, they become less likely to display overconfidence. And overconfidence is most likely to surface when organizational members are considering issues or problems that are outside their area of expertise.[19]

Anchoring Bias   The **anchoring bias** is a tendency to fixate on initial information and fail to adequately adjust for subsequent information.[20] The anchoring bias occurs because our mind appears to give a disproportionate amount of emphasis to the first information it receives. Consider the role of anchoring in negotiations. Anytime a negotiation takes place, so does anchoring. As soon as someone states a number, your ability to ignore that number has been compromised. For instance, when a prospective employer asks how much you were making in your prior job, your answer typically anchors the employer's offer. You may want to keep this in mind when you negotiate your salary, but remember to set the anchor only as high as you ethically can.

Confirmation Bias   The rational decision-making process assumes that we objectively gather information. But we don't. We *selectively* gather it. The **confirmation bias** represents a specific case of selective perception. We seek out information that reaffirms our past choices, and we discount information that contradicts them. We also tend to accept at face value information that confirms our preconceived views, whereas we are critical and skeptical of information that challenges these views. Therefore, the information we gather is typically biased toward supporting views we already hold. This confirmation bias influences where we go to collect evidence because we tend to seek out sources most likely to tell us what we want to hear. It also leads us to give too much weight to supporting information and too little to contradictory information.

Availability Bias   Many more people fear flying than fear driving in a car. But if flying on a commercial airline were as dangerous as driving, the equivalent of two 747s filled to capacity would have to crash every week, killing all aboard, to match the risk of being killed in a car accident. Yet the media gives much more attention to air accidents, so we tend to overstate the risk of flying and understate the risk of driving.

This illustrates the **availability bias**, which is the tendency for people to base their judgments on information that is readily available to them.[21] Events that evoke emotions, that are particularly vivid, or that have occurred more recently tend to be more available in our memory. As a result, we tend to overestimate the chances of unlikely events such as an airplane crash. The availability bias can also explain why managers, when doing annual performance appraisals, tend to give more weight to recent employee behaviors than to behaviors of 6 or 9 months ago.

Escalation of Commitment   Another distortion that creeps into decisions in practice is a tendency to escalate commitment when making a series of decisions.[22] **Escalation of commitment** refers to staying with a decision even when there is clear evidence that it's wrong. For example, consider a friend who has been dating his girlfriend for several years. Although he admits to you that things aren't going too well in the relationship, he says he is still going to marry her. His justification: "I have a lot invested in the relationship!"

It has been well documented that individuals escalate commitment to a failing course of action when they view themselves as responsible for the failure.[23] That is, they "throw good money after bad" to demonstrate that their initial decision wasn't wrong and to avoid having to admit that they made a mistake.[24] Escalation of commitment has obvious implications for managerial decisions. Many an organization has suffered large losses because a manager was determined to prove his original decision was right by continuing to commit resources to what was a lost cause from the beginning.

Hindsight Bias   The **hindsight bias** is the tendency to believe falsely, after the outcome of an event is actually known, that we'd have accurately predicted that outcome.[25] When something happens and we have accurate feedback on the outcome, we seem to be pretty good at concluding that the outcome was relatively obvious. Do you think the 9/11 terrorist attacks should have been prevented? We'll never know, but we have to realize that things always seem much clearer when we know all the facts (or the connections among the facts). As Malcolm Gladwell, author of *Blink* and *The Tipping Point*, writes, "What is clear in hindsight is rarely clear before the fact. It's an obvious point, but one that nonetheless bears repeating, particularly when we're in the midst of assigning blame for the surprise attack of September 11th."[26]

The hindsight bias reduces our ability to learn from the past. It permits us to think that we're better at making predictions than we really are and can result in our being more confident about the accuracy of future decisions than we have a right to be. If, for instance, your actual predictive accuracy is only 40 percent, but you think it's 90 percent, you're likely to become falsely overconfident and less vigilant in questioning your predictive skills.

ORGANIZATIONAL CONSTRAINTS ON DECISION MAKING

Having examined the rational decision-making model, bounded rationality, and some of the most salient biases and errors in decision making, we turn here to a discussion of organizational constraints. Organizations can constrain decision makers, creating deviations from the rational model. For instance, managers shape their decisions to reflect the organization's performance evaluation and reward system, to comply with the organization's formal regulations, and to meet organizationally imposed time constraints. Previous organizational decisions also act as precedents to constrain current decisions.

Performance Evaluation   Managers are strongly influenced in their decision making by the criteria on which they are evaluated. If a division manager believes the manufacturing plants under his responsibility are operating best when he hears nothing negative, we shouldn't be surprised to find his plant managers spending a good part of their time ensuring that negative information doesn't reach him.

Reward Systems   The organization's reward system influences decision makers by suggesting to them what choices are preferable in terms of personal payoff. For example, if the organization rewards risk aversion, managers are more likely to make conservative decisions. From the 1930s through the mid-1980s, General Motors consistently gave out promotions and bonuses to managers who kept a low profile and avoided controversy. The result was that GM managers became very adept at dodging tough issues and passing controversial decisions on to committees.

Formal Regulations   David Gonzalez, a shift manager at a Taco Bell restaurant in San Antonio, Texas, describes constraints he faces on his job: "I've got rules and regulations covering almost every decision I make—from how to make a burrito to how often I need to clean the restrooms. My job doesn't come with much freedom of choice." David's situation is not unique. All but the smallest of organizations create rules and policies to program decisions, which are intended to get individuals to act in the intended manner. And of course, in so doing, they limit the decision maker's choices.

System-Imposed Time Constraints   Organizations impose deadlines on decisions. For instance, a report on new-product development may have to be ready for the executive committee to review by the first of the month. Almost all important decisions come with explicit deadlines. These conditions create time pressures on decision makers and often make it difficult, if not impossible, to gather all the information they might like to have before making a final choice.

Historical Precedents   Decisions aren't made in a vacuum. They have a context. In fact, individual decisions are accurately characterized as points in a stream of decisions. Decisions made in the past are ghosts that continually haunt current choices—that is, commitments that have already been made constrain current options. It's common knowledge that the largest determinant of the size of any given year's budget is last year's budget.[27] Choices made today, therefore, are largely a result of choices made over the years.

WHAT ABOUT ETHICS IN DECISION MAKING?

Ethical considerations should be an important criterion in organizational decision making. This is certainly truer today than at any time in the recent past, given the increasing scrutiny business is under to behave in an ethical and socially responsible way. In this section, we present three different ways to frame decisions ethically.

Three Ethical Decision Criteria

An individual can use three different criteria in making ethical choices.[28] The first is the *utilitarian* criterion, in which decisions are made solely on the basis of their outcomes or consequences. The goal of **utilitarianism** is to provide the greatest good for the greatest number. This view tends to dominate business decision making. It is consistent with goals such as efficiency, productivity, and high profits. By maximizing profits, for instance, a business executive can argue that he is securing the greatest good for the greatest number—as he hands out dismissal notices to 15 percent of his employees.

Another ethical criterion is to focus on *rights*. This calls on individuals to make decisions consistent with fundamental liberties and privileges, as set forth in documents such as the Bill of Rights. An emphasis on rights in decision making means respecting and protecting the basic rights of individuals, such as the right to privacy, to free speech, and to due process. For instance, this criterion protects **whistle-blowers** when they reveal unethical practices by their organization to the press or government agencies, on the grounds of their right to free speech.

A third criterion is to focus on *justice*. This requires individuals to impose and enforce rules fairly and impartially so that there is an equitable distribution of benefits and costs. Union members typically favor this view. It justifies paying people the same wage for a given job, regardless of performance differences, and using seniority as the primary determination in making layoff decisions.

Each of these criteria has advantages and liabilities. A focus on utilitarianism promotes efficiency and productivity, but it can result in ignoring the rights of some individuals, particularly those with minority representation in the organization. The use of rights as a criterion protects individuals from injury and is consistent with freedom and privacy, but it can create an overly legalistic work environment that hinders productivity and efficiency. A focus on justice protects the interests of the underrepresented and less powerful, but it can encourage a sense of entitlement that reduces risk taking, innovation, and productivity.

Decision makers, particularly in for-profit organizations, tend to feel safe and comfortable when they use utilitarianism. A lot of questionable actions can be justified when framed as being in the best interests of "the organization" and stockholders. But many critics of business decision makers argue that this perspective needs to change.[29] Increased concern in society about individual rights and social justice suggests the need for managers to develop ethical standards based on nonutilitarian criteria. This presents a solid challenge to today's managers because making decisions using criteria such as individual rights and social justice involves far more ambiguities than using utilitarian criteria such as effects on efficiency and profits. This helps to explain why managers are increasingly criticized for their actions. Raising prices, selling products with questionable effects on consumer health, closing down inefficient plants, polluting the environment, moving production overseas to cut costs, and similar decisions can be justified in utilitarian terms. But that may no longer be the single criterion by which good decisions should be judged.

Improving Creativity in Decision Making

Although following the steps of the rational decision-making model will often improve decisions, a rational decision maker also needs **creativity**, that is, the ability to produce novel and useful ideas.[30] These are ideas that are different from what's been done before but that are appropriate to the problem or opportunity presented.

Why is creativity important to decision making? It allows the decision maker to more fully appraise and understand the problem, including seeing problems others can't see. Such thinking is becoming more important. Experts estimate that the United States alone will add 10 million "creative class" jobs—in science, technology, entertainment, design, and entrepreneurship—over the next decade. And both companies and business schools are trying to increase the creative potential of their employees and graduates.[31] L'Oréal puts its managers through creative exercises, such as cooking or making music, and University of Chicago's business school has added a requirement for MBA students to make short movies about their experiences.

Creative Potential   Most people have creative potential they can use when confronted with a decision-making problem. But to unleash that potential, they have to get out of the psychological ruts many of us fall into and learn how to think about a problem in divergent ways.

People differ in their inherent creativity, and exceptional creativity is scarce. We all know of creative geniuses in science (Albert Einstein), art (Pablo Picasso), and business (Steve Jobs). But what about the typical individual? People who score high on openness to experience (see Chapter 2), for example, are more likely than others to be creative. Intelligent people also are more likely than others to be creative.[32]

> —Creativity allows the decision maker to more fully appraise and understand the problem, including seeing problems others can't see.

Three-Component Model of Creativity   Given that most people have the capacity to be at least somewhat creative, what can individuals and organizations do to stimulate employee creativity? The best answer to this question lies in the **three-component model of creativity**.[33] Based on an extensive body of research, this model proposes that individual creativity essentially requires expertise, creative-thinking skills, and intrinsic task motivation . Studies confirm that the higher the level of each of these three components, the higher the creativity.

Expertise is the foundation for all creative work. The film writer, producer, and director Quentin Tarantino spent his youth working in a video rental store, where he built up an encyclopedic knowledge of movies. The potential for creativity is enhanced when individuals have abilities, knowledge, proficiencies, and similar expertise in their field of endeavor. For example, you wouldn't expect someone with a minimal knowledge of programming to be very creative as a software engineer.

The second component is *creative-thinking skills*. This encompasses personality characteristics associated with creativity, the ability to use analogies, and the talent to see the familiar in a different light.

Research suggests that we are more creative when we're in good moods, so if we need to be creative, we should do things that make us happy, such as listening to music we enjoy, eating foods we like, watching funny movies, or socializing with others.[34]

Evidence also suggests that being around others who are creative can actually make us more inspired, especially if we're creatively "stuck."[35] One study found that "weak ties" to creative people—knowing creative people but not all that closely—facilitates creativity because the people are there as a resource if we need them, but they are not so close as to stunt our own independent thinking.[36]

The effective use of analogies allows decision makers to apply an idea from one context to another. One of the most famous examples in which analogy resulted in a creative breakthrough was Alexander Graham Bell's observation that it might be possible to apply the way the ear operates to his "talking box." He noticed that the bones in the ear are operated by a delicate, thin membrane. He wondered why, then, a thicker and stronger piece of membrane shouldn't be able to move a piece of steel. From that analogy, the telephone was conceived.

Some people have developed their creative skills because they are able to see problems in a new way. They're able to make the strange familiar and the familiar strange.[37] For instance, most of us think of hens laying eggs. But how many of us have considered that a hen is only an egg's way of making another egg?

The final component in the three-component model of creativity is *intrinsic task motivation*. This is the desire to work on something because it's interesting, involving, exciting, satisfying, or personally challenging. This motivational component is what turns creative *potential* into *actual* creative ideas. It determines the extent to which individuals fully engage their expertise and creative skills. Creative people often love their work, to the point of seeming obsessive. Our work environment can have a significant effect on intrinsic motivation. Stimulants that foster creativity include a culture that encourages the flow of ideas; fair and constructive judgment of ideas; rewards and recognition for creative work; sufficient financial, material, and information resources; freedom to decide what work is to be done and how to do it; a supervisor who communicates effectively, shows confidence in others, and supports the work group; and work group members who support and trust each other.[38]

GLOBAL IMPLICATIONS

In considering whether there are global differences in the concepts we've discussed in this chapter, let's consider the three areas that have attracted the most research: (1) attributions, (2) decision making, and (3) ethics.

Attributions   Although research on cultural differences in perception is just starting to accumulate, there has been some research on cultural differences in attributions. The evidence is mixed, but most of it suggests that there *are* cultural differences across cultures in the attributions people make.[39] For instance, a study of Korean managers found that, contrary to the self-serving bias, they tended to accept responsibility for group failure "because I was not a capable leader" instead of attributing failure to group members.[40] Attribution theory was developed largely based on experiments with U.S. and Western European workers. But the Korean study suggests caution in making attribution theory predictions in non-Western societies, especially in countries with strong collectivist traditions.

Decision Making   The rational model makes no acknowledgment of cultural differences, nor does the bulk of OB research literature on decision making. A 2007 review of cross-cultural OB research covered 25 areas, but cultural influence on decision making was not among them. Another 2007 review identified 15 topics, but the result was the same: no research on culture and decision making.[41] It seems that most OB research assumes that culture doesn't matter to decision making.

But Indonesians, for instance, don't necessarily make decisions the same way Canadians do. Therefore, we need to recognize that the cultural background of a decision maker can have a significant influence on the selection of problems, the depth of analysis, the importance placed on logic and rationality, and whether organizational decisions should be made autocratically by an individual manager or collectively in groups.[42]

Cultures differ, for example, in terms of time orientation, the importance of rationality, their belief in the ability of people to solve problems, and their preference for collective decision making. Differences in time orientation help us understand why managers in Egypt make decisions at a much slower and more deliberate pace than their U.S. counterparts. Although rationality is valued in North America, that's not true elsewhere in the world. A North American manager might make an important decision intuitively but knows it's important to appear to proceed in a rational fashion because rationality is highly valued in the West. In countries such as Iran, where rationality is not as paramount as other factors, efforts to appear rational are not necessary.

Some cultures emphasize solving problems, whereas others focus on accepting situations as they are. The United States falls in the first category; Thailand and Indonesia are examples of the second. Because problem-solving managers believe they can and should change situations to their benefit, U.S. managers might identify a problem long before their Thai or Indonesian counterparts would choose to recognize it as such. Decision making by Japanese managers is much more group oriented than in the United States. The Japanese value conformity and cooperation. So before Japanese CEOs make an important decision, they collect a large amount of information, which they use in consensus-forming group decisions.

In short, we have reason to believe there are important cultural differences in decision making. Unfortunately, though, there is not yet much research to substantiate these beliefs. OB is a research-based discipline, but research does not always respond quickly to important practical concerns.

Ethics What is seen as an ethical decision in China may not be seen as such in Canada. The reason is that there are no global ethical standards.[43] Contrasts between Asia and the West provide an illustration.[44] Because bribery is commonplace in countries such as China, an Australian working in China might face a dilemma: Should I pay a bribe to secure business if it is an accepted part of that country's culture? A manager of a large U.S. company operating in China caught an employee stealing. Following company policy, she fired him and turned him over to the local authorities. Later, she was horrified to learn that the employee had been summarily executed.[45]

Although ethical standards may seem ambiguous in the West, criteria defining right and wrong are actually much clearer in the West than in Asia. Few issues are black and white in Asia; most are gray. The need for global organizations to establish ethical principles for decision makers in countries such as India and China and to modify them to reflect cultural norms may be critical if high standards are to be upheld and if consistent practices are to be achieved.

IMPLICATIONS FOR MANAGERS

Perception Individuals behave in a given manner based not on the way their external environment actually is but, rather, on what they see or believe it to be. It's the employee's perception of a situation that becomes the basis for behavior. Therefore, to be able to influence productivity, it's necessary to assess how workers perceive their jobs.

Dissatisfaction with working conditions or the belief that promotion opportunities in the organization lacking are judgments based on attempts to create meaning out of one's job. The employee's conclusion that a job is good or bad is an interpretation. Managers must spend time understanding how each individual interprets reality, and when there is a significant difference between what is seen and what exists, the managers must try to eliminate the distortions. Failure to deal with the differences when individuals perceive the job in negative terms will result in increased absenteeism and turnover and lower job satisfaction.

Individual Decision Making What can managers do to improve their decision making? We offer five suggestions:

1. *Analyze the situation.* Adjust your decision-making approach to the national culture you're operating in and to the criteria your organization evaluates and rewards. For instance, if you're in a country that doesn't value rationality, don't feel compelled to follow the rational decision-making model or even to try to make your decisions appear rational.

2. Similarly, organizations differ in terms of the importance they place on risk, the use of groups, and the like. *Adjust your decision approach to ensure that it's compatible with the organization's culture.*

3. *Be aware of biases and then try to minimize their impact.* Exhibit 3-3 offers some suggestions.

EXHIBIT 3-3   Reducing Biases and Errors

Focus on Goals. Without goals, you can't be rational, you don't know what information you need, you don't know which information is relevant and which is irrelevant, you'll find it difficult to choose between alternatives, and you're far more likely to experience regret over the choices you make. Clear goals make decision making easier and help you eliminate options that are inconsistent with your interests.

Look for Information That Disconfirms Your Beliefs. One of the most effective means for counteracting overconfidence and the confirmation and hindsight biases is to actively look for information that contradicts your beliefs and assumptions. When we overtly consider various ways we could be wrong, we challenge our tendencies to think we're smarter than we actually are.

Don' Try to Create Meaning out of Random Events. The educated mind has been trained to look for cause-and-effect relationships. When something happens, we ask why. And when we can't find reasons, we often invent them. You have to accept that there are events in life that are outside your control. Ask yourself if patterns can be meaningfully explained or whether they are merely coincidence. Don't attempt to create meaning out of coincidence.

Increase Your Options. No matter how many options you've identified, your final choice can be no better than the best of the option set you've selected. This argues for increasing your decision alternatives and for using creativity in developing a wide range of diverse choices. The more alternatives you can generate, and the more diverse those alternatives, the greater your chance of finding an outstanding one.

Source: S. P. Robbins, *Decide & Conquer Make Winning Decisions and Take Control of Your Life* (Upper Saddle River, NJ; Financial Times/Prentice Hall, 2004), pp. 164-168.

4. *Combine rational analysis with intuition.* These are not conflicting approaches to decision making. By using both, you can actually improve your decision-making effectiveness. As you gain managerial experience, you should feel increasingly confident in imposing your intuitive processes on top of your rational analysis.

5. *Enhance your creativity.* Look for novel solutions to problems, attempt to see problems in new ways, and use analogies. In addition, try to remove work and organizational barriers that might impede your creativity.

Job Attitudes

1. Contrast the three components of an attitude.
2. Summarize the relationship between attitudes and behavior.
3. Compare and contrast the major job attitudes.
4. Define *job satisfaction* and show how it can be measured.
5. Summarize the main causes of job satisfaction, and identify four employee responses to dissatisfaction.
6. Show whether job satisfaction is a relevant concept in countries other than the United States.

We seem to have attitudes toward everything, whether it's about our leaders, our college or university, our families, or ourselves. In this chapter, we look at attitudes, their link to behavior, and how employees' satisfaction or dissatisfaction with their jobs affects the workplace.

ATTITUDES

Attitudes are evaluative statements—either favorable or unfavorable—about objects, people, or events. They reflect how we feel about something. When I say "I like my job," I am expressing my attitude about work.

Attitudes are complex. If you ask people about their attitude toward religion, Paris Hilton, or the organization they work for, you may get a simple response, but the reasons underlying the response are probably complex. In order to fully understand attitudes, we need to consider their fundamental properties or components.

What Are the Main Components of Attitudes?

Typically, researchers have assumed that attitudes have three components: cognition, affect, and behavior.[1] Let's look at each.

The statement "my pay is low" is a description. It is the **cognitive component** of an attitude—the aspect of an attitude that is a description of or belief in the way things are. It sets the stage for the more critical part of an attitude—its **affective component**. Affect is the emotional or feeling segment of an attitude and is reflected in the statement "I am angry over how little I'm paid." Finally, and we'll discuss this issue at considerable length later in this section, affect can lead to behavioral outcomes. The **behavioral component** of an attitude refers to an intention to behave in a certain way toward someone or something (to continue the example, "I'm going to look for another job that pays better").

To view attitudes as made up of three components—cognition, affect, and behavior—is helpful in understanding their complexity and the potential relationship between attitudes and behavior. Keep in mind that these components are closely related, and cognition and affect in particular are inseparable in many ways. For example, imagine you concluded that someone had just treated you unfairly. Aren't you likely to have feelings about that, occurring virtually instantaneously with the thought? Thus, cognition and affect are intertwined.

Exhibit 4-1 illustrates how the three components of an attitude are related. In this example, an employee didn't get a promotion he thought he deserved; a coworker received it instead. The employee's attitude toward his supervisor is illustrated as follows: the employee thought he deserved the promotion (cognition), the employee

EXHIBIT 4-1   The Components of an Attitude

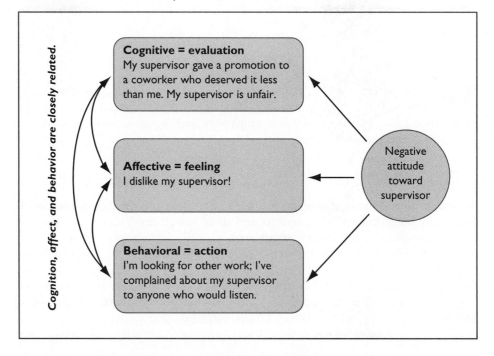

strongly dislikes his supervisor (affect), and the employee is looking for another job (behavior). As previously noted, although we often think that cognition causes affect, which then causes behavior, in reality these components are often difficult to separate.

In organizations, attitudes are important for their behavioral component. If workers believe, for example, that supervisors, auditors, bosses, and time-and-motion engineers are all in conspiracy to make employees work harder for the same or less money, it makes sense to try to understand how these attitudes formed, their relationship to actual job behavior, and how they might be changed.

Does Behavior Always Follow from Attitudes?

Early research on attitudes assumed that they were causally related to behavior; that is, the attitudes people hold determine what they do. Common sense, too, suggests a relationship. Isn't it logical that people watch television programs they like, or that employees try to avoid assignments they find distasteful?

However, in the late 1960s, this assumed effect of attitudes on behavior was challenged by a review of the research.[2] One researcher—Leon Festinger—argued that attitudes *follow* behavior. Did you ever notice how people change what they say so it doesn't contradict what they do? Perhaps a friend of yours has consistently argued that the quality of U.S. cars isn't up to that of imports and that he'd never own anything but a Japanese or German car. But his dad gives him a late-model Ford Mustang, and suddenly U.S. cars aren't so bad. Festinger argued that these cases of attitude following behavior illustrate the effects of **cognitive dissonance**.[3] *Cognitive dissonance* refers to any incompatibility an individual might perceive between two or more attitudes or between behavior and attitudes. Festinger argued that any form of inconsistency is uncomfortable and that individuals will attempt to reduce the dissonance and, hence, the discomfort. They will seek a stable state, in which there is a minimum of dissonance.

Research has generally concluded that people seek consistency among their attitudes and between their attitudes and their behavior.[4] They do this by altering either the attitudes or the behavior or by developing a rationalization for the discrepancy. Tobacco executives provide an example.[5] How, you might wonder, do these people cope with the ongoing barrage of data linking cigarette smoking and negative health outcomes? They can deny that any clear causation between smoking and cancer, for instance, has been established. They can brainwash themselves by continually articulating the benefits of tobacco. They can acknowledge the negative consequences of smoking but rationalize that people are going to smoke and that tobacco companies merely promote freedom of choice. They can accept the research evidence and begin actively working to make less dangerous cigarettes or at least reduce their availability to more vulnerable groups, such as teenagers. Or they can quit their job because the dissonance is too great.

No individual, of course, can completely avoid dissonance. You know that cheating on your income tax is wrong, but you "fudge" the numbers a bit every year and hope you're not audited. Or you tell your children to floss their teeth every day, but *you* don't. So how do people cope? Festinger would propose that the desire to reduce dissonance depends on the *importance* of the elements creating it and the degree of *influence* the individual believes he has over the elements; individuals will be more motivated to reduce dissonance when the attitudes or behavior are important or when they believe that the dissonance is due to something they can control. A third factor is the *rewards* of dissonance; high rewards accompanying high dissonance tend to reduce the tension inherent in the dissonance because they allow us to easily rationalize it.

These moderating factors suggest that just individuals who experience dissonance will not necessarily move directly toward reducing it. If the issues underlying the dissonance are of minimal importance, if individuals perceive the dissonance is externally imposed and substantially uncontrollable, or if rewards are significant enough to offset it, an individual will not be under great tension to reduce the dissonance.

Although Festinger questioned the attitudes–behavior relationship by arguing that, in many cases, attitudes follow behavior, other researchers asked whether there was any relationship at all. More recent research shows that attitudes predict future behavior and confirmed Festinger's original belief that certain "moderating variables" can strengthen the link.[6]

Below we review some of the more important variables that moderate the attitudes–behavior relationship. Though the research on these moderating variables was inspired by Festinger's work, they tend to assume, unlike Festinger's dissonance theory, that attitudes lead to behavior (and thus are distinct from the cognitive dissonance moderating factors reviewed previously).

Moderating Variables   The most powerful moderators of the attitudes–behavior relationship are the *importance* of the attitude, its *correspondence to behavior*, its *accessibility*, whether *social pressures* exist, and whether a person has *direct experience* with the attitude.

Important attitudes reflect fundamental values, self-interest, or identification with individuals or groups that a person values. Attitudes that individuals consider important tend to show a strong relationship to behavior.

The more closely the attitude and the behavior are matched or correspond, the stronger the relationship. Specific attitudes tend to predict specific behaviors, whereas general attitudes tend to best predict general behaviors. For instance, asking someone specifically about her intention to stay with an organization for the next 6 months is likely to better predict turnover for that person than if you asked her how satisfied she was with her job overall. On the other hand, overall job satisfaction would better predict a general behavior such as whether the individual was engaged in her work or motivated to contribute to her organization.[7]

Attitudes we remember easily (i.e., are more accessible) are more likely to predict our behavior. Interestingly, you're more likely to remember attitudes you frequently express. So the more you talk about your attitude on a subject, the more you're likely to remember it, and the more likely it is to shape your behavior.

Discrepancies between attitudes and behavior are more likely to occur when social pressures to behave in certain ways hold exceptional power. This situation tends to characterize behavior in organizations. It may explain why an employee who holds strong anti-union attitudes attends pro-union organizing meetings or why tobacco executives, who are not smokers themselves and who tend to believe the research linking smoking and cancer, don't actively discourage others from smoking in their offices.

Finally, the attitudes–behavior relationship is likely to be much stronger if attitude refers to something with which the individual has direct personal experience. Asking college students with no significant work experience how they would respond to working for an authoritarian supervisor is far less likely to predict actual behavior than asking that same question of employees who have actually worked for such an individual.

What Are the Major Job Attitudes?

A person can have thousands of attitudes, but OB focuses our attention on a very limited number of work-related attitudes. These tap positive or negative evaluations that employees hold about aspects of their work environment. Most of the research in OB has looked at three attitudes: job satisfaction, job involvement, and organizational commitment.[8] A few other attitudes attracting attention from researchers include perceived organizational support and employee engagement; we'll also discuss these.

Job Satisfaction   The term **job satisfaction** describes a positive feeling about a job, resulting from an evaluation of its characteristics. A person with a high level of job satisfaction holds positive feelings about his or her job, whereas a dissatisfied person holds negative feelings. When people speak of employee attitudes, they usually mean job satisfaction. In fact, the two are frequently used interchangeably. Because of the high importance OB researchers have given to job satisfaction, we'll review this attitude in detail shortly.

Job Involvement   Related to job satisfaction is **job involvement**.[9] Job involvement measures the degree to which people identify psychologically with their job and consider their perceived performance level important to self-worth. Employees with a high level of job involvement strongly identify with and really care about the kind of work they do. Another closely related concept is **psychological empowerment**, which is employees' beliefs in the degree to which they influence their work environment, their competence, the meaningfulness of their job, and the perceived autonomy in their work.[10] For example, one study of nursing managers in Singapore found that good leaders empower their employees by involving them in decisions, making them feel their work is important, and giving them discretion to "do their own thing."[11]

—Individuals have many kinds of attitudes about their job; of the main job attitudes, organizational commitment and job satisfaction are the most widely studied.

High levels of both job involvement and psychological empowerment are positively related to organizational citizenship and job performance. In addition, high job involvement has been found to be related to a reduced number of absences and lower resignation rates.[12]

Organizational Commitment   The third job attitude we'll discuss is **organizational commitment**, a state in which an employee identifies with a particular organization and its goals and wishes to maintain membership in the organization. So, high job involvement means identifying with your specific job, whereas high organizational commitment means identifying with your employing organization.

There are three separate dimensions to organizational commitment:[13]

1. *Affective commitment.* An **affective commitment** is an emotional attachment to the organization and a belief in its values. For example, a PETCO employee may be affectively committed to the company because of its involvement with animals.

2. *Continuance commitment.* A **continuance commitment** is the perceived economic value of remaining with an organization compared to leaving it. An employee may be committed to an employer because she is paid well and feels it would hurt her family to quit.

3. *Normative commitment.* A **normative commitment** is an obligation to remain with the organization for moral or ethical reasons. For example, an employee who is spearheading a new initiative may remain with an employer because he feels he would "leave the employer in the lurch" if he left.

A positive relationship appears to exist between organizational commitment and job productivity, but it is a modest one.[14] A review of twenty-seven studies suggested that the relationship between commitment and performance is strongest for new employees, and it is considerably weaker for more experienced employees.[15] And, as with job involvement, the research evidence demonstrates negative relationships between organizational commitment and both absenteeism and turnover.[16] In general, affective commitment seems more strongly related to organizational outcomes such as performance and turnover than the other two commitment dimensions. One study found that affective commitment was a significant predictor of various outcomes (perception of task characteristics, career satisfaction, intent to leave) in 72 percent of the cases, compared with only 36 percent for normative commitment and 7 percent for continuance commitment.[17] The weak results for continuance commitment make sense in that it really isn't a strong commitment at all. Rather than an allegiance (affective commitment) or an obligation (normative commitment) to an employer, a continuance commitment describes an employee who is "tethered" to an employer simply because there isn't anything better available.

There is reason to believe that the concept of commitment may be less important to employers and employees today than it was previously. The unwritten loyalty contract that existed 30 years ago between employees and employers has been seriously damaged, and the notion of employees staying with a single organization for most of their career has become increasingly irrelevant. Given that, "measures of employee–firm attachment, such as commitment, are problematic for new employment relations."[18] This suggests that *organizational commitment* is probably less important as a work-related attitude than it was previously. In its place, we might expect something akin to *occupational commitment* to become a more relevant variable because it better reflects today's fluid workforce.[19]

Perceived Organizational Support   **Perceived organizational support (POS)** is the degree to which employees believe the organization values their contribution and cares about their well-being (for example, an employee believes his organization would be accomodating if he had a child-care problem or would forgive an honest mistake on his part). Research shows that people perceive their organization as supportive when rewards are deemed fair, when employees have a voice in decisions, and when their supervisors are seen as supportive.[20] Although less research has linked POS to OB outcomes than is the case with other job attitudes, some findings suggest that employees with strong POS perceptions are more likely to have higher levels of organizational citizenship behaviors and job performance.[21]

Employee Engagement   A new concept is **employee engagement**, an individual's involvement with, satisfaction with, and enthusiasm for, the work she does. For example, we might ask employees about the availability of resources and the opportunities to learn new skills, whether they feel their work is important and meaningful, and whether their interactions with coworkers and supervisors are rewarding. Highly engaged employees have a passion for their work and feel a deep connection to their company; disengaged employees have essentially "checked out"—putting time but not energy or attention into their work. A recent study of nearly 8,000 business units in thirty-six companies found that, compared with other companies, those whose employees had high-average levels of engagement had higher levels of customer satisfaction, were more productive, had higher profits, and had lower levels of turnover and accidents.[22] Molson Coors found that engaged employees were five times less likely to have safety incidents, and when one did occur, it was much less serious, and less costly, for the engaged employee than for a disengaged one ($63 per incident versus $392). Engagement becomes a real concern for most organizations because surveys indicate that few employees—between 17 percent and 29 percent—are highly engaged by their work. Caterpillar set out to increase employee engagement and concluded that its initiative resulted in an 80 percent drop in grievances and a 34 percent increase in highly satisfied customers.[23]

Because of some of these promising findings, employee engagement has attracted quite a following in many business organizations and management consulting firms. However, the concept is relatively new, so we have a lot to learn about how engagement relates to other concepts, such as job satisfaction, organizational commitment, job involvement, or intrinsic motivation, to do one's job well. Engagement may be broad enough that it captures the intersection of these variables. In other words, it may be what these attitudes have in common.

Are These Job Attitudes Really All That Distinct?   You might wonder whether these job attitudes are really distinct. After all, if people feel deeply involved in their job (high job involvement), isn't it probable that they like it (high job satisfaction)? Similarly, won't people who think their organization is supportive (high perceived organizational support) also feel committed to it (strong organizational commitment)? Evidence suggests that these attitudes are highly related, perhaps to a troubling degree. For example, the correlation between perceived organizational support and affective commitment is very strong.[24] The problem is that a strong correlation means the variables may be redundant (so, for example, if you know someone's affective commitment, you basically know her perceived organizational support).

But why is this redundancy so troubling? Why have two steering wheels on a car when you need only one? Why have two concepts—going by different labels—when you need only one? Redundancy is inefficient and confusing. Although we OB researchers like proposing new attitudes, often we haven't been good at showing how they compare and contrast with each other. There is some measure of distinctiveness among these attitudes, but they overlap greatly. The overlap may exist for various reasons, including the employee's personality. Some people are predisposed to be positive or negative about almost everything. If someone tells you she loves her company, it may not mean a lot if she is positive about everything else in her life. Or the overlap may mean that some organizations are just all-around better places to work than others. This may mean that if you, as a manager, know someone's level of job satisfaction you know most of what is needed to know about the person's perception of the organization.

JOB SATISFACTION

We have already discussed job satisfaction briefly. Because it is the most widely studied job attitude, let's dissect the concept more carefully. How do we measure job satisfaction? How satisfied are employees in their jobs? What causes an employee to have a high level of job satisfaction? How do dissatisfied and satisfied employees affect an organization?

Measuring Job Satisfaction

We've defined job satisfaction as a positive feeling about a job resulting from an evaluation of its characteristics. This definition is clearly a very broad one. Yet breadth is inherent in the concept. Remember, a person's job is more than just the obvious activities of shuffling papers, writing programming code, waiting on customers, or driving a truck. Jobs require interacting with coworkers and bosses, following organizational rules and policies, meeting performance standards, living with working conditions that are often less than ideal, and the like. This means that an employee's assessment of how satisfied he is with the job is a complex summation of a number of discrete job elements. How, then, do we measure the concept?

The two most widely used approaches are a single global rating and a summation score made up of a number of job facets. The single global rating method is nothing more than responses to a few general questions, such as "All things considered, how satisfied are you with your job?" Respondents circle a number between one and five that corresponds to answers from "highly satisfied" to "highly dissatisfied." The other approach—a summation of job facets—is more sophisticated. It identifies key elements in a job and asks for the employee's feelings about each. Typical elements here are the nature of the work, supervision, present pay, promotion opportunities, and relations with coworkers.[25] Respondents rate them on a standardized scale, and researchers add the ratings to create an overall job satisfaction score.

Is one of these approaches superior to the other? Intuitively, summing up responses to a number of job factors seems likely to achieve a more accurate evaluation of job satisfaction. The research, however, doesn't support the intuition.[26] This is one of those rare instances in which simplicity seems to work as well as complexity, and comparisons of the two methods indicate that one is essentially as valid as the other. The best explanation for this outcome is that the concept of job satisfaction is inherently so broad that a few general questions capture its essence. Another explanation may be that some important facets are left out of the summation of job facets. Both methods are helpful. For example, the global rating method isn't very time consuming, which frees managers to address other workplace issues and problems. And the summation of job facets helps managers zero in on where problems exist, making it easier to deal with unhappy employees and solve problems faster and more accurately.

How Satisfied Are People in Their Jobs?

Are most people satisfied with their jobs? The answer seems to be a qualified "yes" in the United States and in most other developed countries. Independent studies conducted among U.S. workers over the past 30 years generally indicate that more workers are satisfied with their jobs than are dissatisfied.[27] However, a caveat needs to be mentioned. Research shows that satisfaction levels vary a lot, depending on which facet of job satisfaction you're talking about. As shown in Exhibit 4-2, people are, on average, satisfied with their jobs overall, with the work itself, and with their supervisors and coworkers. However, they tend to be less satisfied with their pay and with promotion opportunities. It's not really clear why people dislike their pay and promotion

EXHIBIT 4-2   Average Job Satisfaction Levels by Facet

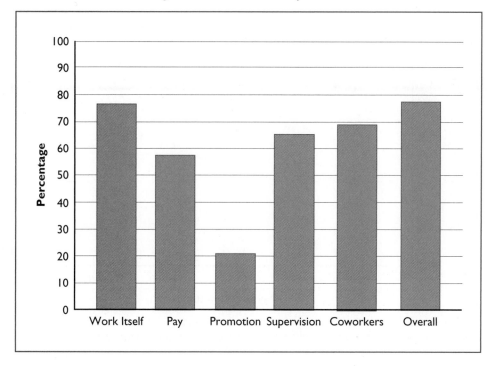

possibilities more than other aspects of their jobs, but what *is* clear is that most employees are relatively dissatisfied with these aspects of their jobs.

What Causes Job Satisfaction?

Think about the best job you've ever had. What made it so? Chances are you probably liked the work you did. In fact, of the major job-satisfaction facets (work itself, pay, advancement opportunities, supervision, coworkers), enjoying the work is almost always the one most strongly correlated with high levels of overall job satisfaction. Interesting jobs that provide training, variety, independence, and control satisfy most employees.[28] In other words, most people prefer work that is challenging and stimulating over work that is predictable and routine.

You've probably noticed that pay comes up often when people discuss job satisfaction. There is an interesting relationship between salary and job satisfaction. For people who are poor (for example, living below the poverty line) or who live in poor countries, pay does correlate with job satisfaction and with overall happiness. But, once an individual reaches a level of comfortable living (in the United States, that occurs at about $40,000 a year, depending on the region and family size), the relationship virtually disappears. In other words, people who earn $80,000 are, on average, no happier with their jobs than those who earn close to $40,000. Take a look at Exhibit 4-3, which shows the relationship between the average pay for a job and the average level of job satisfaction. As you can see, there isn't much of a relationship

EXHIBIT 4-3   Relationship Between Average Pay in a Job and Job Satisfaction of Employees in That Job

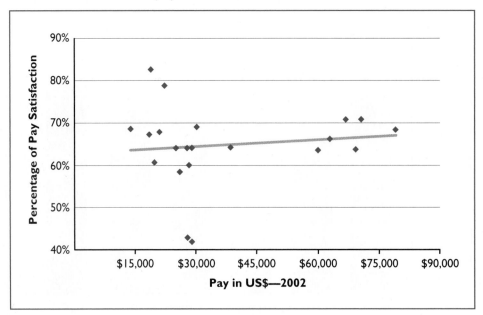

Source: T. A. Judge, R. F. Piccolo, N. P. Podsakoff, J. C. Shaw, and B. L. Rich, "Can Happiness Be "Earned"?: The Relationship Between Pay and Job Satisfaction," working paper, University of Florida, 2005.

there. Jobs that are compensated handsomely have average job satisfaction levels no higher than those that are paid much less. To further illustrate this point, one researcher even found no significant difference when he compared the overall well-being of the richest people on the Forbes 400 list with that of Maasai herdsmen in East Africa.[29]

Money does motivate people, as we will discover in Chapters 5 and 6. But what motivates us is not necessarily the same as what makes us happy. A recent poll by UCLA and the American Council on Education found that entering college freshmen rated becoming "very well off financially" first on a list of nineteen goals, ahead of choices such as helping others, raising a family, or becoming proficient in an academic pursuit. Maybe your goal isn't to be happy. But if it is, money's probably not going to do much to get you there.[30]

The Impact of Satisfied and Dissatisfied Employees on the Workplace

There are consequences when employees like their jobs and when they dislike their jobs. One theoretical model—the exit–voice–loyalty–neglect framework—is helpful in understanding the consequences of dissatisfaction. This framework has four responses, which differ from one another along two dimensions: constructive/destructive and active/passive. These responses are defined as follows:[31]

■ *Exit.* The **exit** response involves directing behavior toward leaving the organization, including looking for a new position as well as resigning.

- *Voice.* The **voice** response involves actively and constructively attempting to improve conditions, including suggesting improvements, discussing problems with superiors, and undertaking some forms of union activity.

- *Loyalty.* The **loyalty** response involves passively but optimistically waiting for conditions to improve, including speaking up for the organization in the face of external criticism and trusting the organization and its management to "do the right thing."

- *Neglect.* The **neglect** response involves passively allowing conditions to worsen, including chronic absenteeism or lateness, reduced effort, and increased error rate.

Exit and neglect behaviors encompass our performance variables—productivity, absenteeism, and turnover. But this model expands employee response to include voice and loyalty—constructive behaviors that allow individuals to tolerate unpleasant situations or to revive satisfactory working conditions. It helps us to understand situations, such as those sometimes found among unionized workers, for whom low job satisfaction is coupled with low turnover.[32] Union members often express dissatisfaction through the grievance procedure or through formal contract negotiations. These voice mechanisms allow them to continue in their jobs while convincing themselves that they are acting to improve the situation.

—Job satisfaction is related to organizational effectiveness—a large study found that business units whose employees had high-average levels of engagement had higher levels of customer satisfaction and lower levels of turnover and accidents. All else equal, it clearly behooves organizations to have a satisfied workforce.

As helpful as this framework is in presenting the possible consequences of job dissatisfaction, it's quite general. We now discuss more specific outcomes of job satisfaction and dissatisfaction in the workplace.

Job Satisfaction and Job Performance   Some researchers used to believe that the relationship between job satisfaction and job performance was a management myth. But a review of 300 studies suggested that the correlation is pretty strong.[33] As we move from the individual level to that of the organization, we also find support for the satisfaction–performance relationship.[34] When satisfaction and productivity data are gathered for the organization as a whole, we find that organizations with more satisfied employees tend to be more effective than organizations with fewer satisfied employees.

Job Satisfaction and OCB   It seems logical to assume that job satisfaction should be a major determinant of an employee's organizational citizenship behavior (OCB). Satisfied employees would seem more likely to talk positively about the organization, help others, and go beyond the normal expectations in their job. Moreover, satisfied employees might be more prone to go beyond the call of duty because they want to reciprocate their positive experiences. Consistent with this thinking, evidence suggests that job satisfaction is moderately correlated with OCBs, such that people who are more satisfied with their jobs are more likely to engage in OCBs.[35]

Why do those satisfied with their jobs contribute more OCBs? Research indicates that fairness perceptions explain the relationship, at least in part.[36] What does this mean? Basically, job satisfaction comes down to conceptions of fair outcomes, treatment, and procedures. If you don't feel that your supervisor, the organization's procedures, or pay policies are fair, your job satisfaction is likely to suffer significantly. However, when you perceive organizational processes and outcomes to be fair, trust develops. And when you trust your employer, you're more willing to voluntarily engage in behaviors that go beyond your formal job requirements.

—*Most employees are satisfied with their jobs; when they're not, however, a host of actions in response to the dissatisfaction might be expected.*

Job Satisfaction and Customer Satisfaction   As we noted in Chapter 1, employees in service jobs often interact with customers. Since the management of service organizations should be concerned with pleasing those customers, it is reasonable to ask: Is employee satisfaction related to positive customer outcomes? For frontline employees who have regular contact with customers, the answer is "yes."

The evidence indicates that satisfied employees increase customer satisfaction and loyalty.[37] Why? In service organizations, customer retention and defection are highly dependent on how frontline employees deal with customers. Satisfied employees are more likely to be friendly, upbeat, and responsive—which customers appreciate. And because satisfied employees are less prone to turnover, customers are more likely to encounter familiar faces and receive experienced service. These qualities build customer satisfaction and loyalty. The relationship also seems to apply in reverse: Dissatisfied customers can increase an employee's job dissatisfaction. Employees who have regular contact with customers report that rude, thoughtless, or unreasonably demanding customers adversely affect the employees' job satisfaction.

A number of companies are acting on this evidence. Service-oriented businesses such as FedEx, Southwest Airlines, Four Seasons Hotels, American Express, and Office Depot obsess about pleasing their customers. Toward that end, they also focus on building employee satisfaction—recognizing that employee satisfaction will go a long way toward contributing to their goal of having happy customers. These firms seek to hire upbeat and friendly employees, they train employees in the importance of customer service, they reward customer service, they provide positive employee work climates, and they regularly track employee satisfaction through attitude surveys.

Job Satisfaction and Absenteeism   We find a consistent negative relationship between satisfaction and absenteeism, but the correlation is moderate to weak.[38] Although it certainly makes sense that dissatisfied employees are more likely to miss work, other factors have an impact on the relationship and reduce the correlation coefficient. For example, organizations that provide liberal sick leave benefits are encouraging all their employees—including those who are highly satisfied—to take days off. Assuming that you have a reasonable number of varied interests, you can find work satisfying and yet still want to take off to enjoy a 3-day weekend or tan yourself on a warm summer day if those days come free with no penalties.

An excellent illustration of how satisfaction directly leads to attendance, when there is minimal impact from other factors, is a study done at Sears, Roebuck.[39] Sears had a policy of not permitting employees to be absent from work for avoidable reasons without penalty. The occurrence of a freak April 2 snowstorm in Chicago created the opportunity to compare employee attendance at the Chicago office with attendance in New York, where the weather was quite nice. (Satisfaction data were available on employees at both locations.) The storm crippled Chicago's transportation system, and individuals knew they could miss work this day with no penalty. If satisfaction leads to attendance when there are no outside factors, the more satisfied employees should have come to work in Chicago, whereas dissatisfied employees should have stayed home. The study found that on this particular April 2, absenteeism rates in New York were just as high for satisfied groups of workers as for dissatisfied groups.

But in Chicago, the workers with high satisfaction scores did indeed have a much higher attendance than did those with lower satisfaction levels, exactly what we would have expected if satisfaction is negatively correlated with absenteeism.

Job Satisfaction and Turnover   Satisfaction is also negatively related to turnover, but the correlation is stronger than what we found for absenteeism.[40] Yet, again, other factors, such as labor-market conditions, expectations about alternative job opportunities, and length of tenure with the organization, are important constraints on an employee's decision to leave her current job.[41]

Evidence indicates that an important moderator of the satisfaction–turnover relationship is the employee's level of performance.[42] Specifically, level of satisfaction is less important in predicting turnover for superior performers. Why? The organization typically makes considerable efforts to keep these people. They get pay raises, praise, recognition, increased promotional opportunities, and so forth. Just the opposite tends to apply to poor performers. The organization makes few attempts to retain them. There may even be subtle pressures to encourage them to quit. We would expect, therefore, that job satisfaction is more important in influencing poor performers to stay than in influencing superior performers to stay. Regardless of level of satisfaction, the latter are more likely to remain with the organization because the receipt of recognition, praise, and other rewards gives them more reasons to do so.

Job Satisfaction and Workplace Deviance   Job dissatisfaction predicts a lot of specific behaviors, including unionization attempts, substance abuse, stealing at work, undue socializing, and tardiness. Researchers argue that these behaviors are indicators of a broader syndrome that we would term *deviant behavior in the workplace* (or *employee withdrawal*).[43] The key is that if employees don't like their work environment, they'll respond somehow. It is not always easy to forecast exactly *how* they'll respond. One worker's response might be to quit. Another might take work time to surf the Internet, take work supplies home for personal use, and so on. In short, evidence indicates that workers who don't like their jobs "get even" in various ways—and because employees can be quite creative in the ways they do that—controlling one behavior, such as having an absence control policy, leaves the root cause untouched. If employers want to control the undesirable consequences of job dissatisfaction, they should attack the source of the problem—the dissatisfaction—rather than try to control the different responses.

Managers Often "Don't Get It"   Given the evidence we've just reviewed, it should come as no surprise that job satisfaction can affect the bottom line. One study by a management consulting firm separated large organizations into high morale (where more than 70 percent of employees expressed overall job satisfaction) and medium or low morale groups (lower than 70 percent). The stock prices of companies in the high-morale group grew 19.4 percent, compared with 10 percent for the medium- or low-morale group. Despite these results, many managers are unconcerned about job satisfaction of their employees. Still others overestimate the degree to which their employees are satisfied with their jobs, so they don't think there's a problem when there is. One study of 262 large employers found that 86 percent of senior managers believed their organization treated its employees well, but only 55 percent of the employees agreed. Another study found 55 percent of managers thought morale was good in their organization, compared to only 38 percent of employees.[44] Managers first need to care about job satisfaction, and then they need to measure it rather than just assume that everything is going well.

GLOBAL IMPLICATIONS

Is Job Satisfaction a U.S. Concept?   Most of the research on job satisfaction has been conducted in the United States. So, we might ask: Is job satisfaction a U.S. concept? The evidence strongly suggests that this is *not* the case; people in other cultures can and do form judgments of job satisfaction. Moreover, it appears that similar factors cause, and result from, job satisfaction across cultures. For example, we noted earlier that pay is positively, but relatively weakly, related to job satisfaction. This relationship appears to hold in other industrialized nations as well as in the United States.

Are Employees in Western Cultures More Satisfied with Their Jobs?   Although job satisfaction appears to be a relevant concept across cultures, that doesn't mean there are no cultural differences in job satisfaction. Evidence suggests that employees in Western cultures have higher levels of job satisfaction than those in Eastern cultures.[45] Exhibit 4-4 provides the results of a global study of the job satisfaction levels of workers in 15 countries. (This study included 23 countries, but for presentation purposes, we report the results for only the largest.) As the exhibit shows, the highest levels of job satisfaction appear to be in the United States and Western Europe. Is the reason that employees in Western cultures have better jobs? Or are individuals in Western cultures simply more positive (and less self-critical)? Although both factors are probably at play, evidence suggests that individuals in

EXHIBIT 4-4   Average Levels of Job Satisfaction by Country

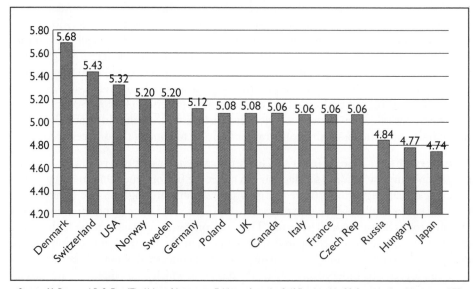

Source: M. Benz and B. S. Frey, "The Value of Autonomy: Evidence from the Self-Employed in 23 Countries," working paper 173, Institute for Empirical Research in Economics, University of Zurich, November 2003 (http://ssrn.com/abstract-475140).

Note: Scores represent average job-satisfaction levels in each country as rated on a 1 = very dissatisfied to 10 = very satisfied scale.

Eastern cultures value negative emotions more than do individuals in Western cultures, whereas those in Western cultures tend to emphasize positive emotions and individual happiness.[46] That may be why employees in Western cultures such as the United States and Scandinavia are more likely to have higher levels of job satisfaction.

IMPLICATIONS FOR MANAGERS

Managers should be interested in their employees' attitudes because attitudes give warnings of potential problems and because they influence behavior. Satisfied and committed employees, for instance, have lower rates of turnover, absenteeism, and withdrawal behaviors. They also perform better on the job. Given that managers want to keep resignations and absences down—especially among their most productive employees—they'll want to do things that generate positive job attitudes. As one review put it, "A sound measurement of overall job attitude is one of the most useful pieces of information an organization can have about its employees."[47]

The most important thing managers can do to raise employee satisfaction is to focus on the intrinsic parts of the job, such as making the work challenging and interesting. Although paying employees poorly will likely not attract high-quality employees to the organization, or keep high performers, managers should realize that high pay alone is unlikely to create a satisfying work environment. Creating a satisfied workforce is hardly a guarantee of successful organizational performance, but evidence strongly suggests that whatever managers can do to improve employee attitudes will likely result in heightened organizational effectiveness.

CHAPTER 5

Motivation Concepts

After studying this chapter, you should be able to:

1. Describe the three key elements of motivation.
2. Identify four early theories of motivation and evaluate their applicability today.
3. Compare and contrast goal-setting theory and self-efficacy theory.
4. Demonstrate how organizational justice is a refinement of equity theory.
5. Apply the key tenets of expectancy theory to motivating employees.
6. Explain to what degree motivation theories are culture bound.

Motivation is one of the most frequently researched topics in OB. One reason for its popularity is revealed in a recent Gallup poll, which found that a majority of U.S. employees—55 percent—have no enthusiasm for their work.[1] Moreover, another study suggested that, by workers' own reports, they waste roughly 2 hours per day, not counting lunch and scheduled breaks (the biggest time-wasters were Internet surfing and talking with coworkers).[2] Clearly, motivation seems to be an issue. The good news is that all this research provides us with considerable insights into how to improve motivation.

In this chapter, we'll review the basics of motivation, assess a number of motivation theories.

DEFINING MOTIVATION

We define **motivation** as the processes that account for an individual's intensity, direction, and persistence of effort toward attaining a goal.[3] Although general motivation is concerned with effort toward *any* goal, we'll narrow the focus to *organizational* goals in order to reflect our singular interest in work-related behavior.

The three key elements in our definition are intensity, direction, and persistence. *Intensity* is concerned with how hard a person tries. This is the element most of us focus on when we talk about motivation. However, high intensity is unlikely to lead to favorable job-performance outcomes unless the effort is channeled in a *direction* that benefits the organization. Therefore, we have to consider the quality of effort as well as its intensity. Effort that is directed toward, and consistent with, the organization's goals is the kind of effort that we should be seeking. Finally, motivation has a *persistence* dimension. This is a measure of how long a person can maintain effort. Motivated individuals stay with a task long enough to achieve their goal.

EARLY THEORIES OF MOTIVATION

The 1950s were a fruitful period in the development of motivation concepts. Four specific theories were formulated during this period, which although heavily attacked and now questionable in terms of validity, are probably still the best-known explanations for employee motivation. As you'll see later in this chapter, we have since developed more valid explanations of motivation, but you should know these early theories for at least two reasons: (1) They represent a foundation from which contemporary theories have grown, and (2) practicing managers still regularly use these theories and their terminology in explaining employee motivation.

Hierarchy of Needs Theory

It's probably safe to say that the most well-known theory of motivation is Abraham Maslow's **hierarchy of needs**.[4] Maslow hypothesized that within every human being, there exists a hierarchy of five needs:

1. *Physiological.* Includes hunger, thirst, shelter, sex, and other bodily needs
2. *Safety.* Security and protection from physical and emotional harm
3. *Social.* Affection, belongingness, acceptance, and friendship
4. *Esteem.* Internal factors such as self-respect, autonomy, and achievement, and external factors such as status, recognition, and attention
5. *Self-actualization.* Drive to become what one is capable of becoming; includes growth, achieving one's potential, and self-fulfillment

As each of these needs becomes substantially satisfied, the next need becomes dominant. In terms of Exhibit 5-1, the individual moves up the steps of the hierarchy. From the standpoint of motivation, the theory would say that, although no need is ever fully gratified, a substantially satisfied need no longer motivates. So if you want to motivate someone, according to Maslow, you need to understand what level of the hierarchy that person is currently on and focus on satisfying the needs at or above that level.

Maslow separated the five needs into higher and lower orders. Physiological and safety needs were described as **lower-order needs** and social, esteem, and self-actualization as **higher-order needs**. The differentiation between the two orders was made on the premise that higher-order needs are satisfied internally (within the person), whereas lower-order needs are predominantly satisfied externally (by things such as pay, union contracts, and tenure).

Maslow's needs theory has received wide recognition, particularly among practicing managers. This can be attributed to the theory's intuitive logic and ease of understanding. Unfortunately, however, research does not validate the theory. Maslow

EXHIBIT 5-1   Maslow's Hierarchy of Needs

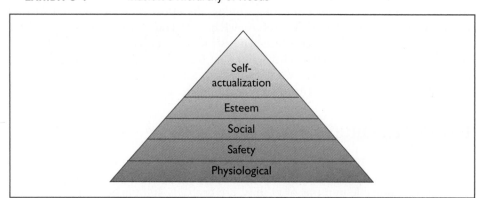

Source: A. H. Maslow, *Motivation and Personality,* 3rd ed., R. D. Frager and J. Fadiman (eds.). © 1997. Adapted by permission of Pearson Education, Inc., Upper Saddle River, New Jersey.

provided no empirical substantiation, and several studies that sought to validate the theory found no support for it.[5]

Old theories, especially ones that are intuitively logical, apparently die hard. Although the hierarchy of needs theory and its terminology have remained popular with practicing managers, there is little evidence that needs structures are organized along the dimensions proposed by Maslow, that unsatisfied needs motivate, or that a satisfied need activates movement to a new needs level.[6]

Theory X and Theory Y

Douglas McGregor proposed two distinct views of human beings: one basically negative, labeled **Theory X**, and the other basically positive, labeled **Theory Y**.[7] After viewing the way in which managers dealt with employees, McGregor concluded that managers' views of the nature of human beings are based on a certain grouping of assumptions and that managers tend to mold their behavior toward employees according to these assumptions.

Under Theory X, managers believe that employees inherently dislike work and must therefore be directed or even coerced into performing it. In contrast to these negative views about the nature of human beings, under Theory Y, managers assume that employees can view work as being as natural as rest or play, and therefore the average person can learn to accept, and even seek, responsibility.

To understand Theory X and Theory Y more fully, think in terms of Maslow's hierarchy. Theory Y assumes that higher-order needs dominate individuals. McGregor himself held to the belief that Theory Y assumptions were more valid than Theory X. Therefore, he proposed such ideas as participative decision making, responsible and challenging jobs, and good group relations as approaches that would maximize an employee's job motivation.

Unfortunately, there is no evidence to confirm that either set of assumptions is valid or that accepting Theory Y assumptions and altering one's actions accordingly will lead to more motivated workers. OB theories need to have empirical support before we can accept them. Such empirical support is lacking for Theory X and Theory Y as it is for the hierarchy of needs theory.

Two-Factor Theory

Psychologist Frederick Herzberg proposed the **two-factor theory**—also called *motivation-hygiene theory*.[8] Believing that an individual's relation to work is basic and that one's attitude toward work can very well determine success or failure, Herzberg investigated the question "What do people want from their jobs?" He asked people to describe, in detail, situations in which they felt exceptionally *good* or *bad* about their jobs. The responses were then tabulated and categorized.

From the categorized responses, Herzberg concluded that the replies people gave when they felt good about their jobs were significantly different from the replies given when they felt bad. As shown in Exhibit 5-2, certain characteristics tend to be consistently related to job satisfaction and others to job dissatisfaction. Intrinsic factors such as advancement, recognition, responsibility, and achievement seem to be related to job satisfaction. Respondents who felt good about their work tended to attribute these factors to themselves. On the other hand, dissatisfied respondents tended to cite extrinsic factors, such as supervision, pay, company policies, and working conditions.

EXHIBIT 5-2   Comparison of Satisfiers and Dissatisfiers

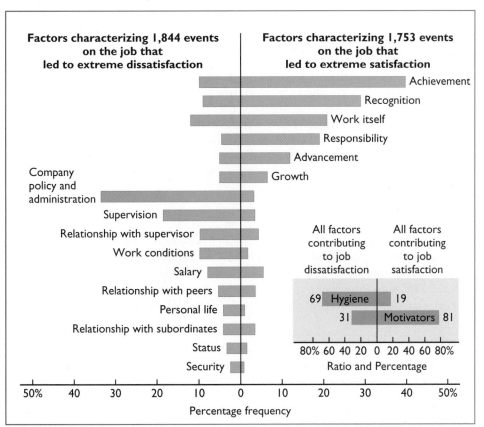

The data suggest, said Herzberg, that the opposite of satisfaction is not dissatisfaction, as was traditionally believed. Removing dissatisfying characteristics from a job does not necessarily make the job satisfying. Herzberg proposed that his findings indicated the existence of a dual continuum: The opposite of "satisfaction" is "no satisfaction," and the opposite of "dissatisfaction" is "no dissatisfaction."

According to Herzberg, the factors that lead to job satisfaction are separate and distinct from those that lead to job dissatisfaction. Therefore, managers who seek to eliminate factors that can create job dissatisfaction may bring about peace but not necessarily motivation. They will be placating their workforce rather than motivating workers. As a result, Herzberg characterized conditions surrounding the job such as quality of supervision, pay, company policies, physical working conditions, relations with others, and job security as **hygiene factors**. When they're adequate, people will not be dissatisfied; neither will they be satisfied. If we want to motivate people on their jobs, Herzberg suggested emphasizing factors associated with the work itself or with outcomes directly derived from it, such as promotional opportunities, opportunities for personal growth, recognition, responsibility, and achievement. These are the characteristics that people find intrinsically rewarding.

Despite its broad appeal, the two-factor theory has not been well supported in the literature, and it has many detractors.[9] The criticisms of the theory include the following:

1. The procedure that Herzberg used is limited by its methodology. When things are going well, people tend to take credit themselves. Contrarily, they blame failure on the extrinsic environment.
2. The reliability of Herzberg's methodology is questioned. Raters have to make interpretations, so they may contaminate the findings by interpreting one response in one manner while treating a similar response differently.
3. No overall measure of satisfaction was utilized. A person may dislike part of a job yet still think the job is acceptable overall.
4. Herzberg assumed a relationship between satisfaction and productivity, but the research methodology he used looked only at satisfaction and not at productivity. To make such research relevant, one must assume a strong relationship between satisfaction and productivity.

Regardless of the criticisms, Herzberg's theory has been widely read, and few managers are unfamiliar with its recommendations.

It's important to realize that even though we may intuitively *like* a theory, that does not mean that we should accept it. Many managers find need theories intuitively appealing, but remember that at one time the world seemed intuitively flat. Sometimes science backs up intuition, and sometimes it doesn't. In the case of the two-factor theory—as with the hierarchy of needs and Theory X/Theory Y—it doesn't.

McClelland's Theory of Needs

McClelland's theory of needs was developed by David McClelland and his associates.[10] The theory focuses on three needs, defined as follows:

- *Need for achievement (nAch)* is the drive to excel, to achieve in relation to a set of standards, to strive to succeed.
- *Need for power (nPow)* is the need to make others behave in a way in which they would not have behaved otherwise.

■ *Need for affiliation (nAff)* is the desire for friendly and close interpersonal relationships.

Of the three needs, McClelland and subsequent researchers focused most of their attention on nAch. High achievers perform best when they perceive their probability of success as 0.5—that is, when they estimate that they have a 50–50 chance of success. They dislike gambling with high odds because they get no achievement satisfaction from success that comes by pure chance. Similarly, they dislike low odds (high probability of success) because then there is no challenge to their skills. They like to set goals that require stretching themselves a little.

Relying on an extensive amount of research, we can make some reasonably well-supported predictions of the relationship between achievement need and job performance. Although less research has been done on power and affiliation needs, there are consistent findings there, too. First, when jobs have a high degree of personal responsibility and feedback and an intermediate degree of risk, high achievers are strongly motivated. High achievers, for example, are successful in entrepreneurial activities such as running their own businesses and managing self-contained units within large organizations.[11] Second, a high need to achieve does not necessarily make someone a good manager, especially in large organizations. People with a high achievement need are interested in how well they do personally and not in influencing others to do well. High-nAch salespeople do not necessarily make good sales managers, and the good general manager in a large organization does not typically have a high need to achieve.[12] Third, the needs for affiliation and power tend to be closely related to managerial success. The best managers are high in their need for power and low in their need for affiliation. In fact, a high power motive may be a requirement for managerial effectiveness.[13]

As you might have gathered, of the early theories of motivation, McClelland's has had the best research support. Unfortunately, it has less practical effect than the others. Because McClelland argued that the three needs are subconscious—meaning that we may be high on these needs but not know it—measuring them is not easy. In the most common approach, a trained expert presents pictures to individuals, asks them to tell a story about each, and then scores their responses in terms of the three needs. However, because measuring the needs is time consuming and expensive, few organizations have been willing to invest time and resources in measuring McClelland's concept.

CONTEMPORARY THEORIES OF MOTIVATION

The previously described theories are well known but, unfortunately, have either not held up well under close examination or fallen out of favor. However, there are a number of contemporary theories, and they have one thing in common: Each has a reasonable degree of valid supporting documentation. Of course, this doesn't mean that the theories we are about to introduce are unquestionably right. We call them "contemporary theories" not because they were all developed recently but because they represent the current state of thinking in explaining employee motivation.

Cognitive Evaluation Theory

Cognitive evaluation theory proposes that the introduction of extrinsic rewards, such as pay, for work effort that was previously intrinsically rewarding due to the pleasure associated with the content of the work itself tends to decrease overall motivation. Cognitive evaluation theory has been extensively researched, and a large number of studies have supported it.[14] As we'll show, the major implications of this theory relate to work rewards.

Historically, motivation theorists generally assumed that intrinsic rewards such as interesting work were independent of extrinsic rewards such as high pay. But cognitive evaluation theory suggests otherwise. It argues that when extrinsic rewards are used by organizations as payoffs for superior performance, the intrinsic rewards, which are derived from individuals doing what they like, are reduced. In other words, when extrinsic rewards are given to someone for performing an interesting task, it causes intrinsic interest in the task itself to decline.

Why would such an outcome occur? The popular explanation is that an individual experiences a loss of control over her own behavior so that the previous intrinsic motivation diminishes. Furthermore, the elimination of extrinsic rewards can produce a shift—from an external to an internal explanation—in an individual's perception of causation of why she works on a task. If you're reading a novel a week because your English literature instructor requires you to, you can attribute your reading behavior to an external source. However, after the course is over, if you find yourself continuing to read a novel every week, your natural inclination is to say, "I must enjoy reading novels because I'm still reading one every week."

If the cognitive evaluation theory is valid, it should have major implications for managerial practices. It has been a truism among compensation specialists for years that if pay or other extrinsic rewards are to be effective motivators, they should be made contingent on an individual's performance. But cognitive evaluation theorists would argue that this will only tend to decrease the internal satisfaction that the individual receives from doing the job. In fact, if cognitive evaluation theory is correct, it would make sense to make an individual's pay *noncontingent* on performance in order to avoid decreasing intrinsic motivation.

We noted earlier that the cognitive evaluation theory has been supported in a number of studies. Yet it has also been met with attacks, specifically on the methodology used in these studies and in the interpretation of the findings.[15] But where does this theory stand today? Can we say that when organizations use extrinsic motivators such as pay and promotions and verbal rewards to stimulate workers' performance, they do so at the expense of reducing intrinsic interest and motivation in the work being done? The answer is not a simple "yes" or a simple "no."

Extrinsic rewards that are verbal (for example, receiving praise from a supervisor or coworker) or tangible (for example, money) can actually have different effects on individuals' intrinsic motivation. That is, verbal rewards increase intrinsic motivation, whereas tangible rewards undermine it. When people are told they will receive a tangible reward, they come to count on it and focus more on the reward than on the task.[16] Verbal rewards, however, seem to keep people focused on the task and encourage them to do it better.

What does all of this mean? It means choose your job carefully. Make sure you're choosing to do something for reasons other than extrinsic rewards. For organizations, managers need to provide intrinsic rewards in addition to extrinsic incentives. In other words, managers need to make the work interesting, provide recognition, and support employee growth and development. Employees who feel that what they do is within their control and a result of free choice are likely to be more motivated by their work and committed to their employers.

Goal-Setting Theory

Gene Broadwater, coach of the Hamilton High School cross-country team, gave his squad these last words before they approached the starting line for the league championship race: "Each one of you is physically ready. Now, get out there and do your best. No one can ever ask more of you than that."

You've heard the sentiment a number of times yourself: "Just do your best." But is that really good advice? The research on **goal-setting theory** answers this question, and the findings, as you'll see, are impressive in terms of the effect that goal specificity, challenge, and feedback have on performance.

In the late 1960s, Edwin Locke proposed that intentions to work toward a goal are a major source of work motivation.[17] That is, goals tell an employee what needs to be done and how much effort will need to be expended. The evidence strongly supports the value of goals. More to the point, we can say that specific goals increase performance; that difficult goals, when accepted, result in higher performance than do easy goals; and that feedback leads to higher performance than does nonfeedback.[18]

Specific goals produce a higher level of output than does the generalized goal of "do your best." Why? The specificity of the goal itself seems to act as an internal stimulus. For instance, when a trucker commits to making twelve round-trip hauls between Toronto and Buffalo, New York, each week, this intention gives him a specific objective to try to attain. We can say that, all things being equal, the trucker with a specific goal will outperform a counterpart operating with no goals or the generalized goal of "do your best."

—In general, managers should make goals specific and difficult—managers should set the highest goals to which employees will commit.

If factors such as acceptance of the goals are held constant, we can also state that the more difficult the goal, the higher the level of performance. Of course, it's logical to assume that easier goals are more likely to be accepted. But once a hard task is accepted, the employee can be expected to exert a high level of effort to try to achieve it.

But why are people motivated by difficult goals? First, difficult goals direct our attention to the task at hand and away from irrelevant distractions. Challenging goals get our attention and thus tend to help us focus. Second, difficult goals energize us because we have to work harder to attain them. For example, think of your study habits. Do you study as hard for an easy exam as you do for a difficult one? Probably not. Third, when goals are difficult, people persist in trying to attain them. Finally, difficult goals lead us to discover strategies that help us perform the job or task more effectively. If we have to struggle for a way to solve a difficult problem, we often think of a better way to go about it.

People do better when they get feedback on how well they are progressing toward their goals because feedback helps to identify discrepancies between what they have done and what they want to do—that is, feedback acts to guide behavior. But all feedback is not equally potent. Self-generated feedback—for which employees are able to monitor their own progress—has been shown to be a more powerful motivator than externally generated feedback.[19]

If employees have the opportunity to participate in setting their own goals, will they try harder? The evidence is mixed regarding the superiority of participative over assigned goals.[20] In some cases, collaboratively set goals elicited superior performance, whereas in other cases, individuals performed best when assigned goals by their boss. However, a major advantage of participation may be in increasing acceptance of the goal itself as a desirable one toward which to work. As we'll note shortly, commitment is important. If participation isn't used, then the individual assigning the goal needs to clearly explain the purpose and importance of the goal.

Are there any contingencies in goal-setting theory, or can we take it as a universal truth that difficult and specific goals will *always* lead to higher performance? In addition to feedback, three other factors have been found to influence the goals–performance relationship: goal commitment, task characteristics, and national culture.

First, goal-setting theory presupposes that an individual is committed to the goal—that is, an individual is determined not to lower or abandon the goal. Goal commitment is most likely to occur when goals are made public, and when the goals are self-set rather than assigned. Second, research indicates that goal-setting theory doesn't work equally well on all tasks. The evidence suggests that goals seem to have a more substantial effect on performance when tasks are simple rather than complex, well learned rather than novel, and independent rather than interdependent.[21] On interdependent tasks, group goals are preferable. Finally, goal-setting theory is culture bound. It's well adapted to countries such as the United States and Canada because its key components align reasonably well with North American cultures. But we can't expect goal setting to necessarily lead to higher employee performance in countries, such as Portugal or Chile, where concrete, individualized objectives may be rejected by more employees.

Our overall conclusion is that intentions—as articulated in terms of difficult and specific goals—are a potent motivating force. The motivating power of goal-setting theory has been demonstrated on more than 100 tasks involving more than 40,000 participants in many different kinds of industries—from lumber, to insurance, to automobiles. Basically, setting specific, challenging goals for employees is the best thing managers can do to improve performance.

Implementing the Goal-Setting Theory   Goal-setting theory has an impressive base of research support. But as a manager, how do you make it operational? That's often left up to the individual manager or leader. Some managers explicitly set aggressive performance targets—what General Electric called "stretch goals." For example, some CEOs, such as Procter & Gamble's A. G. Laffey and SAP's Hasso Plattner, are known for setting demanding performance goals. The problem with leaving it up to the individual manager is that, in many cases, managers don't set goals. A recent survey revealed that when asked whether their job had clearly defined goals, only a minority of employees agreed.[22]

A more systematic way to utilize goal setting is with a management by objectives program. **Management by objectives (MBO)** emphasizes collaboratively set goals that are tangible, verifiable, and measurable. As depicted in Exhibit 5-3, the organization's overall objectives are translated into specific objectives for each succeeding level (that is, divisional, departmental, individual) in the organization. But because lower-unit managers jointly participate in setting their own goals, MBO works from the "bottom up" as well as from the "top down." The result is a hierarchy that links objectives at one level to those at the the next level. And for the individual employee, MBO provides specific personal performance objectives.

Four ingredients are common to MBO programs: goal specificity, participation in decision making (including participation in the setting of goals or objectives), an explicit time period, and performance feedback.[23] Many of the elements in MBO programs match propositions of goal-setting theory. For example, having an explicit time

EXHIBIT 5-3   Cascading of Objectives

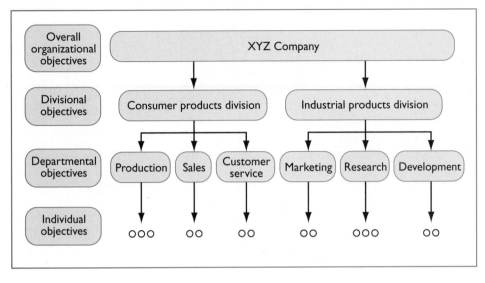

period to accomplish objectives matches goal-setting theory's emphasis on goal specificity. Similarly, we noted earlier that feedback about goal progress is a critical element
of the goal-setting theory. The only area of possible disagreement between MBO and
the goal-setting theory relates to the issue of participation: MBO strongly advocates
it, whereas the goal-setting theory demonstrates that managers assigning goals is usually just as effective.

Self-Efficacy Theory

Self-efficacy (also known as *social cognitive theory* or *social learning theory*) refers to an
individual's belief that he or she is capable of performing a task. The higher your self-
efficacy, the more confidence you have in your ability to succeed in a task. So, in difficult situations, people with low self-efficacy are more likely to lessen their effort or
give up altogether, whereas those with high self-efficacy will try harder to master the
challenge. In addition, individuals high in self-efficacy seem to respond to negative
feedback with increased effort and motivation, whereas those low in self-efficacy are
likely to lessen their effort when given negative feedback.[24] How can managers help
their employees achieve high levels of self-efficacy? By bringing together the goal-
setting theory and self-efficacy theory.

Goal-setting theory and self-efficacy theory don't compete with one another;
rather, they complement each other. As Exhibit 5-4 shows, when a manager sets difficult goals for employees, this leads employees to have a higher level of self-efficacy
and also leads them to set higher goals for their own performance. Why is this the
case? Research has shown that setting difficult goals for people communicates confidence. For example, imagine that your boss sets a high goal for you, and you learn it is
higher than the goals she has set for your coworkers. How would you interpret this?
As long as you didn't feel you were being picked on, you would probably think, "Well,
I guess my boss thinks I'm capable of performing better than others." This then sets
into motion a psychological process in which you're more confident in yourself

EXHIBIT 5-4   Joint Effects of Goals and Self-Efficacy on Performance

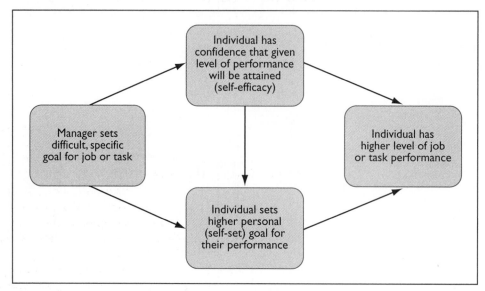

Source: Based on E. A. Locke and G. P. Latham, "Building a Practically Useful Theory of Goal Setting and Task Motivation: A 35-Year Odyssey," *American Psychologist,* September 2002, pp. 705–717.

(higher self-efficacy) and you set higher personal goals, causing you to perform better both in the workplace and outside it.

The researcher who developed self-efficacy theory, Albert Bandura, argues that there are four ways self-efficacy can be increased:[25]

1. *Enactive mastery*—gaining relevant experience with the task or job. If you've been able to perform the job successfully in the past, then you're more confident you'll be able to do it in the future.

2. *Vicarious modeling*—becoming more confident because you see someone else doing the task. For example, if your friend loses weight, then it increases your confidence that you can lose weight, too.

3. *Verbal persuasion*—becoming more confident because someone convinces you that you have the skills necessary to be successful. Motivational speakers use this tactic a lot.

4. *Arousal*—becoming more confident because one is "psyched up" and performs better. But when arousal is not relevant to the task, then arousal hurts performance. In other words, if the task is something that requires a steady, lower-key perspective (say, carefully editing a manuscript), arousal may in fact hurt performance.

Note that intelligence and personality are absent from Bandura's list. A lot of research shows that intelligence and personality (especially conscientiousness and emotional stability) can increase self-efficacy.[26] Those individual traits are so strongly related to self-efficacy (people who are intelligent, conscientiousness, and emotionally stable are much more likely to have high self-efficacy than those who score low on these characteristics) that some researchers would argue that self-efficacy is more a reflection of individual differences than is produced by situational interventions.[27] One of the primary reasons why certain people have high self-efficacy is because of their

—Managers will increase employees' motivation by increasing their confidence in successfully completing the task (self-efficacy).

personality and intelligence. Although Bandura strongly disagrees with this conclusion, more research on the issue is needed.

Equity Theory

In organizations, we often compare what we put into our jobs to what we get out of our jobs. **Equity theory** proposes that these comparisons can affect motivation. Specifically, employees compare their job inputs (effort, experience, education, competence) and outcomes (salary levels, raises, recognition) to those of others. We perceive our outcomes in relation to our inputs, and then we compare our outcome–input ratio with the outcome–input ratio of relevant others, as shown in Exhibit 5-5. If we perceive our ratio to be equal to that of the relevant others with whom we compare ourselves, a state of equity is said to exist; we perceive our situation as fair and that justice prevails. When we see the ratio as unequal, we experience equity tension. When we see ourselves as underrewarded, the tension creates anger; when we see ourselves as overrewarded, the tension creates guilt. J. Stacy Adams has proposed that this negative state of tension provides the motivation to do something to correct it.[28]

The referent that an employee selects adds to the complexity of equity theory. There are four referent comparisons that an employee can use:

1. *Self–inside.* An employee's experiences in a different position inside the employee's current organization
2. *Self–outside.* An employee's experiences in a situation or position outside the employee's current organization
3. *Other–inside.* Another individual or group of individuals inside the employee's organization
4. *Other–outside.* Another individual or group of individuals outside the employee's organization

Employees might compare themselves to friends, neighbors, coworkers, or colleagues in other organizations or compare their present job with past jobs. Which referent an employee chooses will be influenced by the information the employee holds about referents as well as by the attractiveness of the referent. This has led to focusing on moderating variables, such as gender. Research shows, for example, that both men

EXHIBIT 5-5   Equity Theory

Ratio Comparisons*	Perception
$\dfrac{O}{I_A} < \dfrac{O}{I_B}$	Inequity due to being underrewarded
$\dfrac{O}{I_A} = \dfrac{O}{I_B}$	Equity
$\dfrac{O}{I_A} > \dfrac{O}{I_B}$	Inequity due to being overrewarded

*Where $\dfrac{O}{I_A}$ represents the employee; and $\dfrac{O}{I_B}$ represents relevant others; O = outcomes; and I = inputs.

and women prefer same-sex comparisons (i.e., men are more likely to compare themselves to other men than to women, and women are more likely to compare themselves to other women than to men).[29]

What do employees do when they perceive inequity? The theory establishes the following propositions relating to inequitable pay:

A. *Given payment by time, overrewarded employees will produce more than will equitably paid employees.* Hourly and salaried employees will generate high quantity or quality of production in order to increase the input side of the ratio and bring about equity.

B. *Given payment by quantity of production, overrewarded employees will produce fewer, but higher-quality, units than will equitably paid employees.* Individuals paid on a piece-rate basis will increase their effort to achieve equity, which can result in greater quality or quantity. However, increases in quantity will only increase inequity because every unit produced results in further overpayment. Therefore, effort is directed toward increasing quality rather than increasing quantity.

C. *Given payment by time, underrewarded employees will produce less or poorer quality of output.* Effort will be decreased, which will bring about lower productivity or poorer-quality output than equitably paid subjects.

D. *Given payment by quantity of production, underrewarded employees will produce a large number of low-quality units in comparison with equitably paid employees.* Employees on piece-rate pay plans can bring about equity because trading off quality of output for quantity will result in an increase in rewards, with little or no increase in contributions.

Some of these propositions have been supported, but others haven't. First, inequities created by overpayment do not seem to have a very significant impact on behavior in most work situations. Apparently, people have a great deal more tolerance of overpayment inequities than of underpayment inequities or are better able to rationalize them. It's pretty damaging to a theory when one-half of the equation (how people respond to overreward) falls apart. Second, not all people are equity sensitive.[30] For example, there is a small part of the working population who actually prefer that their outcome–input ratios be less than the referent comparison's. Predictions from equity theory are not likely to be very accurate with these "benevolent types."

It's also important to note that although most research on equity theory has focused on pay, employees seem to look for equity in the distribution of other organizational rewards. For instance, it has been shown that the use of high-status job titles as well as large and lavishly furnished offices may function as outcomes for some employees in their equity equation.[31]

—To promote fairness in the workplace, managers should consider openly sharing information on how allocation decisions are made. Fair and open procedures are especially important when the outcome is likely to be viewed negatively by some or all employees.

Finally, recent research has been directed at expanding what is meant by *equity*, or *fairness*.[32] Historically, equity theory focused on **distributive justice**, which is the employee's perceived fairness of the *amount and allocation* of rewards among individuals. However, equity is increasingly thought of from the standpoint of **organizational justice**, which we define as an overall perception of what is fair in the workplace. Employees perceive their organizations as just when they believe the outcomes they have received and the way in which the outcomes were received are fair. One key element of organizational justice is an individual's *perception* of justice. In other words, under organizational justice, fairness or equity can be subjective, and it resides in the perception of the person. What one person may see as unfair another may see as perfectly appropriate. In general, people have an egocentric, or self-serving, bias.

They see allocations or procedures favoring themselves as fair. For example, in a recent poll, 61 percent of respondents said that they are personally paying their fair share of taxes, but an almost equal number (54 percent) of those polled felt the system as a whole is unfair, saying that some people skirt the system.[33] Fairness often resides in the eye of the beholder, and we tend to be fairly self-serving about what we see as fair.

Beyond its focus on perceptions of fairness, the other key element of organizational justice is the view that justice is multidimensional. Organizational justice argues that distributive justice is important. For example, how much we get paid relative to what we think we should be paid (distributive justice) is obviously important. But, according to justice researchers, *how* we get paid is just as important. Exhibit 5-6 shows a model of organizational justice.

Beyond distributive justice, the key addition under organizational justice was **procedural justice**, which is the perceived fairness of the *process* used to determine the distribution of rewards. Two key elements of procedural justice are process control and explanations. *Process control* is the opportunity to present one's point of view about desired outcomes to decision makers. *Explanations* are clear reasons for the outcome that management gives to a person. Thus, for employees to see a process as fair, they need to feel that they have some control over the outcome and feel that they were given an adequate explanation about why the outcome occurred. Also, for procedural fairness, it's important that a manager is *consistent* (across people and over time), is *unbiased*, makes decisions based on *accurate information*, and is *open to appeals*.[34]

EXHIBIT 5-6   Model of Organizational Justice

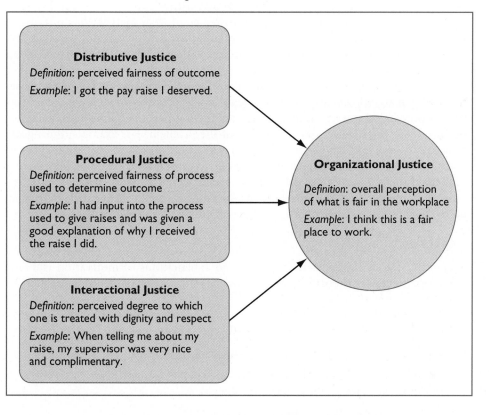

Distributive Justice
Definition: perceived fairness of outcome
Example: I got the pay raise I deserved.

Procedural Justice
Definition: perceived fairness of process used to determine outcome
Example: I had input into the process used to give raises and was given a good explanation of why I received the raise I did.

Interactional Justice
Definition: perceived degree to which one is treated with dignity and respect
Example: When telling me about my raise, my supervisor was very nice and complimentary.

Organizational Justice
Definition: overall perception of what is fair in the workplace
Example: I think this is a fair place to work.

Research shows that the effects of procedural justice become more important when distributive justice is lacking. This makes sense. If we don't get what we want, we tend to focus on *why*. For example, if your supervisor gives a cushy office to a coworker instead of to you, you're much more focused on your supervisor's treatment of you than if you had gotten the office. Explanations are beneficial when they take the form of post hoc excuses (for example, admitting that the act is unfavorable but denying sole responsibility for it) rather than justifications (for example, accepting full responsibility but denying that the outcome is unfavorable or inappropriate).[35] In the office example, an excuse would be "I know this is bad. I wanted to give you the office, but it was not my decision" and a justification would be "Yes, I decided to give the office to Sam, but having the corner office is not that big of a deal."

A recent addition to research on organizational justice is **interactional justice**, which is an individual's perception of the degree to which she is treated with dignity, concern, and respect. When people are treated in an unjust manner (at least in their own eyes), they respond by retaliating (for example, badmouthing a supervisor). Because interactional justice or injustice is intimately tied to the conveyer of the information (usually one's supervisor), whereas procedural injustice often results from impersonal policies, we would expect perceptions of injustice to be more closely related to one's supervisor. Generally, that's what the evidence suggests.[36]

Of these three forms of justice, distributive justice is most strongly related to satisfaction with outcomes (for example, satisfaction with pay) and organizational commitment. Procedural justice relates most strongly to overall job satisfaction, employee trust, withdrawal from the organization, job performance, and citizenship behaviors. There is less evidence on interactional justice.[37]

Managers can take several steps to foster employees' perceptions of fairness. First, they should realize that employees are especially sensitive to unfairness in procedures when bad news has to be communicated (that is, when distributive justice is low). Thus, when managers have bad news to communicate, it's especially important to openly share information about how allocation decisions are made, follow consistent and unbiased procedures, and engage in similar practices to increase the perception of procedural justice. Second, when addressing perceived injustices, managers need to focus their actions on the source of the problem. For example, during one weekend in June 2007, Northwest Airlines was forced to cancel 352 flights because many pilots and flight attendants called in sick to protest their pay. The pilot's union instructed the pilots: "Fly safe. Fly the contract. Don't fly sick. Don't fly fatigued. Don't fly hungry." In a situation like this, Northwest should realize that the remedy needs to be tangible rather than apologies or changes in procedures.[38]

Expectancy Theory

Currently, one of the most widely accepted explanations of motivation is Victor Vroom's **expectancy theory**. Although it has its critics, most of the evidence supports the theory, at least to a moderate degree.[39]

In practical terms, expectancy theory says that employees will be motivated to exert a high level of effort when they believe:

- that effort will lead to a good performance appraisal;
- that a good appraisal will lead to organizational rewards, such as a bonus, a salary increase, or a promotion; and

■ that the rewards will satisfy the employees' personal goals.

The theory, therefore, focuses on three relationships (see Exhibit 5-7):

1. *Effort–performance relationship.* The probability perceived by the individual that exerting a given amount of effort will lead to performance. "If I give a maximum effort, will it be recognized in my performance appraisal?", the employee may ask him- or herself before investing effort in a task. This aspect of expectancy theory suggests that it is critical that an organization's performance appraisal system be fair and unbiased, and that managers are aware of and recognize their employee's efforts.

2. *Performance–reward relationship.* The degree to which the individual believes that performing at a particular level will lead to the attainment of a desired outcome. "If I perform well (i.e., get a good performance review), will it lead to organizational rewards?", the employee may ask him- or herself. Here, it is critical that an organization's pay system reward employees for their performance, and not for other factors such as seniority (which is not within someone's control), "kissing up" to the boss, or other nonperformance factors.

3. *Rewards–personal goals relationship.* The degree to which organizational rewards satisfy an individual's personal goals or needs and the attractiveness of those potential rewards for the individual. "If I'm rewarded, are the rewards ones that I find personally attractive?", the employee may ask him- or herself. Here, it is important that the organization give employees the rewards that they want. A real motivation-killer (and wasted resource) is when the organization spends considerable resources on a reward that employees don't really value (i.e., expensive parties, unwanted perks, etc.).

In principle, expectancy theory helps explain why a lot of workers aren't motivated on their jobs and do only the minimum necessary to get by. But does the theory really work? Attempts to validate the theory have been complicated by methodological, criterion, and measurement problems. As a result, many published studies that purport to support or negate the theory must be viewed with caution. Importantly, most studies have failed to replicate the methodology as it was originally proposed. For example, the theory proposes to explain different levels of effort from the same person under different circumstances, but almost all replication studies have looked at different people. Correcting for this flaw has greatly improved support for the validity of expectancy theory.[40] Some critics suggest that the theory has only limited use, arguing that it tends to be more valid for predicting in situations in which effort–performance and performance–reward linkages are clearly perceived by the individual.[41] Because few individuals perceive a high correlation between performance and rewards in their

EXHIBIT 5-7 Expectancy Theory

Individual effort → ① → Individual performance → ② → Organizational rewards → ③ → Personal goals

① Effort–performance relationship
② Performance–reward relationship
③ Rewards–personal goals relationship

jobs, the theory tends to be idealistic. If organizations actually rewarded individuals for performance rather than according to criteria, such as seniority, effort, skill level, and job difficulty, then the theory's validity might be considerably greater. However, rather than invalidating expectancy theory, this criticism can be used in support of the theory because it explains why a significant segment of the workforce exerts low levels of effort in carrying out job responsibilities.

GLOBAL IMPLICATIONS

In our discussion of the goal-setting theory, we said that care needs to be taken in applying this theory because it assumes cultural characteristics that are not universal. This is true for many of the theories presented in this chapter because most current motivation theories were developed in the United States by and about U.S. adults.[42] For instance, both goal-setting and expectancy theories emphasize goal accomplishment as well as rational and individual thought—characteristics consistent with U.S. culture. Let's take a look at several motivation theories and consider their cross-cultural transferability.

Maslow's needs hierarchy argues that people start at the physiological level and then move progressively up the hierarchy in this order: physiological, safety, social, esteem, and self-actualization. This hierarchy, if it has any application at all, aligns with U.S. culture. In countries, such as Japan, Greece, and Mexico, where uncertainty-avoidance characteristics are strong, security needs would be on top of the hierarchy of needs. Countries that score high on nurturing characteristics—such as Denmark, Sweden, Norway, the Netherlands, and Finland—would have social needs on top.[43] We would predict, for instance, that group work will motivate employees more when the country's culture scores high on the nurturing criterion.

Another motivation concept that clearly has a U.S. bias is the achievement need. The view that a high achievement need acts as an internal motivator presupposes two cultural characteristics—a willingness to accept a moderate degree of risk (which excludes countries with strong uncertainty avoidance characteristics) and a concern with performance (which applies almost singularly to countries with strong achievement characteristics). This combination is found in Anglo-American countries such as the United States, Canada, Australia, and Great Britain.[44] However, these characteristics are relatively absent in countries such as Chile and Portugal.

Equity theory has gained a relatively strong following in the United States. That's not surprising because U.S.-style reward systems are based on the assumption that workers are highly sensitive to equity in reward allocations. And in the United States equity is meant to closely tie pay to performance. However, evidence suggests that in collectivist cultures, especially in the former socialist countries of Central and Eastern Europe, employees expect rewards to reflect their individual needs as well as their performance.[45] Moreover, consistent with a legacy of communism and centrally planned economies, employees exhibited an entitlement attitude—that is, they expected outcomes to be *greater* than their inputs.[46] These findings suggest that U.S.-style pay practices may need modification, especially in Russia and former communist countries, in order to be perceived as fair by employees.

But don't assume there are *no* cross-cultural consistencies. For instance, the desire for interesting work seems important to almost all workers, regardless of their national culture. In a study of seven countries, employees in Belgium, Britain, Israel, and the United States ranked interesting work number one among eleven work goals. And workers in Japan, the

Netherlands, and Germany ranked this factor either second or third.[47] Similarly, in a study comparing job-preference outcomes among graduate students in the United States, Canada, Australia, and Singapore, growth, achievement, and responsibility were rated the top three and had identical rankings.[48] Both of these studies suggest some universality to the importance of intrinsic factors in the two-factor theory.

IMPLICATIONS FOR MANAGERS

The theories we've discussed in this chapter address different outcome variables. Some, for instance, are directed at explaining turnover, whereas others emphasize productivity. The theories also differ in their predictive strength. In this section, we will (1) review the most established motivation theories to determine their relevance in explaining the dependent variables and (2) assess the predictive power of each.

Needs Theories   We introduced four theories that focused on needs: Maslow's hierarchy, McGregor's Theory X and Theory Y, McClelland's needs, and the two-factor theory. None of these theories has found widespread support, although the strongest is probably McClelland's theory, particularly regarding the relationship between achievement and productivity. In general, Maslow's theory is not a particularly valid explanation of motivation.

Goal-Setting Theory   There is little dispute that clear and difficult goals lead to higher levels of employee productivity. This evidence leads us to conclude that goal-setting theory provides one of the most powerful explanations of this dependent variable.

Equity Theory/Organizational Justice   Equity theory deals with productivity, satisfaction, absence, and turnover variables. However, its strongest legacy probably is that it provided the spark for research on organizational justice, which has more support in the literature.

Expectancy Theory   Our final theory, expectancy theory, focuses on performance variables. It has proved to offer a relatively powerful explanation of employee productivity, absenteeism, and turnover. But expectancy theory assumes that employees have few constraints on their decision discretion. Expectancy theory has some validity because for many behaviors people consider expected outcomes. However, the rational model goes only so far in explaining behavior.

Overall, the motivation theories with the most research, and the most recent support, probably deserve the most attention by managers. These theories are goal-setting theory; organizational justice; and, to a lesser degree, expectancy theory. Fortunately, though implementing no theory in the complexities of the workplace is simple, these theories do contain within them practical suggestions for how to make workplaces more motivating.

CHAPTER 6

Motivation: From Concepts to Applications

After studying this chapter, you should be able to:

1. Describe the ways in which employees can be motivated by changing their work environment.
2. Compare and contrast the three main ways jobs can be redesigned.
3. Give examples of employee involvement measures and show how they can motivate employees.
4. Describe the four major strategic rewards decisions.
5. Demonstrate how the different types of variable-pay programs can increase employee motivation.
6. Describe how the application of motivation approaches varies across cultures.

MOTIVATING BY CHANGING THE NATURE OF THE WORK ENVIRONMENT

Increasingly, research on motivation is focused on approaches that link motivational concepts to changes in the way work is structured. Research in **job design** provides evidence that the way the elements in a job are organized can act to increase or decrease effort. This research also offers detailed insights into how we identify those elements. We'll first review the job characteristics model, discuss some ways jobs can be redesigned, and then explore some alternative work arrangements.

The Job Characteristics Model

Developed by J. Richard Hackman and Greg Oldham, the **job characteristics model (JCM)** proposes that any job can be described in terms of five core job dimensions:[1]

1. *Skill variety.* The degree to which a job requires a variety of different activities so the worker can use a number of different skills and talent. For instance, an example of a job scoring high on skill variety would be the job of an owner-operator of a garage who handles the electrical repairs, rebuilds engines, does body work, and interacts with customers. A job scoring low on this dimension would be the job of a body shop worker who sprays paint 8 hours a day.

2. *Task identity.* The degree to which a job requires completion of a whole and identifiable piece of work. An example of a job scoring high on identity would be the job of a cabinetmaker who designs a piece of furniture, selects the wood, builds the object, and finishes it to perfection. A job scoring low on this dimension would be the job of a worker in a furniture factory who operates a lathe solely to make table legs.

3. *Task significance.* The degree to which a job has a substantial impact on the lives or work of other people. An example of a job scoring high on significance would be the job of a nurse handling the diverse needs of patients in a hospital intensive care unit. A job scoring low on this dimension would be the job of a janitor sweeping floors in a hospital.

   —Though there are individual differences, most people respond well to intrinsic job characteristics; the job characteristics model does a good job of summarizing what intrinsic job characteristics might be altered to make the work more interesting and intrinsically motivating for employees.

4. *Autonomy.* The degree to which a job provides substantial freedom, independence, and discretion to the individual in scheduling the work and in determining the procedures to be used in carrying it out. An example of a job scoring high on autonomy is the job of a salesperson who schedules his or her own work each day and decides on the most effective sales approach for each customer without supervision. A job scoring low on this dimension would be the job of a salesperson who is given a set of leads each day and is required to follow a standardized sales script with each potential customer.

5. *Feedback.* The degree to which carrying out the work activities required by a job results in the individual obtaining direct and clear information about the effectiveness of his or her performance. An example of a job with high feedback is the job of a factory worker who assembles iPods and tests them to see if they operate properly. A job scoring low on feedback would be the job of a factory worker who, after assembling an iPod, is required to route it to a quality-control inspector who tests it for proper operation and makes needed adjustments.

Exhibit 6-1 presents the job characteristics model. Note how the first three dimensions—skill variety, task identity, and task significance—combine to create meaningful work. That is, if these three characteristics exist in a job, the model predicts that the incumbent will view the job as being important, valuable, and worthwhile. Note, too, that jobs with high autonomy give job incumbents a feeling of personal responsibility for the results and that, if a job provides feedback, employees will know how effectively they are performing. From a motivational standpoint, the JCM says that individuals obtain internal rewards when they learn (knowledge of results) that they personally (experienced responsibility) have performed well on a task that they care about (experienced meaningfulness). The more these three psychological states are present, the greater will be employees' motivation, performance, and satisfaction and the lower their absenteeism and likelihood of leaving the organization. As Exhibit 6-1 shows, the links between the job dimensions and the outcomes are

EXHIBIT 6-1   The Job Characteristics Model

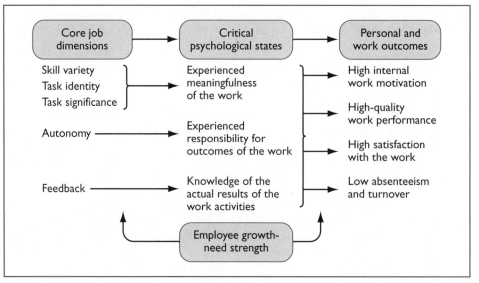

Source: J. R. Hackman and G. R. Oldham, *Work Redesign* © 1980; pp. 78–80. Adapted by permission of Pearson Education, Inc. Upper Saddle River, New Jersey.

moderated or adjusted by the strength of the individual's growth need—that is, by the employee's desire for self-esteem and self-actualization. This means that individuals with a high growth need are more likely to experience the psychological states when their jobs are enriched than are their counterparts with low growth need. Moreover, the individuals with a high growth need will respond more positively to the psychological states when they are present than will individuals with a low growth need.

Jobs that are high on motivating potential must be high on at least one of the three factors that lead to experienced meaningfulness, and they must be high on both autonomy and feedback. If jobs score high on motivating potential, the model predicts that motivation, performance, and satisfaction will be positively affected and that the likelihood of absence and turnover will be reduced.

The JCM has been well researched, with most of the evidence supporting the general framework of the theory—that is, there is a set of job characteristics, and these characteristics affect behavioral outcomes.[2] But it appears that the MPS model doesn't work—that is, we can better derive motivating potential by adding the characteristics rather than using the complex MPS formula.[3] Beyond employee growth-need strength, other variables, such as the employee's perception of his or her work load compared with that of others, may also moderate the link between the core job dimensions and personal and work outcomes.[4] Overall, though, it appears that jobs that have the intrinsic elements of variety, identity, significance, autonomy, and feedback are more satisfying and generate higher performance from people than jobs that lack these characteristics.

How Can Jobs Be Redesigned?

"Every day was the same thing," Frank Greer said. "Stand on that assembly line. Wait for an instrument panel to be moved into place. Unlock the mechanism and drop the panel into the Jeep Liberty as it moved by on the line. Then I plugged in the harnessing wires. I repeated that for eight hours a day. I don't care that they were paying me $24 an hour. I was going crazy. I did it for almost a year and a half. Finally, I just said to my wife that this isn't going to be the way I'm going to spend the rest of my life. My brain was turning to Jell-O on that Jeep assembly line. So I quit. Now I work in a print shop and I make less than $15 an hour. But let me tell you, the work I do is really interesting. The job changes all the time, I'm continually learning new things, and the work really challenges me! I look forward every morning to going to work again."

Frank Greer's job at the Jeep plant involved repetitive tasks that provided him with little variety, autonomy, or motivation. In contrast, his job in the print shop is challenging and stimulating. Let's look at some of the ways to put JCM into practice to make jobs more motivating.

Job Rotation   If employees suffer from overroutinization of their work, one alternative is to use **job rotation** (or what many now call *cross-training*). We define this practice as the periodic shifting of an employee from one task to another. When an activity is no longer challenging, the employee is rotated to another job, usually at the same level, that has similar skill requirements. Singapore Airlines, one of the best-rated airlines in the world, uses job rotation extensively. For example, a ticket agent may take on the duties of a baggage handler. Job rotation is one of the reasons Singapore Airlines is rated as a highly desirable place to work. Many manufacturing firms have adopted job rotation as a means of increasing flexibility and avoiding layoffs. For instance, managers at Apex Precision Technologies, a custom-machine shop in Indiana, continually train workers on all of the company's equipment so they can be moved around in response to the requirements of incoming orders.

The strengths of job rotation are that it reduces boredom, increases motivation through diversifying the employee's activities, and helps employees better understand how their work contributes to the organization. Job rotation also has indirect benefits for the organization because when employees have a wider range of skills management has more flexibility in scheduling work, adapting to changes, and filling vacancies. However, job rotation is not without drawbacks. Training costs are increased and productivity is reduced by moving a worker into a new position just when efficiency at the prior job is creating organizational economies. Job rotation also creates disruptions. Members of the work group have to adjust to the new employee and supervisors may also have to spend more time answering questions and monitoring the work of recently rotated employees.

Job Enlargement   More than 35 years ago, the idea of expanding jobs horizontally, or what we call **job enlargement** grew in popularity. Increasing the number and variety of tasks that an individual performed resulted in jobs with more diversity. Instead of only sorting the incoming mail by department, for instance, a mail sorter's job could be enlarged to include physically delivering the mail to the various departments or running outgoing letters through the postage meter. The difference between job rotation and job enlargement may seem subtle. However, in job rotation, jobs are not redesigned. Employees simply move from one job to another, but the nature of the work does not change. Job enlargement, however, involves actually changing the job.

Efforts at job enlargement have met with less-than-enthusiastic results.[5] One employee who experienced such a redesign on his job remarked, "Before I had one lousy job. Now, through enlargement, I have three!" However, there have been some successful applications of job enlargement. The housekeeping job in some small hotels, for example, includes not only cleaning bathrooms, making beds, and vacuuming but also replacing burned-out light bulbs, providing turn-down service, and restocking mini-bars.

Job Enrichment   **Job enrichment** refers to the vertical expansion of jobs. It increases the degree to which the worker controls the planning, execution, and evaluation of the work. An enriched job organizes tasks so as to allow the worker to do a complete activity, increases the employee's freedom and independence, increases responsibility, and provides feedback so individuals will be able to assess and correct their own performance.[6]

How does management enrich an employee's job? Exhibit 6-2 offers suggested guidelines based on the job characteristics model. *Combining tasks* takes existing and fractionalized tasks and puts them back together to form a new and larger module of work. *Forming natural work units* means that an employee's tasks create an identifiable and meaningful whole. *Establishing client relationships* increases the direct relationships between workers and their clients (these may be an internal customer as well as someone outside the organization). *Expanding jobs vertically* gives employees responsibilities and control that were formerly reserved for management. *Opening feedback channels* lets employees know how well they are performing their jobs and whether their performance is improving, deteriorating, or remaining at a constant level.

The overall evidence on job enrichment generally shows that it reduces absenteeism and turnover costs and increases satisfaction, but on the critical issue of productivity, the evidence is inconclusive.[7] Some recent evidence suggests that job enrichment works best when it compensates for poor feedback and reward systems.[8]

EXHIBIT 6-2   Guidelines for Enriching a Job

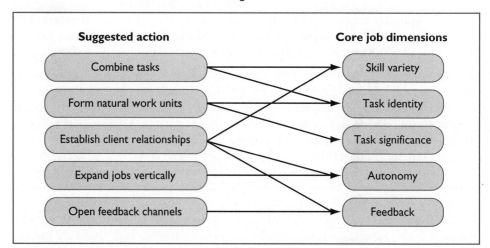

Source: J. R. Hackman and J. L. Suttle (eds.), *Improving Life at Work* (Glenview, IL: Scott Foresman, 1977), p. 138. Reprinted by permission of Richard Hackman and J. Lloyd Suttle.

Alternative Work Arrangements

Beyond redesigning the nature of the work itself and involving employees in decisions, another approach to making the work environment more motivating is to alter work arrangements. We'll discuss three alternative work arrangements: flextime, job sharing, and telecommuting. With increasing advances in technology, all of these alternative work arrangements have become more popular.

Flextime   The term **flextime** is short for "flexible work time." It allows employees some discretion over when they arrive at work and when they leave. Employees have to work a specific number of hours a week, but they are free to vary the hours of work, within certain limits. As shown in Exhibit 6-3, each day consists of a common core, usually 6 hours, with a flexibility band surrounding the core. For example, exclusive of a 1-hour lunch break, the core may be 9 A.M. to 3 P.M., with the office actually opening at 6 A.M. and closing at 6 P.M. All employees are required to be at their jobs during the common core period, but they are allowed to accumulate their other 2 hours before and/or after the core time. Some flextime programs allow extra hours to be accumulated and turned into a free day off each month.

Flextime has become an extremely popular scheduling option. The proportion of full-time U.S. employees on flextime more than doubled between the late 1980s and 2005. Approximately 43 percent of the U.S. full-time workforce now has flexibility in their daily arrival and departure times.[9] And this is not just a U.S. phenomenon. In Germany, for instance, 29 percent of businesses have flextime for their employees.[10]

The benefits claimed for flextime are numerous. They include reduced absenteeism, increased productivity, reduced overtime expenses, reduced hostility toward management, reduced traffic congestion around work sites, elimination of tardiness, and increased autonomy and responsibility for employees that may increase employee job satisfaction. But beyond the claims, what's flextime's record?

Most of the performance evidence stacks up favorably. Flextime tends to reduce absenteeism and frequently improves worker productivity,[11] probably for several reasons. Employees can schedule their work hours to align with personal demands, thus reducing tardiness and absences, and employees can adjust their work activities to those hours in which they are individually most productive.

Flextime's major drawback is that it's not applicable to every job. It works well with clerical tasks for which an employee's interaction with people outside his or her department is limited. It is not a viable option for receptionists, sales personnel in retail stores, or similar jobs for which comprehensive service demands that people be at their workstations at predetermined times.

EXHIBIT 6-3   Example of a Flextime Schedule

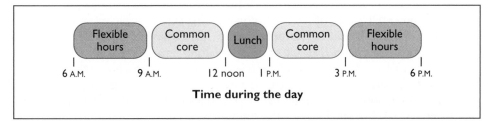

Job Sharing   A recent work scheduling innovation is **job sharing**. It allows two or more individuals to split a traditional 40-hour-a-week job. So, for example, one person might perform the job from 8 A.M. to noon, while another performs the same job from 1 P.M. to 5 P.M.; or the two could work full, but alternate, days. Approximately 31 percent of large organizations now offer their employees job sharing.[12] However, despite its availability, it doesn't seem to be widely adopted by employees. This is probably because of the difficulty of finding compatible partners to share a job and the negative perceptions historically held of individuals not completely committed to their job and employer.

Job sharing allows an organization to draw on the talents of more than one individual in a given job. A bank manager who oversees two job sharers describes it as an opportunity to get two heads but "pay for one." It also opens up the opportunity to acquire skilled workers—for instance, women with young children and retirees—who might not be available on a full-time basis. Many Japanese firms are increasingly considering job sharing—but for a very different reason.[13] Because Japanese executives are extremely reluctant to fire people, job sharing is seen as a potentially humanitarian means for avoiding layoffs due to overstaffing.

From the employee's perspective, job sharing increases flexibility. As such, it can increase motivation and satisfaction for those to whom a 40-hour-a-week job is just not practical. However, the major drawback from management's perspective is finding compatible pairs of employees who can successfully coordinate the intricacies of one job.

Telecommuting   It might be close to the ideal job for many people. No commuting, flexible hours, freedom to dress as you please, and few or no interruptions from colleagues. It's called **telecommuting**, and it refers to employees who do their work at home at least 2 days a week on a computer that is linked to their office.[14] (A closely related term—*virtual office*—is increasingly being used to describe employees who work out of their home on a relatively permanent basis.)

Recent estimates indicate that between 9 million and 24 million people telecommute in the United States, depending on exactly how the term is defined.[15] This translates to about 10 percent or more of the U.S. workforce. The concept is also catching on elsewhere in the world. In Finland, Sweden, Britain, and Germany, telecommuters represent 17, 15, 8, and 6 percent of their workforces, respectively.[16]

What kinds of jobs lend themselves to telecommuting? Three categories have been identified as most appropriate: routine information-handling tasks, mobile activities, and professional and other knowledge-related tasks.[17] Writers, attorneys, analysts, and employees who spend the majority of their time on computers or the telephone are natural candidates for telecommuting. For instance, telemarketers, customer-service representatives, reservation agents, and product-support specialists spend most of their time on the phone. As telecommuters, they can access information on their computers at home as easily as in the company's office.

The potential pluses of telecommuting for management include a larger labor pool from which to select, higher productivity, less turnover, improved morale, and reduced office-space costs. The major downside for management is less direct supervision of employees. In addition, in today's team-focused workplace, telecommuting may make it more difficult for management to coordinate teamwork. From the employee's standpoint, telecommuting offers a considerable increase in flexibility. But not without costs. For employees with a high social need, telecommuting can increase feelings of isolation and reduce job satisfaction. And all telecommuters potentially suffer from the "out of sight, out of mind" effect. Employees who aren't at their desks, who miss meetings, and who don't share in day-to-day informal workplace interactions may be at a disadvantage when it comes to raises and promotions. It can be easy for bosses to overlook or undervalue the contribution of employees whom they don't see regularly.

EMPLOYEE INVOLVEMENT

We define **employee involvement** as a participative process that uses the input of employees to increase their commitment to the organization's success. The underlying logic is that if we involve workers in the decisions that affect them and increase their autonomy and control over their work lives, employees will become more motivated, more committed to the organization, more productive, and more satisfied with their jobs.[18]

Examples of Employee Involvement Programs

Let's look at the two major forms of employee involvement—participative management and representative participation—in more detail.

Participative Management   The distinct characteristic common to all **participative management** programs is the use of joint decision making. That is, subordinates actually share a significant degree of decision-making power with their immediate superiors. Participative management has, at times, been promoted as a panacea for poor morale and low productivity. But for it to work, the issues in which employees get involved must be relevant to their interests so they'll be motivated, employees must have the competence and knowledge to make a useful contribution, and there must be trust and confidence between all parties involved.[19]

Dozens of studies have been conducted on the participation–performance relationship. The findings, however, are mixed.[20] A careful review of the research seems to show that participation typically has only a modest influence on variables such as employee productivity, motivation, and job satisfaction. Of course, this doesn't mean that the use of participative management can't be beneficial under the right conditions. What it says, however, is that the use of participation is not a sure means for improving employee performance.

Representative Participation   Almost every country in Western Europe has some type of legislation that requires companies to practice **representative participation**. That is, rather than participating directly in decisions, workers are represented by a small group of employees who actually participate. Representative participation has been called "the most widely legislated form of employee involvement around the world."[21] The goal of representative participation is to redistribute power within an organization, putting labor on a more equal footing with the interests of management and stockholders.

The two most common forms representative participation takes are works councils and board representatives.[22] Works councils are

> —As opposed to research on the job characteristics model and work redesign, which is mostly favorable, the research evidence on employee involvement programs is decidedly mixed. It is not clear that employee involvement programs have fulfilled their promise.

groups of nominated or elected employees who must be consulted when management makes decisions involving personnel. Board representatives are employees who sit on a company's board of directors and represent the interests of the firm's employees.

The overall influence of representative participation on working employees seems to be minimal.[23] For instance, the evidence suggests that workers' councils are dominated by management and have little impact on employees or the organization. Although this form of employee involvement might increase the motivation and satisfaction of the individuals who are doing the representing, there is little evidence that this trickles down to the operating employees whom they represent. Overall, "the greatest value of representative participation is symbolic. If one is interested in changing employee attitudes or in improving organizational performance, representative participation would be a poor choice."[24]

USING REWARDS TO MOTIVATE EMPLOYEES

As we saw in Chapter 4, pay is not a primary factor driving job satisfaction. However, it does motivate people, and companies often underestimate the importance of pay in keeping top talent. A 2006 study found that whereas only 45 percent of employers thought that pay was a key factor in losing top talent, 71 percent of top performers indicated that it was a top reason.[25]

Given that pay is so important, we need to understand what to pay employees and how to pay them. To do that, management must make some strategic decisions. In this section, we consider four major strategic rewards decisions that need to be made: (1) what to pay employees, (2) how to pay individual employees, (3) what benefits to offer, and (4) how to construct employee recognition programs.

What to Pay: Establishing a Pay Structure

There are many ways to pay employees. The process of initially setting pay levels can be rather complex and entails balancing *internal equity*—the worth of the job to the organization (usually established through a technical process called job evaluation)—and *external equity*—the external competitiveness of an organization's pay relative to pay elsewhere in its industry (usually established through pay surveys). Obviously, the best pay system pays the job what it is worth (internal equity) while also paying competitively relative to the labor market.

Some organizations prefer to be pay leaders by paying above the market, whereas some may lag behind the market because they can't afford to pay market rates, or they are willing to bear the costs of paying below the market (namely, higher turnover as people are lured to better-paying jobs). Wal-Mart, for example, pays less than its competitors and often outsources jobs overseas. Chinese workers in Shenzhen earn $120 a month (that's $1,440 per year) to make stereos for Wal-Mart. Of the 6,000 factories that are worldwide suppliers to Wal-Mart, 80 percent are located in China. In fact, one-eighth of all Chinese exports to the United States go to Wal-Mart.[26]

Pay more, and you may get better-qualified, more highly motivated employees who will stay with the organization longer. But pay is often the single highest operating cost for an organization, which means that paying too much can make the organization's products or services too expensive. It's a strategic decision an organization must make, with clear trade-offs.

How to Pay: Rewarding Individual Employees Through Variable-Pay Programs

"Why should I put any extra effort into this job?" asked Anne Garcia, a fourth-grade elementary schoolteacher in Denver, Colorado. "I can excel or I can do the bare minimum. It makes no difference. I get paid the same. Why do anything above the minimum to get by?"

Comments similar to Anne's have been voiced by schoolteachers for decades because pay increases were tied to seniority. Recently, however, a number of schools have begun revamping their compensation systems to motivate people like Anne to strive for excellence in their jobs.

A number of organizations—business firms as well as school districts and other government agencies—are moving away from paying people based solely on credentials or length of service and toward using variable-pay programs. Piece-rate plans, merit-based pay, bonuses, profit-sharing, gainsharing, and employee stock ownership plans are all forms of **variable-pay programs**. Instead of paying a person only for time on the job or seniority, a variable-pay program bases a portion of an employee's pay on some individual and/or organizational measure of performance. Earnings therefore fluctuate up and down with the measure of performance. Variable-pay plans have long been used to compensate salespeople and executives. Today, more than 70 percent of U.S. companies have some form of variable-pay plan, up from only about 5 percent in 1970.[27] Unfortunately, recent survey data indicate that most employees still don't see a strong connection between pay and performance. Only 29 percent say that when they do a good job, their performance is rewarded.[28]

—Variable-pay plans, when properly designed and administered, do appear to enhance employee motivation.

It is precisely the fluctuation in variable pay that has made these programs attractive to management. It turns part of an organization's fixed labor costs into a variable cost, thus reducing expenses when performance declines. So when the U.S. economy encountered a recession in 2001 and experienced a similar downturn in 2008, companies with variable pay were able to reduce their labor costs much faster than companies that had maintained non-performance-based compensation systems.[29] In addition, when pay is tied to performance, the employee's earnings recognize contribution rather than being a form of entitlement. Low performers find, over time, that their pay stagnates, whereas high performers enjoy pay increases commensurate with their contributions.

What are the specific forms of variable pay? There are seven major types of variable-pay programs:

1. *Piece-Rate Pay* In **piece-rate pay plans**, workers are paid a fixed sum for each unit of production completed. When an employee gets no base salary and is paid only for what he or she produces, this is a pure piece-rate plan. People who work in ballparks selling peanuts and soda are frequently paid this way. If they sell only forty bags of peanuts, their take is only $40. The harder they work and the more peanuts they sell, the more they earn. The limitation of these plans is that they're not feasible for many jobs. For example, Alabama college football coach Nick Saban earns $4 million per year. That salary is paid regardless of how many games he wins. Would it be better to pay Saban, say, $500,000 for each win? It seems unlikely he would accept such a deal, and it may cause unanticipated consequences as well (such as cheating). So, although incentives are motivating and relevant for some jobs, it is unrealistic to think they can constitute the only piece of some employees' pay.

2. *Merit-Based Pay* Unlike piece-rate plans, which pay based on objective output, **merit-based pay plans** are based on performance appraisal ratings. A main advantage of merit pay plans is that they allow employers to differentiate pay based on performance so that those people thought to be high performers are given bigger raises. The plans can be motivating because, if they are designed correctly, individuals perceive a strong relationship between their performance and the rewards they receive. One of the limitations of merit pay plans is that the merit pay is as valid or invalid as the performance ratings on which it is based. Another limitation of merit pay is that sometimes the pay-raise pool fluctuates based on economic conditions or other factors that have little to do with an individual employee's performance. One year, a colleague at a top university who performed very well in teaching and research was given a pay raise of $300. Why? Because the pay-raise pool was very small. Yet that is hardly pay-for-performance.

3. *Bonuses* For many jobs, annual bonuses are a significant component of the total compensation. Many companies now routinely reward production employees with bonuses in the thousands of dollars when company profits improve. Steel company Nucor, for example, guarantees its employees only about $10/hour, but its bonuses can be substantial; the average Nucor worker made roughly $91,000 last year. One advantage of bonuses over merit pay is that **bonuses** reward employees for recent performance rather than historical performance. The incentive effects of performance should be higher because, rather than paying people for performance that may have occurred years ago (and was rolled into their base pay), bonuses reward only recent performance. The downside of bonuses is that employees may view them negatively—after all, any worker would choose a $5,000 raise rolled into her base pay over a one-time payment of $5,000.

4. *Skill-Based Pay* **Skill-based pay** is an alternative to job-based pay. Rather than having an individual's job title define his or her pay category, skill-based pay (also called *competency-based* or *knowledge-based pay*) sets pay levels on the basis of how many skills employees have or how many jobs they can do. For instance, employees at American Steel & Wire can boost their annual salaries by up to $12,480 by acquiring as many as ten new skills. For employers, the lure of skill-based pay plans is that they increase the flexibility of the workforce: Filling staffing needs is easier when employee skills are interchangeable. Skill-based pay also facilitates communication across the organization because people gain a better understanding of each others' jobs. The main downside of skill-based pay is that people can "top out"—that is, they can learn all the skills the program calls for them to learn. This can frustrate employees after they've become challenged by an environment of learning, growth, and continual pay raises. There is also a problem created by paying people for acquiring skills for which there may be no immediate need. This happened at IDS Financial Services.[30] The company found itself paying people more money even though there was little immediate use for their new skills. IDS eventually dropped its skill-based pay plan and replaced it with one that equally balances individual contribution and gains in work-team productivity.

5. *Profit-Sharing Plans* **Profit-sharing plans** are organization-wide programs that distribute compensation based on some established formula designed around a company's profitability. These can be direct cash outlays or, particularly in the case of top managers, allocations of stock options. When you read about executives like Reuben Mark, the CEO at Colgate-Palmolive, earning $148 million in a year, almost all this comes from cashing in stock options previously granted based on company profit performance. Not all profit-sharing plans, though, need be so grand in scale. Jacob Luke, 13, started his own lawn-mowing business after getting a mower from his uncle. Jacob employs his brother, Isaiah, and friend, Marcel Monroe, and pays them each 25 percent of the profits he makes on each yard.

6. *Gainsharing* A variable-pay program that has gotten a great deal of attention in recent years is **gainsharing**.[31] This is a formula-based group incentive plan. Improvements in group productivity from one period to another determine the total amount of money that is to be allocated. Gainsharing's popularity seems to be narrowly focused among large manufacturing companies such as Champion Spark Plug and Mead Paper. For instance, approximately 45 percent of Fortune 1000 firms have implemented gainsharing plans.[32] Gainsharing is different from profit-sharing in that rewards are tied to productivity gains rather than on profits. Employees in a gainsharing plan can receive incentive awards even when the organization isn't profitable.

7. *Employee Stock Ownership Plans* **Employee stock ownership plans (ESOPs)** are company-established benefit plans in which employees acquire stock, often at below-market prices, as part of their benefits. Companies as varied as Publix Supermarkets and W.L. Gore & Associates are now over 50 percent employee owned. But most of the 10,000 or so ESOPs in the United States are in small, privately held companies.[33] The research on ESOPs indicates that they increase employee satisfaction; however, their impact on performance is less clear. It appears that, in addition to merely having a financial stake in the company, employees need to be kept regularly informed of the status of the business and also have the opportunity to exercise influence over it. The evidence consistently indicates that it takes ownership and a participative style of management to achieve significant improvements in an organization's performance.[34]

Evaluation of Variable Pay   Do variable-pay programs increase motivation and productivity? The answer is a qualified "yes." For example, studies generally support the idea that organizations with profit-sharing plans have higher levels of profitability than those without them.[35] Similarly, gainsharing has been found to improve productivity in a majority of cases and often has a positive impact on employee attitudes.[36] Another study found that whereas piece-rate pay-for-performance plans stimulated higher levels of productivity, this positive effect was not observed for risk-averse employees. Thus, in general, what economist Ed Lazear has said seems generally right: employees "respond to prices just as economic theory predicts. Claims by sociologists and others that monetizing incentives may actually reduce output are unambiguously refuted by the data." But that doesn't mean everyone responds positively to variable-pay plans.[37]

What Benefit to Offer: Flexible Benefits

Flexible benefits allow each employee to put together a benefits package individually tailored to his or her own needs and situation. It replaces the traditional "one-benefit-plan-fits-all" programs that dominated organizations for more than 50 years.[38] Consistent with expectancy theory's thesis that organizational rewards should be linked to each individual employee's goals, flexible benefits individualize rewards by allowing each employee to choose the compensation package that best satisfies his or her current needs. The average organization provides fringe benefits worth approximately 40 percent of an employee's salary. Traditional benefits programs were designed for the typical employee of the 1950s—a male with a wife and two children at home. Less than 10 percent of employees now fit this stereotype. About 25 percent of today's employees are single, and one-third are part of two-income families with no children. Traditional programs don't meet their diverse needs, but flexible benefits do. They can be uniquely tailored to accommodate differences in employee needs based on age, marital status, spouses' benefit status, number and age of dependents, and the like.

The three most popular types of benefits plans are modular plans, core-plus options, and flexible spending accounts.[39] *Modular plans* are predesigned packages of benefits, with each module put together to meet the needs of a specific group of employees. So a module designed for single employees with no dependents might include only essential benefits. Another, designed for single parents, might have additional life insurance, disability insurance, and expanded health coverage. *Core-plus plans* consist of a core of essential benefits and a menu-like selection of other benefit options from which employees can select and add to the core. Typically, each employee is given "benefit credits," which allow the "purchase" of additional benefits that uniquely meet his or her needs. *Flexible spending plans* allow employees to set aside up to the dollar amount offered in the plan to pay for particular services. It's a convenient way, for example, for employees to pay for health care and dental premiums. Flexible spending accounts can increase employee take-home pay because employees don't have to pay taxes on the dollars they spend out of these accounts.

Intrinsic Rewards: How to Construct Employee Recognition Programs

Laura Schendell makes only $8.50 per hour working at her fast-food job in Pensacola, Florida, and the job isn't very challenging or interesting. Yet Laura talks enthusiastically about her job, her boss, and the company that employs her. "What I like is the fact that Guy [her supervisor] appreciates the effort I make. He compliments me regularly in front of the other people on my shift, and I've been chosen Employee of the Month twice in the past six months. Did you see my picture on that plaque on the wall?"

Organizations are increasingly recognizing what Laura Schendell knows: Important work rewards can be both intrinsic and extrinsic. Rewards are intrinsic in the form of employee recognition programs and extrinsic in the form of compensation systems. In this section, we will deal with ways in which managers can reward and motivate employee performance.

Employee recognition programs range from a spontaneous and private "thank you" up to widely publicized formal programs in which specific types of behavior are encouraged and the procedures for attaining recognition are clearly identified. Some research has suggested that whereas financial incentives may be more motivating in the short term, in the long run, nonfinancial incentives are more motivating.[40]

Nichols Foods Ltd., a British bottler of soft drinks and syrups, has a comprehensive recognition program.[41] The central hallway in its production area is lined with "bragging boards," where the accomplishments of various individuals and teams are regularly updated. Monthly awards are presented to people who have been nominated by peers for extraordinary effort on the job. Also, monthly award winners are eligible for further recognition at an annual off-site meeting for all employees. In contrast, most managers use a far more informal approach. Julia Stewart, president of Applebee's restaurants, frequently leaves sealed notes on the chairs of employees after everyone has gone home.[42] These notes explain how critical Stewart thinks the person's work is or how much she appreciates the completion of a recent project. Stewart also relies heavily on voice mail messages left after office hours to tell employees how appreciative she is for a job well done.

A few years ago, 1,500 employees were surveyed in a variety of work settings to find out what they considered to be the most powerful workplace motivator. Their response? Recognition, recognition, and more recognition.[43]

An obvious advantage of recognition programs is that they are inexpensive (praise, of course, is free!). It shouldn't be surprising, therefore, to find that employee recognition programs have grown in popularity. A 2002 survey of 391 companies found that 84 percent had some program to recognize worker achievements and that 4 in 10 said they were doing more to foster employee recognition than they had been just a year earlier.[44]

Despite the increased popularity of employee recognition programs, critics argue that these programs are highly susceptible to political manipulation by management.[45] When applied to jobs where performance factors are relatively objective, such as sales, recognition programs are likely to be perceived by employees as fair. However, in most jobs, the criteria for good performance aren't self-evident, which allows managers to manipulate the system and recognize their favorite employees. Abuse of such a system can undermine the value of recognition programs and lead to demoralizing employees.

GLOBAL IMPLICATIONS

Do the motivational approaches discussed in this chapter vary by culture? Because we've discussed some very different approaches in this chapter, let's break down our analysis by approach. Not every approach has been studied by cross-cultural researchers, so we don't discuss every motivational approach. However, we consider cross-cultural differences in the following approaches: (1) job characteristics and job enrichment, (2) telecommuting, (3) variable pay, (4) flexible benefits, and (5) employee involvement.

Job Characteristics and Job Enrichment   Although a few studies have tested the job characteristics model in different cultures, the results aren't very consistent. One study suggested that when employees are "other-oriented" (that is, concerned with the welfare of others at work), the relationship between intrinsic job characteristics and job satisfaction was weaker. As the authors note, because the job characteristics model is relatively individualistic (considering the relationship between the employee and his or her work), this suggests that job enrichment strategies may not have the same effects in more collectivistic cultures that they do in individualistic cultures (as in the United States).[46] However, another study suggested that the degree to which jobs had intrinsic job characteristics predicted job satisfaction and job involvement equally well for U.S., Japanese, and Hungarian employees.[47]

Telecommuting   Does the degree to which employees telecommute vary by nation? Does its effectiveness depend on culture? First, one study suggests that telecommuting is more common in the United States than in all the European Union (EU) nations except the Netherlands. In the study, 24.6 percent of U.S. employees engaged in telecommuting, compared to only 13.0 percent of EU employees. Of the EU countries, the Netherlands had the highest rate of telecommuting (26.4 percent); the lowest rates were in Spain (4.9 percent) and Portugal (3.4 percent). Thus, telecommuting appears to be more common in the United States than in Europe. What about the rest of the world? Unfortunately, there are very little data comparing telecommuting rates in other parts of the world. Similarly, we don't really know whether telecommuting works better in the United States than in other countries. However, the same study that compared telework rates between the United States and the EU determined that employees in Europe appeared to have the same level of interest in telework: Regardless of country, interest is higher among employees than among employers.[48]

Variable Pay   You'd probably think that individual pay systems (such as merit pay or pay-for-performance) would work better in individualistic cultures like the United States than in collectivistic cultures like China or Venezuela. Similarly, you'd probably hypothesize that group-based rewards such as gainsharing or profit-sharing would work better in collectivistic cultures than in individualistic cultures. Unfortunately, there isn't much research on the issue. One recent study did suggest, though, that beliefs about the fairness of a group incentive plan were more predictive of pay satisfaction for employees in the United States than for employees in Hong Kong. One interpretation of these findings is that U.S. employees are more critical in appraising a group pay plan, and therefore it's more critical that the plan be communicated clearly and administered fairly.[49]

Flexible Benefits   Today, almost all major corporations in the United States offer flexible benefits. And they're becoming the norm in other countries, too. For instance, a recent survey of 136 Canadian organizations found that 93 percent have adopted or will adopt flexible benefits in the near term.[50] A similar survey of 307 firms in the United Kingdom found that although only 16 percent have flexible benefits programs in place, another 60 percent are either in the process of implementing them or are seriously considering it.[51] We don't yet know whether employee reactions to flexible benefits vary by culture.

Employee Involvement   Employee involvement programs differ among countries.[52] For instance, a study comparing the acceptance of employee involvement programs in four countries, including the United States and India, confirmed the importance of modifying practices to reflect national culture.[53] Specifically, although U.S. employees readily accepted these programs, managers in India who tried to empower their employees through employee involvement programs were rated low by those employees. Employee satisfaction also decreased. These reactions are consistent with India's high power–distance culture, which accepts and expects differences in authority.

IMPLICATIONS FOR MANAGERS

We've presented a number of motivation theories and applications in Chapter 5 and in this chapter. Although it's always dangerous to synthesize a large number of complex ideas into a few simple guidelines, the following suggestions summarize the essence of what we know about motivating employees in organizations.

Recognize Individual Differences   Managers should be sensitive to individual differences. For example, employees from Asian cultures prefer not to be singled out as special because it makes them uncomfortable.

Employees have different needs. Don't treat them all alike. Moreover, spend the time necessary to understand what's important to each employee. This allows you to individualize goals, level of involvement, and rewards to align with individual needs. Also, design jobs to align with individual needs and therefore maximize the motivation potential in jobs.

Use Goals and Feedback   Employees should have firm, specific goals, and they should get feedback on how well they are faring in pursuit of those goals.

Allow Employees to Participate in Decisions That Affect Them   Employees can contribute to a number of decisions that affect them: setting work goals, choosing their own benefits packages, solving productivity and quality problems, and the like. This can increase employee productivity, commitment to work goals, motivation, and job satisfaction.

Link Rewards to Performance   Rewards should be contingent on performance. Importantly, employees must perceive a clear linkage between performance and rewards. Regardless of how closely rewards are actually correlated to performance criteria, if individuals perceive this relationship to be low, the results will be low performance, a decrease in job satisfaction, and an increase in turnover and absenteeism.

Check the System for Equity   Employees should perceive rewards as equating with the inputs they bring to the job. At a simplistic level, this should mean that experience, skills, abilities, effort, and other obvious inputs should explain differences in performance and, hence, pay, job assignments, and other obvious rewards.

CHAPTER 7

Emotions and Moods

1. Differentiate emotions from moods and list the basic emotions and moods.
2. Identify the sources of emotions and moods.
3. Show the impact emotional labor has on employees.
4. Contrast the evidence for and against the existence of emotional intelligence.
5. Apply concepts about emotions and moods to specific OB issues.
6. Contrast the experience, interpretation, and expression of emotions across cultures.

Given the obvious role that emotions play in our work and everyday lives, it might surprise you to learn that, until recently, the field of OB has given the topic of emotions little or no attention.[1] How could this be? We can offer two possible explanations.

The first is the *myth of rationality*. From the late nineteenth century and the rise of scientific management until very recently, the protocol of the work world was to keep a damper on emotions. A well-run organization didn't allow employees to express frustration, fear, anger, love, hate, joy, grief, and similar feelings. The prevailing thought was that such emotions were the antithesis of rationality. Even though researchers and managers knew that emotions were an inseparable part of everyday life, they tried to create organizations that were emotion free. That, of course, wasn't possible.

The second explanation is that many believed that emotions of any kind are disruptive. When researchers considered emotions, they looked at strong negative emotions—especially anger—that interfered with an employee's ability to work effectively. They rarely viewed emotions as constructive or contributing to enhanced performance.

Certainly some emotions, particularly when exhibited at the wrong time, can hinder employee performance. But this doesn't change the fact that employees bring their emotional sides with them to work every day and that no study of OB would be comprehensive without considering the role of emotions in workplace behavior.

WHAT ARE EMOTIONS AND MOODS?

Although we don't want to belabor definitions, before we can proceed with our analysis, we need to clarify three terms that are closely intertwined: *affect, emotions,* and *moods.*

Affect is a generic term that covers a broad range of feelings that people experience. It's an umbrella concept that encompasses both emotions and moods. **Emotions** are intense feelings that are directed at someone or something. **Moods** are feelings that tend to be less intense than emotions and that often (though not always) lack a contextual stimulus.[2]

Most experts believe that emotions are more fleeting than moods. For example, if someone is rude to you, you'll feel angry. That intense feeling of anger probably comes and goes fairly quickly, maybe even in a matter of seconds. When you're in a bad mood, though, you can feel bad for several hours.

Emotions are reactions to a person (for example, seeing a friend at work may make you feel glad) or event (for example, dealing with a rude client may make you feel angry). You show your emotions when you're "happy about something, angry at someone, afraid of something."[3] Moods, in contrast, aren't usually directed at a person or an event. But emotions can turn into moods when you lose focus on the event or object that started the feeling. And, by the same token, good or bad moods can make you more emotional in response to an event. So when a colleague criticizes how you spoke to a client, you might become angry at him; that is, you show emotion (anger) toward a specific object (your colleague). But as the specific emotion dissipates, you might just feel generally dispirited. You can't attribute this feeling to any single event; you're just not your normal self. You might then overreact to other events. This affect state describes a mood. Exhibit 7-1 shows the relationships among affect, emotions, and moods.

EXHIBIT 7-1   Affect, Emotions, and Moods

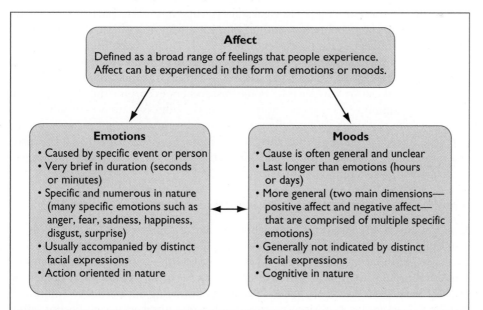

Affect
Defined as a broad range of feelings that people experience. Affect can be experienced in the form of emotions or moods.

Emotions
- Caused by specific event or person
- Very brief in duration (seconds or minutes)
- Specific and numerous in nature (many specific emotions such as anger, fear, sadness, happiness, disgust, surprise)
- Usually accompanied by distinct facial expressions
- Action oriented in nature

Moods
- Cause is often general and unclear
- Last longer than emotions (hours or days)
- More general (two main dimensions—positive affect and negative affect—that are comprised of multiple specific emotions)
- Generally not indicated by distinct facial expressions
- Cognitive in nature

First, as the exhibit shows, *affect* is a broad term that encompasses emotions and moods. Second, there are differences between emotions and moods. Some of these differences—that emotions are more likely to be caused by a specific event, and emotions are more fleeting than moods—were just discussed. Other differences are subtler. For example, unlike moods, emotions tend to be more clearly revealed with facial expressions (for example, anger, disgust). Also, some researchers speculate that emotions may be more action-oriented—they may lead us to some immediate action—whereas moods may be more cognitive, meaning they may cause us to think or brood for a while.[4]

Finally, the exhibit shows that emotions and moods can mutually influence each other. For example, an emotion, if it's strong and deep enough, can turn into a mood: Getting your dream job may generate the emotion of joy, but it also can put you in a good mood for several days. Similarly, if you're in a good or bad mood, it might make you experience a more intense positive or negative emotion than would otherwise be the case. For example, if you're in a bad mood, you might "blow up" in response to a coworker's comment when normally it would have just generated a mild reaction. Because emotions and moods can mutually influence each other, there will be many points throughout the chapter where emotions and moods will be closely connected.

Although affect, emotions, and moods are separable in theory, in practice the distinction isn't always crystal clear. In fact, in some areas, researchers have studied mostly moods, and in other areas, mainly emotions. So, when we review the OB topics on emotions and moods, you may see more information on emotions in one area and moods in another. This is simply the state of the research.

Also, the terminology can be confusing. For example, the two main mood dimensions are positive affect and negative affect, yet we have defined affect more broadly than mood. So, although the topic can be fairly dense in places, hang in there. The material is interesting—and applicable to OB.

The Basic Emotions

How many emotions are there? In what ways do they vary? There are dozens of emotions, including anger, contempt, enthusiasm, envy, fear, frustration, disappointment, embarrassment, disgust, happiness, hate, hope, jealousy, joy, love, pride, surprise, and sadness. Many researchers have agreed on six essentially universal emotions—anger, fear, sadness, happiness, disgust, and surprise—with most other emotions subsumed under one of these six categories.[5] Some researchers even plot these six emotions along a continuum: happiness—surprise—fear—sadness—anger—disgust.[6] The closer any two emotions are to each other on this continuum, the more likely it is that people will confuse them. For instance, we sometimes mistake happiness for surprise, but rarely do we confuse happiness and disgust. In addition, as we'll see later on, cultural factors can also influence interpretations.

The Basic Moods: Positive and Negative Affect

One way to classify emotions is by whether they are positive or negative. Positive emotions—such as joy and gratitude—express a favorable evaluation or feeling. Negative emotions—such as anger or guilt—express the opposite. When we group emotions into positive and negative categories, they become mood states because we are now looking at them more generally instead of isolating one particular emotion. In Exhibit 7-2, excited is a specific emotion that is a pure marker of high positive affect,

EXHIBIT 7-2   The Structure of Moods

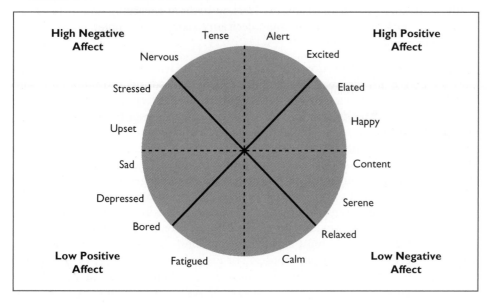

whereas boredom is a pure marker of low positive affect. Similarly, nervous is a pure marker of high negative affect, whereas relaxed is a pure marker of low negative affect. Finally, some emotions—such as contentment (a mixture of high positive affect and low negative affect) and sadness (a mixture of low positive affect and high negative affect)—are in between. You'll notice that this model does not include all emotions. There are two reasons. First, we can fit other emotions such as enthusiasm or depression into the model, but we're short on space. Second, some emotions, such as surprise, don't fit well because they're not as clearly positive or negative.

So, we can think of **positive affect** as a mood dimension consisting of positive emotions such as excitement, self-assurance, and cheerfulness at the high end and boredom, sluggishness, and tiredness at the low end. **Negative affect** is a mood dimension consisting of nervousness, stress, and anxiety at the high end and relaxation, tranquility, and poise at the low end. (Note that positive and negative affects *are* moods. We're using these labels, rather than *positive mood* and *negative mood* because that's how researchers label them.) Research shows that there is a **positivity offset**, meaning that at zero input (when nothing in particular is going on), most individuals experience a mildly positive mood.[7] So, for most people, positive moods are somewhat more common than negative moods—even at work.

The Function of Emotions

Do Emotions Make Us Irrational?   How often have you heard someone say, "Oh, you're just being emotional"? The statement implies that being emotional is being irrational. However, the research is increasingly showing that emotions are actually critical to rational thinking.[8] Why? Because our emotions provide important information about how we understand the world around us. Although we might think of a computer as intellectually superior, a human so void of emotion would be unable to function. Think about a manager making a decision to fire an employee. Would you really want the manager to make the decision without regarding either his or the employee's emotions? The key to good decision making is to employ both thinking *and* feeling in one's decisions.

What Functions Do Emotions Serve?   Why do we have emotions? What role do they serve? We just discussed one function—that we need them to think rationally. Charles Darwin, however, took a broader approach. In *The Expression of the Emotions in Man and Animals*, Darwin argued that emotions developed over time to help humans solve problems. Emotions are useful, he said, because they motivate people to engage in actions that are important for survival—actions such as foraging for food, seeking shelter, choosing mates, guarding against predators, and predicting others' behaviors. For example, disgust (an emotion) motivates us to avoid dangerous or harmful things (such as rotten foods). Excitement (also an emotion) motivates us to take on situations in which we require energy and initiative (for example, tackling a new career).

Drawing from Darwin are researchers who focus on **evolutionary psychology**. This field of study says we must experience emotions—whether they are positive or negative—because they serve a purpose.[9] For example, you would probably consider jealousy to be a negative emotion. Evolutionary psychologists would argue that it exists in people because it has a useful purpose. Mates may feel jealousy to increase the chance that their genes, rather than a rival's genes, are passed on to the next generation.[10] Although we tend to think of anger as being "bad," it actually can help us protect our rights when we feel they're being violated. For example, a person showing anger when she's double-crossed by a colleague is serving a warning for others not to repeat the same behavior. Consider another example. Rena Weeks was a secretary at a prominent law firm. Her boss wouldn't stop touching and grabbing her. His treatment of her made her angry. So she did more than quit—she sued, and won a multimillion-dollar case.[11] It's not that anger is always good. But as with all other emotions, it exists because it serves a useful purpose. Positive emotions also serve a purpose. For example, a service employee who feels empathy for a customer may provide better customer service than a seemingly unfeeling employee.

But some researchers are not firm believers of evolutionary psychology. Why? Think about fear (an emotion). It's just as easy to think of the harmful effects of fear as it is the beneficial effects. For example, running in fear from a predator increases the likelihood of survival. But what benefit does freezing in fear serve? Evolutionary psychology provides an interesting perspective on the functions of emotions, but it's difficult to know whether this perspective is valid all the time.[12]

Sources of Emotions and Moods

Have you ever said, "I got up on the wrong side of the bed today"? Have you ever snapped at a coworker or family member for no particular reason? If you have, it probably makes you wonder where emotions and moods come from. Here we discuss some of the primary influences on moods and emotions.

Day of the Week and Time of the Day   Are people in their best moods on the weekends? Well, sort of. As Exhibit 7-3 shows, people tend to be in their worst moods (highest negative affect and lowest positive affect) early in the week and in their best moods (highest positive affect and lowest negative affect) late in the week.[13]

EXHIBIT 7-3   Our Moods Are Affected by the Day of the Week

Source: D. Watson, *Mood and Temperament* (New York: Guilford Press, 2000).

What about time of the day? (See Exhibit 7-4.) We often think that people differ, depending on whether they are "morning" or "evening" people. However, the vast majority of us follow the same pattern. Regardless of what time people go to bed at night or get up in the morning, levels of positive affect tend to peak around the halfway point between waking and sleeping. Negative affect, however, shows little fluctuation throughout the day.[14] This basic pattern seems to hold whether people describe themselves as morning people or evening people.

What does this mean for organizational behavior? Monday morning is probably not the best time to ask someone for a favor or convey bad news. Our workplace interactions will probably be more positive from midmorning onward and also later in the week.

Weather   When do you think you would be in a better mood—when it's 70 degrees and sunny or when it's a gloomy, cold, rainy day? Many people believe their mood is tied to the weather. Although some early evidence suggested a link between weather and mood, a more recent expert suggests that there is less of a link than you might think. One expert concluded, "Contrary to the prevailing cultural view, these data indicate that people do not report a better mood on bright and sunny days (or, conversely, a worse mood on dark and rainy days)."[15]

Stress   As you might imagine, stress affects emotions and moods. For example, students have higher levels of fear before an exam, but their fear dissipates once the exam is over.[16] At work, stressful daily events (for example, a nasty e-mail, an impending deadline, the loss of a big sale, being reprimanded by your boss) negatively affect employees' moods. Also, the effects of stress build over time. As the authors of one study note, "a constant diet of even low-level stressful events has the potential to cause

EXHIBIT 7-4   Our Moods Are Affected by the Time of the Day

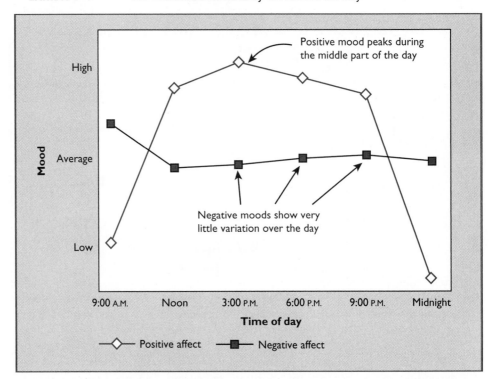

Source: D. Watson, *Mood and Temperament* (New York: Guilford Press, 2000).

workers to experience gradually increasing levels of strain over time."[17] Such mounting levels of stress and strain at work can worsen our moods, and we experience more negative emotions. Consider the following entry from a worker's blog: "i'm in a bit of a blah mood today . . . physically, i feel funky, though and the weather out combined with the amount of personal and work i need to get done are getting to me." Although sometimes we thrive on stress, for most of us, like this blogger, stress takes a toll on our mood.[18]

Social Activities   Do you tend to be happiest when you are out with friends? For most people, social activities increase positive mood and have little effect on negative mood. But do people in positive moods seek out social interactions, or do social interactions cause people to be in good moods? It seems that both are true.[19] And does the *type* of social activity matter? Indeed it does. Research suggests that physical (skiing or hiking with friends), informal (going to a party), or epicurean (eating with others) activities are more strongly associated with increases in positive mood than formal (attending a meeting) or sedentary (watching TV with friends) events.[20]

Sleep   U.S. adults report that they sleep less than they did a generation ago.[21] Does lack of sleep make people grumpier? Sleep quality does affect mood. Undergraduates and adult workers who are sleep deprived report greater feelings of fatigue, anger, and hostility.[22] One of the reasons less sleep, or poor sleep quality, puts people in a bad mood is that it impairs decision making and makes it difficult to control emotions.

A recent study suggests that poor sleep the previous night also impairs people's job satisfaction the next day, mostly because people feel fatigued, irritable, and less alert.[23]

Exercise   You often hear that people should exercise to improve their mood. But does "sweat therapy" really work? It appears so. Research consistently shows that exercise enhances people's positive mood.[24] It appears that the therapeutic effects of exercise are strongest for those who are depressed. Although the effects of exercise on moods are consistent, they are not terribly strong. So, exercise may help put you in a better mood, but don't expect miracles.

Age   Do you think that young people experience more extreme, positive emotions (so-called "youthful exuberance") than older people do? If you answered "yes," you were wrong. One study of people aged 18 to 94 years revealed that negative emotions seem to occur less as people get older. Periods of highly positive moods lasted longer for older individuals, and bad moods faded for them more quickly than for younger people.[25] The study implies that emotional experience tends to improve with age, so that as we get older, we experience fewer negative emotions and our positive emotions tend to linger longer. Some things do improve with age!

Gender   The common belief is that women are more emotional than men. Is there any truth to this? The evidence does confirm that women are more emotionally expressive than are men; they experience emotions more intensely, they tend to "hold onto" emotions longer than men, and they display more frequent expressions of both positive and negative emotions, except anger. Although there may be innate differences between the genders, research suggests that emotional differences also are due to the different ways men and women have been socialized.[26] Men are taught to be tough and brave. Showing emotion is inconsistent with this image. Women, in contrast, are socialized to be nurturing. For instance, women are expected to express more positive emotions on the job (shown by smiling) than men, and they do.[27]

EMOTIONAL LABOR

If you've ever had a job working in retail sales or waiting on tables in a restaurant, you know the importance of projecting a friendly demeanor and smiling. Even though there were days when you didn't feel cheerful, you knew management expected you to be upbeat when dealing with customers. So you faked it, and in so doing, you expressed emotional labor.

Every employee expends physical and mental labor when they put their bodies and cognitive capabilities, respectively, into their job. But jobs also require **emotional labor**. Emotional labor is an employee's expression of organizationally desired emotions during interpersonal transactions at work.[28]

The concept of emotional labor emerged from studies of service jobs. Airlines expect their flight attendants, for instance, to be cheerful; we expect funeral directors to be sad; and we expect doctors to be emotionally neutral. But really, emotional labor is relevant to almost every job. Your managers expect you, for example, to be courteous, not hostile, in interactions with coworkers. The true challenge arises when employees have to project one emotion while simultaneously feeling another. This disparity is **emotional dissonance**, and it can take a heavy toll on employees. Bottled-up feelings of frustration, anger, and resentment can eventually lead to emotional exhaustion and burnout.[29]

Emotional labor creates dilemmas for employees. There are people with whom you have to work that you just plain don't like. Maybe you consider their personality abrasive. Maybe you know they've said negative things about you behind your back. Regardless, your job requires you to interact with these people on a regular basis. So you're forced to feign friendliness.

It can help you, on the job especially, if you separate emotions into *felt* or *displayed emotions*.[30] **Felt emotions** are an individual's actual emotions. In contrast, **displayed emotions** are those that the organization requires workers to show and considers appropriate in a given job. They're not innate; they're learned. "The ritual look of delight on the face of the first runner-up as the new Miss America is announced is a product of the display rule that losers should mask their sadness with an expression of joy for the winner."[31] Similarly, most of us know that we're expected to act sad at funerals, regardless of whether we consider the person's death to be a loss, and to pretend to be happy at weddings, even if we don't feel like celebrating.[32]

Effective managers have learned to be serious when giving an employee a negative performance evaluation and to hide their anger when they've been passed over for promotion. And a salesperson who hasn't learned to smile and appear friendly, regardless of his true feelings at the moment, isn't typically going to last long on most sales jobs. How we *experience* an emotion isn't always the same as how we *show* it.

Yet another point is that displaying fake emotions requires us to suppress the emotions we really feel (not showing anger toward a customer, for example). In other words, the individual has to "act" to keep her job. **Surface acting** is hiding one's inner feelings and forgoing emotional expressions in response to display rules. For example, when a worker smiles at a customer even when he doesn't feel like it, he is surface acting. **Deep acting** is trying to modify one's true inner feelings based on display rules. A health care provider trying to genuinely feel more empathy for her patients is deep acting. Surface acting deals with one's *displayed* emotions, and deep acting deals with one's *felt* emotions. Research shows that surface acting is more stressful to employees than deep acting because it entails feigning one's true emotions.[33]

EMOTIONAL INTELLIGENCE

Diane Marshall is an office manager. Her awareness of her own and others' emotions is almost nil. She's moody and unable to generate much enthusiasm or interest in her employees. She doesn't understand why employees get upset with her. She often overreacts to problems and chooses the most ineffectual responses to emotional situations.[34] Diane Marshall has low emotional intelligence. **Emotional intelligence (EI)** is a person's ability to (1) be self-aware (to recognize her own emotions when she experiences them), (2) detect emotions in others, and (3) manage emotional cues and information. People who know their own emotions and are good at reading emotion cues—for instance, knowing why they're angry and how to express themselves without violating norms—are most likely to be effective.[35]

Several studies suggest that EI plays an important role in job performance. One study looked at the characteristics of engineers at Lucent Technologies who were rated as stars by their peers. The researchers concluded that stars were better at relating to others; that is, it was EI, not IQ, that characterized high performers. Another illuminating study looked at the successes and failures of eleven American presidents—from Franklin Roosevelt to Bill Clinton. They were evaluated on six qualities—communication, organization, political skill, vision, cognitive style, and emotional intelligence. It was found that the key quality that differentiated the successful (such as Roosevelt, Kennedy, and Reagan) from the unsuccessful (such as Johnson, Carter, and Nixon) was emotional intelligence.[36]

EI has been a controversial concept in OB. It has supporters and detractors. In the following sections, we will review the arguments for and against the viability of EI in OB.

> —People who know their own emotions and are good at reading others' emotions may be more effective in their jobs.

The Case for EI

The arguments in favor of EI include its intuitive appeal, the fact that EI predicts criteria that matter, and the idea that EI is biologically based.

Intuitive Appeal   There's a lot of intuitive appeal to the EI concept. Almost everyone would agree that it is good to possess street smarts and social intelligence. People who can detect emotions in others, control their own emotions, and handle social interactions well will have a powerful leg up in the business world, so the thinking goes. As just one example, partners in a multinational consulting firm who scored above the median on an EI measure delivered $1.2 million more in business than did the other partners.[37]

EI Predicts Criteria That Matter   More and more evidence is suggesting that a high level of EI means a person will perform well on the job. One study found that EI predicted the performance of employees in a cigarette factory in China.[38] Another study found that being able to recognize emotions in others' facial expressions and to emotionally "eavesdrop" (that is, pick up subtle signals about people's emotions) predicted peer ratings of how valuable those people were to their organization.[39] Finally, a review of fifty-nine studies indicated that, overall, EI correlated moderately with job performance.[40]

EI Is Biologically Based   One study has shown that people with damage to the part of the brain that governs emotional processing (lesions in an area of the prefrontal cortex) score significantly lower than others on EI tests. Even though these brain-damaged people scored no lower on standard measures of intelligence than people without the same brain damage, they were still impaired in normal decision making. Specifically, when people were playing a card game in which there is a reward (money) for picking certain types of cards and a punishment (a loss of money) for picking other types of cards, the participants with no brain damage learned to succeed in the game, whereas the performance of the brain-damaged group worsened over time. This study suggests that EI is neurologically based in a way that's unrelated to standard measures of intelligence and that people who suffer neurological damage score lower on EI and make poorer decisions than people who are healthier in this regard.[41]

The Case Against EI

For all its supporters, EI has just as many critics. Its critics say that EI is vague and impossible to measure, and they question its validity.

EI Is Too Vague a Concept   To many researchers, it's not clear what EI is. Is it a form of intelligence? Most of us wouldn't think that being self-aware or self-motivated or having empathy is a matter of intellect. So, is EI a misnomer? Moreover, many times different researchers focus on different skills, making it difficult to get a definition of EI. One researcher may study self-discipline. Another may study empathy. Another may look at self-awareness. As one reviewer noted, "The concept of EI has now become so broad and the components so variegated that...it is no longer even an intelligible concept."[42]

EI Can't Be Measured   Many critics have raised questions about measuring EI. Because EI is a form of intelligence, for instance, there must be right and wrong answers about it on tests, they argue. Some tests do have right and wrong answers, although the validity of some of the questions on these measures is questionable. For example, one measure asks you to associate particular feelings with specific colors, as if purple always makes us feel cool and not warm. Other measures are self-reported, meaning there is no right or wrong answer. For example, an EI test question might ask you to respond to the statement, "I'm good at 'reading' other people." In general, the measures of EI are diverse, and researchers have not subjected them to as much rigorous study as they have measures of personality and general intelligence.[43]

The Validity of EI Is Suspect   Some critics argue that because EI is so closely related to intelligence and personality, once you control for these factors, EI has nothing unique to offer. There is some foundation to this argument. EI appears to be highly correlated with measures of personality, especially emotional stability.[44] But there hasn't been enough research on whether EI adds insight beyond measures of personality and general intelligence in predicting job performance. Still, among consulting firms and in the popular press, EI is wildly popular. For example, one company's promotional materials for an EI measure claimed, "EI accounts for more than 85 percent of star performance in top leaders."[45] To say the least, it's difficult to validate this statement with the research literature.

Weighing the arguments for and against EI, it's still too early to tell whether the concept is useful. It *is* clear, though, that the concept is here to stay.

OB APPLICATIONS OF EMOTIONS AND MOODS

In this section, we assess how an understanding of emotions and moods can improve our ability to explain and predict the selection process in organizations, decision making, creativity, motivation, leadership, interpersonal conflict, negotiation, customer service, job attitudes, and deviant workplace behaviors. We also look at how managers can influence our moods.

Selection

One implication from the evidence to date on EI is that employers should consider it a factor in hiring employees, especially in jobs that demand a high degree of social interaction. In fact, more and more employers are starting to use EI measures to hire people. A study of U.S. Air Force recruiters showed that top-performing recruiters exhibited high levels of EI. Using these findings, the Air Force revamped its selection criteria. A follow-up investigation found that future hires who had high EI scores were 2.6 times more successful than those who didn't. At L'Oréal, salespersons selected on EI scores outsold those hired using the company's old selection procedure. On an annual basis, salespeople selected on the basis of emotional competence sold $91,370 more than other salespeople did, for a net revenue increase of $2,558,360.[46]

Decision Making

As you saw in Chapter 3, traditional approaches to the study of decision making in organizations have emphasized rationality. More and more OB researchers, though, are finding that moods and emotions have important effects on decision making.

Positive moods and emotions seem to help decision making. People in good moods or those experiencing positive emotions are more likely than others to use heuristics, or rules of thumb, to help make good decisions quickly. Positive emotions also enhance problem-solving skills so that positive people find better solutions to problems.[47]

OB researchers continue to debate the role of negative emotions and moods in decision making. Although one often-cited study suggested that depressed people reach more accurate judgments,[48] more recent evidence has suggested that people who are depressed make poorer decisions. Why? Because depressed people are slower at processing information and tend to weigh all possible options rather than the most likely ones.[49] Although it would seem that weighing all possible options is a good thing, the problem is that depressed people search for the perfect solution when there rarely is any solution perfect.

Creativity

People who are in good moods tend to be more creative than people in bad moods.[50] They produce more ideas, others think their ideas are more original, and they tend to identify more creative options to problems. It seems that people who are experiencing positive moods or emotions are more flexible and open in their thinking, which may explain why they're more creative.[51] Supervisors should actively try to keep employees happy because doing so creates more good moods (employees like their leaders to encourage them and provide positive feedback on a job well done), which in turn leads people to be more creative.[52]

Some researchers, however, do not believe that a positive mood makes people more creative. They argue that when people are in positive moods, they may relax ("If I'm in a good mood, things must be going okay, and I must not need to think of new ideas") and not engage in the critical thinking necessary for some forms of creativity.[53] However, this view is controversial.[54] Until there are more studies on the subject, we can safely conclude that for many tasks, positive moods increase our creativity.

—Positive emotions can increase problem-solving skills and help us understand and analyze new information.

Motivation

Two studies have highlighted the importance of moods and emotions on motivation. The first study had two groups of people solve a number of word puzzles. One group saw a funny video clip, which was intended to put the group in a good mood before having to solve the puzzles. The other group was not shown the clip and just started working on solving the word puzzles right away. The results? The positive-mood group reported higher expectations of being able to solve the puzzles, worked harder at them, and solved more puzzles as a result.[55]

The second study found that giving people feedback—whether real or fake—about their performance influenced their mood, which then influenced their motivation.[56] So a cycle can exist in which positive moods cause people to be more creative, which leads to positive feedback from those observing their work. This positive feed-back then further reinforces their positive mood, which may then make them perform even better, and so on.

Both of these studies highlight the effects of mood and emotions on motivation and suggest that organizations that promote positive moods at work are likely to have more motivated workers.

Leadership

Effective leaders rely on emotional appeals to help convey their messages. In fact, the expression of emotions in speeches is often the critical element that makes us accept or reject a leader's message. "When leaders feel excited, enthusiastic, and active, they may be more likely to energize their subordinates and convey a sense of efficacy, competence, optimism, and enjoyment."[57] Politicians, as a case in point, have learned to show enthusiasm when talking about their chances of winning an election, even when polls suggest otherwise.

Corporate executives know that emotional content is critical if employees are to buy into their vision of their company's future and accept change. When higher-ups offer new visions, especially when the visions contain distant or vague goals, it is often difficult for employees to accept those visions and the changes they'll bring. By arousing emotions and linking them to an appealing vision, leaders increase the likelihood that managers and employees alike will accept change.[58]

Negotiation

Negotiation is an emotional process; however, we often say a skilled negotiator has a "poker face." The founder of Britain's Poker Channel, Crispin Nieboer, stated, "It is a game of bluff and there is fantastic human emotion and tension, seeing who can bluff the longest."[59] Several studies have shown that a negotiator who feigns anger has an advantage over the opponent. Why? Because when a negotiator shows anger, the opponent concludes that the negotiator has conceded all that she can, so the opponent gives in.[60]

Displaying a negative emotion (such as anger) can be effective, but feeling bad about your performance appears to impair future negotiations. Individuals who do poorly in a negotiation experience negative emotions, develop negative perceptions of their counterpart, and are less willing to share information or be cooperative in future negotiations.[61] Interestingly, then, although moods and emotions have benefits at work, in negotiation, unless we're putting up a false front (feigning anger), it seems that emotions may impair negotiator performance. In fact, a 2005 study found that people who suffered damage to the emotional centers of their brains may be the *best* negotiators because they're not likely to overcorrect when faced with negative outcomes.[62]

Customer Service

A worker's emotional state influences customer service, which influences levels of repeat business and levels of customer satisfaction.[63] Providing quality customer service makes demands on employees because it often puts them in a state of emotional dissonance. Over time, this state can lead to job burnout, declines in job performance, and lower job satisfaction.[64]

In addition, employees' emotions may transfer to the customer. Studies indicate a matching effect between employee and customer emotions, an effect that is called **emotional contagion**—the "catching" of emotions from others.[65] How does emotional contagion work? The primary explanation is that when someone experiences positive emotions and laughs and smiles at you, you begin to copy that person's behavior. So when employees express positive emotions, customers tend to respond positively. Emotional contagion is important because when customers catch the positive moods or emotions of employees they shop longer. But what about negative emotions and moods? Are they contagious, too? Absolutely. When an employee feels unfairly treated by a customer, for example, it's harder for him to display the positive emotions his organization expects of him.[66]

Job Attitudes

Ever hear the advice "Never take your work home with you," meaning that people should forget about their work once they go home? As it turns out, that's easier said than done. Several studies have shown that people who had a good day at work tend to be in a better mood at home that evening. And people who had a bad day tend to be in a bad mood once they're at home. Evidence also suggests that people who have a stressful day at work have trouble relaxing after they get off work.[67]

Even though people do emotionally take their work home with them, by the next day, the effect is usually gone.[68] So, although it may be difficult or even unnatural to "never take your work home with you," it doesn't appear that, for most people, a negative mood resulting from a bad day at work carries over to the next day.

Deviant Workplace Behaviors

Negative emotions can lead to a number of deviant workplace behaviors.

Anyone who has spent much time in an organization realizes that people often behave in ways that violate established norms and that threaten the organization, its members, or both. These actions are called *workplace deviant behaviors*.[69] Many of these deviant behaviors can be traced to negative emotions.

For instance, envy is an emotion that occurs when you resent someone for having something that you don't have but that you strongly desire—such as a better work assignment, larger office, or higher salary.[70] It can lead to malicious deviant behaviors. An envious employee, for example, could then act hostilely by backstabbing another employee, negatively distorting others' successes, and positively distorting his own accomplishments. Evidence suggests that people who feel negative emotions, particularly those who feel angry or hostile, are more likely than people who don't feel negative emotions to engage in deviant behavior at work.[71]

How Managers Can Influence Moods

In general, you can improve people's moods by showing them a funny video clip, giving them a small bag of candy, or even having them taste a pleasant beverage. But what can companies do to improve their employees' moods? Managers can use humor and give their employees small tokens of appreciation for work well done. Also, research indicates that when leaders are in good moods, group members are more positive, and as a result, the members cooperate more.[72]

Finally, selecting positive team members can have a contagion effect as positive moods transmit from team member to team member. One study of professional cricket teams (cricket is a sport played in countries such as Great Britain and India that's a little like baseball) found that players' happy moods affected the moods of their team members and also positively influenced their performance.[73] It makes sense, then, for managers to select team members who are predisposed to experience positive moods.

GLOBAL IMPLICATIONS

Does the degree to which people *experience* emotions vary across cultures? Do people's *interpretations* of emotions vary across cultures? Finally, do the norms for the *expression* of emotions differ across cultures? Let's tackle each of these questions.

Does the Degree to Which People Experience Emotions Vary Across Cultures?
Yes. In China, for example, people report experiencing fewer positive and negative emotions than people in other cultures, and the emotions they experience are less intense than what other cultures report. Compared with Mainland Chinese, Taiwanese are more like U.S. workers in their experience of emotions: On average, Taiwanese report more positive and fewer negative emotions than their Chinese counterparts.[74] In general, people in most cultures appear to experience certain positive and negative emotions, but the frequency of their experience and their intensity varies to some degree.[75]

Do People's Interpretations of Emotions Vary Across Cultures?
In general, people from all over the world interpret negative and positive emotions the same way. We all view negative emotions, such as hate, terror, and rage, as dangerous and destructive. And we all desire positive emotions, such as joy, love, and happiness. However, some cultures value certain emotions more than others. For example, U.S. culture values enthusiasm, whereas the Chinese consider negative emotions to be more useful and constructive than do people in the United States. In general, pride is seen as a positive emotion in Western, individualistic cultures such as the United States, but Eastern cultures such as China and Japan tend to view pride as undesirable.[76]

Do the Norms for the Expression of Emotions Differ Across Cultures?
Absolutely. For example, Muslims see smiling as a sign of sexual attraction, so women have learned not to smile at men.[77] And research has shown that in collectivist countries people are more likely to believe the emotional displays of another have something to do with their own relationship with the person expressing the emotion, whereas people in individualistic cultures don't think that another's emotional expressions are directed at them. Evidence indicates that in the United States there's a bias against expressing emotions, especially intense negative emotions. French retail clerks, in contrast, are infamous for being surly toward customers. (A report from the French government itself confirmed this.) There are also reports that serious German shoppers have been turned off by Wal-Mart's friendly greeters and helpful personnel.[78]

In general, and not surprisingly, it's easier for people to accurately recognize emotions within their own culture than in other cultures. For example, a Chinese businessperson is more likely to accurately label the emotions underlying the facial expressions of a fellow Chinese colleague than those of a U.S. colleague.[79]

Interestingly, some cultures lack words for standard U.S. emotional terms such as *anxiety*, *depression*, and *guilt*. Tahitians, as a case in point, don't have a word directly equivalent to *sadness*. When Tahitians are sad, their peers attribute their state to a physical illness.[80] Our discussion illustrates the need to consider the fact that cultural factors influence what managers think is emotionally appropriate.[81] What's acceptable in one culture may seem extremely unusual or even dysfunctional in another. Managers need to know the emotional norms in each culture they do business in or with so they don't send unintended signals or misread the reactions of others. For example, a U.S. manager in Japan should know that although U.S. culture tends to view smiling positively, the Japanese attribute frequent smiling to a lack of intelligence.[82]

—*Managers need to know the emotional norms in each culture they do business in so they don't send unintended signals or misread the reactions of locals.*

IMPLICATIONS FOR MANAGERS

Emotions and moods are similar in that both are affective in nature. But they're also different— moods are more general and less contextual than emotions. And events do matter. The time of day and day of the week, stressful events, social activities, and sleep patterns are some of the factors that influence emotions and moods.

Emotions and moods have proven themselves to be relevant for virtually every OB topic we study. Increasingly, organizations are selecting employees they believe have high levels of emotional intelligence. Emotions, especially positive moods, appear to facilitate effective decision making and creativity. Although the research is relatively recent, research suggests that mood is linked to motivation, especially through feedback, and that leaders rely on emotions to increase their effectiveness. The display of emotions is important to negotiation and customer service, and the experience of emotions is closely linked to job attitudes and behaviors that follow from attitudes, such as deviant behavior in the workplace.

Can managers control their colleagues' and employees' emotions and moods? Certainly there are limits, both practical and ethical. Emotions and moods are a natural part of an individual's makeup. Where managers err is in ignoring their coworkers' and employees' emotions and assessing others' behavior as if it were completely rational. As one consultant aptly put it, "You can't divorce emotions from the workplace because you can't divorce emotions from people."[83] Managers who understand the role of emotions and moods will significantly improve their ability to explain and predict their coworkers' and employees' behavior.

CHAPTER 8

Foundations of Group Behavior

After studying this chapter, you should be able to:

1. Define *group* and differentiate between different types of groups.
2. Identify the five stages of group development.
3. List and define the five properties of groups.
4. Demonstrate how norms and status exert influence on an individual's behavior.
5. Contrast the strengths and weaknesses of group decision making.
6. Evaluate evidence for cultural differences in status and social loafing as well as the effects of diversity in groups.

DEFINING AND CLASSIFYING GROUPS

A **group** is defined as two or more individuals, interacting and interdependent, who have come together to achieve particular objectives. Groups can be either formal or informal. By **formal groups**, we mean those defined by the organization's structure, with designated work assignments establishing tasks. In formal groups, the behaviors that team members should engage in are stipulated by and directed toward organizational goals. The six members making up an airline flight crew are an example of a formal group. In contrast, **informal groups** are alliances that are neither formally structured nor organizationally determined. These groups are natural formations in the work environment that appear in response to the need for social contact. Three employees from different departments who regularly eat lunch or have coffee together are an example of an informal group. These types of interactions among individuals, even though informal, deeply affect their behavior and performance.

It's possible to further subclassify groups as command, task, interest, or friendship groups.[1] Command and task groups are dictated by formal organization, whereas interest and friendship groups are informal alliances.

A **command group** is determined by the organization chart. It is composed of the individuals who report directly to a given manager plus the manager. An elementary school principal and her eighteen teachers form a command group, as do a director of postal audits and his five inspectors.

Task groups, also organizationally determined, represent individuals working together to complete a job task. However, a task group's boundaries are not limited to its immediate hierarchical superior. It can cross command relationships. For instance, if a college student is accused of a campus crime, dealing with the problem might require communication and coordination among the dean of academic affairs, the dean of students, the registrar, the director of security, and the student's advisor. Such a formation would constitute a task group. It should be noted that all command groups are also task groups, but because task groups can cut across the organization, the reverse need not be true.

People who may or may not be aligned into common command or task groups may affiliate to attain a specific objective with which each is concerned. This is an **interest group**. Employees who band together to have their vacation schedules altered, to support a peer who has been fired, or to seek improved working conditions represent the formation of a united body to further their common interest.

> —Groups can be formal as well as informal, and that regardless of the type of group, group norms, roles, and identities have powerful effects on individuals' behavior.

Groups often develop because the individual members have one or more common characteristics. We call these formations **friendship groups**. Social alliances, which frequently extend outside the work situation, can be based on similar age or ethnic heritage, support for Notre Dame football, interest in the same alternative rock band, or the holding of similar political views, to name just a few such characteristics.

There is no single reason why individuals join groups. Because most people belong to a number of groups, it's obvious that different groups provide different benefits to their members. Exhibit 8-1 summarizes the most popular reasons people have for joining groups.

EXHIBIT 8-1   Why Do People Join Groups?

Security.   By joining a group, individuals can reduce the insecurity of "standing alone." People feel stronger, have fewer self-doubts, and are more resistant to threats when they are part of a group.

Status.   Inclusion in a group that is viewed as important by others provides recognition and status for its members.

Self-esteem.   Groups can provide people with feelings of self-worth. That is, in addition to conveying status to those outside the group, membership can also give increased feelings of worth to the group members themselves.

Affiliation.   Groups can fulfill social needs. People enjoy the regular interaction that comes with group membership. For many people, these on-the-job interactions are their primary source for fulfilling their needs for affiliation.

Power.   What cannot be achieved individually often becomes possible through group action. There is power in numbers.

Goal achievement.   There are times when it takes more than one person to accomplish a particular task—there is a need to pool talents, knowledge, or power in order to complete a job. In such instances, management will rely on the use of a formal group.

STAGES OF GROUP DEVELOPMENT

Groups generally pass through a standardized sequence in their evolution. We call this sequence the five-stage model of group development. Although research indicates that not all groups follow this pattern,[2] it is a useful framework for understanding group development. In this section, we describe the five-stage general model and an alternative model for temporary groups with deadlines.

The Five-Stage Model

As shown in Exhibit 8-2, the **five-stage group-development model** characterizes groups as proceeding through five distinct stages: forming, storming, norming, performing, and adjourning.[3]

The first stage, **forming**, is characterized by a great deal of uncertainty about the group's purpose, structure, and leadership. Members "test the waters" to determine what types of behaviors are acceptable. This stage is complete when members have begun to think of themselves as part of a group.

The **storming stage** is one of intragroup conflict. Members accept the existence of the group, but there is resistance to the constraints that the group imposes on individuality. Furthermore, there is conflict over who will control the group. When this stage is complete, there will be a relatively clear hierarchy of leadership within the group.

The third stage is one in which close relationships develop and the group demonstrates cohesiveness. There is now a strong sense of group identity and camaraderie. This **norming stage** is complete when the group structure solidifies and the group has assimilated a common set of expectations of what defines correct member behavior.

The fourth stage is **performing**. The structure at this point is fully functional and accepted. Group energy has moved from getting to know and understand each other to performing the task at hand.

For permanent work groups, performing is the last stage in the group development. However, for temporary committees, teams, task forces, and similar groups that have a limited task to perform, there is an **adjourning stage**. In this stage, the group prepares for its disbandment.

Many interpreters of the five-stage model have assumed that a group becomes more effective as it progresses through the first four stages. Although this assumption may be generally true, what makes a group effective is more complex than this model acknowledges.[4] Under some conditions, high levels of conflict may be conducive to high group performance. So we might expect to find situations in which groups in

EXHIBIT 8-2   Stages of Group Development

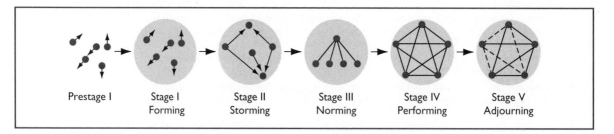

| Prestage I | Stage I Forming | Stage II Storming | Stage III Norming | Stage IV Performing | Stage V Adjourning |

Stage II outperform those in Stage III or IV. Similarly, groups do not always proceed clearly from one stage to the next. Sometimes, in fact, several stages go on simultaneously, as when groups are storming and performing at the same time. Groups even occasionally regress to previous stages. Therefore, even the strongest proponents of this model do not assume that all groups follow its five-stage process precisely or that Stage IV is always the most preferable.

GROUP PROPERTIES: ROLES, NORMS, STATUS, SIZE, AND COHESIVENESS

Work groups are not unorganized mobs. Work groups have properties that shape the behavior of members and make it possible to explain and predict a large portion of individual behavior within the group as well as the performance of the group itself. Some of these properties are: (1) roles, (2) norms, (3) status, (4) group size, and (5) the degree of group cohesiveness.

Group Property 1: Roles

Shakespeare said, "All the world's a stage, and all the men and women merely players." Using the same metaphor, all group members are actors, each playing a **role**. By this term, we mean a set of expected behavior patterns attributed to someone occupying a given position in a social unit. The understanding of role behavior would be dramatically simplified if each of us chose one role and "played it out" regularly and consistently. Unfortunately, we are required to play a number of diverse roles, both on and off our jobs. One of the tasks in understanding behavior is grasping the role that a person is currently playing. We are all required to play a number of roles, and our behavior varies with the role we are playing. Different groups impose different role requirements on individuals. We can think of group roles in four ways: role identity, role perception, role expectations, and role conflict.

Role Identity   Certain attitudes and actual behaviors are consistent with a role, and they create the **role identity**. People have the ability to shift roles rapidly when they recognize that a situation and its demands clearly require major changes. One fascinating example illustrating the power of role identity is Stanford University psychologist Philip Zimbardo's prison experiment.[5] Zimbardo and his associates created a "prison" in the basement of the Stanford psychology building, hired, at $15 a day, two dozen emotionally stable, physically healthy, law-abiding students who scored "normal average" on extensive personality tests; randomly assigned them the role of either "guard" or "prisoner"; and established some basic rules. The simulation actually proved *too successful* in demonstrating how quickly individuals learn new roles. The researchers had to stop it after only six days because those individuals assigned as guards became abusive to those individuals assigned as prisoners. And remember, these were individuals chosen precisely for their normalcy and emotional stability. Zimbardo's experiment shows that individuals will often do anything as long as it's consistent with their role identity.

Role Perception   Our view of how we're supposed to act in a given situation is a **role perception**. Based on an interpretation of how we believe we are supposed to behave, we engage in certain types of behavior. Where do we get these perceptions?

We get them from stimuli all around us—friends, books, television. For example, we may form an impression of the work of doctors from watching *Grey's Anatomy*. Of course, the primary reason apprenticeship programs exist in many trades and professions is to allow beginners to watch an "expert" so they can learn to act as they are supposed to. When role perceptions come together, they often form a role identity.

Role Expectations   **Role expectations** are defined as the way others believe you should act in a given situation. How you behave is determined to a large extent by the role defined in the context in which you are acting. For instance, the role of a U.S. federal judge is viewed as having propriety and dignity, whereas a football coach is seen as aggressive, dynamic, and inspiring to his players. To return to the Stanford prison experiment, the guard role identity led individuals to expect that they needed to act authoritatively toward the prisoners. Thus, if role perceptions often lead to role identities, role identities, in turn, often lead to role expectations.

Role Conflict   When an individual is confronted by divergent role expectations, the result is **role conflict**. It exists when an individual finds that compliance with one role requirement may make it difficult to comply with another. At the extreme, it would include situations in which two or more role expectations are mutually contradictory.

Group Property 2: Norms

Did you ever notice that golfers don't speak while their partners are putting on the green or that employees don't criticize their bosses in public? Why? The answer is norms.

All groups have established **norms**—that is, acceptable standards of behavior that are shared by the group's members. Norms can cover virtually any aspect of group behavior. Probably the most common group norm is a *performance norm*. Work groups typically provide their members with explicit cues to how hard they should work, how to get the job done, what their level of output should be, what level of tardiness is appropriate, and the like. These norms are extremely powerful in affecting an individual employee's performance—they are capable of significantly modifying a performance prediction that was based solely on the employee's ability and level of personal motivation.

The **Hawthorne Studies** provide striking evidence for the power of norms over group members. First, though, let's describe the studies. In these studies, researchers at Western Electric were studying the effects of illumination and other working conditions on employees. Contrary to their expectations, researchers found that in no case was the increase or decrease in output in proportion to the increase or decrease in illumination. So the researchers introduced a control group: An experimental group was presented with varying intensity of illumination, whereas the controlled unit worked under a constant illumination intensity, only to find that output rose for *both* the control group and the experimental group. What became evident was that the groups' performance was significantly affected by being observed. In essence, workers in the illumination and experiments were reacting to the increased attention they were receiving, and their performance expectations and norms increased in turn.

Though this is the most often-cited finding of the Hawthorne Studies, a follow-up study showed the power of group norms on individuals. In this study, a sophisticated pay plan was set up to ascertain its effect on employee motivation. The assumption was that individual workers would maximize their productivity when they saw that it was directly related to economic rewards. The most important finding to come out of this study was that employees did not individually maximize their outputs. Rather, their output became controlled by a group norm that defined a proper day's work. Output was not only being restricted, but individual workers were giving erroneous reports. The total for a week would check with the total week's output, but the daily reports showed a steady level of output, regardless of actual daily production. What was going on?

Interviews determined that the group was operating well below its capability and was leveling output in order to protect itself. Members were afraid that if they significantly increased their output, the unit incentive rate would be cut, the expected daily output would be increased, layoffs might occur, or slower workers would be reprimanded. So the group established its idea of a fair output—neither too much nor too little. They helped each other out to ensure that their reports were nearly level.

The norms the group established included a number of don'ts. *Don't* be a rate-buster, turning out too much work. *Don't* be a chiseler, turning out too little work. *Don't* be a squealer on any of your peers. How did the group enforce these norms? Their methods were neither gentle nor subtle. They included sarcasm, name-calling, ridicule, and even physical punches to the upper arm of any member who violated the group's norms. Members would also ostracize individuals whose behavior was against the group's interest.

The Hawthorne Studies made an important contribution to our understanding of group behavior—particularly the significant place that norms have in determining individual work behavior.

Conformity   As a member of a group, you desire acceptance by the group. Because of your desire for acceptance, you are susceptible to conforming to the group's norms. There is considerable evidence that groups can place strong pressures on individual members to change their attitudes and behaviors to conform to the group's standard.[6]

Do individuals conform to the pressures of all the groups to which they belong? Obviously not, because people belong to many groups, and their norms vary. In some cases, they may even have contradictory norms. So what do people do? They conform to the important groups to which they belong or hope to belong. The important groups have been called **reference groups**, and they're characterized as ones in which a person is aware of other members, defines himself or herself as a member or would like to be a member, and feels that the group members are significant to him or her.[7] The implication, then, is that all groups do not impose equal conformity pressures on their members.

—Conformity is a problem with groups; managers should encourage group leaders to actively seek input from all members and avoid expressing their own opinions, especially in the early stages of deliberation.

The impact that group pressures for **conformity** can have on an individual member's judgment and attitudes was demonstrated in the now-classic studies by Solomon Asch.[8] Asch made up groups of seven or eight people, who sat around a table and were asked to compare two cards held by the experimenter. One card had one line, and the other had three lines of varying length. As shown in Exhibit 8-3, one of the lines on the three-line card was identical to the line on the one-line card. Also, as shown in Exhibit 8-3, the difference in line length was quite obvious; in fact, under ordinary conditions, subjects made fewer than 1 percent errors. The object was to announce aloud which of the three lines matched the single line. But what happens if

EXHIBIT 8-3   Examples of Cards Used in Asch's Study

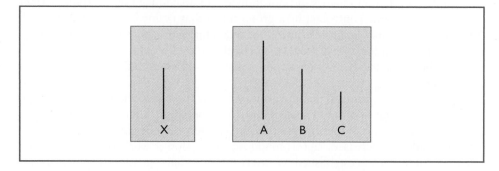

the members in the group begin to give incorrect answers? Will the pressures to conform result in an unsuspecting subject (USS) altering an answer to align with the others? That was what Asch wanted to know. So he arranged the group so that only the USS was unaware that the experiment was "fixed." The seating was prearranged: The USS was placed so as to be one of the last to announce a decision.

The experiment began with several sets of matching exercises. All the subjects gave the right answers. On the third set, however, the first subject gave an obviously wrong answer—for example, saying "C" in Exhibit 8-3. The next subject gave the same wrong answer, and so did the others until it got to the unknowing subject. He knew "B" was the same as "X," yet everyone else had said "C." The decision confronting the USS was this: Do you publicly state a perception that differs from the preannounced position of the others in your group? Or do you give an answer that you strongly believe is incorrect in order to have your response agree with that of the other group members?

The results obtained by Asch demonstrated that over many experiments and many trials 75 percent of the subjects gave at least one answer that conformed—that is, that they knew was wrong but that was consistent with the replies of other group members—and the average for conformers was 37 percent. What meaning can we draw from these results? They suggest that there are group norms that press us toward conformity; that is, we desire to be one of the group and avoid being visibly different.

The preceding conclusions are based on research that was conducted 50 years ago. Has time altered their validity? And should we consider these findings generalizable across cultures? The evidence indicates that there have been changes in the level of conformity over time; and Asch's findings are culture bound.[9] Specifically, levels of conformity have steadily declined since Asch's studies in the early 1950s. In addition, conformity to social norms is higher in collectivist cultures than in individualistic cultures. Nevertheless, even in individualistic countries, you should consider conformity to norms to still be a powerful force in groups.

Deviant Workplace Behavior   Ted Vowinkel is frustrated by a coworker who constantly spreads malicious and unsubstantiated rumors about him. Debra Hundley is tired of a member of her work team who, when confronted with a problem, takes out his frustration by yelling and screaming at her and other work team members. And Rhonda Lieberman recently quit her job as a dental hygienist after being constantly sexually harassed by her employer.

What do these three episodes have in common? They represent employees being exposed to acts of deviant workplace behavior.[10] **Deviant workplace behavior**

EXHIBIT 8-4   Typology of Deviant Workplace Behavior

Category	Examples
Production	Leaving early
	Intentionally working slowly
	Wasting resources
Property	Sabotage
	Lying about hours worked
	Stealing from the organization
Political	Showing favoritism
	Gossiping and spreading rumors
	Blaming coworkers
Personal aggression	Sexual harassment
	Verbal abuse
	Stealing from coworkers

Source: Adapted from S. L. Robinson and R. J. Bennett, "A Typology of Deviant Workplace Behaviors: A Multidimensional Scaling Study," *Academy of Management Journal,* April 1995, p. 565.

(also called *antisocial behavior* or *workplace incivility*) is voluntary behavior that violates significant organizational norms and, in doing so, threatens the well-being of the organization or its members. Exhibit 8-4 provides a typology of deviant workplace behaviors, with examples of each.

Few organizations will admit to creating or condoning conditions that encourage and maintain deviant norms. Yet they exist. Employees report, for example, an increase in rudeness and disregard toward others by bosses and coworkers in recent years. And nearly half of employees who have suffered this incivility report that it has led them to think about changing jobs, with 12 percent actually quitting because of it.[11]

As with norms in general, individual employees' antisocial actions are shaped by the group context within which they work. Evidence demonstrates that the antisocial behavior exhibited by a work group is a significant predictor of an individual's antisocial behavior at work.[12] In other words, deviant workplace behavior is likely to flourish where it's supported by group norms. What this means for managers is that when deviant workplace norms surface, employee cooperation, commitment, and motivation are likely to suffer. This, in turn, can lead to reduced employee productivity and job satisfaction and increased turnover.

In addition, just being part of a group can increase an individual's deviant behavior. In other words, someone who ordinarily wouldn't engage in deviant behavior might be more likely to do so when working in a group. In fact, a recent study suggests that, compared with individuals working alone, those working in a group were more likely to lie, cheat, and steal. As shown in Exhibit 8-5, in this study, no individual working alone lied, but 22 percent of those working in groups did. Moreover, individuals working in groups also were more likely to cheat (55 percent of individuals working in a group cheated on a task versus 23 percent of individuals working alone) and steal (29 percent of individuals working in a group stole compared to only 10 percent working alone).[13] Groups provide a shield of anonymity so that someone who ordinarily might be afraid of getting caught for stealing can rely on the fact that other group members had the same opportunity or reason to steal.

EXHIBIT 8-5   Groups and Deviant Behavior

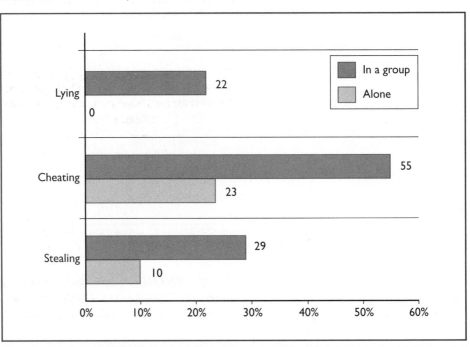

Source; A. Erez, H. Elms, and E. Fong, "Lying, Cheating, Stealing: Groups and the Ring of Gyges," paper presented at the Academy of Management Annual Meeting, Honolulu, HI, August 8, 2005.

Group Property 3: Status

Status—that is, a socially defined position or rank given to groups or group members by others—permeates every society. Even the smallest group will develop roles, rights, and rituals to differentiate its members. Status is an important factor in understanding human behavior because it is a significant motivator and has major behavioral consequences when individuals perceive a disparity between what they believe their status to be and what others perceive it to be.

What Determines Status?   According to **status characteristics theory**, status tends to be derived from one of three sources:[14]

1. *The power a person wields over others.* Because they likely control the group's resources, people who control the outcomes of a group through their power tend to be perceived as high status.

2. *A person's ability to contribute to a group's goals.* People whose contributions are critical to the group's success tend to have high status.

3. *An individual's personal characteristics.* Someone whose personal characteristics are positively valued by the group (for example, good looks, intelligence, money, or a friendly personality) typically has higher status than someone who has fewer valued attributes.

Status and Norms   Status has been shown to have some interesting effects on the power of norms and pressures to conform. For instance, high-status members of groups are often given more freedom to deviate from norms than are other group members. High-status people are also better able to resist conformity pressures than their lower-status peers. An individual who is highly valued by a group but who doesn't much need or care about the social rewards the group provides is particularly able to pay minimal attention to conformity norms.[15]

Status and Group Interaction   Interaction among members of groups is influenced by status. We find, for instance, that high-status people tend to be more assertive.[16] They speak out more often, criticize more, state more commands, and interrupt others more often. But status differences actually inhibit diversity of ideas and creativity in groups because lower-status members tend to be less active participants in group discussions. In situations in which lower-status members possess expertise and insights that could aid the group, their expertise and insights are not likely to be fully utilized, thus reducing the group's overall performance.

Group Property 4: Size

Does the size of a group affect the group's overall behavior? The answer to this question is a definite "yes," but the effect is contingent on what dependent variables you look at.[17] The evidence indicates, for instance, that smaller groups are faster at completing tasks than are larger ones and that individuals perform better in smaller groups than in larger ones.[18] However, for groups engaged in problem solving, large groups consistently get better marks than their smaller counterparts, at least up to a point (approximately seven members).[19]

One of the most important findings related to the size of a group has been labeled **social loafing**. Social loafing is the tendency for individuals to expend less effort when working collectively than when working individually.[20] It directly challenges the logic that the productivity of the group as a whole should at least equal the sum of the productivity of the individuals in that group.

A common stereotype about groups is that the sense of team spirit spurs individual effort and enhances the group's overall productivity. But that stereotype may be wrong. In the late 1920s, German psychologist Max Ringelmann compared the results of individual and group performance on a rope-pulling task.[21] He expected that the group's effort would be equal to the sum of the efforts of individuals within the group. That is, three people pulling together should exert three times as much pull on the rope as one person, and eight people should exert eight times as much pull. Ringelmann's results, however, didn't confirm his expectations. One person pulling on a rope alone exerted an average of 63 kilograms of force. In groups of three, the per-person force dropped to 53 kilograms. And in groups of eight, it fell to only 31 kilograms per person.

Replications of Ringelmann's research with similar tasks have generally supported his findings.[22] Group performance increases with group size, but the addition of new members to the group has diminishing returns on productivity.

What causes this social loafing effect? It may be due to a belief that others in the group are not carrying their fair share. If you see others as lazy or inept, you can reestablish equity by reducing your effort. Another explanation is the dispersion of responsibility. Because the results of the group cannot be attributed to any single person, the relationship between an individual's input and the group's output is clouded. In such situations, individuals may be tempted to become "free riders" and coast on the group's efforts. In other words, there will be a reduction in efficiency when individuals think that their contribution cannot be measured.

There are several ways to prevent social loafing: (1) Set group goals so that the group has a common purpose to strive toward; (2) increase intergroup competition, which again focuses the group on the shared outcome; (3) engage in peer evaluation so that each person's contribution to the group is evaluated by each group member; and (4) if possible, distribute group rewards, in part, based on each member's unique contributions.[23] Although none of these actions is a "magic bullet" that will prevent social loafing in all cases, they should help minimize its effect.

Group Property 5: Cohesiveness

Groups differ in their **cohesiveness**—that is, the degree to which members are attracted to each other and are motivated to stay in the group.[24] For instance, some work groups are cohesive because the members have spent a great deal of time together, or the group's small size facilitates high interaction, or the group has experienced external threats that have brought members close together. Cohesiveness is important because it has been found to be related to group productivity.[25]

Studies consistently show that the relationship between cohesiveness and productivity depends on the performance-related norms established by the group.[26] If performance-related norms are high (for example, high output, quality work, cooperation with individuals outside the group), a cohesive group will be more productive than will a less cohesive group. But if cohesiveness is high and performance norms are low, productivity will be low. If cohesiveness is low and performance norms are high, productivity increases, but it increases less than in the high-cohesiveness/high-norms situation. When cohesiveness and performance-related norms are both low, productivity tends to fall into the low-to-moderate range.

What can you do to encourage group cohesiveness? You might try one or more of the following suggestions: (1) Make the group smaller, (2) encourage agreement with group goals, (3) increase the time members spend together, (4) increase the status of the group and the perceived difficulty of attaining membership in the group, (5) stimulate competition with other groups, (6) give rewards to the group rather than to individual members, and (7) physically isolate the group.[27]

GROUP DECISION MAKING

The belief—characterized by juries—that two heads are better than one has long been accepted as a basic component of North American and many other countries' legal systems. This belief has expanded to the point that, today, many decisions in organizations are made by groups, teams, or committees.[28] In this section, we will discuss group decision making.

Groups Versus the Individual

Decision-making groups may be widely used in organizations, but does that imply that group decisions are preferable to those made by an individual alone? The answer to this question depends on a number of factors. Let's begin by looking at the strengths and weaknesses of group decision making.[29]

Strengths of Group Decision Making   Groups generate *more complete information and knowledge*. By aggregating the resources of several individuals, groups bring more input into the decision process. In addition to more input, groups can bring hetero-geneity to the decision process. They offer *increased diversity of views*. This opens up the opportunity for more approaches and alternatives to be considered. Finally, groups lead to increased *acceptance of a solution*. Many decisions fail after the final choice is made because people don't accept the solution. Group members who partic-ipated in making a decision are likely to enthusiastically support the decision and encourage others to accept it.

Weaknesses of Group Decision Making   In spite of the pluses noted, group deci-sions have their drawbacks. They're time consuming because groups typically take more time to reach a solution than would be the case if an individual were making the decision. There are *conformity pressures in groups*. The desire by group members to be accepted and considered an asset to the group can result in squashing any overt dis-agreement. Group discussion can be *dominated by one or a few members*. If this dominant coalition is composed of low- and medium-ability members, the group's overall effectiveness will suffer. Finally, group decisions suffer from *ambiguous responsibility*. In an individual decision, it's clear who is accountable for the final outcome. In a group decision, the responsi-bility of any single member is watered down.

—Group decision making is not always better than individual decision making.

Effectiveness and Efficiency   Whether groups are more effective than individuals depends on the criteria you use to define effectiveness. In terms of *accuracy*, group decisions are generally more accurate than the decisions of the average individual in a group, but they are less accurate than the judgments of the most accurate group mem-ber.[30] If decision effectiveness is defined in terms of *speed*, individuals are superior. If *creativity* is important, groups tend to be more effective than individuals. And if effec-tiveness means the degree of *acceptance* the final solution achieves, the nod again goes to the group.[31]

But effectiveness cannot be considered without also assessing efficiency. In terms of efficiency, groups almost always stack up as a poor second to the individual decision maker. With few exceptions, group decision making consumes more work hours than if one were to compare the group's combined effort to the same group of individuals working alone. In deciding whether to use groups, then, consideration should be given to assessing whether increases in effectiveness are more than enough to offset the reductions in efficiency.

Groupthink and Groupshift

Two by-products of group decision making have received a considerable amount of attention from researchers in OB. As we'll show, these two phenomena have the potential to affect a group's ability to appraise alternatives objectively and to arrive at quality decision solutions.

The first phenomenon, called **groupthink**, is related to norms. It describes situ-ations in which group pressures for conformity deter the group from critically appraising unusual, minority, or unpopular views. Groupthink is a disease that attacks many groups and can dramatically hinder their performance. The second phenome-non we will discuss is called **groupshift**. It indicates that, in discussing a given set of alternatives and arriving at a solution, group members tend to exaggerate the initial positions they hold. In some situations, caution dominates, and there is a conservative shift. More often, however, the evidence indicates that groups tend toward a risky shift. Let's look at each of these phenomena in more detail.

Groupthink   Have you ever felt like speaking up in a meeting, a classroom, or an informal group but decided against it? One reason may have been shyness. On the other hand, you may have been a victim of groupthink, a phenomenon that occurs when group members become so enamored of seeking concurrence that the norm for consensus overrides the realistic appraisal of alternative courses of action and the full expression of deviant, minority, or unpopular views. It describes a deterioration in an individual's mental efficiency, reality testing, and moral judgment as a result of group pressures.[32]

We have all seen the symptoms of the groupthink phenomenon:

1. Group members rationalize any resistance to the assumptions they have made. No matter how strongly the evidence may contradict their basic assumptions, members behave so as to reinforce those assumptions continually.

2. Members apply direct pressures on those who momentarily express doubts about any of the group's shared views or who question the validity of arguments supporting the alternative favored by the majority.

3. Members who have doubts or hold differing points of view seek to avoid deviating from what appears to be group consensus by keeping silent about misgivings and even minimizing to themselves the importance of their doubts.

4. There appears to be an illusion of unanimity. If someone doesn't speak, it's assumed that he or she is in full accord. In other words, abstention becomes viewed as a "yes" vote.[33]

In studies of historic American foreign policy decisions, these symptoms were found to prevail when government policy-making groups failed—unpreparedness at Pearl Harbor in 1941, the U.S. invasion of North Korea, the Bay of Pigs fiasco, the escalation of the Vietnam War, and the evaluation of intelligence information about the presence of weapons of mass destruction (WMD) in Iraq.[34] More recently, the *Challenger* and *Columbia* space shuttle disasters and the failure of the main mirror on the *Hubble* telescope have been linked to decision processes at NASA in which groupthink symptoms were evident.[35] And groupthink was found to be a primary factor leading to setbacks at both British Airways and retailer Marks & Spencer as they tried to implement globalization strategies.[36]

What can managers do to minimize groupthink?[37] First, they can monitor group size. People grow more intimidated and hesitant as group size increases, and, although there is no magic number that will eliminate groupthink, individuals are likely to feel less personal responsibility when groups get larger than seven to ten. Managers should also encourage group leaders to play an impartial role. Leaders should actively seek input from all members and avoid expressing their own opinions, especially in the early stages of deliberation. In addition, managers should appoint one group member to play the role of devil's advocate; this member's role is to overtly challenge the majority position and offer divergent perspectives.

Groupshift   In comparing the outcomes of group decisions with the individual decisions of members within the group, evidence suggests that there are differences. In some cases, group decisions are more conservative than individual decisions. More often, the shift is toward greater risk.[38]

What appears to happen in groups is that the discussion leads to a significant shift in the positions of members toward a more extreme position in the direction in which they were already leaning before the discussion. So conservative types become more cautious, and more aggressive types take on more risk. The group discussion tends to exaggerate the initial position of the group.

Groupshift can be viewed as actually a special case of groupthink. The decision of the group reflects the dominant decision-making norm that develops during the group's discussion. Whether the shift in the group's decision is toward greater caution or more risk depends on the dominant prediscussion norm.

The greater occurrence of the shift toward risk has generated several explanations for the phenomenon.[39] It's been argued, for instance, that discussion creates familiarization among the members. As they become more comfortable with each other, they also become more bold and daring. Another argument is that most societies in developed nations value risk, that they admire individuals who are willing to take risks, and that group discussion motivates members to show that they are at least as willing as their peers to take risks. The most plausible explanation of the shift toward risk, however, seems to be that the group diffuses responsibility. Group decisions free any single member from accountability for the group's final choice. Greater risk can be taken because even if the decision fails no one member can be held wholly responsible.

So how should you use the findings on groupshift? You should recognize that group decisions exaggerate the initial position of the individual members, that the shift has been shown more often to be toward greater risk, and that whether a group will shift toward greater risk or caution is a function of the members' prediscussion inclinations.

Having discussed group decision making and its pros and cons, we now turn to the techniques by which groups make decisions. These techniques reduce some of the dysfunctional aspects of group decision making.

Group Decision-Making Techniques

The most common form of group decision making takes place in **interacting groups**. In these groups, members meet face-to-face and rely on both verbal and nonverbal interaction to communicate with each other. But as our discussion of groupthink demonstrated, groups do not always work in the way that we think they should. That holds true with group decision making, too. Here we review the most common group decision-making technique—brainstorming—and an alternative—the nominal group technique.

Brainstorming is meant to overcome pressures for conformity in an interacting group that retard the development of creative alternatives.[40] It does this by utilizing an idea-generation process that specifically encourages any and all alternatives while withholding any criticism of those alternatives.

In a typical brainstorming session, six to twelve people sit around a table. The group leader states the problem in a clear manner so that it is understood by all participants. Members then "freewheel" as many alternatives as they can in a given length of time. No criticism is allowed, and all the alternatives are recorded for later discussion and analysis. One idea stimulates others, and judgments of even the most bizarre suggestions are withheld until later to encourage group members to "think the unusual."

Brainstorming may indeed generate ideas—but not in a very efficient manner. Research consistently shows that individuals working alone generate more ideas than a group in a brainstorming session. Why? One of the primary reasons is because of "production blocking." In other words, when people are generating ideas in a group, there are many people talking at once, which blocks the thought process and eventually impedes the sharing of ideas.[41] The following technique goes further than brainstorming by offering a method that helps groups arrive at a preferred solution.[42]

The **nominal group technique** restricts discussion or interpersonal communication during the decision-making process, hence the term *nominal*. Group members are all physically present, as in a traditional committee meeting, but members operate independently. Specifically, a problem is presented and then the group takes the following steps:

1. Members meet as a group, but before any discussion takes place, each member independently writes down ideas on the problem.
2. After this silent period, each member presents one idea to the group. Each member takes a turn, presenting a single idea, until all ideas have been presented and recorded. No discussion takes place until all ideas have been recorded.
3. The group discusses the ideas for clarity and evaluates them.
4. Each group member silently and independently rank-orders the ideas. The idea with the highest aggregate ranking determines the final decision.

The chief advantage of the nominal group technique is that it permits a group to meet formally but does not restrict independent thinking, as does an interacting group. Research generally shows that nominal groups outperform brainstorming groups.[43]

GLOBAL IMPLICATIONS

As in most other areas of OB, most of the research on groups has been conducted in North America, but that situation is changing quickly. There are three areas of group research where cross-cultural issues are particularly important.

Status and Culture   Do cultural differences affect status? The answer is a resounding "yes."

The importance of status does vary between cultures. The French, for example, are highly status conscious. Countries also differ on the criteria that create status. For instance, status for Latin Americans and Asians tends to be derived from family position and formal roles held in organizations. In contrast, although status is still important in countries such as the United States and Australia, it is often bestowed more for accomplishments than on the basis of titles and family trees.[44]

The message here is to make sure you understand who and what holds status when interacting with people from a culture different from your own. A U.S. manager who doesn't understand that physical office size is not a measure of a Japanese executive's position or who fails to grasp the importance the British place on family genealogy and social class is likely to unintentionally offend his overseas counterparts and, in so doing, lessen his interpersonal effectiveness.

Social Loafing   Social loafing appears to have a Western bias. It's consistent with individualistic cultures, such as the United States and Canada, that are dominated by self-interest. It is *not* consistent with collective societies, in which individuals are motivated by in-group goals. For instance, in studies comparing employees from the United States with employees from the People's Republic of China and Israel (both collectivist societies), the Chinese and Israelis showed no propensity to engage in social loafing.

Group Diversity   More and more research is being done on how diversity influences group performance. Some of this research looks at cultural diversity, and some of it considers diversity on other characteristics (such as race or gender). Collectively, the research points to both benefits and costs of group diversity.

In terms of costs, diversity appears to lead to increased group conflict, especially in the early stages of a group's tenure. This conflict often results in lower group morale and group members dropping out. One study of groups that were either culturally diverse (composed of people from different countries) or homogeneous (composed of people from the same country) found that, on a wilderness survival exercise, the diverse and homogenous groups performed equally well, but the diverse groups were less satisfied with their groups, were less cohesive, and had more conflict.[45]

In terms of the benefits to diversity, more evidence is accumulating that, over time, culturally and demographically diverse groups may perform better, if they can get over their initial conflicts. Why might this be the case?

Research shows that surface-level diversity—observable characteristics such as national origin, race, and gender—actually cues people to possible differences in deep-level diversity—underlying attitudes, values, and opinions. One researcher argues, "The mere presence of diversity you can see, such as a person's race or gender, actually cues a team that there's likely to be differences of opinion." Although those differences of opinion can lead to conflict, they also provide an opportunity to solve problems in unique ways.

One study of jury behavior, for example, found that diverse juries were more likely to deliberate longer, share more information, and make fewer factual errors when discussing evidence. Interestingly, two studies of MBA student groups found that surface-level diversity led to greater openness even when there was no deep-level diversity. In such cases, the surface-level diversity of a group may subconsciously cue team members to be more open-minded in their views.[46]

IMPLICATIONS FOR MANAGERS

A number of group properties show a relationship with performance. Among the most prominent are role perception, norms, status differences, size of the group, and cohesiveness.

There is a positive relationship between role perception and an employee's performance evaluation. The degree of congruence that exists between an employee and the boss in the perception of the employee's job influences the degree to which the boss will judge that employee as an effective performer. To the extent that the employee's role perception fulfills the boss's role expectations, the employee will receive a higher performance evaluation.

Norms control group member behavior by establishing standards of right and wrong. The norms of a given group can help to explain the behaviors of its members for managers. When norms support high output, managers can expect individual performance to be markedly higher than when group norms aim to restrict output. Similarly, norms that support antisocial behavior increase the likelihood that individuals will engage in deviant workplace activities.

Status inequities create frustration and can adversely influence productivity and the willingness to remain with an organization. Among individuals who are equity sensitive, incongruence is likely to lead to reduced motivation and an increased search for ways to bring about fairness (for example, taking another job).

The impact of size on a group's performance depends on the type of task in which the group is engaged. Larger groups are more effective at fact-finding activities. Smaller groups are more effective at action-taking tasks. Our knowledge of social loafing suggests that, if management uses larger groups, efforts should be made to provide measures of individual performance within the group.

Cohesiveness can play an important function in influencing a group's level of productivity. Whether it does depends on the group's performance-related norms.

CHAPTER 9

Understanding Work Teams

After studying this chapter, you should be able to:

1. Contrast groups and teams, and analyze the growing popularity of using teams in organizations.
2. Compare and contrast four types of teams.
3. Identify the characteristics of effective teams.
4. Show how organizations can create team players.
5. Decide when to use individuals instead of teams.
6. Show how the understanding of teams differs in a global context.

Having discussed groups in Chapter 8, now we'll turn our attention to a particular type of group, namely work teams. Approximately 80 percent of *Fortune* 500 companies now have half or more of their employees on teams. And 68 percent of small U.S. manufacturers are using teams in their production areas.[1] Thus, teams are increasingly becoming the primary means for organizing work in contemporary business firms.

WHY HAVE TEAMS BECOME SO POPULAR?

How do we explain the current popularity of teams? As organizations have restructured themselves to compete more effectively and efficiently, they have turned to teams as a better way to use employee talents. Management has found that teams are more flexible and responsive to changing events than are traditional departments or other forms of permanent groupings. Teams have the capability to quickly assemble, deploy, refocus, and disband. But don't overlook the motivational properties of teams. Consistent with our discussion in Chapter 6 of the role of employee involvement as a motivator, teams facilitate employee participation in operating decisions. So another explanation for the popularity of teams is that they are an effective means for management to democratize their organizations and increase employee motivation.

The fact that organizations have turned to teams doesn't necessarily mean they're always effective. Decision makers, as humans, can be swayed by fads and herd mentality. Are teams truly effective? What conditions affect their potential? How do teams work together? These are some of the questions we'll answer in this chapter.

DIFFERENCES BETWEEN GROUPS AND TEAMS

Groups and teams are not the same thing. In this section, we define and clarify the difference between work groups and work teams.[2]

In Chapter 8, we defined a *group* as two or more individuals, interacting and interdependent, who have come together to achieve particular objectives. A **work group** is a group that interacts primarily to share information and to make decisions to help each member perform within his or her area of responsibility.

Work groups have no need or opportunity to engage in collective work that requires joint effort. So their performance is merely the summation of each group member's individual contribution. There is no positive synergy that would create an overall level of performance that is greater than the sum of the inputs.

A **work team** generates positive synergy through coordinated effort. The individual efforts result in a level of performance that is greater than the sum of those individual inputs. Exhibit 9-1 highlights the differences between work groups and work teams.

These definitions help clarify why so many organizations have recently restructured work processes around teams. Management is looking for positive synergy that will allow the organizations to increase performance. The extensive use of teams creates the *potential* for an organization to generate greater outputs with no increase in inputs. Notice, however, that we said *potential*. There is nothing inherently magical in the creation of teams that ensures the achievement of positive synergy. Merely calling a *group* a *team* doesn't automatically increase its performance. As we show later in this

EXHIBIT 9-1   Comparing Work Groups and Work Teams

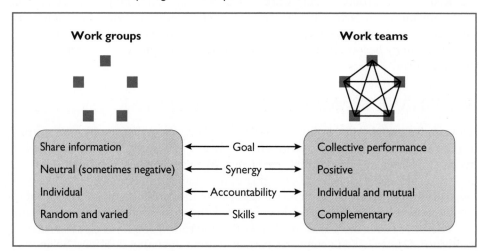

Work groups		Work teams
Share information	←— Goal —→	Collective performance
Neutral (sometimes negative)	←— Synergy —→	Positive
Individual	←— Accountability —→	Individual and mutual
Random and varied	←— Skills —→	Complementary

chapter, effective teams have certain common characteristics. If management hopes to gain increases in organizational performance through the use of teams, it needs to ensure that its teams possess these characteristics.

TYPES OF TEAMS

Teams can do a variety of things. They can make products, provide services, negotiate deals, coordinate projects, offer advice, and make decisions. In this section, we'll describe the four most common types of teams you're likely to find in an organization: *problem-solving teams, self-managed work teams, cross-functional teams,* and *virtual teams* (see Exhibit 9-2).

Problem-Solving Teams

Twenty years ago or so, teams were just beginning to grow in popularity, and most of those teams took similar form. They were typically composed of five to twelve hourly employees from the same department who met for a few hours each week to discuss ways of improving quality, efficiency, and the work environment. We call these **problem-solving teams**.

In problem-solving teams, members share ideas or offer suggestions on how work processes and methods can be improved; they rarely have the authority to uni-laterally implement any of their suggested actions. For instance, Merrill Lynch cre-ated a problem-solving team to specifically figure out ways to reduce the number of days it took to open up a new cash management account.[3] By suggesting cuts in the number of steps in the process from forty-six to thirty-six, the team was able to reduce the average number of days from fifteen to eight.

Self-Managed Work Teams

Although problem-solving teams involve employees in decisions, they "only" make recommendations. Some organizations have gone further and created teams that can not only solve problems but implement solutions and take responsibility for outcomes.

Self-managed work teams are groups of employees (typically ten to fifteen in number) who perform highly related or interdependent jobs and take on many of the responsibilities of their former supervisors. Typically, these tasks involve planning and scheduling work, assigning tasks to members, making operating decisions, taking action on problems, and working with suppliers and customers. Fully self-managed

EXHIBIT 9-2   Four Types of Teams

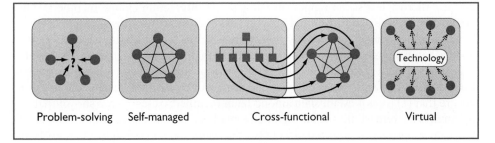

| Problem-solving | Self-managed | Cross-functional | Virtual |

work teams even select their own members and have the members evaluate each other's performance. As a result, supervisory positions take on decreased importance and may even be eliminated.

Business periodicals have been chock-full of articles describing successful applications of self-managed teams. But a word of caution needs to be offered: The overall research on the effectiveness of self-managed work teams has not been uniformly positive.[4] Moreover, although individuals on these teams do tend to report higher levels of job satisfaction compared to other individuals, they also sometimes have higher absenteeism and turnover rates. Inconsistency in findings suggests that the effectiveness of self-managed teams depends on the strength and makeup of team norms, the type of tasks the team undertakes, and the reward structure the team operates under—each of which can significantly influence how well the team performs.

Cross-Functional Teams

The Boeing Company created a team made up of employees from production, planning, quality, tooling, design engineering, and information systems to automate shims on the company's C-17 program. The team's suggestions resulted in drastically reduced cycle time and cost as well as improved quality on the C-17 program.[5]

This Boeing example illustrates the use of **cross-functional teams**. These are teams made up of employees from about the same hierarchical level but from different work areas, who come together to accomplish a task.

Cross-functional teams are an effective means for allowing people from diverse areas within an organization (or even between organizations) to exchange information, develop new ideas and solve problems, and coordinate complex projects. Of course, cross-functional teams are no picnic to manage. Their early stages of development are often very time consuming, as members learn to work with diversity and complexity. It takes time to build trust and teamwork, especially among people from different backgrounds with different experiences and perspectives.

Virtual Teams

The previously described types of teams do their work face-to-face. **Virtual teams** use computer technology to tie together physically dispersed members in order to achieve a common goal.[6] They allow people to collaborate online—using communication links such as wide-area networks, video conferencing, or e-mail—whether they're only a room away or continents apart. Virtual teams are so pervasive, and technology has advanced so far, that it's probably a bit of a misnomer to call these teams "virtual." Nearly all teams today do at least some of their work remotely.

Despite their ubiquity, virtual teams face special challenges. They may suffer because there is less social rapport and less direct interaction among members. They aren't able to duplicate the normal give-and-take of face-to-face discussion. Especially when members haven't personally met, virtual teams tend to be more task oriented and exchange less social–emotional information than face-to-face teams. Not surprisingly, virtual team members report less satisfaction with the group interaction process than do face-to-face teams. For virtual teams to be effective, management should ensure that (1) trust is established among team members (research has shown that one inflammatory remark in a team member e-mail can severely undermine team trust); (2) team progress is monitored closely (so the team doesn't lose sight of its goals and no team member "disappears"); and (3) the efforts and products of the virtual team are publicized throughout the organization (so the team does not become invisible).[7]

Creating Effective Teams

Many have tried to identify factors related to team effectiveness. However, recent studies have organized what was once a "veritable laundry list of characteristics" into a relatively focused model.[8] Exhibit 9-3 summarizes what we currently know about what makes teams effective. As you'll see, it builds on many of the group concepts introduced in Chapter 8.

The following discussion is based on the model in Exhibit 9-3. Keep in mind two caveats before we proceed. First, teams differ in form and structure. Because the model we present attempts to generalize across all varieties of teams, you need to be careful not to rigidly apply the model's predictions to all teams. You should use the model as a guide. Second, the model assumes that it's already been determined that teamwork is

EXHIBIT 9-3 Team Effectiveness Model

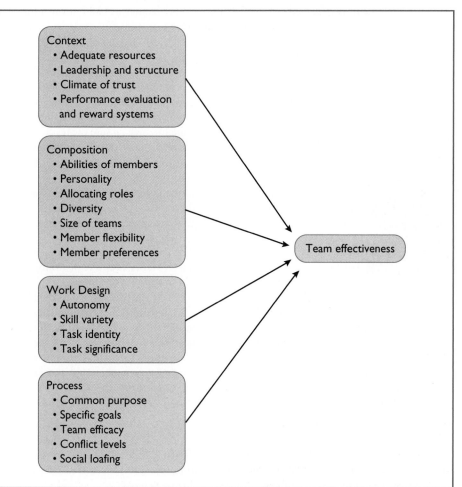

preferable to individual work. Creating "effective" teams in situations in which individuals can do the job better is equivalent to solving the wrong problem perfectly.

The key components of effective teams can be subsumed into four general categories. First are the resources and other *contextual* influences that make teams effective. The second relates to the team's *composition*. The third category is *work design*. Finally, *process* variables reflect those things that go on in the team that influences effectiveness. What does *team effectiveness* mean in this model? Typically, it has included objective measures of the team's productivity, managers' ratings of the team's performance, and aggregate measures of member satisfaction.

Context: What Factors Determine Whether Teams Are Successful

Four contextual factors appear to be most significantly related to team performance:

1. *Adequate Resources* Teams are part of a larger organization system. As such, every work team relies on resources outside the group to sustain it. A scarcity of resources directly reduces the ability of a team to perform its job effectively. As one set of researchers concluded, after looking at thirteen factors potentially related to group performance, "perhaps one of the most important characteristics of an effective work group is the support the group receives from the organization."[9] This support includes timely information, proper equipment, adequate staffing, encouragement, and administrative assistance.

2. *Leadership and Structure* Teams can't function if they can't agree on who is to do what and ensure that all members contribute equally in sharing the work load. Agreeing on the specifics of work and how they fit together to integrate individual skills requires team leadership and structure. Leadership is especially important in **multi-team systems**—where different teams need to coordinate their efforts to produce a desired outcome. In such systems, leaders need to empower teams by delegating responsibility to them, and they need to play the role of facilitator, making sure the teams are coordinating their efforts so that they work together rather than against one another.[10]

3. *Climate of Trust* Members of effective teams trust each other. And they also exhibit trust in their leaders.[11] Interpersonal trust among team members facilitates cooperation, reduces the need to monitor each others' behavior, and bonds members around the belief that others on the team won't take advantage of them. Team members, for instance, are more likely to take risks and expose vulnerabilities when they believe they can trust others on their team. Similarly, as discussed in Chapter 11, trust is the foundation of leadership. Trust in leadership is important in that it allows a team to be willing to accept and commit to its leader's goals and decisions.

   —Team composition matters—the optimal way to construct teams depends on the ability, skill, or trait under consideration.

4. *Performance Evaluation and Reward Systems* How do you get team members to be both individually and jointly accountable? The traditional, individually oriented evaluation and reward system must be modified to reflect team performance.[12] Individual performance evaluations and incentives may interfere with the development of high-performance teams. So in addition to evaluating and rewarding employees for their individual contributions, management should consider group-based appraisals, profit-sharing, gainsharing, small-group incentives, and other system modifications that reinforce team effort and commitment.

Team Composition

The team composition category includes variables that relate to how teams should be staffed. In this section, we address the ability and personality of team members, diversity, size of the team, and members' preference for teamwork.

Abilities of Members   Part of a team's performance depends on the knowledge, skills, and abilities of its individual members.[13] It's true that we occasionally read about an athletic team composed of mediocre players who, because of excellent coaching, determination, and precision teamwork, beats a far more talented group of players. But such cases make the news precisely because they represent an aberration. As the old saying goes, "The race doesn't always go to the swiftest nor the battle to the strongest, but that's the way to bet." A team's performance is not merely the summation of its individual members' abilities. However, these abilities set parameters for what members can do and how effectively they will perform on a team.

To perform effectively, a team requires three different types of skills. First, it needs people who have *technical expertise*. Second, it needs people who have the *problem-solving* and *decision-making skills* to be able to identify problems, generate alternatives, evaluate those alternatives, and make competent choices. Finally, teams need people who have good listening, feedback, conflict resolution, and other *interpersonal skills*.

Research on the skills and abilities of team members has revealed some interesting insights into team composition and performance. First, when the task entails considerable thought (for example, solving a complex problem such as reengineering an assembly line), high-ability teams (that is, teams composed of mostly intelligent members) do better than lower-ability teams, especially when the work load is distributed evenly. (That way, team performance does not depend on the weakest link.) High-ability teams are also more adaptable to changing situations in that they can more effectively adapt prior knowledge to suit a set of new problems.

Second, although high-ability teams generally have an advantage over lower-ability teams, this is not always the case. For example, when tasks are simple (for example, tasks that individual team members might be able to solve on their own), high-ability teams do not perform as well, perhaps because, in such tasks, high-ability teams become bored and turn their attention to other activities that are more stimulating, whereas low-ability teams stay on task. High-ability teams should be "saved" for tackling the tough problems. So matching team ability to the complexity of the task is important.

Finally, the ability of the team's *leader* also matters. Research shows that smart team leaders help less intelligent team members when they struggle with a task. But a less intelligent leader can neutralize the effect of a high-ability team.[14]

Personality of Members   We demonstrated in Chapter 2 that personality has a significant influence on individual employee behavior. This can also be extended to team behavior. Many of the dimensions identified in the Big Five personality model have been shown to be relevant to team effectiveness. A recent review of the literature suggested that three of the Big Five traits were especially important for team performance.[15] Specifically, teams that rate higher on mean levels of conscientiousness and openness to experience tend to perform better. Moreover, the minimum level of team member agreeableness also matters: Teams did worse when they had one or more highly disagreeable members. Perhaps one bad apple *can* spoil the whole bunch!

Research has also provided us with a good idea about why these personality traits are important to teams. Conscientious people are valuable in teams because they're good at backing up other team members, and they're also good at sensing when that support is truly needed. Open team members communicate better with one another and throw out more ideas, which leads teams composed of open people to be more creative and innovative.[16]

Even if an organization does a really good job of selecting individuals for team roles, most likely they'll find there aren't enough, say, conscientious people to go around. Suppose an organization needs to create 20 teams of 4 people each and has 40 highly conscientious people and 40 who score low on conscientiousness. Would the organization be better off (A) putting all the conscientious people together (forming 10 teams with the highly conscientious people and 10 teams of members low on conscientiousness) or (B) "seeding" each team with 2 people who scored high and 2 who scored low on conscientiousness?

Perhaps surprisingly, the evidence tends to suggest that option A is the best choice; performance across the teams will be higher if the organization forms 10 highly conscientious teams and 10 teams low in conscientiousness. "This may be because, in such teams, members who are highly conscientious not only must perform their own tasks but also must perform or redo the tasks of low-conscientious members. It may also be because such diversity leads to feelings of contribution inequity."[17]

Diversity of Members   In Chapter 8, we discussed research on the effect of diversity on groups. How does *team* diversity affect *team* performance?

Many of us hold the optimistic view that diversity should be a good thing—diverse teams should benefit from differing perspectives and do better. Unfortunately, the evidence appears to favor the pessimists. One review concluded, "Studies on diversity in teams from the last 50 years have shown that surface-level social-category differences such as race/ethnicity, gender, and age tend to . . . have negative effects" on the performance of teams.[18] As in the literature on groups, there is some evidence that the disruptive effects of diversity decline over time, but unlike in group literature, there is less evidence that diverse teams perform better eventually.

One of the pervasive problems with teams is that although diversity may have real potential benefits, a team is deeply focused on commonly held information. But if diverse teams are to realize their creative potential, they need to focus not on their similarities but on their differences. There is some evidence, for example, that when team members believe others have more expertise, they will work to support those members, leading to higher levels of effectiveness.[19] The key is for diverse teams to communicate what they uniquely know and also what they don't know.

Size of Teams   The president of AOL Technologies says the secret to a great team is to "think small. Ideally, your team should have seven to nine people."[20] His advice is supported by evidence.[21] Generally speaking, the most effective teams have five to nine members; experts suggest using the smallest number of people who can do the task. Unfortunately, there is a pervasive tendency for managers to err on the side of making teams too large. Although a minimum of four or five may be necessary to develop diversity of views and skills, managers seem to seriously underestimate how coordination problems can exponentially increase as team members are added.

—By matching individual preferences with team role demands, managers increase the likelihood that the team members will work well together.

When teams have excess members, cohesiveness and mutual accountability decline, social loafing increases, and more and more people do less talking relative to others. Moreover, large teams have trouble coordinating with one another, especially when under time pressure. So in designing effective teams, managers should try to keep them at nine or fewer members. If a natural working unit is larger and you want a team effort, consider breaking the group into subteams.[22]

Member Preferences Not every employee is a team player. Given the option, many employees will select themselves *out* of team participation. When people who would prefer to work alone are required to team up, there is a direct threat to the team's morale and to individual member satisfaction.[23] This suggests that, when selecting team members, individual preferences should be considered along with abilities, personalities, and skills. High-performing teams are likely to be composed of people who prefer working as part of a group.

Work Design

Effective teams need to work together and take collective responsibility for completing significant tasks. An effective team must be more than a "team in name only."[24] Based on terminology introduced in Chapter 6, the work-design category includes variables such as freedom and autonomy, the opportunity to use different skills and talents (skill variety), the ability to complete a whole and identifiable task or product (task identity), and work on a task or project that has a substantial impact on others (task significance). The evidence indicates that these characteristics enhance member motivation and increase team effectiveness.[25] These work-design characteristics motivate because they increase members' sense of responsibility and ownership of the work and because they make the work more interesting to perform.

Team Processes

The final category related to team effectiveness is process variables. These include member commitment to a common purpose, establishment of specific team goals, team efficacy, a managed level of conflict, and minimization of social loafing.

Why are processes important to team effectiveness? One way to answer this question is to return to the topic of social loafing. We found that 1+1+1 doesn't necessarily add up to 3. In team tasks for which each member's contribution is not clearly visible, there is a tendency for individuals to decrease their effort. Social loafing, in other words, illustrates a process loss as a result of using teams. But team processes should produce positive results. That is, teams should create outputs greater than the sum of their inputs. The development of creative alternatives by a diverse group would be one such instance. Exhibit 9-4 illustrates how group processes can have an impact on a group's actual effectiveness.[26] Research teams are often used in research laboratories because they can draw on the diverse skills of various individuals to produce more meaningful research as a team than could be generated by all the researchers working independently; that is, they produce positive synergy. Their process gains exceed their process losses.

EXHIBIT 9-4   Effects of Group Processes

Potential group effectiveness + Process gains − Process losses = Actual group effectiveness

Common Plan and Purpose   An effective team has a common plan and purpose that provides direction, momentum, and commitment for members.[27] This purpose is a vision, or master, plan. It's broader than specific goals.

Members of successful teams put a tremendous amount of time and effort into discussing, shaping, and agreeing on a purpose that belongs to them both collectively and individually. This common purpose, when accepted by the team, becomes the equivalent of what celestial navigation is to a ship captain: it provides direction and guidance under any and all conditions. Like the proverbial ship following the wrong course, teams that don't have good planning skills are doomed; perfectly executing the wrong plan is a lost cause.[28] Effective teams also show **reflexivity**, meaning that they reflect on and adjust their master plan when necessary. A team has to have a good plan, but it also has to be willing and able to adapt when conditions call for it.[29]

Specific Goals   Successful teams translate their common purpose into specific, measurable, and realistic performance goals. Just as we demonstrated in Chapter 5 how goals lead individuals to higher performance, goals also energize teams. Specific goals facilitate clear communication. They also help teams maintain their focus on getting results.

—As long as it remains focused on the task, conflicts stimulate discussion, promote critical assessment of problems and options, and can lead to better team decisions.

Also, consistent with the research on individual goals, team goals should be challenging. Difficult goals have been found to raise team performance on those criteria for which they're set. So, for instance, goals for quantity tend to raise quantity, goals for speed tend to raise speed, goals for accuracy raise accuracy, and so on.[30]

Team Efficacy   Effective teams have confidence in themselves. They believe they can succeed. We call this *team efficacy*.[31] Success breeds success. Teams that have been successful raise their beliefs about future success, which, in turn, motivates them to work harder. What, if anything, can management do to increase team efficacy? Two possible options are helping the team to achieve small successes and providing skill training. Small successes build team confidence. As a team develops an increasingly stronger performance record, it also increases the collective belief that future efforts will lead to success. In addition, managers should consider providing training to improve members' technical and interpersonal skills. The greater the abilities of team members, the greater the likelihood that the team will develop confidence and the capability to deliver on that confidence.

Mental Models   Effective teams have accurate and common **mental models**—knowledge and beliefs (a "psychological map") about how the work gets done. If team members have the wrong mental models, which is particularly likely to happen with teams under acute stress, their performance suffers.[32] For example, in the Iraq war, many military leaders said they underestimated the power of the insurgency and the infighting among Iraqi religious sects. The similarity of team members' mental models matters, too. If team members have different ideas about how to do things, the teams will fight over how to do things rather than focus on what needs to be done.[33]

Conflict Levels   Conflict on a team isn't necessarily bad. As discussed in more depth in Chapter 13, teams that are completely void of conflict are likely to become apathetic and stagnant. So conflict can actually improve team effectiveness.[34] But not all types of conflict. Relationship conflicts—those based on interpersonal incompatibilities, tension, and animosity toward others—are almost always dysfunctional. However, on teams performing nonroutine activities, disagreements among members about task content (called *task conflicts*) is not detrimental. In fact, it is often beneficial because it reduces the likelihood of groupthink. Task conflicts stimulate discussion, promote critical assessment of problems and options, and can lead to better team decisions. So, effective teams can be characterized as having an appropriate level of conflict.

Social Loafing   We talked in Chapter 8 about the fact that individuals can hide inside a group. They can engage in social loafing and coast on the group's effort because their individual contributions can't be identified. Effective teams fight this tendency by holding themselves accountable at both the individual and team levels. Successful teams make members individually and jointly accountable for the team's purpose, goals, and approach.[35] Therefore, members should be clear on what they are individually responsible for and what they are jointly responsible for.

TURNING INDIVIDUALS INTO TEAM PLAYERS

To this point, we've made a strong case for the value and growing popularity of teams, but many people are not inherently team players. There are also many organizations that have historically nurtured individual accomplishments. Finally, countries differ in terms of how they rate on individualism and collectivism. Teams fit well with countries that score high on collectivism. But what if an organization wants to introduce teams into a work population that is made up largely of individuals born and raised in an individualistic society? A veteran employee of a large company, who had done well working in an individualistic company in an individualist country, described the experience of joining a team: "I'm learning my lesson. I just had my first negative performance appraisal in 20 years."[36]

So what can organizations do to enhance team effectiveness—to turn individual contributors into team members? The following are the primary options managers have for trying to turn individuals into team players.

Selection: Hiring Team Players   Some people already possess the interpersonal skills to be effective team players. When hiring team members, in addition to the technical skills required to fill the job, care should be taken to ensure that candidates can fulfill their team roles as well as technical requirements.[37] Very disagreeable or unconscientious people, for example, are probably not your first choice as team members.

Training: Creating Team Players   A large proportion of people raised on the importance of individual accomplishments can be trained to become team players. Training specialists conduct exercises that allow employees to experience the satisfaction that teamwork can provide. They typically offer workshops to help employees improve their problem-solving, communication, negotiation, conflict-management, and coaching skills. Emerson Electric's Specialty Motor Division in Missouri, for instance, has achieved remarkable success in getting its 650-member workforce not only to accept but to welcome team training.[38] Outside consultants were brought in to give workers practical skills for working in teams. After less than one year, employees were enthusiastically accepting the value of teamwork.

Rewarding: Providing Incentives to Be a Good Team Player   An organization's reward system needs to be reworked to encourage cooperative efforts rather than competitive ones.[39] For instance, Hallmark Cards, Inc., added to its basic individual-incentive system an annual bonus based on achievement of team goals. Trigon Blue Cross/Blue Shield changed its system to reward an even split between individual goals and team-like behaviors.[40]

BEWARE! TEAMS AREN'T ALWAYS THE ANSWER

Teamwork takes more time and often more resources than individual work. For instance, teams have increased communication demands, conflicts to be managed, and meetings to be run. So the benefits of using teams have to exceed the costs. And that's not always the case.[41] In the excitement to enjoy the benefits of teams, some managers have introduced them into situations in which the work is better done by individuals. Before you rush to implement teams, you should carefully assess whether the work requires or will benefit from a collective effort.

How do you know if the work of your group would be better done in teams? It's been suggested that three tests be applied to see if a team fits the situation.[42] First, can the work be done better by more than one person? A good indicator is the complexity of the work and the need for different perspectives. Simple tasks that don't require diverse input are probably better left to individuals. Second, does the work create a common purpose or set of goals for the people in the group that is more than the aggregate of individual goals? For instance, many new-car dealer service departments have introduced teams that link customer-service personnel, mechanics, parts special-ists, and sales representatives. Such teams can better manage collective responsibility for ensuring that customer needs are properly met. The final test to assess whether teams fit the situation is to determine whether the members of the group are interde-pendent. Using teams makes sense when there is interdependence between tasks—when the success of the whole depends on the success of each one *and* the success of each one depends on the success of the others. Soccer, for instance, is an obvious *team* sport. Success requires a great deal of coordination between interdependent players. Conversely, except possibly for relays, swim teams are not really teams. They're groups of individuals, performing individually, whose total performance is merely the aggregate summation of their individual performances.

GLOBAL IMPLICATIONS

Although research on global considerations in the use of teams is just beginning, three areas are particularly worth mentioning: the extent of teamwork, self-managed teams, and team cultural diversity.

Extent of Teamwork   Although the use of work teams is pervasive in the United States, some evidence suggests that the extent of teamwork—the degree to which teams deeply affect the way work is done—is not as significant in the United States as in other countries. One study comparing U.S. workers to Canadian and Asian workers revealed that 51 percent of workers in Asia-Pacific and 48 percent of Canadian employees report high levels of teamwork. But only about one-third (32 percent) of U.S. employees say their organization has a high level of teamwork.[43] Thus, although teamwork is widely used in the United States, this evidence suggests that there still is a heavy role for individual contributions. Given that U.S. culture is highly individualistic, that may continue to be true for quite some time.

Self-Managed Teams   Although self-managed teams have not proven to be the panacea many thought they would be, special care needs to be taken when introducing self-managed teams globally. For instance, evidence suggests that these types of teams have not fared well in Mexico, largely due to the culture's low tolerance of ambiguity and uncertainty and employees' strong respect for hierarchical authority.[44] Thus, in countries that are relatively high in power distance—meaning that roles of leaders and followers are clearly delineated—a team may need to be structured so that leadership roles are spelled out and power relationships are identified.

Team Cultural Diversity and Team Performance   Earlier, we discussed research on team diversity in terms of factors such as race or gender. But what about diversity created by national differences? Like the earlier research, evidence indicates that these elements of diversity interfere with team processes, at least in the short term.[45] Cultural diversity does seem to be an asset for tasks that call for a variety of viewpoints. But culturally heterogeneous teams have more difficulty learning to work with each other and solving problems. The good news is that these difficulties seem to dissipate with time. Although newly formed culturally diverse teams underperform newly formed culturally homogeneous teams, the differences disappear after about 3 months.[46] The reason is that it takes culturally diverse teams a while to learn how to work through disagreements and different approaches to solving problems.

IMPLICATIONS FOR MANAGERS

Few trends have influenced employee jobs as much as the massive movement to introduce teams into the workplace. The shift from working alone to working on teams requires employees to cooperate with others, share information, confront differences, and minimize personal interests for the greater good of the team. Effective teams have common characteristics:

- Adequate resources
- Effective leadership
- A climate of trust
- A performance evaluation and reward system that reflects team contributions

Effective teams have individuals with technical expertise, as well as problem-solving, decision-making, and interpersonal skills; team members also have high scores on the personality characteristics of agreeableness, conscientiousness, and openness to experience. Effective teams also tend to be small—with fewer than ten people—preferably made up of individuals with diverse backgrounds. They have members who fill role demands, are flexible, and prefer to be part of a group. The work that members do provides freedom and autonomy, the opportunity to use different skills and talents, the ability to complete a whole and identifiable task or product, and work that has a substantial impact on others. Also, effective teams have members committed to a common purpose, specific team goals, members who believe in the team's capabilities, a manageable level of conflict, and a minimal degree of social loafing.

Because individualistic organizations and societies attract and reward individual accomplishments, it is more difficult to create team players in these environments. To make the conversion, management should select individuals with the interpersonal skills to be effective team players, provide training to develop teamwork skills, and reward individuals for cooperative efforts.

Communication

1. Describe the communication process and distinguish between formal and informal channels of communication.
2. Contrast downward, upward, and lateral communication and provide examples of each.
3. Contrast oral, written, and nonverbal communication.
4. Contrast formal communication networks and the grapevine.
5. Identify common barriers to effective communication.
6. Show how to overcome the potential problems in cross-cultural communication.

No individual, group, or organization can exist without communication: the transfer of meaning among its members. It is only through transmitting meaning from one person to another that information and ideas can be conveyed. Communication, however, is more than merely imparting meaning. It must also be understood. In a group in which one member speaks only German and the others do not know German, the individual speaking German will not be fully understood. Therefore, **communication** must include both the *transfer and the understanding of meaning*.

Before making too many generalizations concerning communication and problems in communicating effectively, we need to describe the communication process.

THE COMMUNICATION PROCESS

Before communication can take place, a purpose, expressed as a message to be conveyed, is needed. It passes between a sender and a receiver. The message is encoded (converted to a symbolic form) and passed by way of some medium (channel) to the receiver, who retranslates (decodes) the message initiated by the sender. The result is transfer of meaning from one person to another.[1]

EXHIBIT 10-1   The Communication Process

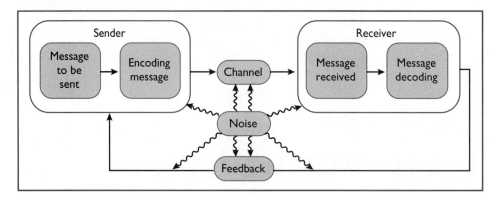

Exhibit 10-1 depicts this **communication process**. The key parts of this model include (1) the sender, (2) encoding, (3) the message, (4) the channel, (5) decoding, (6) the receiver, (7) noise, and (8) feedback.

The *sender* initiates a message by encoding a thought. The *message* is the actual physical product from the sender's *encoding*. When we speak, the speech is the message. When we write, the writing is the message. When we gesture, the movements of our arms and the expressions on our faces are the message. The *channel* is the medium through which the message travels. It is selected by the sender, who must determine whether to use a formal or informal channel. **Formal channels** are established by the organization and transmit messages that are related to the professional activities of members. They traditionally follow the authority chain within the organization. Other forms of messages, such as personal or social, follow **informal channels** in the organization. These informal channels are spontaneous and emerge as a response to individual choices.[2] The *receiver* is the object to whom the message is directed. But before the message can be received, the symbols in it must be translated into a form that can be understood by the receiver. This step is the *decoding* of the message. *Noise* represents communication barriers that distort the clarity of the message. Examples of possible noise sources include perceptual problems, information overload, semantic difficulties, or cultural differences. The final link in the communication process is a feedback loop. *Feedback* is the check on how successful we have been in transferring our messages as originally intended. It determines whether understanding has been achieved.

DIRECTION OF COMMUNICATION

Communication can flow vertically or laterally. The vertical dimension can be further divided into downward and upward directions.[3]

Downward Communication

Communication that flows from one level of a group or organization to a lower level is *downward communication*. When we think of managers communicating with employees, the downward pattern is the one we are usually thinking of. It's used by group leaders and managers to assign goals, provide job instructions, inform employees of policies and procedures, point out problems that need attention, and offer feedback about performance. But downward communication doesn't have to be oral or face-to-face contact. When management sends letters to employees' homes to advise them of the organization's new sick leave policy, it's using downward communication. Another example of downward communication is an e-mail from a team leader to the members of her team, reminding them of an upcoming deadline.

—Downward, upward, and lateral directions of communication have their own challenges; understand and manage these unique challenges.

When engaging in downward communication, managers must explain the reasons *why* a decision was made. One study found that employees were twice as likely to be committed to changes when the reasons behind them were fully explained. Although this may seem like common sense, many managers feel they are too busy to explain things, or that explanations will "open up a big can of worms." Evidence clearly indicates, though, that explanations increase employee commitment and support of decisions.[4]

Another problem in downward communication is its one-way nature; generally, managers inform employees but rarely solicit their advice or opinions. The best communicators are those who explain the reasons behind their downward communications, but also solicit upward communication from the employees they supervise. That leads us to the next direction: upward communication.

Upward Communication

Upward communication flows to a higher level in the group or organization. It's used to provide feedback to higher-ups, inform them of progress toward goals, and relay current problems. Upward communication keeps managers aware of how employees feel about their jobs, coworkers, and the organization in general. Managers also rely on upward communication for ideas on how things can be improved.

Given that job responsibilities of most managers and supervisors have expanded, upward communication is increasingly difficult because managers are overwhelmed and easily distracted. To engage in effective upward communication, try to reduce distractions (meet in a conference room if you can, rather than your boss's office or cubicle), communicate in headlines not paragraphs (your job is to get your boss's attention, not to engage in a meandering discussion), support your headlines with actionable items (what you believe should happen), and prepare an agenda to make sure you use your boss's attention well.[5]

Lateral Communication

When communication takes place among members of the same work group, among members of work groups at the same level, among managers at the same level, or among any other horizontally equivalent personnel, we describe it as *lateral communications*.

Why would there be a need for horizontal communications if a group or an organization's vertical communications are effective? The answer is that horizontal communication is often necessary to save time and facilitate coordination. In some cases, such lateral relationships are formally sanctioned. More often, they are informally created to short-circuit the vertical hierarchy and expedite action. So lateral communications can, from management's viewpoint, be good or bad. Because strict adherence to the formal vertical structure for all communications can impede the efficient and accurate transfer of information, lateral communications can be beneficial. In such cases, they occur with the knowledge and support of superiors. But they can create dysfunctional conflicts when the formal vertical channels are breached, when members go above or around their superiors to get things done, or when bosses find out that actions have been taken or decisions have been made without their knowledge.

INTERPERSONAL COMMUNICATION

How do group members transfer meaning between and among each other? There are three basic methods. People essentially rely on oral, written, and nonverbal communication.

Oral Communication

The chief means of conveying messages is *oral communication*. Speeches; formal one-on-one and group discussions; and the informal rumor mill, or grapevine, are popular forms of oral communication.

The advantages of oral communication are speed and feedback. A verbal message can be conveyed and a response received in a minimal amount of time. If the receiver is unsure of the message, rapid feedback allows for early detection by the sender and, hence, allows for early correction. As one professional put it, "Face-to-face communication on a consistent basis is still the best way to get information to and from employees."[6]

The major disadvantage of oral communication surfaces whenever a message has to be passed through a number of people. The more people a message must pass through, the greater the potential distortion. If you've ever played the game "telephone," you know the problem. Each person interprets the message in his or her own way. The message's content, when it reaches its destination, is often very different from that of the original. In an organization, where decisions and other communiqués are verbally passed up and down the authority hierarchy, there are considerable opportunities for messages to become distorted.

Written Communication

Written communications include memos, letters, fax transmissions, e-mail, instant messaging, organizational periodicals, notices placed on bulletin boards, or any other device that is transmitted via written words or symbols.

Why would a sender choose to use written communications? They're often tangible and verifiable. When they're printed or electronically saved, both the sender and receiver have a record of the communication; and the message can be stored for an indefinite period. If there are questions concerning the content of the message, it is physically available for later reference. This feature is particularly important for complex and lengthy communications. The marketing plan for a new product, for instance, is likely to contain a number of tasks spread out over several months. By putting it in writing, those who have to initiate the plan can readily refer to it over the life of the plan. A final benefit of all written communication comes from the process itself. People are usually more careful with the written word than with the oral word. They're forced to think more thoroughly about what it is they want to convey in a written message than in a spoken one. Thus, written communications are more likely to be well thought out, logical, and clear.

Of course, written messages do have drawbacks. They're time consuming. You could convey far more information to a college instructor in a 1-hour oral exam than in a 1-hour written exam. In fact, you could probably say the same thing in 10 to 15 minutes that it would take you an hour to write. So, although writing may be more precise, it also consumes a great deal of time. The other major disadvantage is feedback, or lack of it. Oral communication allows the receiver to respond rapidly to what he thinks he hears. Written communication, however, does not have a built-in feedback mechanism. The result is that mailing a memo is no assurance that it has been received, and, if received, there is no guarantee the recipient will interpret it as the sender intended. The latter point is also relevant in oral communiqués, except it's easy in such cases merely to ask the receiver to summarize what you've said. An accurate summary presents feedback evidence that the message has been received and understood.

Nonverbal Communication

Every time we verbally give a message to someone, we also impart a nonverbal message.[7] In some instances, the nonverbal component may stand alone. For example, in a singles bar, a glance, a stare, a smile, a frown, and a provocative body movement all convey meaning. Therefore, no discussion of communication would be complete without consideration of *nonverbal communication*—which includes body movements, the intonations or emphasis we give to words, facial expressions, and the physical distance between the sender and receiver.

> —Oral, written, and nonverbal communication forms or mediums of communication have their unique purposes, and specific limitations; utilize each medium when optimal, and try to avoid their limitations.

It can be argued that every *body movement* has a meaning, and no movement is accidental. The two most important messages that body language conveys are (1) the extent to which an individual likes another and is interested in his or her views and (2) the relative perceived status between a sender and receiver. For instance, we're more likely to position ourselves closer to people we like and touch them more often. Similarly, if you feel that you're of higher status than another, you're more likely to display body movements—such as crossed legs or a slouched seated position—that reflect a casual and relaxed manner.[8]

Body language adds to, and often complicates, verbal communication. A body position or movement does not by itself have a precise or universal meaning, but when it is linked with spoken language, it gives fuller meaning to a sender's message.

If you read the verbatim minutes of a meeting, you wouldn't grasp the impact of what was said in the same way you would if you had been there or if you saw the meeting on video. Why? There is no record of nonverbal communication. The emphasis given to words or phrases is missing. Exhibit 10-2 illustrates how *intonations* can change the meaning of a message. *Facial expressions* also convey meaning. A snarling face says something different than a smile. Facial expressions, along with intonations, can show arrogance, aggressiveness, fear, shyness, and other characteristics that would never be communicated if you read a transcript of what had been said.

The way individuals space themselves in terms of *physical distance* also has meaning. What is considered proper spacing is largely dependent on cultural norms. For example, what is considered a business-like distance in some European countries would be viewed as intimate in many parts of North America. If someone stands closer to you than is considered appropriate, it may indicate aggressiveness or sexual interest; if farther away than usual, it may mean disinterest or displeasure with what is being said.

EXHIBIT 10-2   Intonations: It's the Way You Say It!

Change your tone and you change your meaning:

Placement of the emphasis	What it means
Why don't I take **you** to dinner tonight?	I was going to take someone else.
Why don't **I** take you to dinner tonight?	Instead of the guy you were going with.
Why **don't** I take you to dinner tonight?	I'm trying to find a reason why I **shouldn't** take you.
Why don't I take you to dinner tonight?	Do you have a problem with me?
Why don't I **take** you to dinner tonight?	Instead of going on your own.
Why don't I take you to **dinner** tonight?	Instead of lunch tomorrow.
Why don't I take you to dinner **tonight**?	Not tomorrow night.

Source: Based on M. Kiely, "When 'No' Means 'Yes,'" *Marketing*, October 1993, pp. 7–9. Reproduced in A. Huczynski and D. Buchanan, *Organizational Behavior*, 4th ed. (Essex, England: Pearson Education, 2001), p. 194.

It's important for the receiver to be alert to these nonverbal aspects of communication. You should look for nonverbal cues as well as listen to the literal meaning of a sender's words. You should particularly be aware of contradictions between the messages. Your boss may say she is free to talk to you about a pressing budget problem, but you may see nonverbal signals suggesting that this is not the time to discuss the subject. Regardless of what is being said, an individual who frequently glances at her wristwatch is giving the message that she would prefer to terminate the conversation. We misinform others when we express one message verbally, such as trust, but nonverbally communicate a contradictory message that reads, "I don't have confidence in you."

ORGANIZATIONAL COMMUNICATION

In this section, we move from interpersonal communication to organizational communication. Our first focus will be to describe and distinguish formal networks and the grapevine. In the following section, we discuss technological innovations in communication.

Formal Small-Group Networks

Formal organizational networks can be very complicated. They can, for instance, include hundreds of people and a half-dozen or more hierarchical levels. To simplify our discussion, we've condensed these networks into three common small groups of five people each (see Exhibit 10-3). These three networks are the chain, wheel, and all channel. Although these three networks have been simplified, they allow us to describe the unique qualities of each.

The *chain* rigidly follows the formal chain of command. This network approximates the communication channels you might find in a rigid three-level organization. The *wheel* relies on a central figure to act as the conduit for all of the group's communication. It simulates the communication network you would find on a team with a strong leader. The *all-channel* network permits all group members to actively communicate with each other. The all-channel network is most often characterized in practice by self-managed teams, in which all group members are free to contribute and no one person takes on a leadership role.

EXHIBIT 10-3   Three Common Small-Group Networks

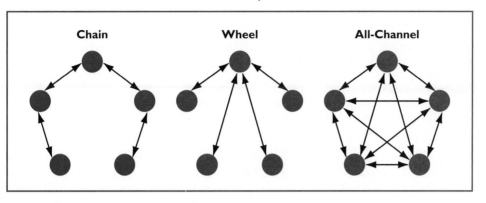

As Exhibit 10-4 demonstrates, the effectiveness of each network depends on the dependent variable you're concerned about. For instance, the structure of the wheel facilitates the emergence of a leader, the all-channel network is best if you are concerned with having high member satisfaction, and the chain and the wheel are best if accuracy is most important. Exhibit 10-4 leads us to the conclusion that no single network will be best for all occasions.

The Grapevine

The formal system is not the only communication network in a group or organization. There is also an informal one, called the **grapevine**. Although the grapevine may be informal, it's still an important source of information. For instance, a survey found that 75 percent of employees hear about matters first through rumors on the grapevine.[9]

The grapevine has three main characteristics.[10] First, it is not controlled by management. Second, it is perceived by most employees as being more believable and reliable than formal communiqués issued by top management. Finally, it is largely used to serve the self-interests of the people within it.

Is the information that flows along the grapevine accurate? The evidence indicates that about 75 percent of what is carried is accurate.[11] But what conditions foster an active grapevine? What gets the rumor mill rolling?

It's frequently assumed that rumors start because they make titillating gossip. This is rarely the case. Rumors emerge as a response to situations that are *important* to us, when there is *ambiguity*, and under conditions that arouse *anxiety*.[12] The fact that work situations frequently contain these three elements explains why rumors flourish in organizations. The secrecy and competition that typically prevail in large

EXHIBIT 10-4   Small-Group Networks and Effective Criteria

Criteria	Chain	Networks Wheel	All Channel
Speed	Moderate	Fast	Fast
Accuracy	High	High	Moderate
Emergence of a leader	Moderate	High	None
Member satisfaction	Moderate	Low	High

EXHIBIT 10-5   Suggestions for Reducing the Negative Consequences of Rumors

1. Announce timetables for making important decisions.
2. Explain decisions and behaviors that may appear inconsistent or secretive.
3. Emphasize the downside, as well as the upside, of current decisions and future plans.
4. Openly discuss worst-case possibilities—it is almost never as anxiety provoking as the unspoken fantasy.

Source: Adapted from L. Hirschhorn, "Managing Rumors," in L. Hirschhorn (ed.), *Cutting Back* (San Francisco: Jossey-Bass, 1983), pp. 54–56. With permission.

organizations—around issues such as the appointment of new bosses, the relocation of offices, downsizing decisions, and the realignment of work assignments—create conditions that encourage and sustain rumors on the grapevine. A rumor will persist either until the wants and expectations creating the uncertainty underlying the rumor are fulfilled or until the anxiety is reduced.

What can we conclude from the preceding discussion? Certainly the grapevine is an important part of any group or organization communication network and is well worth understanding. It gives managers a feel for the morale of their organization, identifies issues that employees consider important, and helps tap into employee anxieties. The grapevine also serves employees' needs: Small talk serves to create a sense of closeness and friendship among those who share information, although research suggests that it often does so at the expense of those in the "out" group.[13]

Can management entirely eliminate rumors? No. What management should do, however, is minimize the negative consequences of rumors by limiting their range and impact. Exhibit 10-5 offers a few suggestions for minimizing those negative consequences.

Electronic Communications

An indispensable—and in 71 percent of cases, the primary—medium of communication in today's organizations is electronic. Electronic communications include e-mail, instant messaging, text messaging, networking software, Internet or Web logs (blogs), and video conferencing. Let's discuss each in turn.

E-mail   E-mail uses the Internet to transmit and receive computer-generated text and documents. Its growth has been spectacular, and its use is now so pervasive that it's hard to imagine life without it.

E-mail, of course, is not without drawbacks. The following are some of the most significant limitations of e-mail and what organizations should do to reduce or eliminate these problems:

- *Misinterpreting the message.* It's true that we often misinterpret verbal messages, but the potential for misinterpretation with e-mail is even greater. One research team at New York University found that we can accurately decode an e-mail's intent and tone only 50 percent of the time, yet most of us vastly overestimate our ability to send and interpret clear messages. If you're sending an important message, make sure you reread it for clarity. And if you're upset about the presumed tone of someone else's message, keep in mind that you may be misinterpreting it.[14]

- *Communicating negative messages.* When companies have negative information to communicate, managers need to think carefully. E-mail may not be the best way to communicate the message. When Radio Shack decided to lay off 400 employees, it drew down an avalanche of scorn inside and outside the company by doing it via e-mail. Employees need to be careful communicating negative messages via e-mail, too. Justen Deal, 22, wrote an e-mail critical of some strategic decisions made by his employer, pharmaceutical giant Kaiser Permanente. In the e-mail, he criticized the "misleadership" of Kaiser CEO George Halvorson and questioned the financing of several information technology projects. Within hours, Deal's computer was seized; he was later fired.[15]

- *Overuse of e-mail.* An estimated 6 trillion e-mails are sent every year, and someone has to answer all those messages! As people become established in their careers and their responsibilities expand, so do their inboxes. A survey of Canadian managers revealed that 58 percent spent 2 to 4 hours per day reading and responding to e-mails. Some people, such as venture capitalist Fred Wilson, have become so overwhelmed by e-mail that they've declared "e-mail bankruptcy." Recording artist Moby sent an e-mail to all those in his address book announcing that he was taking a break from e-mail for the rest of the year. Although you probably don't want to declare e-mail bankruptcy, or couldn't get away with it even if you did, you should use e-mail judiciously, especially when you're contacting people inside the organization who may already be wading through many e-mail messages every day.[16]

- *E-mail emotions.* We tend to think of e-mail as a sort of sterile, faceless form of communication. But that doesn't mean it's unemotional. As you no doubt know, e-mails are often highly emotional. One CEO said, "I've seen people not talk to each other, turf wars break out and people quit their jobs as a result of e-mails." E-mail tends to have a disinhibiting effect on people; senders write things they'd never be comfortable saying in person. When others send flaming messages, remain calm and try not to respond in kind. Also, when writing new e-mails, try to temper your own tendencies to quickly fire off messages.[17]

- *Privacy concerns.* There are two privacy issues with e-mail. First, you need to be aware that your e-mails may be, and often are, monitored. Also, you can't always trust that the recipient of your e-mail will keep it confidential. For these reasons, you shouldn't write anything you wouldn't want made public. Before Wal-Mart fired marketing VP Julie Roehm, its managers examined her e-mails for evidence of an inappropriate romantic relationship. Second, you need to exercise caution in forwarding e-mail from your company's e-mail account to a personal, or "public," (for example, Gmail, Yahoo!, MSN) e-mail account. These accounts often aren't as secure as corporate accounts, so when you forward a company e-mail to them, you may be violating your organization's policy or unintentionally disclosing confidential data. Many employers hire vendors that sift through e-mails, using software to catch not only the obvious ("insider trading") but the vague ("that thing we talked about") or guilt ridden ("regret"). Another survey revealed that nearly 40 percent of companies have employees whose only job is to read other employees' e-mail. You are being watched—so be careful what you e-mail![18]

Instant Messaging and Text Messaging   Like e-mail, instant messaging (IM) and text messaging (TM) use electronic messages. Unlike e-mail, though, IM and TM are either in "real" time (IM) or use portable communication devices (TM). In just a few years, IM/TM has become pervasive. As you no doubt know from experience, IM is usually sent via desktop or laptop computers, whereas TM is transmitted via cell phones or handheld devices such as Blackberrys or iPhones.

The growth of TM has been spectacular. In 2001, for instance, just 8 percent of U.S. employees were using it. Now that number is more than 50 percent.[19] Why? Because IM and TM represent fast and inexpensive means for managers to stay in touch with employees and for employees to stay in touch with each other. In an increasing number of cases, this isn't just a luxury, it's a business imperative. For example, Bill Green, CEO of the consulting firm Accenture, doesn't have a permanent office. Since he's on the road all the time, visiting Accenture's 100 locations scattered across the globe, TM is essential for him keep in touch. Although there aren't many other examples so dramatic, the great advantage of TM is that it is flexible; with it, you can be reached almost anywhere, anytime.[20]

Despite their advantages, IM and TM aren't going to replace e-mail. E-mail is still probably a better device for conveying long messages that need to be saved. IM is preferable for one- or two-line messages that would just clutter up an e-mail inbox. On the downside, some IM/TM users find the technology intrusive and distracting. Their continual presence can make it hard for employees to concentrate and stay focused. For example, a survey of managers revealed that in 86 percent of meetings, at least some participants checked TM. Finally, because instant messages can be intercepted easily, many organizations are concerned about the security of IM/TM.[21]

One other point: It's important to not let the informality of text messaging ("omg! r u serious? brb") spill over into business e-mails. Many prefer to keep business communication relatively formal. By making sure your professional communications are, well, professional, you'll show yourself to be mature and serious.

Networking Software   Nowhere has communication been transformed more than in the area of networking. You are doubtless familiar with and perhaps a user of social networking platforms such as Facebook and MySpace.

Rather than being one huge site, Facebook, which has 30 million active users, is actually composed of separate networks based on schools, companies, or regions. It might surprise you to learn that individuals over the age of 25 are the fastest-growing users of Facebook.

More than 100 million users have created accounts at MySpace. This site averages more than 40 billion hits per month. MySpace profiles contain two "blurbs": "About Me" and "Who I'd Like to Meet" sections. Profiles can also contain "Interests" and "Details" sections, photos, blog entries, and other details. Compared to Facebook, MySpace is relatively more likely to be used for purely personal reasons, as illustrated by the "Friends Space" portion of a user's account.

To get the most out of social networks, while avoiding irritating your contacts, use them "for high-value items only"—not as an everyday or even every-week tool. Also, remember that a prospective employer might check your MySpace or Facebook entry. In fact, some entrepreneurs have developed software that mines such Web sites for companies (or individuals) that want to check up on a job applicant (or potential date). So keep in mind that what you post may be read by people other than your intended contacts.[22]

Web Logs (Blogs)   Sun Microsystems CEO Jonathan Schwartz is a big fan of Web logs (**blogs**), Web sites about a single person or company that are usually updated daily. He encourages his employees to have them and has one himself (http://blogs.sun.com/jonathan). Schwartz's blog averages 400,000 hits per month, and Schwartz allows Sun customers to post comments about the company's products on its Web site.

Obviously, Schwartz is not the only fan of blogs. Experts estimate that more than 10 million U.S. workers have blogs, and nearly 40 million people read blogs on a regular basis. Thousands of Microsoft employees have blogs and Google, GM, Nike, IBM, and many other large organizations also have corporate blogs.

So what's the downside? Although some companies have policies in place governing the content of blogs, many don't, and 39 percent of individual bloggers say they have posted comments that could be construed as harmful to their company's reputation. Many bloggers think their personal blogs are outside their employer's purview, but if someone else in a company happens to read a blog entry, there is nothing to keep him or her from sharing that information with others, and the employee could be dismissed as a result. Schwartz says that Sun would not fire an employee over any blog entry short of one that broke the law. "Our blogging policy is 'Be authentic. Period,'" he says. But most organizations are unlikely to be so forgiving of any blog entry that might cast a negative light on them.

One legal expert notes, "Employee bloggers mistakenly believe that the First Amendment gives them the right to say whatever they want on their personal blogs. Wrong!" Also, beware of posting personal blog entries at work. More than three-quarters of employers actively monitor employees' Web site connections. In short, if you are going to have a personal blog, maintain a strict work–personal "firewall."[23]

Video Conferencing   *Video conferencing* permits employees in an organization to have meetings with people at different locations. Live audio and video images of members allow them to see, hear, and talk with each other. Video conferencing technology, in effect, allows employees to conduct interactive meetings without the necessity of everyone being physically in the same location.

In the late 1990s, video conferencing was basically conducted from special rooms equipped with television cameras, located at company facilities. More recently, cameras and microphones are being attached to individual computers, allowing people to participate in video conferences without leaving their desks. As the cost of this technology drops, video conferencing is likely to be increasingly seen as an alternative to expensive and time-consuming travel.

Knowledge Management

Our final topic under organizational communication is **knowledge management (KM)**. This is a process of organizing and distributing an organization's collective wisdom so the right information gets to the right people at the right time. When done properly, KM provides an organization with both a competitive edge and improved organizational performance because it makes its employees smarter. It can also help control leaks of vital company information so that an organization's competitive advantage is preserved for as long as possible. Despite its importance, KM gets low marks from most business leaders. When consulting firm Bain & Co. asked 960 executives about the effectiveness of twenty-five management tools, KM ranked near the bottom of the list. One expert concluded, "Most organizations are still managing as if we were in the industrial era."[24]

Effective KM begins by identifying what knowledge matters to the organization.[25] Management needs to review processes to identify those that provide the most value. Then it can develop computer networks and databases that can make that information readily available to the people who need it the most. But KM won't work unless the culture supports sharing of information. As we'll show in Chapter 12, information that is important and scarce can be a potent source of power. And people who hold that power are often reluctant to share it with others. So KM requires an organizational culture that promotes, values, and rewards sharing knowledge. Finally, KM must provide the mechanisms and the motivation for employees to share knowledge that employees find useful on the job and enables them to achieve better performance. *More* knowledge isn't necessarily *better* knowledge. Information overload needs to be avoided by designing the system to capture only pertinent information and then organizing it so it can be quickly accessed by the people whom it can help.

Finally, security is a huge concern with any KM system. A Merrill Lynch survey of fifty executives found that 52 percent rated leaks of company information as their number-one information security concern, topping viruses and hackers. In response, most companies actively monitor employee Internet use and e-mail records, and some even use video surveillance and record phone conversations. Necessary though they may be, such surveillance and monitoring practices may seem invasive to employees. An organization can buttress employee concerns by involving them in the creation of information-security policies and giving them some control over how their personal information is used.[26]

BARRIERS TO EFFECTIVE COMMUNICATION

A number of barriers can retard or distort effective communication. In this section, we highlight the most important of these barriers.

Filtering

Filtering refers to a sender's purposely manipulating information so it will be seen more favorably by the receiver. For example, when a manager tells his boss what he feels his boss wants to hear, he is filtering information.

The major determinant of filtering is the number of levels in an organization's structure. The more vertical levels in the organization's hierarchy, the more opportunities there are for filtering. But you can expect some filtering to occur wherever there are status differences. Factors such as fear of conveying bad news and the desire to please one's boss often lead employees to tell their superiors what they think those superiors want to hear, thus distorting upward communications.

Selective Perception

We have mentioned selective perception before in this book. It appears again here because the receivers in the communication process selectively see and hear based on their needs, motivations, experience, background, and other personal characteristics. Receivers also project their interests and expectations into communications as they decode them. An employment interviewer who expects a female job applicant to put her family ahead of her career is likely to see that in female applicants, regardless of whether the applicants actually feel that way. As we said in Chapter 3, we don't see reality; we interpret what we see and call it reality.

Information Overload

Individuals have a finite capacity for processing data. When the information we have to work with exceeds our processing capacity, the result is **information overload**. And with e-mails, IM, phone calls, faxes, meetings, and the need to keep current in one's field, the potential for today's managers and professionals to suffer from information overload is high.

What happens when individuals have more information than they can sort out and use? They tend to select, ignore, pass over, or forget information. Or they may put off further processing until the overload situation is over. In any case, the result is lost information and less effective communication.

Emotions

How the receiver feels at the time of receipt of a communication influences how he or she interprets it. The same message received when you're angry or distraught is often interpreted differently than it is when you're happy. Extreme emotions such as jubilation or depression are most likely to hinder effective communication. In such instances, we are most prone to disregard our rational and objective thinking processes and substitute emotional judgments.

Language

Even when we're communicating in the same language, words mean different things to different people. Age and context are two of the biggest factors that influence the language a person uses and the definitions he or she gives to words.

When Michael Schiller, a business consultant, was talking with his 15-year-old daughter about where she was going with her friends, he told her, "You need to recognize your ARAs and measure against them." Schiller said that in response, his daughter "looked at him like he was from outer space." (For the record, ARA stands for accountability, responsibility, and authority.) Those of you new to corporate lingo may find acronyms such as ARA, words such as "skeds" (schedules), or phrases such as "bake your noodle" (provide a service) to be bewildering, much in the same way that your parents may be mystified by the slang of your generation.[27]

The point is that although you and I probably speak a common language—English—our use of that language is far from uniform. If we knew how each of us modified the language, communication difficulties would be minimized. The problem is that members in an organization usually don't know how those with whom they interact have modified the language. Senders tend to assume that the words and terms they use mean the same to the receiver as they do to them. This assumption is often incorrect.

> —A number of barriers—such as culture—often retard or distort effective communication; understand these barriers as a means of overcoming them.

Communication Apprehension

Another major barrier to effective communication is that some people—an estimated 5 to 20 percent of the population[28]—suffer from debilitating **communication apprehension**, or anxiety. Lots of people dread speaking in front of a group, but communication apprehension is a more serious problem because it affects a whole category of communication techniques. People who suffer from it experience undue tension and anxiety in oral communication, written communication, or both.[29] For example, oral apprehensives may find it extremely difficult to talk with others face-to-face or may become extremely anxious when they have to use the telephone. As a result, they may rely on memos or faxes to convey messages when a phone call would be not only faster but more appropriate.

GLOBAL IMPLICATIONS

Effective communication is difficult under the best of conditions. Cross-cultural factors clearly create the potential for increased communication problems. This is illustrated in Exhibit 10-6. A gesture that is well understood and acceptable in one culture can be meaningless or lewd in another. Unfortunately, as business has become more global,

EXHIBIT 10-6   Hand Gestures Mean Different Things in Different Countries

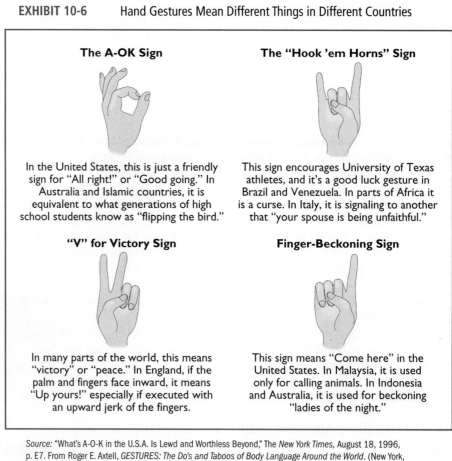

The A-OK Sign

In the United States, this is just a friendly sign for "All right!" or "Good going." In Australia and Islamic countries, it is equivalent to what generations of high school students know as "flipping the bird."

The "Hook 'em Horns" Sign

This sign encourages University of Texas athletes, and it's a good luck gesture in Brazil and Venezuela. In parts of Africa it is a curse. In Italy, it is signaling to another that "your spouse is being unfaithful."

"V" for Victory Sign

In many parts of the world, this means "victory" or "peace." In England, if the palm and fingers face inward, it means "Up yours!" especially if executed with an upward jerk of the fingers.

Finger-Beckoning Sign

This sign means "Come here" in the United States. In Malaysia, it is used only for calling animals. In Indonesia and Australia, it is used for beckoning "ladies of the night."

Source: "What's A-O-K in the U.S.A. Is Lewd and Worthless Beyond," The *New York Times,* August 18, 1996, p. E7. From Roger E. Axtell, *GESTURES: The Do's and Taboos of Body Language Around the World.* (New York, NY: John Wiley & Sons, 1991). Copyright © 1991. This material is used by permission of Wiley.

companies' communication approaches have not kept pace. Only 18 percent of companies have documented strategies for communicating with employees across cultures, and only 31 percent of companies require that corporate messages be customized for consumption in other cultures.[30]

Cultural Barriers   One author has identified four specific problems related to language difficulties in cross-cultural communications.[31]

First, there are *barriers caused by semantics*. As we've noted previously, words mean different things to different people. This is particularly true for people from different national cultures. Some words, for instance, don't translate between cultures.

Second, there are *barriers caused by word connotations*. Words imply different things in different languages. Negotiations between American and Japanese executives, for instance, can be difficult because the Japanese word *hai* translates as "yes," but its connotation is "yes, I'm listening" rather than "yes, I agree."

Third, there are *barriers caused by tone differences*. In some cultures, language is formal, and in others, it's informal. In some cultures, the tone changes, depending on the context: People speak differently at home, in social situations, and at work. Using a personal, informal style in a situation in which a more formal style is expected can be embarrassing and off-putting.

Fourth, there are *barriers caused by differences among perceptions*. People who speak different languages actually view the world in different ways. Eskimos perceive snow differently because they have many words for it. Thais perceive "no" differently than do Americans because the former have no such word in their vocabulary.

A Cultural Guide   When communicating with people from a different culture, what can you do to reduce misperceptions, misinterpretations, and misevaluations? You can begin by trying to assess (and deal with) the cultural barriers. In addition, the following four rules can be helpful:[32]

1. *Assume differences until similarity is proven.*   Most of us assume that others are more similar to us than they actually are. But people from different countries are often very different from us. You are therefore far less likely to make an error if you assume that others are different from you rather than assume similarity until difference is proven.
2. *Emphasize description rather than interpretation or evaluation.*   Interpreting or evaluating what someone has said or done, in contrast to description, is based more on the observer's culture and background than on the observed situation. As a result, delay judgment until you've had sufficient time to observe and interpret the situation from the differing perspectives of all the cultures involved.
3. *Practice empathy.*   Before sending a message, put yourself in the recipient's shoes. What are his or her values, experiences, and frames of reference? What do you know about his or her education, upbringing, and background that can give you added insight? Try to see the other person as he or she really is, as best you can.
4. *Treat your interpretations as a working hypothesis.*   Once you've developed an explanation for a new situation or think you empathize with someone from a foreign culture, treat your interpretation as a hypothesis that needs further testing rather than as a certainty. Carefully assess the feedback provided by recipients to see if it confirms your hypothesis. For important decisions or communiqués, you can also check with other foreign and home-country colleagues to make sure that your interpretations are on target.

IMPLICATIONS FOR MANAGERS

A careful review of this chapter yields a common theme regarding the relationship between communication and employee satisfaction: The less the uncertainty, the greater the satisfaction. Distortions, ambiguities, and incongruities in communications all increase uncertainty and, hence, have a negative impact on satisfaction.[33]

The less distortion that occurs in communication, the more that goals, feedback, and other management messages to employees will be received as they were intended.[34] This, in turn, should reduce ambiguities and clarify the group's task. Extensive use of vertical, lateral, and informal channels will increase communication flow, reduce uncertainty, and improve group performance and satisfaction. We should also expect incongruities between verbal and nonverbal communiqués to increase uncertainty and to reduce satisfaction.

Paying close attention to communication effectiveness is all the more important given the ways in which communication technology has transformed the workplace. Despite the great advantages of electronic communication formats, the pitfalls are numerous. Because we gather so much meaning from how a message is communicated (voice tone, facial expressions, body language), the potential for misunderstandings in electronic communication is great. E-mail, IM, and TM, and networking software are vital aspects of organizational communication, but we need to use these tools wisely, or we'll not be as effective as managers as we might be.

Finally, there are a lot of barriers to effective communication, such as culture. By keeping these barriers in mind, we can overcome them and increase our communication effectiveness.

Leadership

In this chapter, we'll look at the basic approaches to determining what makes an effective leader and what differentiates leaders from nonleaders. First, we'll present theories of leadership. Then, we'll discuss challenges to the meaning and importance of leadership. But before we review these approaches, let's first clarify what we mean by the term *leadership.*

WHAT IS LEADERSHIP?

Leadership and *management* are two terms that are often confused. What's the difference between them?

John Kotter of the Harvard Business School argues that management is about coping with complexity.[1] Good management brings about order and consistency by drawing up formal plans, designing rigid organization structures, and monitoring results against the plans. Leadership, in contrast, is about coping with change. Leaders establish direction by developing a vision of the future; then they align people by communicating this vision and inspiring them to overcome hurdles.

Although Kotter provides separate definitions of the two terms, both researchers and practicing managers frequently make no such distinctions. So we need to present leadership in a way that can capture how it is used in theory and practice.

We define **leadership** as the ability to influence a group toward the achievement of a vision or set of goals. The source of this influence may be formal, such as that provided by the possession of managerial rank in an organization. Because management positions come with some degree of formally designated authority, a person may assume a leadership role simply because of the position he or she holds in the organization. But not all leaders are managers, nor, for that matter, are all managers leaders. Just because an organization provides its managers with certain formal rights is no assurance that they will be able to lead effectively. We find that nonsanctioned leadership—that is, the ability to influence that arises outside the formal structure of the organization—is often as important or more important than formal influence. In other words, leaders can emerge from within a group as well as by formal appointment to lead a group.

—In today's dynamic world, leadership has the ability to influence a group toward the achievement of a vision or set of goals.

One last comment before we move on: Organizations need strong leadership *and* strong management for optimal effectiveness. In today's dynamic world, we need leaders to challenge the status quo, to create visions of the future, and to inspire organizational members to want to achieve the visions. We also need managers to formulate detailed plans, create efficient organizational structures, and oversee day-to-day operations.

In two major sections that follow, we present traditional and contemporary theories of leadership. Our objective in reviewing these theories is to give you an idea of the ingredients of effective leadership.

TRADITIONAL THEORIES OF LEADERSHIP

Trait Theories

Trait theories of leadership differentiate leaders from nonleaders by focusing on personal qualities and characteristics. The search for personality, social, physical, or intellectual attributes that would describe leaders and differentiate them from nonleaders goes back to the earliest stages of leadership research.

Research efforts at isolating leadership traits resulted in a number of dead ends. For instance, a review in the late 1960s of 20 different studies identified nearly 80 leadership traits, but only 5 of these traits were common to 4 or more of the investigations.[2] By the 1990s, after numerous studies and analyses, about the best thing that could be said was that most "leaders are not like other people," but the particular traits that were isolated varied a great deal from review to review.[3] It was a pretty confusing state of affairs.

A breakthrough, of sorts, came when researchers began organizing traits around the Big Five personality framework (see Chapter 2).[4] It became clear that most of the dozens of traits emerging in various leadership reviews could be subsumed under one of the Big Five traits and that this approach resulted in consistent and strong support for traits as predictors of leadership. For instance, ambition and energy—two common traits of leaders—are part of extraversion. Rather than focus on these two specific traits, it is better to think of them in terms of the more general trait of extraversion.

A comprehensive review of the leadership literature, when organized around the Big Five traits, has found that extraversion is the most important trait of effective leaders.[5] But results show that extraversion is more strongly related to leader emergence than to leader effectiveness. This is not totally surprising since sociable and dominant people are more likely to assert themselves in group situations. Although the assertive nature of extraverts is a positive, leaders need to make sure they're not too assertive—one study found that leaders who scored very high on assertiveness were less effective than those who were moderately high.[6]

Conscientiousness and openness to experience also showed strong and consistent relationships to leadership, though not quite as strong as extraversion. The traits of agreeableness and emotional stability weren't as strongly correlated with leadership. Overall, it does appear that the trait approach does have something to offer. Leaders who are extraverted (individuals who like being around people and are able to assert themselves), conscientious (individuals who are disciplined and keep commitments they make), and open (individuals who are creative and flexible) do seem to have an advantage when it comes to leadership, suggesting that good leaders do have key traits in common.

Recent studies are indicating that another trait that may indicate effective leadership is emotional intelligence (EI), which we discussed in Chapter 7. Advocates of EI argue that without it, a person can have outstanding training, a highly analytical mind, a compelling vision, and an endless supply of terrific ideas but still not make a great leader.[7] Despite these claims for its importance, the link between EI and leadership effectiveness is much less investigated than other traits. Until more rigorous evidence accumulates, we can't be confident about the connection.

Behavioral Theories

The failures of early trait studies led researchers in the late 1940s through the 1960s to go in a different direction. These **behavioral theories of leadership** were so named because they focused on observable behaviors, as opposed to underlying traits, exhibited by specific leaders. They wondered if there was something unique in the way that effective leaders behave. One relative advantage of the behavioral approach is that, since behaviors can be learned, we could *train* people to be leaders.

Ohio State Studies The most comprehensive and replicated of the behavioral theories resulted from research that began at Ohio State University in the late 1940s.[8] Researchers at Ohio State sought to identify independent dimensions of leader behavior. Beginning with over 1,000 dimensions, they eventually narrowed the list to two categories that substantially accounted for most of the leadership behavior described by employees. They called these two dimensions *initiating structure* and *consideration*.

Initiating structure refers to the extent to which a leader is likely to define and structure his or her role and those of employees in the search for goal attainment. It includes behavior that attempts to organize work, work relationships, and goals. A leader characterized as high in initiating structure could be described as someone who "assigns group members to particular tasks," "expects workers to maintain definite standards of performance," and "emphasizes the meeting of deadlines."

Consideration is described as the extent to which a person is likely to have job relationships that are characterized by mutual trust, respect for employees' ideas, and regard for their feelings. We could describe a leader high in consideration as one who helps employees with personal problems, is friendly and approachable, treats all employees as equals, and expresses appreciation and support. A recent survey of employees revealed that, when asked to indicate the factors that most motivated them at work, 66 percent mentioned appreciation. This speaks to the motivating potential of considerate leadership behavior.[9]

At one time, the results of the Ohio State studies were thought to be disappointing. One 1992 review concluded, "Overall, the research based on a two-factor conceptualization of leadership behavior has added little to our knowledge about effective leadership."[10] However, a more recent review suggests that this two-factor conceptualization was given a premature burial. A review of 160 studies found that both initiating structure and consideration were associated with effective leadership. Specifically, consideration was more strongly related to the behavior of the individual. In other words, the followers of leaders who were high in consideration were more satisfied with their jobs and more motivated and also had more respect for their leader. Initiating structure, however, was more strongly related to higher levels of group and organization productivity and more positive performance evaluations.

University of Michigan Studies   Leadership studies undertaken at the University of Michigan's Survey Research Center, at about the same time as those being conducted at Ohio State, had similar research objectives: to locate behavioral characteristics of leaders that appeared to be related to measures of performance effectiveness.

The Michigan group also came up with two dimensions of leadership behavior that they labeled *employee oriented* and *production oriented*. **Employee-oriented leaders** were described as emphasizing interpersonal relations; they took a personal interest in the needs of their employees and accepted individual differences among members. The **production-oriented leaders**, in contrast, tended to emphasize the technical or task aspects of their jobs—their main concern was in accomplishing each group's tasks, and the group members were a means to that end. These dimensions—employee oriented and production oriented—are closely related to the Ohio State dimensions. Employee-oriented leadership is similar to consideration, and production-oriented leadership is similar to initiating structure. In fact, most leadership researchers use the terms synonymously.

The conclusions arrived at by the Michigan researchers strongly favored the leaders who were employee oriented in their behavior. Employee-oriented leaders were associated with higher group productivity and higher job satisfaction. Production-oriented leaders tended to be associated with low group productivity and lower job satisfaction. Although the Michigan studies emphasized employee-oriented leadership (or consideration) over production-oriented leadership (or initiating structure), the Ohio State studies garnered more research attention and suggested that *both* consideration and initiating structure are important to effective leadership.[11] Blake and Mouton used the Ohio State and Michigan studies in proposing a **managerial grid** (sometimes called the *leadership grid*) based on the styles of *concern for people* and *concern for production*, which essentially represent the Ohio State dimensions of consideration and initiating structure or the Michigan dimensions of employee oriented and production oriented. They argued that leaders could increase their effectiveness by demonstrating higher concern for people and higher concern for production.

Summary of Trait Theories and Behavioral Theories

Judging from the evidence, the behavioral theories, like the trait theories, add to our understanding of leadership effectiveness. Leaders who have certain traits and who display consideration and structuring behaviors, do appear to be more effective. Perhaps trait theories and behavioral theories should be integrated. For example, you would think that conscientious leaders (conscientiousness is a trait) are more likely to be structuring

(structuring is a behavior). And maybe extraverted leaders (extraversion is a trait) are more likely to be considerate (consideration is a behavior). Unfortunately, we can't be sure there is a connection. Future research is needed to integrate these approaches.

Contingency Theories

Though the trait and behavioral theories contribute to our understanding of leadership, predicting leadership success is more complex than isolating a few traits or preferable behaviors. **Contingency theories** were developed to focus on situational influences on leadership effectiveness suggested that under condition *a*, style *x* would be appropriate, whereas style *y* would be more suitable for condition *b*, and style *z* would be more suitable for condition *c*. But what were the conditions *a*, *b*, *c*, and so forth? We shall consider two contingency theories: the *Fiedler model* and the *leader–member exchange theory*.

Fiedler Model The first comprehensive contingency model for leadership was developed by Fred Fiedler.[12] The **Fiedler contingency model** proposes that effective group performance depends on the proper match between the leader's style and the degree to which the situation gives control to the leader.

Fiedler believes a key factor in leadership success is the individual's basic leadership style. So he begins by trying to find out the basic style. Fiedler created the **least preferred coworker (LPC) questionnaire** for this purpose; it purports to measure whether a person is task or relationship oriented. The LPC questionnaire contains sets of 16 contrasting adjectives (such as pleasant–unpleasant, efficient–inefficient, open–guarded, supportive–hostile). It asks respondents to think of all the coworkers they have ever had and to describe the one person they *least enjoyed* working with by rating that person on a scale of 1 to 8 for each of the 16 sets of contrasting adjectives. Fiedler believes that based on the respondents' answers to this LPC questionnaire, he can determine their basic leadership styles. If the least preferred coworker is described in relatively positive terms (a high LPC score), then the respondent is primarily interested in good personal relations with this coworker. That is, if you essentially describe the person you are least able to work with in favorable terms, Fiedler would label you *relationship oriented*. In contrast, if the least preferred coworker is seen in relatively unfavorable terms (a low LPC score), the respondent is interested primarily in productivity and thus would be labeled *task oriented*. About 16 percent of respondents score in the middle range. Such individuals cannot be classified as either relationship oriented or task oriented and thus fall outside the theory's predictions. The rest of our discussion, therefore, relates to the 84 percent who score in either the high or low range of the LPC.

Fiedler assumes that an individual's leadership style is fixed. If a situation requires a task-oriented leader and the person in that leadership position is relationship oriented, either the situation has to be modified or the leader replaced to achieve optimal effectiveness.

After an individual's basic leadership style has been assessed through the LPC, management must match the leader with the situation. Fiedler has identified three contingency dimensions that, he argues, define the key situational factors that determine leadership effectiveness:

1. *Leader–member relations:* The degree of confidence, trust, and respect members have in a leader
2. *Task structure:* The degree to which job assignments are structured or unstructured

3. *Position power:* The degree of influence a leader has over power variables such as hiring, firing, discipline, promotions, and salary increases

The next step in the Fiedler model is to evaluate the situation in terms of these three contingency variables:

- Leader–member relations are either good or poor.
- Task structure is either high or low.
- Position power is either strong or weak.

Fiedler states that the better the leader–member relations, the more highly structured the job, and the stronger the position power, the more control the leader has. For instance, a very favorable situation (in which the leader would have a great deal of control) might involve a payroll manager who is well respected and whose employees have confidence in her (good leader–member relations), for which the activities to be done—such as wage computation, check writing, report filing—are specific and clear (high task structure), and for whom the job provides considerable freedom for the manager to reward and punish her employees (strong position power). However, an unfavorable situation might involve the disliked chairperson of a voluntary United Way fund-raising team with very little control in the job. Altogether, by compiling the three contingency dimensions, we find eight potential situations or categories in which leaders could find themselves (see Exhibit 11-1).

With the knowledge of an individual's LPC and an assessment of the three contingency dimensions, the Fiedler model proposes matching them up to achieve maximum leadership effectiveness. Based on his research, Fiedler concluded that task-oriented

EXHIBIT 11-1   Findings from the Fiedler Model

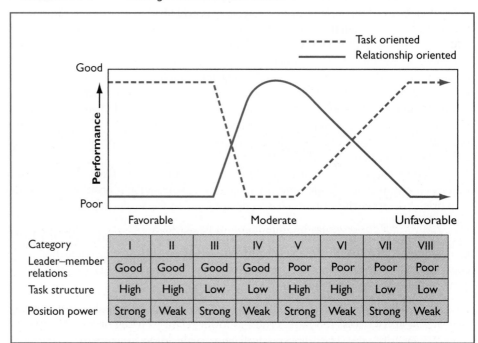

Category	I	II	III	IV	V	VI	VII	VIII
Leader–member relations	Good	Good	Good	Good	Poor	Poor	Poor	Poor
Task structure	High	High	Low	Low	High	High	Low	Low
Position power	Strong	Weak	Strong	Weak	Strong	Weak	Strong	Weak

leaders tend to perform better in situations that were very favorable to them and in situations that were very unfavorable (see Exhibit 11-1). So Fiedler would predict that when faced with a category I, II, III, VII, or VIII situation, task-oriented leaders perform better. Relationship-oriented leaders, however, perform better in moderately favorable situations—categories IV through VI. In recent years, Fiedler has condensed these eight situations into three. He now says that task-oriented leaders perform best in situations of high and low control, whereas relationship-oriented leaders perform best in situations of moderate control.

You would apply Fiedler's findings by matching leaders and situations. Individuals' LPC scores would determine the types of situations for which they were best suited. Such situations would be defined by evaluating the three contingency factors of leader–member relations, task structure, and position power. But remember that Fiedler views an individual's leadership style as being fixed. Therefore, leader effectiveness can be improved in only two ways:

1. *Change the leader to fit the situation:* As in a baseball game, a manager can put a right-handed pitcher or a left-handed pitcher into the game, depending on the situational characteristics of the hitter. So, for instance, if a group situation rates as highly unfavorable but is currently led by a relationship-oriented manager, the group's performance could be improved by replacing that manager with one who is task oriented.

2. *Change the situation to fit the leader:* That could be done by restructuring tasks or increasing or decreasing the power that the leader has to control factors such as salary increases, promotions, and disciplinary actions.

As a whole, reviews of the major studies that tested the overall validity of the Fiedler model lead to a generally positive conclusion. Considerable evidence supports at least substantial parts of the model.[13] If predictions from the model use only three categories rather than the original eight, ample evidence supports Fiedler's conclusions. But problems with the LPC and the practical use of the model must be addressed. For instance, the logic underlying the LPC is not well understood, and studies have shown that respondents' LPC scores are not stable. Also, the contingency variables are complex and difficult for practitioners to assess. It's often difficult in practice to determine how good the leader–member relations are, how structured the task is, and how much position power the leader has.

Leader–Member Exchange Theory   The leadership theories we've covered to this point have largely assumed that leaders treat all of their individual followers in the same manner. They assume leaders use a fairly homogeneous style with all of the people in their work units. But think about your experiences in groups. Did you notice that leaders often act differently toward different people? Did the leader tend to have favorites who made up his or her in-group? If you answered "yes" to both these questions, you're acknowledging the foundation of leader–member exchange theory. The **leader–member exchange (LMX) theory** argues that because of time pressures, leaders establish a special relationship with small group of their followers. These individuals make up the *in-group:* They are trusted, get a disproportionate amount of the leader's attention, and are more likely to receive special privileges. Other followers fall into the *out-group:* They get less of the leader's time, few of the preferred rewards that the leader controls, and have leader–follower relations based on formal authority interactions. LMX is a contingency theory because the leader's actions vary depending on their relationship with each of their followers. Unlike LPC theory, however, the contingency is not the leader's environment but instead is the leader's unique relationship with each of his or her followers.

The theory proposes that early in the history of the interaction between a leader and a given follower, the leader implicitly categorizes the follower as an *in* or an *out* and that relationship is relatively stable over time. Leaders induce LMX by rewarding those employees with whom they want a closer linkage and punishing those with whom they do not. But for the LMX relationship to remain intact, the leader and the follower must invest in the relationship.

How the leader chooses who falls into each category is unclear, but evidence suggests that leaders tend to choose in-group members because they have attitude and personality characteristics that are similar to their own or a higher level of competence than do out-group members (see Exhibit 11-2).[14] For instance, followers who have a mastery orientation—who place high priority on learning what is required to perform the job well—develop closer leader–member exchanges because such employees turn to their supervisors for sources of valuable information and experience. As a result, employees are provided with prospects for skill development and self-improvement that can further benefit the organization.[15] However, communicating frequently with a supervisor appears to be helpful only for high-LMX employees, probably because supervisors perceive frequent communication from low-LMX employees as annoying and a waste of their time.[16] The key point to note here is that even though it is the leader who is doing the choosing, it is the follower's characteristics that drive the leader's categorizing decision.

Research to test LMX theory has been generally supportive. More specifically, the theory and research surrounding it provide substantive evidence of the following:

- Leaders do differentiate among followers.
- These disparities are far from random.
- Followers with in-group status will have higher performance ratings, lower turnover intentions, greater satisfaction with their superiors, and higher overall satisfaction than will the out-group.[17]

EXHIBIT 11-2   Leader–Member Exchange Theory

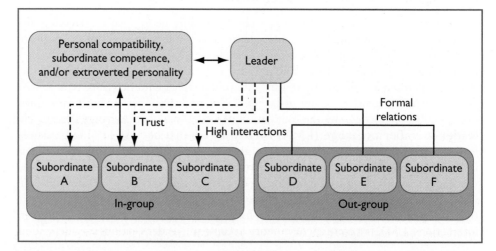

These positive findings for in-group members shouldn't be totally surprising given our knowledge of the self-fulfilling prophecy. Leaders invest their resources with those they expect to perform best. And with the belief that in-group members are the most competent, leaders treat them as such and unwittingly fulfill their prophecies.[18]

CONTEMPORARY APPROACHES TO LEADERSHIP

Traditional approaches to leadership—those we've just considered—ignore the importance of the leader as a communicator. **Framing** is a way of communicating to shape meaning. It's a way for leaders to influence how others see and understand events. It includes selecting and highlighting one or more aspects of a subject while excluding others. Framing is especially important to an aspect of leadership ignored in the traditional theories: the ability of the leader to inspire others to act beyond their immediate self-interests.

In this section, we present two contemporary leadership theories with a common theme. They view leaders as individuals who inspire followers through their words, ideas, and behaviors. These theories are charismatic leadership and transformational leadership. Then we consider the newest contemporary approach, one that considers the authentic and ethical aspects of leadership.

Charismatic Leadership

John F. Kennedy, Martin Luther King, Jr., Ronald Reagan, Bill Clinton, Mary Kay Ash (founder of Mary Kay Cosmetics), and Steve Jobs (co-founder of Apple Computer) are individuals frequently cited as being charismatic leaders. So what do they have in common?

What Is Charismatic Leadership? Max Weber, a sociologist, was the first scholar to discuss charismatic leadership. More than a century ago, he defined *charisma* (from the Greek for "gift") as "a certain quality of an individual personality, by virtue of which he or she is set apart from ordinary people and treated as endowed with supernatural, superhuman, or at least specifically exceptional powers or qualities."

The first researcher to consider charismatic leadership in terms of OB was Robert House. According to House's **charismatic leadership theory**, followers make attributions of heroic or extraordinary leadership abilities when they observe certain behaviors.[19] There have been a number of studies that have attempted to identify the characteristics of the charismatic leader. One of the best reviews of the literature has documented four—they have a vision, they are willing to take personal risks to achieve that vision, they are sensitive to follower needs, and they exhibit behaviors that are out of the ordinary.[20] These characteristics are described in Exhibit 11-3.

Are Charismatic Leaders Born or Made? Are charismatic leaders born with their qualities? Or can people actually learn how to be charismatic leaders? The answer to both questions is "yes."

Although a small minority thinks that charisma is inherited and therefore cannot be learned, most experts believe that individuals also can be trained to exhibit charismatic behaviors and can thus enjoy the benefits that accompany being labeled "a charismatic leader."[21] After all, just because we inherit certain tendencies doesn't mean that we can't learn to change. One set of authors proposes that a person can

EXHIBIT 11-3   Key Characteristics of Charismatic Leaders

1. *Vision and articulation.* Has a vision—expressed as an idealized goal—that proposes a future better than the status quo and is able to clarify the importance of the vision in terms that are understandable to others.

2. *Personal risk.* Willing to take on high personal risk, incur high costs, and engage in self-sacrifice to achieve the vision.

3. *Sensitivity to follower needs.* Perceptive of others' abilities and responsive to their needs and feelings.

4. *Unconventional behavior.* Engages in behaviors that are perceived as novel and counter to norms.

Source: Based on J. A. Conger and R. N. Kanungo, *Charismatic Leadership in Organizations* (Thousand Oaks, CA: Sage Publications, 1998), p. 94.

learn to become charismatic by following a three-step process.[22] First, an individual needs to develop an aura of charisma by maintaining an optimistic view; using passion as a catalyst for generating enthusiasm; and communicating with the whole body, not just with words. Second, an individual draws others in by creating a bond that inspires others to follow. Third, the individual brings out the potential in followers by tapping into their emotions.

The three-step approach seems to work, as evidenced by researchers who have succeeded in actually scripting undergraduate business students to "play" charismatic.[23] The students were taught to articulate an overarching goal, communicate high performance expectations, exhibit confidence in the ability of followers to meet these expectations, and empathize with the needs of their followers; they learned to project a powerful, confident, and dynamic presence; and they practiced using a captivating and engaging voice tone. To further capture the dynamics and energy of charisma, the leaders were trained to evoke charismatic nonverbal characteristics: They alternated between pacing and sitting on the edges of their desks, leaned toward the subjects, maintained direct eye contact, and had relaxed postures and animated facial expressions. These researchers found that the students could learn how to project charisma. Moreover, followers of these leaders had higher task performance, task adjustment, and adjustment to the leader and to the group than did followers who worked under groups led by noncharismatic leaders.

How Charismatic Leaders Influence Followers   How do charismatic leaders actually influence followers? The evidence suggests a four-step process.[24] It begins by the leader articulating an appealing **vision**. A vision is a long-term strategy for how to attain a goal or goals. The vision provides a sense of continuity for followers by linking the present with a better future for the organization. For example, at Apple, Steve Jobs championed the iPod, noting, "It's as Apple as anything Apple has ever done." The creation of the iPod achieved Apple's goal of offering groundbreaking and easy-to-use-technology. Apple's strategy was to create a product that had a user-friendly interface where songs could be quickly uploaded and easily organized. It was the first major-market device to link data storage capabilities with music downloading.

Next, the leader conveys, through words and actions, a new set of values and, by his or her behavior, sets an example for followers to imitate. One study of Israeli bank employees showed, for example, that charismatic leaders were more effective because their employees personally identified with the leaders. Finally, the charismatic leader engages in emotion-inducing and often unconventional behavior to demonstrate courage and convictions about the vision. There is an emotional contagion in charismatic leadership whereby followers "catch" the emotions their leader is conveying.[25] The next time you see Martin Luther King, Jr.'s "I Have a Dream" speech, focus on the reactions of the crowd, and it will bring to light how a charismatic leader can spread his emotion to his followers.

Does Effective Charismatic Leadership Depend on the Situation? There is an increasing body of research that shows impressive correlations between charismatic leadership and high performance and satisfaction among followers.[26] People working for charismatic leaders are motivated to exert extra work effort and, because they like and respect their leader, express greater satisfaction. It also appears that organizations with charismatic CEOs are more profitable. And charismatic college professors enjoy higher course evaluations.[27] However, there is a growing body of evidence indicating that charisma may not always be generalizable; that is, its effectiveness may depend on the situation. Charisma appears to be most successful when the follower's task has an ideological component or when the environment involves a high degree of stress and uncertainty.[28] This may explain why, when charismatic leaders surface, it's likely to be in politics, religion, wartime, or when a business firm is in its infancy or facing a life-threatening crisis. For example, in the early 1970s, when Chrysler Corp. was on the brink of bankruptcy, it needed a charismatic leader with unconventional ideas like Lee Iacocca to reinvent the company. In 1997, when Apple Computer was floundering and lacking direction, the board persuaded charismatic co-founder Steve Jobs to return as interim CEO and to inspire the company to return to its innovative roots.

In addition to ideology and uncertainty, another situational factor limiting charisma appears to be level in the organization. Remember that the creation of a vision is a key component of charisma. But visions typically apply to entire organizations or major divisions. They tend to be created by top executives. Charisma therefore probably has more direct relevance to explaining the success and failures of chief executives than of lower-level managers. So even though an individual may have an inspiring personality, it's more difficult to utilize the person's charismatic leadership qualities in lower-level management jobs. Lower-level managers *can* create visions to lead their units. It's just harder to define such visions and align them with the larger goals of the organization as a whole.

Finally, charismatic leadership may affect some followers more than others. Research suggests, for example, that people are especially receptive to charismatic leadership when they sense a crisis, when they are under stress, or when they fear for their lives. More generally, some people's personalities are especially susceptible to charismatic leadership.[29] Consider self-esteem. If an individual lacks self-esteem and questions his self-worth, he is more likely to absorb a leader's direction rather than establish his own way of leading or thinking.

The Dark Side of Charismatic Leadership Charismatic business leaders like AIG's Hank Greenberg, GE's Jack Welch, Tyco's Dennis Kozlowski, Southwest Airlines' Herb Kelleher, Disney's Michael Eisner, and HP's Carly Fiorina became celebrities on the order of David Beckham and Madonna. Every company wanted a charismatic CEO. And to attract these people, boards of directors gave them unprecedented autonomy and resources. They had private jets at their beck and call, use of $30 million penthouses, interest-free loans to buy beach homes and artwork, security staffs provided by their companies, and similar benefits befitting royalty. One study showed that charismatic CEOs were able to use their charisma to leverage higher salaries even when their performance was mediocre.[30]

Unfortunately, charismatic leaders who are larger-than-life don't necessarily act in the best interests of their organizations.[31] Many of these leaders used their power to remake their companies in their own image. These leaders often completely blurred the boundary separating their personal interests from their organization's interests. The perils of this ego-driven charisma at its worst are leaders who allow their self-interest and personal goals to override the goals of the organization. Intolerant of criticism, they surround themselves with yes people who are rewarded for pleasing the leader and create a climate where people are afraid to question or challenge the "king" or "queen" when they think he or she is making a mistake. The results at companies such as Enron, Tyco, WorldCom, and HealthSouth were leaders who recklessly used organizational resources for their personal benefit and executives who broke laws and crossed ethical lines to generate financial numbers that temporarily inflated stock prices and allowed leaders to cash in millions of dollars in stock options.

We don't mean to suggest that charismatic leadership isn't effective. Overall, its effectiveness is well supported. The point is that a charismatic leader isn't always the answer. Yes, an organization with a charismatic leader at the helm is more likely to be successful, but that success depends, to some extent, on the situation and on the leader's vision. Some charismatic leaders—Hitler, for example—are all too successful at convincing their followers to pursue a vision that can be disastrous.

Now we turn our attention to a related theory, transformational leadership. Although the theories share many similarities, they also have their differences. We'll explicitly compare the two theories after first reviewing the basic tenets of the transformational leadership theory.

Transformational Leadership

A stream of research has focused on differentiating transformational leaders from transactional leaders.[32] Most of the leadership theories presented earlier—both the Ohio State studies and Fiedler's model—have concerned **transactional leaders**. These kinds of leaders guide or motivate their followers in the direction of established goals by clarifying role and task requirements. **Transformational leaders** inspire followers to transcend their own self-interests for the good of the organization and are capable of having a profound and extraordinary effect on their followers. They pay attention to the concerns and developmental needs of individual followers; they change followers' awareness of issues by helping them to look at old problems in new ways; and they are able to excite, arouse, and inspire followers to put out extra effort to achieve group goals. Exhibit 11-4 briefly identifies and defines the characteristics that differentiate these two types of leaders.

Transactional and transformational leadership shouldn't be viewed as opposing approaches to getting things done. Transformational and transactional leadership complement each other, but that doesn't mean they're equally important. Transformational leadership builds *on top of* transactional leadership and produces levels of follower effort and performance that go beyond what would occur with a transactional approach

EXHIBIT 11-4   Characteristics of Transactional and Transformational Leaders

---

Transactional Leader

Contingent Reward: Contracts exchange of rewards for effort, promises rewards for good performance, recognizes accomplishments.

Management by Exception (active): Watches and searches for deviations from rules and standards, takes correct action.

Management by Exception (passive): Intervenes only if standards are not met.

Laissez-Faire: Abdicates responsibilities, avoids making decisions.

Transformational Leader

Idealized Influence: Provides vision and sense of mission, instills pride, gains respect and trust.

Inspirational Motivation: Communicates high expectations, uses symbols to focus efforts, expresses important purposes in simple ways.

Intellectual Stimulation: Promotes intelligence, rationality, and careful problem solving.

Individualized Consideration: Gives personal attention, treats each employee individually, coaches, advises.

Source: B. M. Bass, "From Transactional to Transformational Leadership: Learning to Share the Vision," *Organizational Dynamics,* Winter 1990, p. 22. Reprinted by permission of the publisher, American Management Association, New York. All rights reserved.

alone. But the reverse isn't true. So if you are a good transactional leader but do not have transformational qualities, you'll likely only be a mediocre leader. The best leaders are transactional *and* transformational.

Full Range of Leadership Model   Exhibit 11-5 shows the full range of the leadership model. Laissez-faire is the most passive and therefore the least effective of the leader behaviors. Leaders using this style are rarely viewed as effective. Management by exception—regardless of whether it is active or passive—is slightly better than laissez-faire, but it's still considered ineffective leadership. Leaders who practice management by exception leadership tend to be available only when there is a problem, which is often too late. Contingent reward leadership can be an effective style of leadership. However, leaders will not get their employees to go above and beyond the call of duty when practicing this style of leadership. Only with the four remaining leadership styles—which are all aspects of transformational leadership—are leaders able to motivate followers to perform above expectations and transcend their own self-interest for the sake of the organization. Individualized consideration, intellectual stimulation, inspirational motivation, and idealized influence all result in extra effort from workers, higher productivity, higher morale and satisfaction, higher organizational effectiveness, lower turnover, lower absenteeism, and greater organizational adaptability. Based on this model, leaders are generally most effective when they regularly use each of the four transformational behaviors.

How Transformational Leadership Works   In the past few years, a great deal of research has been conducted to explain how transformational leadership works. Transformational leaders encourage their followers to be more innovative and creative.[33] Transformational leaders are more effective because they themselves are more creative, but they're also more effective because they encourage those who follow them to be creative, too.

Goals are another key mechanism that explain how transformational leadership works. Followers of transformational leaders are more likely to pursue ambitious

EXHIBIT 11-5　　Full Range of Leadership Model

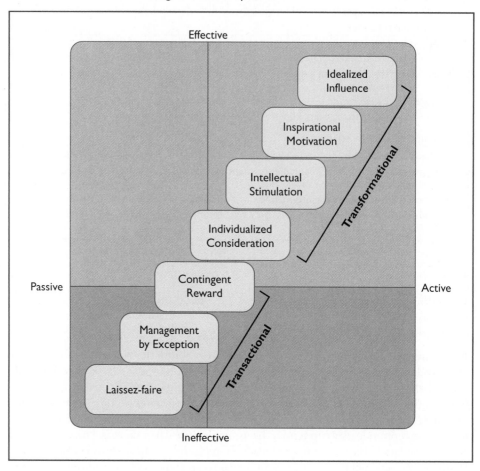

goals, be familiar with and agree on the strategic goals of the organization, and believe that the goals they are pursuing are personally important.[34] Goals are closely linked to our earlier discussion of vision—one might think of a vision as a statement of collective goals. Just as research has shown that vision is important in explaining how charismatic leadership works, research has also shown that vision explains part of the effect of transformational leadership. Indeed, one study found that vision was even more important than a charismatic (effusive, dynamic, lively) communication style in explaining the success of entrepreneurial firms.[35]

Evaluation of Transformational Leadership　　The evidence supporting the superiority of transformational leadership over transactional leadership is impressive. Transformational leadership has been supported in disparate occupations (for example, school principals, marine commanders, ministers, presidents of MBA associations, military cadets, union shop stewards, school teachers, sales reps) and at various job levels. One recent study of R&D firms found, for example, that teams led by project leaders who scored high on transformational leadership produced better-quality products as judged 1 year later and were more profitable 5 years later.[36] A review of eighty-seven studies testing transformational leadership found that it was related to the motivation and satisfaction of followers and to the higher performance and perceived effectiveness of leaders.[37]

Transformational leadership theory is not perfect. There are concerns about whether contingent reward leadership is strictly a characteristic of transactional leaders only. And contrary to the full range of leadership model, contingent reward leadership is sometimes more effective than transformational leadership.

In summary, the overall evidence indicates that transformational leadership is more strongly correlated than transactional leadership with lower turnover rates, higher productivity, lower employee stress and burnout, and higher employee satisfaction.[38] Like charisma, it appears that transformational leadership can be learned. One study of Canadian bank managers found that those managers who underwent transformational leadership training had bank branches that performed significantly better than branches with managers who did not undergo training. Other studies show similar results.[39]

Transformational Leadership Versus Charismatic Leadership　There is some debate about whether transformational leadership and charismatic leadership are the same. The researcher most responsible for introducing charismatic leadership to OB, Robert House, considers them synonymous, calling the differences "modest" and "minor." However, the individual who first researched transformational leadership, Bernard Bass, considers charisma to be part of transformational leadership but argues that transformational leadership is broader than charisma, suggesting that charisma is, by itself, insufficient to "account for the transformational process."[40] Another researcher commented, "The purely charismatic [leader] may want followers to adopt the charismatic's worldview and go no further; the transformational leader will attempt to instill in followers the ability to question not only established views but eventually those established by the leader."[41] Although many researchers believe that transformational leadership is broader than charismatic leadership, studies show that in reality a leader who scores high on transformational leadership is also likely to score high on charisma. Therefore, in practice, measures of charisma and transformational leadership may be roughly equivalent.

AUTHENTIC LEADERSHIP: ARE ETHICS THE FOUNDATION OF LEADERSHIP?

Although charismatic leadership theories and transformational leadership theories have added greatly to our understanding of effective leadership, they do not explicitly deal with the role of ethics and trust. Some scholars have argued that a consideration of ethics and trust is essential to complete the picture of effective leadership. Here we consider these two concepts under the rubric of authentic leadership.[42]

What Is Authentic Leadership?

Douglas R. Conant is not your typical CEO. His style is decidedly understated. When asked to reflect on the strong performance of Campbell Soup, he demurs, "We're hitting our stride a little bit more (than our peers)." He regularly admits mistakes and often says, "I can do better." Conant appears to be a good exemplar of authentic leadership.[43]

Authentic leaders know who they are, know what they believe in and value, and act on those values and beliefs openly and candidly. Their followers would consider them to be ethical people. The primary quality, therefore, produced by authentic leadership is trust. How does authentic leadership build trust? Authentic leaders share information, encourage open communication, and stick to their ideals. The result: People come to have faith in authentic leaders.

Because the concept is so recent, there hasn't been a lot of research on authentic leadership. However, we believe it's a promising way to think about ethics and trust in leadership because it focuses on the moral aspects of being a leader. Transformational or charismatic leaders can have a vision, and communicate it persuasively, but sometimes the vision is wrong (as in the case of Hitler), or the leader is more concerned with his own needs or pleasures, as in the case with business leaders Tyco ex-CEO Dennis Kozlowski and Enron ex-CEO Enron Jeff Skilling, both of whom are in jail.[44]

> —If we're looking for the best possible leader, it is not enough to be charismatic or visionary—one must also be ethical and authentic.

Ethics and Leadership

The topic of ethics and leadership has received surprisingly little attention. Only recently have ethicists and leadership researchers begun to consider the ethical implications in leadership.[45] Why now? One reason may be the growing general interest in ethics throughout the field of management. Another reason may be the discovery by probing biographers that many of our past leaders—such as Martin Luther King, Jr., John F. Kennedy, and Thomas Jefferson—suffered from ethical shortcomings. Ethical lapses by business leaders are never absent from the headlines. Some companies, like Boeing, are even tying executive compensation to ethics. They've done so to reinforce the idea that "there's no compromise between doing things the right way and performance," in the words of Boeing's CEO Jim McNerney.[46]

Ethics touches on leadership at a number of junctures. Transformational leaders, for instance, have been described by one authority as fostering moral virtue when they try to change the attitudes and behaviors of followers. Charisma, too, has an ethical component. Unethical leaders are more likely to use their charisma to enhance *power* over followers, directed toward self-serving ends. Ethical leaders are considered to use their charisma in a socially constructive way to serve others. There is also the issue of abuse of power by leaders, for example, when they give themselves large salaries, bonuses, and stock options while, at the same time, they seek to cut costs by laying off long-time employees. Because top executives set the moral tone for an organization, they need to set high ethical standards, demonstrate those standards through their own behavior, and encourage and reward integrity in others.

Leadership effectiveness needs to address the *means* a leader uses in trying to achieve goals, as well as the content of those goals. Recently, scholars have tried to integrate ethical and charismatic leadership by advancing the idea of **socialized charismatic leadership**—leadership that conveys values that are other-centered versus self-centered by leaders who model ethical conduct.[47]

Leadership is not value free. Before we judge any leader to be effective, we should consider both the means used by the leader to achieve goals and the moral content of those goals.

CHALLENGES TO THE LEADERSHIP CONSTRUCT

A noted management expert takes issue with the omnipotent role that academicians, practicing managers, and the general public have given to the concept of leadership. He says, "In the 1500s, people ascribed all events they didn't understand to God. Why did the crops fail? God. Why did someone die? God. Now our all-purpose explanation is leadership."[48] He notes that when a company succeeds, people need to give the credit to someone. And that's typically the firm's CEO. Similarly, when a company does poorly, people need someone to blame. CEOs also play this role. But much of an organization's success or failure is due to factors outside the influence of leadership. In many cases, success or failure is just a matter of being in the right or wrong place at a given time.

In this section, we will present two perspectives that challenge the widely accepted belief in the importance of leadership. The first argument proposes that leadership is more about appearances than reality. You don't have to *be* an effective leader as long as you *look* like one. The second argument directly attacks the notion that some leadership *will always be effective*, regardless of the situation. This argument contends that in many situations, whatever actions leaders exhibit are irrelevant.

Leadership as an Attribution

We introduced attribution theory in Chapter 3. As you may remember, it deals with the ways in which people try to make sense out of cause-and-effect relationships. We said that when something happens, we want to attribute it to something else. The **attribution theory of leadership** says that leadership is merely an attribution that people make about other individuals.[49] The attribution theory has shown that people characterize leaders as having such traits as intelligence, an outgoing personality, strong verbal skills, aggressiveness, understanding, and industriousness.[50] At the organizational level, the attribution framework accounts for the conditions under which people use leadership to explain organizational outcomes. Those conditions are extremes in organizational performance. When an organization has either extremely negative or extremely positive performance, people are prone to make leadership attributions to explain the performance.[51] As noted earlier, this tendency helps to account for the vulnerability of CEOs (and high-ranking state officials) when their organizations suffer a major financial setback, regardless of whether they had much to do with it, and it also accounts for why CEOs tend to be given credit for extremely positive financial results—again, regardless of how much or how little they contributed.

One longitudinal study of 128 major U.S. corporations provided important support for the attributional approach. Analyzing top management team members' perceptions of the charisma of their CEOs and their companies' objective performance, this study found that, whereas perceptions of CEO charisma did not lead to objective company performance, company performance did lead to perceptions of charisma.[52]

Following the attribution theory of leadership, we'd say that what's important in being characterized as an "effective leader" is projecting the *appearance* of being a leader rather than focusing on *actual accomplishments*. Leader-wannabes can attempt to shape the perception that they're smart, personable, verbally adept, aggressive, hardworking, and consistent in their style. By doing so, they increase the probability that their bosses, colleagues, and employees will *view* them as an effective leader.

Substitutes for and Neutralizers of Leadership

Contrary to the arguments made throughout this chapter, leadership may not always be important. A theory of leadership suggests that, in many situations, whatever actions leaders exhibit are irrelevant. Certain individual, job, and organizational variables can act as *substitutes* for leadership or *neutralize* the leader's influence on his or her followers.[53]

Neutralizers make it impossible for leader behavior to make any difference to follower outcomes. They negate the leader's influence. Substitutes, however, make a leader's influence not only impossible but also unnecessary. They act as a replacement for the leader's influence. For instance, characteristics of employees such as their experience, training, "professional" orientation, or indifference toward organizational rewards can substitute for, or neutralize the effect of, leadership. Experience and training can replace the need for a leader's support or ability to create structure and reduce task ambiguity. Jobs that are inherently unambiguous and routine or that are intrinsically satisfying may place fewer demands on the leadership variable. Organizational characteristics such as explicit, formalized goals, rigid rules and procedures, and cohesive work groups can also replace formal leadership (see Exhibit 11-6).

This recognition that leaders don't always have an impact on follower outcomes should not be that surprising. After all, we have introduced a number of variables in this text—attitudes, personality, ability, and group norms, to name but a few—that have been documented as having an effect on employee performance and satisfaction. Yet supporters of the leadership concept place an undue burden on this variable for explaining and predicting behavior. It's too simplistic to consider employees as guided to goal accomplishments solely by the actions of their leader. It's important, therefore, to recognize explicitly that leadership is merely another independent variable in our overall OB model. In some situations, it may contribute a lot to explaining employee productivity, absence, turnover, satisfaction, and citizenship behavior, but in other situations, it may contribute little toward that end.

The validity of substitutes and neutralizers is controversial. One of the problems is that the theory is very complicated: There are many possible substitutes for and neutralizers of many different types of leader behaviors across many different situations. Moreover, sometimes the difference between substitutes and neutralizers is fuzzy. For example, if I'm working on a task that's intrinsically enjoyable, the theory predicts that leadership will be less important because the task itself provides enough motivation. But does that mean that intrinsically enjoyable tasks neutralize leadership effects, or substitute for them, or both? Another problem that this review points out is that substitutes for leadership (such as employee characteristics, the nature of the task, and so forth) matter, but it does not appear that they substitute for or neutralize leadership.[54]

FINDING AND CREATING EFFECTIVE LEADERS

We have covered a lot of ground in this chapter on leadership. But the ultimate goal of our review is to answer this question: How can organizations find or create effective leaders? Let's try to answer that question.

EXHIBIT 11-6   Substitutes and Neutralizers for Leadership

Defining Characteristics	Relationship-Oriented Leadership	Task-Oriented Leadership
Individual		
Experience/training	No effect on	Substitutes for
Professionalism	Substitutes for	Substitutes for
Indifference to rewards	Neutralizes	Neutralizes
Job		
Highly structured task	No effect on	Substitutes for
Provides its own feedback	No effect on	Substitutes for
Intrinsically satisfying	Substitutes for	No effect on
Organization		
Explicit, formalized goals	No effect on	Substitutes for
Rigid rules and procedures	No effect on	Substitutes for
Cohesive work groups	Substitutes for	Substitutes for

Source: Based on S. Kerr and J. M. Jermier, "Substitutes for Leadership: Their Meaning and Measurement,"
Organizational Behavior and Human Performance, December 1978, p. 378.

Selecting Leaders

The entire process that organizations go through to fill management positions is essentially an exercise in trying to identify individuals who will be effective leaders. Your search might begin by reviewing the specific requirements for the position to be filled. What knowledge, skills, and abilities are needed to do the job effectively? You should try to analyze the situation to find candidates who will make a proper match.

Testing is useful for identifying and selecting leaders. Personality tests can be used to look for traits associated with leadership—extraversion, conscientiousness, and openness to experience. Interviews also provide an opportunity to evaluate leadership candidates. For instance, we know that experience is a poor predictor of leader effectiveness, but situation-specific experience is relevant. You can use an interview to determine whether a candidate's prior experience fits with the position you're trying to fill. Similarly, the interview is a reasonably good vehicle for identifying the degree to which a candidate has leadership traits such as extraversion, self-confidence, a vision, the verbal skills to frame issues, or a charismatic physical presence.

Training Leaders

Organizations, in aggregate, spend billions of dollars, yen, and euros on leadership training and development.[55] These efforts take many forms—from $50,000 executive leadership programs offered by universities such as Harvard to sailing experiences at the Outward Bound school. Business schools, including some elite programs, such as Dartmouth, MIT, and Stanford, are placing renewed emphasis on leadership development. Some companies, too, place a lot of emphasis on leadership development. For example, Goldman Sachs is well known for developing leaders, so much so that *BusinessWeek* called it the "Leadership Factory."[56]

Although much of the money spent on training may provide dubious benefits, our review suggests that there are some things managers can do to get the maximum effect from their leadership-training budgets.[57]

First, let's recognize the obvious. People are not equally trainable. Leadership training of any kind is likely to be more successful with individuals who are high self-monitors than with low self-monitors. Such individuals have the flexibility to change their behavior.

What kinds of things can individuals learn that might be related to higher leader effectiveness? It may be a bit optimistic to believe that we can teach "vision creation," but we can teach implementation skills. We can train people to develop "an understanding about content themes critical to effective visions."[58] We can also teach skills such as trust building and mentoring. And leaders can be taught situational-analysis skills. They can learn how to evaluate situations, how to modify situations to make them fit better with their style, and how to assess which leader behaviors might be most effective in given situations. A number of companies have recently turned to executive coaches to help senior managers improve their leadership skills.[59]

On an optimistic note, there is evidence suggesting that behavioral training through modeling exercises can increase an individual's ability to exhibit charismatic leadership qualities. The success of the researchers mentioned earlier in actually scripting undergraduate business students to "play" charismatic is a case in point.[60] Finally, there is accumulating research showing that leaders can be trained in transformational leadership skills. Once learned, these skills have bottom-line results, whether in the financial performance of Canadian banks or the training effectiveness of soldiers in the Israeli Defense Forces.[61]

GLOBAL IMPLICATIONS

Most of the research on the leadership theories discussed in this chapter has been conducted in English-speaking countries. Thus, we know very little about how culture might influence their validity, particularly in Eastern cultures. However, a recent analysis of the Global Leadership and Organizational Behavior Effectiveness (GLOBE) research project has produced some useful, if preliminary, insights into cultural issues that leaders need to consider.[62] The GLOBE research program, which we introduced in Chapter 2, has gathered data on approximately 18,000 middle managers in 825 organizations, covering 62 countries. It's the most comprehensive cross-cultural study of leadership ever undertaken. So its findings should not be quickly dismissed.

In one article based on the GLOBE study, the authors sought to answer the practical question of how culture might affect a U.S. manager if he or she had been given 2 years to lead a project in four prototypical countries whose cultures diverged from that of the United States in different ways: Brazil, France, Egypt, and China. Let's consider each case in turn.

Brazil   Based on the GLOBE study findings of the values of Brazilian employees, a U.S. manager leading a team in Brazil would need to be team oriented, participative, and humane. This would suggest that leaders who are high on consideration, who emphasize participative decision making, and who have high LPC scores would be best suited to managing employees in this culture. As one Brazilian manager said in the study, "We do not prefer leaders who take self-governing decisions and act alone without engaging the group. That's part of who we are." Charismatic leadership was one of the most important leadership dimensions in Brazil. According to these authors, Brazilians do not expect grand institutional vision, but do expect a vision for how their work group should function and what its goals should be.

France   Compared to U.S. employees, the French tend to have a more bureaucratic view of leaders and are less likely to expect them to be humane and considerate. Thus, a leader who is high on initiating structure, or relatively task oriented, will do best, and she can make decisions in a relatively autocratic manner. A manager who scores high on consideration (people-oriented) leadership may find that style backfiring in France. As in Brazil, charismatic leadership was considered one of the more important leadership qualities. Because the French are more formal and reserved than Americans, "Grand corporate strategies and visions may be of limited value to a French team." However, French teams do expect their leaders to articulate a strategy for their team and to describe how it will be attained.

—Although the proper leadership style does, to some degree, vary by culture, there are also commonalities across cultures—charismatic/ visionary leadership matters in most countries, even if the particular way it is expressed does vary across cultures.

Egypt   Like those in Brazil, employees in Egypt are more likely to value team-oriented and participative leadership than U.S. employees. However, Egypt is also a relatively high-power-distance culture, meaning that status differences between leaders and followers are expected. How would a U.S. manager be participative and yet act in a manner that shows his or her high level of status? According to the authors, the leaders should ask employees for their opinions, try to minimize conflicts, but also not be afraid to take charge and make the final decision (after consulting team members). Here, too, charismatic leadership matters: "Egyptian employees expect their leaders to develop and communicate heroic and grand strategies. Due to their high institutional collectivism and performance orientation, it is helpful to design and communicate ambitious strategies and put them into the broader context of the corporation."

China   According to the GLOBE study, Chinese culture emphasizes being polite, considerate, and unselfish. But the culture also has a high performance orientation. These two factors suggest that both consideration and initiating structure may be important. Although Chinese culture is relatively participative compared with the United States, there are also status differences between leaders and employees. This suggests that, as in Egypt, a moderately participative style may work best. As with the other nations, charismatic leadership appears to be effective in China as well. The authors note: "Developing an exciting vision is very effective."

In sum, does charismatic/transformational leadership concepts generalize across cultures? The answer seems clearly, to be "yes." The results led two members of the GLOBE team to conclude that "effective business leaders in any country are expected by their subordinates to provide a powerful and proactive vision to guide the company into the future, strong motivational skills to stimulate all employees to fulfill the vision, and excellent planning skills to assist in implementing the vision."

As for the more traditional leadership concepts, there appears to be more variability across cultures in terms of how well they work. A participative leadership style (e.g., high consideration or high LPC) may work well in collectivistic countries like Brazil, but not well in more bureaucratic countries like France.

IMPLICATIONS FOR MANAGERS

Leadership plays a central part in understanding group behavior, for it's the leader who usually provides the direction toward goal attainment. Therefore, a more accurate predictive capability should be valuable in improving group performance.

To some degree, leadership success depends on having "the right stuff." Individuals who have the right traits (are extroverted, conscientious, and open) and exhibit the right behaviors (consideration, initiating structure) are more likely to be effective.

It's also true that leadership success depends on the situation. In particular, the Fiedler model and the LMX theory suggest that aspects of the environment are critical in leadership.

Organizations are increasingly searching for managers who can exhibit transformational leadership qualities. They want leaders with visions and the charisma to carry out those visions. And although true leadership effectiveness may be a result of exhibiting the right behaviors at the right time, the evidence is quite strong that people have a relatively uniform perception of what a leader should look like. Recently, leadership scholars have emphasized the importance of ethics and authenticity—the idea behind that it's not just the vision that matters, but whether it is implemented for the good of the organization (rather than the individual).

For managers concerned with how to fill key positions in their organizations with effective leaders, they should select individuals with certain traits and behavioral tendencies, and they also should pay particular attention to charisma and inspirational qualities. We have also shown that we all can learn to become better leaders by showing these characteristics.

CHAPTER 12

Power and Politics

After studying this chapter, you should be able to:

1. Define *power* and contrast leadership and power.
2. Contrast the five bases of power.
3. Identify nine power or influence tactics and their contingencies.
4. Identify the causes and consequences of political behavior.
5. Apply impression management techniques.
6. Show the influence of culture on the uses and perceptions of politics.

*P*ower and *politics* have been described as the last dirty words. It is easier for most of us to talk about sex or money than it is to talk about power or political behavior. People who have power deny it, people who want it try not to look like they're seeking it, and those who are good at getting it are secretive about how they do so.

In this chapter, we show that power determines what goals a group will pursue and how the group's resources will be distributed among its members. Further, we show how group members with good political skills use their power to influence the distribution of resources in their favor.

A DEFINITION OF *POWER*

Power refers to a capacity that *A* has to influence the behavior of *B* so that *B* acts in accordance with *A*'s wishes.[1] This definition implies a *potential* that need not be actualized to be effective, and a *dependency* relationship.

Power may exist even when it's not used. It is, therefore, a capacity or potential. One can have power but not impose it, but probably the more important aspect of power is that power is a function of **dependency**. The greater *B*'s dependence on *A*, the greater *A*'s power in the relationship. Dependence, in turn, is based on alternatives that *B* perceives and the importance that *B* places on the alternative(s) that *A* controls. A person can have power over you only if he or she controls something you desire. If you want a college degree and have to pass a certain course to get it, and your current instructor is the only faculty member in the college who teaches that course, he or she has power over you. Your alternatives are highly limited, and you place a high degree of importance on obtaining a passing grade.

CONTRASTING LEADERSHIP AND POWER

A careful comparison of our description of power with our description of leadership in the previous chapter reveals that the concepts are closely intertwined. Leaders use power as a means of attaining group goals. Leaders achieve goals, and power is a means of facilitating their achievement.

What differences are there between the two terms? One difference relates to goal compatibility. Power does not require goal compatibility, merely dependence. Leadership, on the other hand, requires some congruence between the goals of the leader and those being led. A second difference relates to the direction of influence. Leadership focuses on the downward influence on one's followers. It minimizes the importance of lateral and upward influence patterns. Power does not. Still another difference deals with research emphasis. Leadership research, for the most part, emphasizes style. It seeks answers to questions such as: How supportive should a leader be? How much decision making should be shared with followers? In contrast, the research on power has tended to encompass a broader area and to focus on tactics for gaining compliance. It has gone beyond the individual as the exerciser of power because power can be used by groups as well as by individuals to control other individuals or groups.

BASES OF POWER

Where does power come from? What is it that gives an individual or a group influence over others? We answer these questions by dividing the bases or sources of power into two general groupings—formal and personal—and then breaking each of these down into more specific categories.[2]

Formal Power

Formal power is based on an individual's position in an organization. Formal power can come from the ability to coerce or reward, or it can come from formal authority.

Coercive Power The **coercive power** base is dependent on fear. A person reacts to this power out of fear of the negative results that might occur if she failed to comply. It rests on the application, or the threat of application, of physical sanctions such as the infliction of pain, the generation of frustration through restriction of movement, or the controlling by force of basic physiological or safety needs.

Reward Power The converse of coercive power is **reward power**. People comply with the wishes or directives of another because doing so produces positive benefits; therefore, one who can distribute rewards that others view as valuable will have power over those others. These rewards can be either financial—such as controlling pay rates, raises, and bonuses—or nonfinancial—including recognition, promotions, interesting work assignments, friendly colleagues, and preferred work shifts or sales territories.

Legitimate Power   In formal groups and organizations, probably the most frequent access to one or more of the power bases is one's structural position. This is called **legitimate power**, which represents the formal authority to control and use organizational resources. Positions of authority include coercive and reward powers. Legitimate power, however, is broader than the power to coerce and reward. Specifically, it includes acceptance by members in an organization of the authority of a position.

> —Formal power can come from the ability to coerce or reward, or it can come from formal authority. However, evidence suggests that informal power, expert and reference power, is the most important to acquire.

Personal Power

You don't have to have a formal position in an organization to have power. Many of the most competent and productive chip designers at Intel, for instance, have power, but they aren't managers and have no formal power. What they have is personal power—power that comes from an individual's unique characteristics. In this section, we look at two bases of personal power: expertise and the respect and admiration of others.

Expert Power   **Expert power** is influence wielded as a result of expertise, special skill, or knowledge. Expertise has become one of the most powerful sources of influence as the world has become more technologically oriented. As jobs become more specialized, we become increasingly dependent on experts to achieve goals. Thus, the importance of expert power may be increasing.

Referent Power   **Referent power** is based on identification with a person who has desirable resources or personal traits. If I like, respect, and admire you, you can exercise power over me because I want to please you. Referent power develops out of admiration of another and a desire to be like that person. One of the ways in which individuals acquire referent power is through charisma. Some people have referent power who, while not in formal leadership positions, nevertheless are able to exert influence over others because of their charismatic dynamism, likability, and emotional effects on us.

Which Bases of Power Are Most Effective?

Of the three bases of formal power (coercive, reward, legitimate) and two bases of personal power (expert, referent), which is most important to have? Interestingly, research suggests pretty clearly that the personal sources of power are most effective. Both expert and referent power are positively related to employees' satisfaction with supervision, their organizational commitment, and their performance, whereas reward and legitimate power seem to be unrelated to these outcomes. Moreover, one source of formal power—coercive power—actually can backfire in that it is negatively related to employee satisfaction and commitment.[3]

POWER TACTICS

What **power tactics** do people use to translate power bases into specific action? That is, what options do individuals have for influencing their bosses, coworkers, or employees? And are some of these options more effective than others? In this section, we review popular tactical options and the conditions under which one may be more effective than another. Although power bases and power tactics are similar concepts, power tactics are more immediate in nature. You might imagine that power tactics, when successfully applied over time, result in an accumulation of a power base.

Research has identified nine distinct influence tactics:[4]

- *Legitimacy.* Relying on one's authority position or stressing that a request is in accordance with organizational policies or rules.
- *Rational persuasion.* Presenting logical arguments and factual evidence to demonstrate that a request is reasonable.
- *Inspirational appeals.* Developing emotional commitment by appealing to a target's values, needs, hopes, and aspirations.
- *Consultation.* Increasing the target's motivation and support by involving him or her in deciding how the plan or change will be accomplished.
- *Exchange.* Rewarding the target with benefits or favors in exchange for following a request.
- *Personal appeals.* Asking for compliance based on friendship or loyalty.
- *Ingratiation.* Using flattery, praise, or friendly behavior prior to making a request.
- *Pressure.* Using warnings, repeated demands, and threats.
- *Coalitions.* Enlisting the aid of other people to persuade the target or using the support of others as a reason for the target to agree.

> —Political influence behaviors are one important means of gaining power and influence. The least widely used influence behaviors—consultation and inspirational appeal—tend to be the least widely used. You should make these influence tactics part of your repertoire.

Some tactics are more effective than others. Specifically, evidence indicates that rational persuasion, inspirational appeals, and consultation tend to be the most effective. On the other hand, pressure tends to frequently backfire and is typically the least effective of the nine tactics.[5] You can also increase your chance of success by using more than one type of tactic at the same time or sequentially, as long as your choices are compatible. For instance, using both ingratiation and legitimacy can lessen the negative reactions that might come from the appearance of being "dictated to" by the boss.

But the effectiveness of some influence tactics depends on the direction of influence. As shown in Exhibit 12-1, studies have found that rational persuasion is the only tactic that is effective across organizational levels. Inspirational appeals work best as a downward-influencing tactic with subordinates. When pressure works, it's generally only to achieve downward influence. And the use of personal appeals and coalitions are most effective with lateral influence attempts. In addition to the direction of influence, a number of other factors have been found to affect which tactics work best. These include the sequencing of tactics, a person's skill in using the tactic, and the culture of the organization.

EXHIBIT 12-1   Preferred Power Tactics by Influence Direction

Upward Influence	Downward Influence	Lateral Influence
Rational persuasion	Rational persuasion	Rational persuasion
	Inspirational appeals	Consultation
	Pressure	Ingratiation
	Consultation	Exchange
	Ingratiation	Legitimacy
	Exchange	Personal appeals
	Legitimacy	Coalitions

Finally, we know that cultures within organizations differ markedly—for example, some are warm, relaxed, and supportive; others are formal and conservative. The organizational culture in which a person works, therefore, will have a bearing on defining which tactics are considered appropriate. Some cultures encourage the use of participation and consultation, some encourage reason, and still others rely on pressure. So the organization itself will influence which subset of power tactics is viewed as acceptable for use.

POLITICS: POWER IN ACTION

When people get together in groups, power will be exerted. People want to carve out a niche from which to exert influence, to earn rewards, and to advance their careers. When employees in organizations convert their power into action, we describe them as being engaged in politics. Those with good political skills have the ability to use their bases of power effectively.[6]

Definition of *Organizational Politics*

There has been no shortage of definitions of *organizational politics*. Essentially, however, they have focused on the use of power to affect decision making in an organization or on behaviors by members that are self-serving and organizationally nonsanctioned. For our purposes, we shall define **political behavior** in organizations as activities that are not required as part of one's formal role in the organization but that influence, or attempt to influence, the distribution of advantages and disadvantages within the organization.[7] This definition encompasses key elements from what most people mean when they talk about organizational politics. Political behavior is outside one's specified job requirements. The behavior requires some attempt to use one's power bases.

A final comment relates to what has been referred to as the "legitimate" dimension in political behavior. **Legitimate political behavior** refers to normal everyday politics—complaining to your supervisor, bypassing the chain of command, forming coalitions, obstructing organizational policies or decisions through inaction or excessive adherence to rules, and developing contacts outside the organization through one's professional activities. On the other hand, there are also **illegitimate political behaviors** that violate the implied rules of the game. Those who pursue such extreme activities are often described as individuals who "play hardball." Illegitimate activities include sabotage, whistle-blowing, and symbolic protests such as wearing unorthodox dress or protest buttons and groups of employees simultaneously calling in sick.

The Reality of Politics

Politics is a fact of life in organizations. People who ignore this do so at their own peril. But why, you may wonder, must politics exist? Isn't it possible for an organization to be politics free? It's *possible* but unlikely.

Organizations are made up of individuals and groups with different values, goals, and interests.[8] This sets up the potential for conflict over resources. Departmental budgets, space allocations, project responsibilities, and salary adjustments are just a few examples of the resources about whose allocation organizational members will disagree.

Resources in organizations are also limited, which often turns potential conflict into real conflict.[9] If resources were abundant, then all the various constituencies within the organization could satisfy their goals. But because they are limited, not everyone's interests can be provided for. Furthermore, whether true or not, gains by one individual or group are often *perceived* as being at the expense of others within the organization. These forces create competition among members for the organization's limited resources.

Finally, because most decisions have to be made in a climate of ambiguity—where facts are rarely fully objective and thus are open to interpretation—people within organizations will use whatever influence they can to taint the facts to support their goals and interests. That, of course, creates the activities we call *politicking*.

Therefore, to answer the earlier question of whether it is possible for an organization to be politics free, we can say "yes," if all members of that organization hold the same goals and interests, if organizational resources are not scarce, and if performance outcomes are completely clear and objective. But that doesn't describe the organizational world that most of us live in.

CAUSES AND CONSEQUENCES OF POLITICAL BEHAVIOR

Factors Contributing to Political Behavior

Not all groups or organizations are equally political. In some organizations, for instance, politicking is overt and rampant, whereas in others, politics plays a small role in influencing outcomes. Why is there such variation? Recent research and observation have identified a number of factors that appear to encourage political behavior. Some are individual characteristics, derived from the unique qualities of the people the organization employs; others are a result of the organization's culture or internal environment. Let's review both factors.

Individual Factors   At the individual level, researchers have identified certain personality traits, needs, and other factors that are likely to be related to political behavior. In terms of traits, we find that employees who are high self-monitors, and people who have a high need for power, are more likely to engage in political behavior.[10] The high self-monitor is more sensitive to social cues, exhibits higher levels of social conformity, and is more likely to be skilled in political behavior than the low self-monitor.

In addition, an individual's investment in the organization, perceived alternatives, and expectations of success will influence the degree to which he or she will pursue illegitimate means of political action.[11] The more a person has invested in the organization in terms of expectations of increased future benefits, the more that person has to lose if forced out and the less likely he or she is to use illegitimate means. The more alternative job opportunities an individual has—due to a favorable job market or the possession of scarce skills or knowledge, a prominent reputation, or influential contacts outside the organization—the more likely that individual is to risk illegitimate political actions. Finally, if an individual has a low expectation of success in using illegitimate means, it is unlikely that he or she will attempt to do so. High expectations of success in the use of illegitimate means are most likely to be the province of both experienced and powerful individuals with polished political skills and inexperienced and naive employees who misjudge their chances.

Organizational Factors   Although we acknowledge the role that individual differences can play in fostering politicking, the evidence more strongly supports the idea that certain situations and cultures promote politics. Specifically, when an organization's resources are declining, when the existing pattern of resources is changing, and when there is opportunity for promotions, politicking is more likely to surface. In addition, cultures characterized by low trust, role ambiguity, unclear performance evaluation systems, zero-sum reward allocation practices, democratic decision making, high pressures for performance, and self-serving senior managers will create breeding grounds for politicking.[12]

The less trust there is within the organization, the higher the level of political behavior and the more likely that the political behavior will be of the illegitimate kind. So high trust should suppress the level of political behavior in general and inhibit illegitimate actions in particular.

Role ambiguity means that the prescribed behaviors of the employee are not clear. There are fewer limits, therefore, to the scope and functions of the employee's political actions. Because political activities are defined as those not required as part of one's formal role, the greater the role ambiguity, the more one can engage in political activity with little chance of it being visible.

The more that an organization's culture emphasizes the zero-sum or win/lose approach to reward allocations, the more employees will be motivated to engage in politicking. The zero-sum approach treats the reward "pie" as fixed so that any gain one person or group achieves has to come at the expense of another person or group. If I win, you must lose! If $15,000 in annual raises is to be distributed among five employees, then any employee who gets more than $3,000 takes money away from one or more of the others. Such a practice encourages making others look bad and increasing the visibility of what you do.

The more pressure that employees feel to perform well, the more likely they are to engage in politicking. When people are held strictly accountable for outcomes, this puts great pressure on them to "look good." If a person perceives that his or her entire career is riding on next quarter's sales figures or next month's plant productivity report, there is motivation to do whatever is necessary to make sure the numbers come out favorably.

Finally, when employees see the people on top engaging in political behavior, especially when they do so successfully and are rewarded for it, a climate is created that supports politicking. Politicking by top management, in a sense, gives permission to those lower in the organization to play politics by implying that such behavior is acceptable.

How Do People Respond to Organizational Politics?

Trish O'Donnell loves her job as a writer on a weekly television comedy series but hates the internal politics. "A couple of the writers here spend more time kissing up to the executive producer than doing any work. And our head writer clearly has his favorites. While they pay me a lot and I get to really use my creativity, I'm sick of having to be on alert for backstabbers and constantly having to self-promote my contributions. I'm tired of doing most of the work and getting little of the credit." Are Trish O'Donnell's comments typical of people who work in highly politicized workplaces? We all know of friends or relatives who regularly complain about the politics at their job, but how do people in general react to organizational politics? Let's look at the evidence.

In our discussion earlier in this chapter of factors that contribute to political behavior, we focused on the favorable outcomes for individuals who successfully engage in politicking. However, for most people—who have modest political skills or are unwilling to play the politics game—outcomes tend to be predominantly negative. Exhibit 12-2 summarizes the extensive research on the relationship between organizational politics and individual outcomes.[13] There is, for instance, very strong evidence indicating that perceptions of organizational politics are negatively related to job satisfaction.[14] The perception of politics also tends to increase job anxiety and stress. This seems to be due to the perception that, by not engaging in politics, a person may be losing ground to others who are active politickers, or, conversely, because of the additional pressures individuals feel because of having entered into and competing in the political arena.[15] Not surprisingly, when politicking becomes too much to handle, it can lead to employees quitting.[16] Finally, there is preliminary evidence suggesting that politics leads to self-reported declines in employee performance. This may occur because employees perceive political environments to be unfair, which demotivates them.[17]

In addition to these conclusions, several interesting qualifiers have been noted. First, the politics–performance relationship appears to be moderated by an individual's understanding of the "hows" and "whys" of organizational politics. "An individual who has a clear understanding of who is responsible for making decisions and why they were selected to be the decision makers would have a better understanding of how and why things happen the way they do than someone who does not understand the decision-making process in the organization."[18] When both politics and understanding are high, performance is likely to increase because the individual will see political actions as an opportunity. This is consistent with what you might expect among individuals with well-honed political skills. But when understanding is low, individuals are more likely to see politics as a threat, which would have a negative effect on job performance. Second, when politics is seen as a threat and consistently responded to with

EXHIBIT 12-2 Employee Responses to Organizational Politics

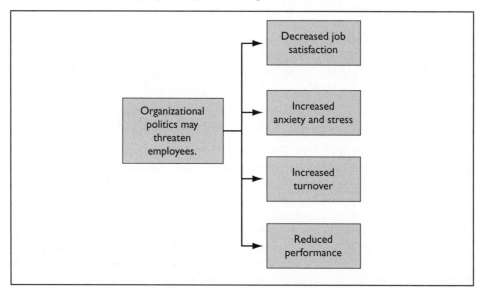

EXHIBIT 12-3   Defensive Behaviors

Avoiding Action

Overconforming. Strictly interpreting your responsibility by saying things like, "The rules clearly state . . ." or "This is the way we've always done it."

Buck passing. Transferring responsibility for the execution of a task or decision to someone else.

Playing dumb. Avoiding an unwanted task by falsely pleading ignorance or inability.

Stretching. Prolonging a task so that one person appears to be occupied—for example, turning a two-week task into a four-month job.

Stalling. Appearing to be more or less supportive publicly while doing little or nothing privately.

Avoiding Blame

Buffing. This is a nice way to refer to "covering your rear." It describes the practice of rigorously documenting activity to project an image of competence and thoroughness.

Playing safe. Evading situations that may reflect unfavorably. It includes taking on only projects with a high probability of success, having risky decisions approved by superiors, qualifying expressions of judgment, and taking neutral positions in conflicts.

Justifying. Developing explanations that lessen one's responsibility for a negative outcome and/or apologizing to demonstrate remorse.

Scapegoating. Placing the blame for a negative outcome on external factors that are not entirely blameworthy.

Misrepresenting. Manipulation of information by distortion, embellishment, deception, selective presentation, or obfuscation.

Avoiding Change

Prevention. Trying to prevent a threatening change from occurring.

Self-protection. Acting in ways to protect one's self-interest during change by guarding information or other resources.

defensiveness, negative outcomes are almost sure to surface eventually. When people perceive politics as a threat rather than as an opportunity, they often respond with **defensive behaviors**—reactive and protective behaviors to avoid action, blame, or change. (Exhibit 12-3 provides some examples of these defensive behaviors.) And defensive behaviors are often associated with negative feelings toward the job and work environment.[19] In the short run, employees may find that defensiveness protects their self-interest. But in the long run, it wears them down. People who consistently rely on defensiveness find that, eventually, it is the only way they know how to behave. At that point, they lose the trust and support of their peers, bosses, employees, and clients.

Impression Management

We know that people have an ongoing interest in how others perceive and evaluate them. For example, North Americans spend billions of dollars on diets, health club memberships, cosmetics, and plastic surgery—all intended to make them more attractive to others. Being perceived positively by others should have benefits for people in organizations. It might, for instance, help them initially to get the jobs they want in an organization and, once hired, to get favorable evaluations, superior salary increases, and more rapid promotions. In a political context, it might help sway the distribution of advantages in their favor. The process by which individuals attempt to control the impression others form of them is called **impression management (IM)**. It's a subject that has gained the attention of OB researchers only recently.[20]

Is everyone concerned with IM? No! Who, then, might we predict to engage in IM? No surprise here. It's our old friend that we introduced in Chapter 2, the high self-monitor.[21] Low self-monitors tend to present images of themselves that are consistent with their personalities, regardless of the beneficial or detrimental effects for them. In contrast, high self-monitors are good at reading situations and molding their appearances and behavior to fit each situation. If you want to control the impression others form of you, what techniques can you use? Exhibit 12-4 summarizes some of the most popular IM techniques and provides an example of each.

Keep in mind that IM does not imply that the impressions people convey are necessarily false (although, of course, they sometimes are).[22] Excuses, for instance, may be offered with sincerity. Referring to the example for excuses used in Exhibit 12-4, you can *actually* believe that ads contribute little to sales in your region. But misrepresentation can have

EXHIBIT 12-4   Impression Management (IM) Techniques

Conformity
Agreeing with someone else's opinion in order to gain his or her approval.
Example: A manager tells his boss, "You're absolutely right on your reorganization plan for the western regional office. I couldn't agree with you more."

Excuses
Explanations of a predicament-creating event aimed at minimizing the apparent severity of the predicament.
Example: Sales manager to boss, "We failed to get the ad in the paper on time, but no one responds to those ads anyway."

Apologies
Admitting responsibility for an undesirable event and simultaneously seeking to get a pardon for the action.
Example: Employee to boss, "I'm sorry I made a mistake on the report. Please forgive me."

Self-Promotion
Highlighting one's best qualities, downplaying one's deficits, and calling attention to one's achievements.
Example: A salesperson tells his boss: "Matt worked unsuccessfully for three years to try to get that account. I sewed it up in six weeks. I'm the best closer this company has."

Flattery
Complimenting others about their virtues in an effort to make oneself appear perceptive and likeable.
Example: New sales trainee to peer, "You handled that client's complaint so tactfully! I could never have handled that as well as you did."

Favors
Doing something nice for someone to gain that person's approval.
Example: Salesperson to prospective client, "I've got two tickets to the theater tonight that I can't use. Take them. Consider it a thank-you for taking the time to talk with me."

Association
Enhancing or protecting one's image by managing information about people and things with which one is associated.
Example: A job applicant says to an interviewer, "What a coincidence. Your boss and I were roommates in college."

Source: Based on B. R. Schlenker, *Impression Management* (Monterey, CA: Brooks/Cole, 1980); W. L. Gardner and M. J. Martinko, "Impression Management in Organizations," *Journal of Management,* June 1988, p. 332; and R. B. Cialdini, "Indirect Tactics of Image Management Beyond Basking," in R. A. Giacalone and P. Rosenfeld (eds.), *Impression Management in the Organization* (Hillsdale, NJ: Lawrence Erlbaum, 1989), pp. 45–71.

a high cost. If the image claimed is false, you may be discredited. If you "cry wolf" once too often, no one is likely to believe you when the wolf really comes. So the impression manager must be cautious not to be perceived as insincere or manipulative.

Are there *situations* in which individuals are more likely to misrepresent themselves or more likely to get away with it? Yes—situations that are characterized by high uncertainty or ambiguity provide relatively little information for challenging a fraudulent claim and reduce the risks associated with misrepresentation.

Most of the studies undertaken to test the effectiveness of IM techniques have related it to two criteria: interview success and performance evaluations. Let's consider each of these.

—Impression management is a specific type of political behavior, designed to alter other's immediate perceptions of us; evidence suggests that the effectiveness of impression management techniques depends on the setting (i.e., self-promotion works better in the interview than for performance evaluation).

The evidence indicates that most job applicants use IM techniques in interviews and that, when IM behavior is used, it works.[23] In one study, for instance, interviewers felt that applicants for a position as a customer service representative who used IM techniques performed better in the interview, and they seemed somewhat more inclined to hire these people.[24] Moreover, when the researchers considered applicants' credentials, they concluded that IM techniques alone influenced the interviewers; that is, it didn't seem to matter if applicants were well qualified or poorly qualified. If they used IM techniques, they did better in the interview.

Research indicates that some IM techniques work better than others in the interview. Researchers have compared applicants who used IM techniques that focused on promoting one's accomplishments (called *self-promotion*) to applicants who used techniques that focused on complimenting the interviewer and finding areas of agreement (referred to as *ingratiation*). In general, applicants appear to use self-promotion more than ingratiation.[25] What's more, self-promotion tactics may be more important to interviewing success. Applicants who work to create an appearance of competence by enhancing their accomplishments, taking credit for successes, and explaining away failures do better in interviews. These effects reach beyond the interview: Applicants who use more self-promotion tactics also seem to get more follow-up job-site visits, even after adjusting for grade-point average, gender, and job type. Ingratiation also works well in interviews, meaning that applicants who compliment the interviewer, agree with his or her opinions, and emphasize areas of fit do better than those who don't employ this tactic.[26]

In terms of performance ratings, the picture is quite different. Ingratiation is positively related to performance ratings, meaning that those who ingratiate with their supervisors get higher performance evaluations. However, self-promotion appears to backfire: Those who self-promote actually seem to receive *lower* performance evaluations.[27] Another study of 760 boards of directors found that individuals who ingratiate themselves to current board members (express agreement with the director, point out shared attitudes and opinions, compliment the director) increase their chances of landing on a board.[28]

What explains these results? If you think about them, they make sense. Ingratiating always works because everyone—both interviewers and supervisors—likes to be treated nicely. However, self-promotion may work only in interviews and backfire on the job because, whereas the interviewer has little idea whether you're blowing smoke about your accomplishments, the supervisor knows because it's his or her job to observe you. Thus, if you're going to self-promote, remember that what works in an interview will not always work once you're on the job.

THE ETHICS OF BEHAVING POLITICALLY

We conclude our discussion of politics by providing some ethical guidelines for political behavior. Although there are no clear-cut ways to differentiate ethical politicking from unethical politicking, there are some questions you should consider. For example, what is the utility of engaging in politicking? Sometimes we engage in political behaviors for little good reason. For example, major league baseball player Al Martin claimed he played football at USC when in fact he never did. Because Martin was playing baseball, not football, there was little to be gained by his lie. Outright lies like this may be a rather extreme example of impression management, but many of us have distorted information to make a favorable impression. The point is that, before we do so, one thing to keep in mind is whether it's really worth the risk. Another question to ask is an ethical one: How does the utility of engaging in the political behavior balance out any harm (or potential harm) it will do to others? For example, complimenting a supervisor on his or her appearance to curry favor is probably much less harmful than grabbing credit for a project that is deserved by others.

Finally, does the political activity conform to standards of equity and justice? Sometimes it is hard to weigh the costs and benefits of a political action, but its ethicality is clear. The department head who inflates the performance evaluation of a favored employee and deflates the evaluation of a disfavored employee—and then uses these evaluations to justify giving the former a big raise and nothing to the latter—has treated the disfavored employee unfairly.

Unfortunately, the answers to these questions are often argued in ways to make unethical practices seem ethical. Powerful people, for example, can become very good at explaining self-serving behaviors in terms of the organization's best interests. Similarly, they can persuasively argue that unfair actions are really fair and just. Our point is that immoral people can justify almost any behavior. Those who are powerful, articulate, and persuasive are most susceptible because they are likely to be able to get away with unethical practices successfully. When faced with an ethical dilemma regarding organizational politics, try to consider the preceding issues (is playing politics worth the risk, and will others be harmed in the process?). If you have a strong power base, recognize the ability of power to corrupt. Remember that it's a lot easier for the powerless than the powerful to act ethically, if for no other reason than they typically have very little political discretion to exploit.

GLOBAL IMPLICATIONS

Although culture might enter any of the topics we've covered to this point, three questions are particularly important: (1) Does culture influence politics perceptions? (2) Does culture affect the power of influence tactics people prefer to use? and (3) Does culture influence the effectiveness of different power tactics?

Politics Perceptions

We noted earlier that when people see their work environment as political, negative consequences in their overall work attitudes and behaviors generally result. Most of the research on politics perceptions has been conducted in the United States. A recent study, however, suggested that politics perceptions have the same negative effects in Nigeria. When employees of two agencies in Nigeria viewed their work environments as political, they reported higher levels of job distress and were less likely to help their coworkers. Thus, although developing countries such as Nigeria are perhaps more ambiguous and more political environments in which to work, the negative consequences appear to be the same as in the United States.[29]

Preference for Power Tactics

Evidence indicates that people in different countries tend to prefer different power tactics.[30] For instance, a study comparing managers in the United States and China found that U.S. managers prefer rational appeal, whereas Chinese managers preferred coalition tactics.[31] These differences tend to be consistent with the values in these two countries. Reason is consistent with the U.S. preference for direct confrontation and the use of rational persuasion to influence others and resolve differences. Similarly, coalition tactics are consistent with the Chinese preference for using indirect approaches for difficult or controversial requests. Research also has shown that individuals in Western, individualistic cultures tend to engage in more self-enhancement (such as self-promotion) behaviors than individuals in Eastern, more collectivistic cultures.[32]

Effectiveness of Power Tactics

Unfortunately, although we know people in different cultures seem to have different preferences for the use of power or influence tactics, there is much less evidence as to whether these tactics work better in some cultures than in others. One study of managers in U.S. culture and three Chinese cultures (People's Republic of China, Hong Kong, Taiwan) found that U.S. managers evaluated "gentle persuasion" tactics such as consultation and inspirational appeal as more effective than did their Chinese counterparts.[33]

IMPLICATIONS FOR MANAGERS

If you want to get things done in a group or organization, it helps to have power. As a manager who wants to maximize your power, you will want to increase others' dependence on you. You can increase your power in relation to your boss by developing knowledge or a skill that she needs and for which she perceives no ready substitute. But power is a two-way street, and you will not be alone in attempting to build your power bases. Others, particularly employees and peers, will be seeking to make you dependent on them. The result is an unending battle. While you seek to maximize others' dependence on you, you will be seeking to minimize your dependence on others. And, of course, others you work with will be trying to do the same.

One way to increase your power in an organization is to, over time, acquire the bases of power that are most useful (expert, referent) and then to use the power tactics (consultation, inspirational appeal) that are most effective. Avoid tactics (like coercion) that tend to backfire (result in resistance and resentment).

The effective manager accepts the political nature of organizations. By assessing behavior in a political framework, you can better predict the actions of others and use this information to formulate political strategies that will gain advantages for you and your work unit.

CHAPTER 13

Conflict and Negotiation

1. Define *conflict*, and differentiate between the traditional, human relations, and interactionist views of conflict.
2. Outline the conflict process.
3. Contrast distributive and integrative bargaining.
4. Apply the five steps of the negotiation process.
5. Show how individual differences influence negotiations.
6. Describe cultural differences in negotiations.

Conflict can often turn personal. It can create chaotic conditions that make it nearly impossible for employees to work as a team. However, conflict also has a less well-known positive side. We'll explain the difference between negative and positive conflicts in this chapter and provide a guide to help you understand how conflicts develop. We'll also present a topic closely akin to conflict: negotiation.

A DEFINITION OF CONFLICT

We can define **conflict**, then, as a process that begins when one party perceives that another party has negatively affected, or is about to negatively affect, something that the first party cares about.[1] This definition is purposely broad. It describes that point in any ongoing activity when an interaction "crosses over" to become an interparty conflict. It encompasses the wide range of conflicts that people experience in organizations—incompatibility of goals, differences over interpretations of facts, disagreements based on behavioral expectations, and the like. Finally, our definition is flexible enough to cover the full range of conflict levels—from overt and violent acts to subtle forms of disagreement.

TRANSITIONS IN CONFLICT THOUGHT

It is entirely appropriate to say there has been conflict over the role of conflict in groups and organizations. One school of thought has argued that conflict must be avoided—that it indicates a malfunctioning within the group. We call this the *traditional* view. Another school of thought, the *human relations* view, argues that conflict is a natural and inevitable outcome in any group and that it need not be evil but rather has the potential to be a positive force in determining group performance. The third, and most recent, perspective proposes not only that conflict can be a positive force in a group but explicitly argues that some conflict is *absolutely necessary* for a group to perform effectively. We label this third school the *interactionist* view. Let's take a closer look at each of these views.

The Traditional View of Conflict

The early approach to conflict assumed that all conflict was bad. Conflict was viewed negatively, and it was used synonymously with such terms as *violence*, *destruction*, and *irrationality* to reinforce its negative connotation. Conflict, by definition, was harmful and was to be avoided. The **traditional view of conflict** was consistent with the attitudes that prevailed about group behavior in the 1930s and 1940s. Conflict was seen as a dysfunctional outcome resulting from poor communication, a lack of openness and trust between people, and the failure of managers to be responsive to the needs and aspirations of their employees.

—Conflict is an inherent part of organizational life. Indeed, some level of conflict is probably necessary for optimal organizational functioning.

The view that all conflict is bad certainly offers a simple approach to looking at the behavior of people who create conflict. Because all conflict is to be avoided, we need merely direct our attention to the causes of conflict and correct those malfunctions to improve group and organizational performance. Although research studies now provide strong evidence to dispute that this approach to conflict reduction results in high group performance, many of us still evaluate conflict situations using this outmoded standard.

The Human Relations View of Conflict

The **human relations view of conflict** argued that conflict was a natural occurrence in all groups and organizations. Because conflict was inevitable, the human relations school advocated acceptance of conflict. Proponents rationalized its existence: It cannot be eliminated, and there are even times when conflict may benefit a group's performance. The human relations view dominated conflict theory from the late 1940s through the mid-1970s.

The Interactionist View of Conflict

Whereas the human relations view accepted conflict, the **interactionist view of conflict** encourages conflict on the grounds that a harmonious, peaceful, tranquil, and cooperative group is prone to becoming static, apathetic, and nonresponsive to needs for change and innovation.[2] The major contribution of the interactionist view, therefore, is encouraging group leaders to maintain an ongoing minimum level of conflict—enough to keep the group viable, self-critical, and creative.

—Task conflict is more constructive than process or, especially, relationship conflict.

The interactionist view does not propose that all conflicts are good. Rather, some conflicts support the goals of the group and improve its performance; these are **functional**, constructive, forms of conflict. In addition, there are conflicts that hinder group performance; these are **dysfunctional**, or destructive, forms of conflict. What differentiates functional from dysfunctional conflict? The evidence indicates that you need to look at the *type* of conflict.[3] Specifically, there are three types: task, relationship, and process.

Task conflict relates to the content and goals of the work. **Relationship conflict** focuses on interpersonal relationships. **Process conflict** relates to how the work gets done. Studies demonstrate that relationship conflicts are almost always dysfunctional.[4] Why? It appears that the friction and interpersonal hostilities inherent in relationship conflicts increase personality clashes and decrease mutual understanding, which hinders the completion of organizational tasks. Unfortunately, managers spend a lot of their time resolving personality conflicts; one survey indicated that 18 percent of managers' time is spent trying to resolve personality conflicts among staff members.[5]

Unlike relationship conflict, low levels of process conflict and low to moderate levels of task conflict are functional. For process conflict to be productive, it must be kept low. Intense arguments about who should do what become dysfunctional when they create uncertainty about task roles, increase the time to complete tasks, and lead to members working at cross purposes. Low-to-moderate levels of task conflict consistently demonstrate a positive effect on group performance because it stimulates discussion of ideas that helps groups perform better.

THE CONFLICT PROCESS

The **conflict process** has five stages: potential opposition or incompatibility, cognition and personalization, intentions, behavior, and outcomes. This process is diagrammed in Exhibit 13-1.

Stage I: Potential Opposition or Incompatibility

The first step in the conflict process is the presence of conditions that create opportunities for conflict to arise. They *need not* lead directly to conflict, but one of these conditions is necessary if conflict is to surface. For simplicity's sake, these conditions (which we can also look at as causes or sources of conflict) have been condensed into three general categories: communication, structure, and personal variables.

Communication Susan's comments illustrate that communication can be a source of conflict.[6] They represent the opposing forces that arise from semantic difficulties, misunderstandings, and "noise" in the communication channels. A review of the research suggests that differing word connotations, jargon, insufficient exchange of information, and noise in the communication channel are all barriers to communication and potential antecedent conditions to conflict. Research has further demonstrated a surprising finding: The potential for conflict increases when either too little or too much communication takes place. Apparently, an increase in communication is

EXHIBIT 13-1   The Conflict Process

functional up to a point, whereupon it is possible to overcommunicate, with a resultant increase in the potential for conflict.

Structure   The term *structure* is used, in this context, to include variables such as size, degree of specialization in the tasks assigned to group members, jurisdictional clarity, member-goal compatibility, leadership styles, reward systems, and the degree of dependence between groups, tenure and ages of group members. Research indicates that size and specialization act as forces to stimulate conflict. The larger the group and the more specialized its activities, the greater the likelihood of conflict. Tenure and conflict have been found to be inversely related. The potential for conflict tends to be greatest when group members are younger and when turnover is high.

   The greater the ambiguity in precisely defining where responsibility for actions lies, the greater the potential for conflict to emerge. Such jurisdictional ambiguities increase intergroup fighting for control of resources and territory. Diversity of goals among groups can also lead to conflict. Reward systems, too, are found to create conflict when one member's gain is at another's expense. Finally, if a group is dependent on another group (in contrast to the two being mutually independent) or if interdependence allows one group to gain at another's expense, opposing forces are stimulated.[7]

Personal Variables   Our last category of potential sources of conflict is personal variables, which include personality, emotions, and values. Evidence indicates that certain personality types—for example, individuals who are highly authoritarian and dogmatic—lead to potential conflict. Emotions can also cause conflict. For example, an employee who shows up to work irate from her hectic morning commute may carry that anger with her to her 9 A.M. meeting. The problem? Her anger can annoy her colleagues, which may lead to a tension-filled meeting.

Stage II: Cognition and Personalization

If the conditions cited in Stage I negatively affect something that one party cares about, the potential for opposition or incompatibility becomes actualized in the second stage.

As we noted in our definition of conflict, perception is required. Therefore, one or more of the parties must be aware of the existence of the antecedent conditions. However, because a conflict is a **perceived conflict** does not mean that it is personalized. In other words, "*A* may be aware that *B* and *A* are in serious disagreement . . . but it may not make *A* tense or anxious, and it may have no effect whatsoever on *A*'s affection toward *B*."[8] It is at the **felt conflict** level, when individuals become emotionally involved, that parties experience anxiety, tension, frustration, or hostility.

Stage II is important because it's where conflict issues tend to be defined. This is the place in the process where the parties decide what the conflict is about. In turn, this "sense making" is critical because the way a conflict is defined goes a long way toward establishing the sort of outcomes that might settle it. So the definition of a conflict is important because it typically delineates the set of possible settlements. Our second point is that emotions play a major role in shaping perceptions.[9]

Stage III: Intentions

Intentions Intervene among people's perceptions and emotions and overt behaviors. These intentions are decisions to act in a given way.

Intentions are separated out as a distinct stage because you have to infer the other's intent to know how to respond to that other's behavior. A lot of conflicts are escalated merely by one party attributing the wrong intentions to the other party. In addition, there is typically a great deal of slippage between intentions and behavior, so behavior does not always accurately reflect a person's intentions.

Using two dimensions—*cooperativeness* (the degree to which one party attempts to satisfy the other party's concerns) and *assertiveness* (the degree to which one party attempts to satisfy his or her own concerns)—we can identify five conflict-handling intentions:

1. *Competing:* assertive and uncooperative, such as when you strive to achieve your goal at the expense of the other party achieving his.
2. *Collaborating:* assertive and cooperative—intending to find a win–win solution that makes both parties happy.
3. *Avoiding:* unassertive and uncooperative, such as when you avoid a conflict based on the hope it will just go away.
4. *Accommodating:* unassertive and cooperative, such as when you give in just to please someone else.
5. *Compromising:* mid-range on both assertiveness and cooperativeness, where the pie is sliced down the middle.

People differ in the degree to which they generally rely on these strategies (e.g., some people are competitive in most situations), but the approach also will vary by the situation (e.g., a strategy one intends to use in a conflict with a loved one will often differ from a conflict with strangers).

Stage IV: Behavior

When most people think of conflict situations, they tend to focus on Stage IV because this is where conflicts become visible. The behavior stage includes the statements, actions, and reactions made by the conflicting parties. These conflict behaviors are usually overt attempts to implement each party's intentions. But these behaviors have a stimulus quality that is separate from intentions. As a result of miscalculations or unskilled enactments, overt behaviors sometimes deviate from original intentions.

It helps to think of Stage IV as a dynamic process of interaction. For example, you make a demand on me, I respond by arguing, you threaten me, I threaten you back, and so on. Exhibit 13-2 provides a way of visualizing conflict behavior. All conflicts exist somewhere along this continuum. At the lower part of the continuum are conflicts characterized by subtle, indirect, and highly controlled forms of tension. An illustration might be a student questioning in class a point the instructor has just made. Conflict intensities escalate as they move upward along the continuum until they become highly destructive. Strikes, riots, and wars clearly fall in this upper range. For the most part, you should assume that conflicts that reach the upper ranges of the continuum are almost always dysfunctional. Functional conflicts are typically confined to the lower range of the continuum.

Stage V: Outcomes

The action–reaction interplay between the conflicting parties results in consequences. As our model (see Exhibit 13-1) demonstrates, these outcomes may be functional in that the conflict results in an improvement in the group's performance or dysfunctional in that it hinders group performance.

Functional Outcomes   How might conflict act as a force to increase group performance? It is hard to visualize a situation in which open or violent aggression could be functional. But there are a number of instances in which it's possible to envision how low or moderate levels of conflict could improve the effectiveness of a group. Because

EXHIBIT 13-2   Conflict-Intensity Continuum

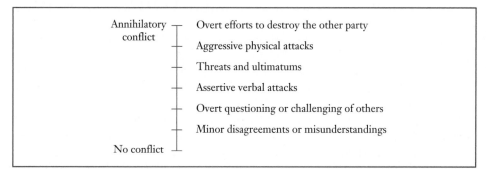

Source: Based on S. P. Robbins, *Managing Organizational Conflict: A Nontraditional Approach* (Upper Saddle River, NJ: Prentice Hall, 1974), pp. 93–97; and F. Glasi., "The Process of Conflict Escalation and the Roles of Third Parties," in G. B. J. Bomers and R. Peterson (eds.), *Conflict Management and Industrial Relations* (Boston: Kluwer-Nijhoff, 1982), pp. 119–140.

people often find it difficult to think of instances in which conflict can be constructive, let's consider some examples and then review the research evidence. Note how all these examples focus on task and process conflicts and exclude the relationship variety.

Conflict is constructive when it improves the quality of decisions, stimulates creativity and innovation, encourages interest and curiosity among group members, provides the medium through which problems can be aired and tensions released, and fosters an environment of self-evaluation and change. The evidence suggests that conflict can improve the quality of decision making by allowing all points, particularly the ones that are unusual or held by a minority, to be weighed in important decisions.[10] Conflict is an antidote for groupthink. It doesn't allow the group to passively "rubber-stamp" decisions that may be based on weak assumptions, inadequate consideration of relevant alternatives, or other debilities. Conflict challenges the status quo and therefore furthers the creation of new ideas, promotes reassessment of group goals and activities, and increases the probability that the group will respond to change.

Research studies in diverse settings confirm the functionality of conflict. Consider the following findings. Conflict can also positively relate to productivity. For instance, it was demonstrated that, among established groups, performance tended to improve more when there was conflict among members than when there was a fairly close agreement. The investigators observed that when groups analyzed decisions that had been made by the individual members of that group, the average improvement among the high-conflict groups was 73 percent greater than that of groups characterized by low-conflict conditions.[11] Others have found similar results: Groups composed of members with different interests tend to produce higher-quality solutions to a variety of problems than do homogeneous groups.[12]

Dysfunctional Outcomes   The destructive consequences of conflict on a group's or an organization's performance are generally well known. A reasonable summary might state: Uncontrolled opposition breeds discontent, which acts to dissolve common ties and eventually leads to the destruction of the group. And, of course, there is a substantial body of literature to document how conflict—the dysfunctional varieties—can reduce group effectiveness.[13] Among the more undesirable consequences are a retarding of communication, reductions in group cohesiveness, and subordination of group goals to the primacy of infighting among members. At the extreme, conflict can bring group functioning to a halt and potentially threaten the group's survival.

The demise of an organization as a result of too much conflict isn't as unusual as it might first appear. For instance, one of New York's best-known law firms, Shea & Gould, closed down solely because the eighty partners just couldn't get along.[14] As one legal consultant familiar with the organization said: "This was a firm that had basic and principled differences among the partners that were basically irreconcilable." That same consultant also addressed the partners at their last meeting: "You don't have an economic problem," he said. "You have a personality problem. You hate each other!"

Creating Functional Conflict   If managers accept the interactionist view toward conflict, what can they do to encourage functional conflict in their organizations?[15]

There seems to be general agreement that creating functional conflict is a tough job, particularly in large U.S. corporations. As one consultant said, "A high proportion of people who get to the top are conflict avoiders. They don't like hearing negatives; they don't like saying or thinking negative things. They frequently make it up the ladder in part because they don't irritate people on the way up." Another suggests that at least 7 out of 10 people in U.S. businesses hush up when their opinions are at odds with those of their superiors, allowing bosses to make mistakes even when they know better.

Such anticonflict cultures may have been tolerable in the past but are not in today's fiercely competitive global economy. Organizations that don't encourage and support dissent may find their survival threatened. Let's look at some approaches organizations are using to encourage their people to challenge the system and develop fresh ideas.

One common ingredient in organizations that successfully create functional conflict is that they reward dissent and punish conflict avoiders. The real challenge for managers, however, is when they hear news they don't want to hear. The news may make their blood boil or their hopes collapse, but they can't show it. They have to learn to take the bad news without flinching. No tirades, no tight-lipped sarcasm, no eyes rolling upward, and no gritting of teeth. Rather, managers should ask calm, even-tempered questions: "Can you tell me more about what happened?" "What do you think we ought to do?" A sincere "Thank you for bringing this to my attention" will probably reduce the likelihood that managers will be cut off from similar communications in the future.

Having considered conflict—its nature, causes, and consequences—we now turn to negotiation. Negotiation and conflict are closely related because negotiation often resolves conflict.

NEGOTIATION

Negotiation permeates the interactions of almost everyone in groups and organizations. There's the obvious: Labor bargains with management. There's the not-so-obvious: Managers negotiate with employees, peers, and bosses; salespeople negotiate with customers; and purchasing agents negotiate with suppliers. And there's the subtle: An employee agrees to answer a colleague's phone for a few minutes in exchange for a past or future benefit. In today's loosely structured organizations, in which members are increasingly finding themselves having to work with colleagues over whom they have no direct authority and with whom they may not even share a common boss, negotiation skills become critical.

We can define **negotiation** as a process in which two or more parties exchange goods or services and attempt to agree on the exchange rate for them.[16] Note that we use the terms *negotiation* and *bargaining* interchangeably. In this section, we contrast two bargaining strategies, provide a model of the negotiation process, ascertain the role of moods and personality traits on bargaining, and review gender and cultural differences in negotiation.

—The most effective negotiators utilize different tactics for distributive and integrative bargaining; the chapter provides clear ways in order for you to improve each type of bargaining.

Bargaining Strategies

There are two general approaches to negotiation—*distributive bargaining* and *integrative bargaining*.[17] As Exhibit 13-3 shows, distributive and integrative bargaining differ in their goal and motivation, focus, interests, information sharing, and duration

EXHIBIT 13-3   Distributive Versus Integrative Bargaining

Bargaining Characteristic	Distributive Bargaining	Integrative Bargaining
Goal	Get as much of the pie as possible	Expand the pie so that both parties are satisfied
Motivation	Win/lose	Win/win
Focus	Positions ("I can't go beyond this point on this issue.")	Interests ("Can you explain why this issue is so important to you?")
Interests	Opposed	Congruent
Information sharing	Low (sharing information will only allow other party to take advantage)	High (sharing information will allow each party to find ways to satisfy interests of each party)
Duration of relationship	Short term	Long term

of relationship. We now define distributive and integrative bargaining and illustrate the differences between these two approaches.

Distributive Bargaining   You see a used car advertised for sale in the newspaper. It appears to be just what you've been looking for. You decide to go out and see the car. It's great, and you want it. The owner tells you the asking price, but you don't want to pay that much. The two of you then negotiate over the price. The negotiating strategy you're engaging in is called **distributive bargaining**. Its most identifying feature is that it operates under zero-sum conditions. That is, any gain I make is at your expense and vice versa. In the used-car example, every dollar you can get the seller to cut from the car's price is a dollar you save. Conversely, every dollar more the seller can get from you comes at your expense. So the essence of distributive bargaining is negotiating over who gets what share of a fixed pie. By **fixed pie**, we mean that the bargaining parties believe there is only a set amount of goods or services to be divvied up. Therefore, fixed pies are zero-sum games in that every dollar in one party's pocket is a dollar out of their counterpart's pocket. When parties believe the pie is fixed, they tend to bargain distributively.

Probably the most widely cited example of distributive bargaining is in labor-management negotiations over wages. Typically, labor's representatives come to the bargaining table determined to get as much money as possible out of management. Because every cent more that labor negotiates increases management's costs, each party bargains aggressively and treats the other as an opponent who must be defeated.

The essence of distributive bargaining is depicted in Exhibit 13-4. Parties *A* and *B* represent two negotiators. Each has a *target point* that defines what he or she would like to achieve. Each also has a *resistance point*, which marks the lowest outcome that is acceptable—the point below which they would break off negotiations rather than accept a less favorable settlement. The area between these two points makes up each one's aspiration range. As long as there is some overlap between *A*'s

EXHIBIT 13-4   Staking Out the Bargaining Zone

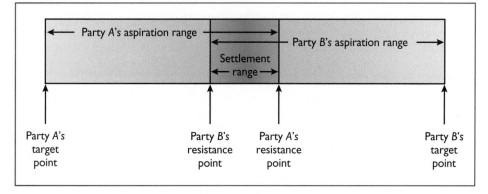

and *B*'s aspiration ranges, there exists a settlement range in which each one's aspirations can be met.

When engaged in distributive bargaining, one of the best things you can do is to make the first offer, and to make it an aggressive one. Research consistently shows that the best negotiators are those who make the first offer, and whose initial offer has very favorable terms. Why is this so? One reason is that making the first offer shows power; research shows that individuals in power are much more likely to make initial offers, speak first at meetings, and thereby gain the advantage. Another reason was mentioned in Chapter 3. Recall that we discussed the anchoring bias, which is the tendency for people to fixate on initial information. Once that anchoring point is set, people fail to adequately adjust it based on subsequent information. A savvy negotiator sets an anchor with the initial offer, and scores of negotiation studies show that such anchors greatly favor the person who sets it.[18]

For example, say you have a job offer, and your prospective employer asks you what sort of starting salary you'd be looking for. You need to realize that you've just been given a great gift—you have a chance to set the anchor, meaning that you should ask for the highest salary that you think the employer could reasonably offer. For most of us, asking for a million dollars is only going to make us look ridiculous, which is why we suggest being on the high end of what you think is reasonable. Too often, we err on the side of caution, being afraid of scaring off the employer and thus settling for too little. It *is* possible to scare off an employer, and it's true that employers don't like candidates to be assertive in salary negotiations, but liking isn't the same as respect or doing what it takes to hire or retain someone.[19] You should realize that what happens much more often is that we ask for less than what we could have gotten.

Integrative Bargaining   A sales representative for a women's sportswear manufacturer has just closed a $15,000 order from a small clothing retailer. The sales rep calls in the order to her firm's credit department and is told that the firm can't approve credit to this customer because of a past slow-payment record. The next day, the sales rep and the firm's credit manager meet to discuss the problem. The sales rep doesn't want to lose the business. Neither does the credit manager, but he also doesn't want to get stuck with an uncollectible debt. The two openly review their options. After considerable discussion, they agree on a solution that meets both their needs: The credit manager will approve the sale, but the clothing store's owner will provide a bank guarantee that will ensure payment if the bill isn't paid within 60 days. This sales-credit negotiation is an example of **integrative bargaining**. In contrast to distributive bargaining, integrative bargaining operates under the assumption that there are one or more settlements that can create a win–win solution.

In terms of intraorganizational behavior, all things being equal, integrative bargaining is preferable to distributive bargaining. Why? Because the former builds long-term relationships. It bonds negotiators and allows them to leave the bargaining table feeling that they have achieved a victory. Distributive bargaining, however, leaves one party a loser. It tends to build animosities and deepen divisions when people have to work together on an ongoing basis. Research shows that over repeated bargaining episodes, when the "losing" party feels positive about the negotiation outcome, he is much more likely to bargain cooperatively in subsequent negotiations. This points to the important advantage of integrative negotiations: Even when you "win," you want your opponent to feel positively about the negotiation.[20]

Why, then, don't we see more integrative bargaining in organizations? The answer lies in the conditions necessary for this type of negotiation to succeed. These include parties who are open with information and candid about their concerns, a sensitivity by both parties to the other's needs, the ability to trust one another, and a willingness by both parties to maintain flexibility. Because these conditions often don't exist in organizations, it isn't surprising that negotiations often take on a "win-at-any-cost" dynamic.

There are some ways to achieve more integrative outcomes. For example, one way to achieve higher joint-gain settlements is to put more issues on the table. The more negotiable issues that are introduced into a negotiation, the more opportunity there is for "logrolling" where issues are traded because of differences in preferences. This creates better outcomes for each side than if each issue were negotiated individually.[21]

Finally, you should realize that compromise may be your worst enemy in negotiating a win–win agreement. This is because compromising reduces the pressure to bargain integratively. After all, if you or your opponent caves in easily, it doesn't require anyone to be creative to reach a settlement. Thus, people end up settling for less than they could have obtained if they had been forced to consider the other party's interests, trade-off issues, and had been creative.[22] Think of the classic example where two sisters are arguing over who gets an orange. Unbeknownst to each other, one sister wants the orange to drink the juice, whereas the other sister wants the orange peel to bake a cake. If one sister simply capitulates and gives the other sister the orange, then they will not be forced to explore their reasons for wanting the orange, and thus they will never find the win–win solution: They could *each* have the orange because they want different parts of it!

The Negotiation Process

Exhibit 13-5 provides a simplified model of the negotiation process. It views negotiation as consisting of five steps: (1) preparation and planning, (2) definition of ground rules, (3) clarification and justification, (4) bargaining and problem solving, and (5) closure and implementation.[23]

EXHIBIT 13-5 The Negotiation Process

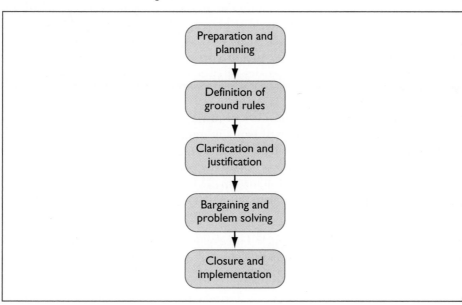

Preparation and
planning

↓

Definition of
ground rules

↓

Clarification and
justification

↓

Bargaining and
problem solving

↓

Closure and
implementation

Preparation and Planning Before you start negotiating, you need to do your homework. What's the nature of the conflict? What's the history leading up to this negotiation? Who's involved and what are their perceptions of the conflict? What do you want from the negotiation? What are *your* goals? If you're a supply manager at Dell Computer, for instance, and your goal is to get a significant cost reduction from your supplier of keyboards, make sure that this goal stays paramount in your discussions and doesn't get overshadowed by other issues. It often helps to put your goals in writing and develop a range of outcomes—from "most hopeful" to "minimally acceptable"—to keep your attention focused.

You also want to prepare an assessment of what you think the other party's goals are. What are they likely to ask for? How entrenched are they likely to be in their position? What intangible or hidden interests may be important to them? What might they be willing to settle on? When you can anticipate your opponent's position, you are better equipped to counter arguments with the facts and figures that support your position.

Once you've gathered your information, use it to develop a strategy. For example, expert chess players have a strategy. They know ahead of time how they will respond to any given situation. As part of your strategy, you should determine yours and the other side's *B*est *A*lternative *T*o a *N*egotiated *A*greement (**BATNA**).[24] Your BATNA determines the lowest value acceptable to you for a negotiated agreement. Any offer you receive that is higher than your BATNA is better than an impasse. Conversely, you shouldn't expect success in your negotiation effort unless you're able to make the other side an offer they find more attractive than their BATNA. If you go into your negotiation having a good idea of what the other party's BATNA is, even if you're not able to meet theirs, you might be able to get them to change it.

Definition of Ground Rules   Once you've done your planning and developed a strategy, you're ready to begin defining the ground rules and procedures with the other party over the negotiation itself. Who will do the negotiating? Where will it take place? What time constraints, if any, will apply? To what issues will negotiation be limited? Will there be a specific procedure to follow if an impasse is reached? During this phase, the parties will also exchange their initial proposals or demands.

Clarification and Justification   When initial positions have been exchanged, both you and the other party will explain, amplify, clarify, bolster, and justify your original demands. This needn't be confrontational. Rather, it's an opportunity for educating and informing each other on the issues, why they are important, and how each arrived at their initial demands. This is the point at which you might want to provide the other party with any documentation that helps support your position.

Bargaining and Problem Solving   The essence of the negotiation process is the actual give-and-take in trying to hash out an agreement. This is where both parties will undoubtedly need to make concessions.

Closure and Implementation   The final step in the negotiation process is formalizing the agreement that has been worked out and developing any procedures that are necessary for implementation and monitoring. For major negotiations—which would include everything from labor-management negotiations to bargaining over lease terms to buying a piece of real estate to negotiating a job offer for a senior management position—this requires hammering out the specifics in a formal contract. For most cases, however, closure of the negotiation process is nothing more formal than a handshake.

Individual Differences in Negotiation Effectiveness

Are some people better negotiators than others? Though the answer to this question might seem obvious, as it turns out the answers are more complex than you might think. Here we discuss three factors that influence how effectively individuals negotiate: personality, mood/emotions, and gender.

Personality Traits in Negotiation   Can you predict an opponent's negotiating tactics if you know something about his or her personality? It's tempting to answer "yes" to this question. For instance, you might assume that high risk takers would be more aggressive bargainers who make fewer concessions. Surprisingly, the evidence hasn't always supported this intuition.[25]

Assessments of the personality–negotiation relationship have been that personality traits have no significant direct effect on either the bargaining process or the negotiation outcomes. However, recent research has started to question the theory that personality and the negotiation process aren't connected. In fact, it appears that several of the Big Five traits are related to negotiation outcomes. For example, negotiators who are agreeable or extraverted are not very successful when it comes to distributive bargaining. Why? Because extraverts are outgoing and friendly, they tend to share more information than they should. And agreeable people are more interested in finding ways to cooperate rather than butt heads. These traits, while slightly helpful in integrative negotiations, are liabilities when interests are opposed. So the best distributive bargainer appears to be a disagreeable introvert—that is, someone who is interested in his own outcomes versus pleasing the other party and having a pleasant social exchange. Research also suggests that intelligence predicts negotiation effectiveness, but, as with personality, the effects aren't especially strong.[26]

Though personality and intelligence do appear to have some influence on negotiation, it's not a strong effect. In a sense, that's good news because it means even if you're an agreeable extrovert, you're not severely disadvantaged when it comes time to negotiate. We all can learn to be better negotiators.

Moods/Emotions in Negotiation   Do moods and emotions influence negotiation? They do, but the way they do appears to depend on the type of negotiation. In distributive negotiations, it appears that negotiators who show anger negotiate better outcomes, because their anger induces concessions from their opponents. This appears to hold true even when the negotiators are instructed to show anger despite not being truly angry.

In integrative negotiations, in contrast, positive moods and emotions appear to lead to more integrative agreements (higher levels of joint gain). This may happen because, as we noted in Chapter 7, positive mood is related to creativity.[27]

Gender Differences in Negotiations   Do men and women negotiate differently? And does gender affect negotiation outcomes? The answer to the first question appears to be no.[28] The answer to the second is a qualified yes.[29]

A popular stereotype is that women are more cooperative and pleasant in negotiations than are men. The evidence doesn't support this belief. However, men have been found to negotiate better outcomes than women, although the difference is relatively small. It's been postulated that this difference might be due to men and women placing divergent values on outcomes. "It is possible that a few hundred dollars more in salary or the corner office is less important to women than forming and maintaining an interpersonal relationship."[30]

The belief that women are "nicer" than men in negotiations is probably due to a confusion between gender and the lower degree of power women typically hold in most large organizations. Because women are expected to be "nice" and men "tough," research shows that, relative to men, women are penalized when they initiate negotiations.[31] What's more, when women and men actually do conform to these stereotypes—women act "nice" and men "tough"—it becomes a self-fulfilling prophecy, reinforcing the stereotypical gender differences between male and female negotiators.[32] Thus, one of the reasons why negotiations favor men is that women are "damned if they do, damned if they don't." Negotiate tough and they are penalized for violating a gender stereotype. Negotiate nice and it only reinforces the stereotype (and is taken advantage of).

In addition to the other party's attitudes and behaviors, the evidence also suggests that women's own attitudes and behaviors hurt them in negotiations. Managerial women demonstrate less confidence in anticipation of negotiating and are less satisfied with their performance after the process is complete, even when their performance and the outcomes they achieve are similar to those for men.[33] This latter conclusion suggests that women may unduly penalize themselves by failing to engage in negotiations when such action would be in their best interests.

GLOBAL IMPLICATIONS

Conflict and Culture

Although there is relatively little research on cross-cultural differences in conflict resolution strategies, some research suggests differences between U.S. and Asian managers. This research indicates that individuals in Japan and in the United States view conflict differently. Compared to Japanese negotiators, their U.S. counterparts are more likely to see offers from their counterparts as unfair and to reject them. Another study revealed that whereas U.S. managers were more likely to use competing tactics in the face of conflicts, compromising and avoiding are the most preferred methods of conflict management in China.[34]

Cultural Differences in Negotiations

Compared to the research on conflict, there is a lot more research on how negotiating styles vary across national cultures.[35] One study compared U.S. and Japanese negotiators. These researchers found that the Japanese negotiators tended to communicate indirectly and adapt their behaviors to the situation. A follow-up study showed that whereas among U.S. managers making early offers led to the anchoring effect we noted when discussing distributive negotiation, for Japanese negotiators, early offers led to more information sharing and better integrative outcomes.[36]

Another study compared North American, Arab, and Russian negotiators.[37] North Americans tried to persuade by relying on facts and appealing to logic. They countered opponents' arguments with objective facts. They made small concessions early in the negotiation to establish a relationship and usually reciprocated opponents' concessions. North Americans treated deadlines as very important. The Arabs tried to persuade by appealing to emotion. They countered opponents' arguments with subjective feelings. They made concessions throughout the bargaining process and almost always reciprocated opponents' concessions. Arabs approached deadlines very casually. The Russians based their arguments on asserted ideals. They made few, if any, concessions. Any concession offered by an opponent was viewed as a weakness and almost never reciprocated. Finally, the Russians tended to ignore deadlines.

Another study looked at verbal and nonverbal negotiation tactics exhibited by North Americans, Japanese, and Brazilians during half-hour bargaining sessions.[38] Some of the differences were particularly interesting. For instance, the Brazilians on average said "no" 83 times, compared to 5 times for the Japanese and 9 times for the North Americans. The Japanese displayed more than 5 periods of silence lasting longer than 10 seconds during the 30-minute sessions. North Americans averaged 3.5 such periods; the Brazilians had none. The Japanese and North Americans interrupted their opponent about the same number of times, but the Brazilians interrupted 2.5 to 3 times more often than the North Americans and the Japanese. Finally, the Japanese and the North Americans had no physical contact with their opponents during negotiations except for handshaking, but the Brazilians touched each other almost 5 times every half hour.

IMPLICATIONS FOR MANAGERS

Managing Conflict

Many people assume that conflict is related to lower group and organizational performance. This chapter has demonstrated that this assumption is often false. Conflict can be either constructive or destructive to the functioning of a group or unit. When it's too high or too low, conflict hinders performance. At an optimal level, there is enough conflict to prevent stagnation, stimulate creativity, allow tensions to be released, and initiate the seeds for change, yet not so much as to be disruptive. As shown in Exhibit 13-6, levels of conflict can be either too high or too low. Either extreme hinders performance. An optimal level is one at which there is

EXHIBIT 13-6 Conflict and Unit Performance

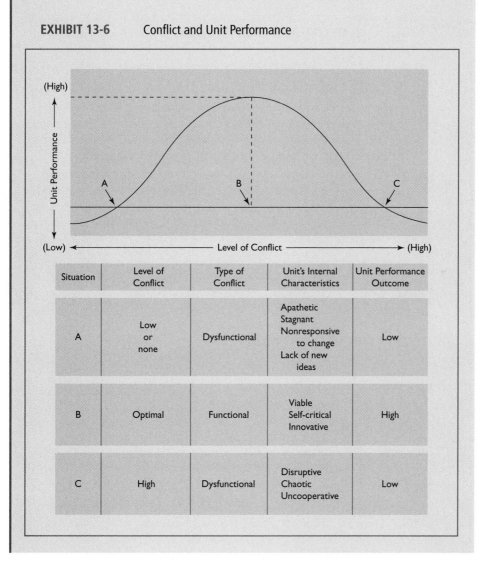

Situation	Level of Conflict	Type of Conflict	Unit's Internal Characteristics	Unit Performance Outcome
A	Low or none	Dysfunctional	Apathetic Stagnant Nonresponsive to change Lack of new ideas	Low
B	Optimal	Functional	Viable Self-critical Innovative	High
C	High	Dysfunctional	Disruptive Chaotic Uncooperative	Low

enough conflict to prevent stagnation, stimulate creativity, allow tensions to be released, and initiate the seeds for change, yet not so much as to be disruptive or to deter coordination of activities.

What advice can we give to managers faced with excessive conflict and the need to reduce it? Don't assume that one conflict-handling approach will always be best! Select the resolution technique appropriate for each situation. Here are some guidelines:[39]

- Use *competition* when quick, decisive action is vital (in emergencies); on important issues, for which unpopular actions need implementing (in cost cutting, enforcing unpopular rules, discipline); on issues vital to the organization's welfare when you know you're right; and against people who take advantage of noncompetitive behavior.

- Use *collaboration* to find an integrative solution when both sets of concerns are too important to be compromised; when your objective is to learn; to merge insights from people with different perspectives; to gain commitment by incorporating concerns into a consensus; and to work through feelings that have interfered with a relationship.

- Use *avoidance* when an issue is trivial or when more important issues are pressing; when you perceive no chance of satisfying your concerns; when potential disruption outweighs the benefits of resolution; to let people cool down and regain perspective; when gathering information supersedes an immediate decision; when others can resolve the conflict more effectively; and when issues seem tangential or symptomatic of other issues.

- Use *accommodation* when finding you are wrong and to allow a better position to be heard, to learn, and to show your reasonableness; when issues are more important to others than to yourself and to satisfy others and maintain cooperation; to build social credits for later issues; to minimize loss when you are outmatched and losing; when harmony and stability are especially important; and to allow subordinates to develop by learning from mistakes.

- Use *compromise* when goals are important but not worth the effort of potential disruption of more assertive approaches; when opponents with equal power are committed to mutually exclusive goals; to achieve temporary settlements of complex issues; to arrive at expedient solutions under time pressure; and as a backup when collaboration or competition is unsuccessful.

Improving Negotiation Skills

The following recommendations should help improve your effectiveness at negotiating:[40]

- *Set ambitious goals.* Research shows that the best agreements are negotiated by people who set goals and make aggressive initial offers. So, set ambitious goals and take the lead by making an aggressive first offer.

- *Pay little attention to initial offers.* Because initial offers often "anchor" negotiations, resist being anchored by the other party's offer. Particularly in distributive negotiations, stick to your goals.

- *Research your opponent.* Acquire as much information as you can about your opponent's interests and goals. What constituencies must he or she appease? What is his or her strategy? This knowledge will help you to better understand your opponent's behavior, predict responses to your offers, and help you to frame solutions in terms of his or her interests.

- *Address the problem, not personalities.* Concentrate on the negotiation issues, not on the personal characteristics of your opponent. When negotiations get tough, avoid the tendency to attack your opponent. It's your opponent's ideas or position that you disagree with, not him or her personally. Separate the person from the problem, and don't personalize differences.

- *Be creative and emphasize win–win solutions.* If conditions are supportive, look for an integrative solution. Frame options in terms of your opponent's interests, and look for solutions that can allow both you and your opponent to declare a victory. Try to create options that may make both parties happy. Remember, no danger lies in putting forward possible solutions as long as all of them are intended to meet your goals.

CHAPTER 14

Foundations of Organization Structure

After studying this chapter, you should be able to:

1. Identify the six elements of an organization's structure.
2. Describe the common organizational designs.
3. Compare and contrast the virtual and boundaryless organizations.
4. Demonstrate how organizational structures differ.
5. Analyze the behavioral implications of different organizational designs.
6. Show how globalization affects organizational structure.

The theme of this chapter is that organizations have different structures and that these structures have a bearing on employee attitudes and behavior. More specifically, in the following pages, we'll define the key components that make up an organization's structure, present half a dozen or so structural design options, identify the contingency factors that make certain structural designs preferable in different situations, and conclude by considering the different effects that various organizational structures have on employee behavior.

WHAT IS ORGANIZATIONAL STRUCTURE?

An **organizational structure** defines how job tasks are formally divided, grouped, and coordinated. There are six key elements that managers need to address when designing their organization's structure: work specialization, departmentalization, chain of command, span of control, centralization and decentralization, and formalization.[1]

EXHIBIT 14-1   Key Design Questions and Answers for Designing the Proper
Organizational Structure

The Key Question	The Answer Is Provided By
1. To what degree are activities subdivided into separate jobs?	Work specialization
2. On what basis will jobs be grouped together?	Departmentalization
3. To whom do individuals and groups report?	Chain of command
4. How many individuals can a manager efficiently and effectively direct?	Span of control
5. Where does decision-making authority lie?	Centralization and decentralization
6. To what degree will there be rules and regulations to direct employees and managers?	Formalization

Exhibit 14-1 presents each of these elements as answers to an important structural question. The following sections describe these six elements of structure.

Work Specialization

Early in the twentieth century, Henry Ford became rich and famous by building automobiles on an assembly line. Every Ford worker was assigned a specific, repetitive task. For instance, one person would just put on the right-front wheel, and someone else would install the right-front door. By breaking jobs up into small standardized tasks, which could be performed over and over again, Ford was able to produce cars at the rate of one every 10 seconds, while using employees who had relatively limited skills.

Ford demonstrated that work can be performed more efficiently if employees are allowed to specialize. Today we use the term **work specialization**, or *division of labor*, to describe the degree to which activities in the organization are subdivided into separate jobs. The essence of work specialization is that rather than an entire job being done by one individual, it is broken down into a number of steps, with each step being completed by a separate individual. In essence, individuals specialize in doing part of an activity rather than the entire activity.

By the late 1940s, most manufacturing jobs in industrialized countries were performed with high work specialization. Because not all employees in an organization have the same skills, management saw specialization as a means to make the most efficient use of its employees' skills. Managers also saw other efficiencies that could be achieved through work specialization. Employee skills at performing a task successfully increase through repetition. Less time is spent in changing tasks, in putting away one's tools and equipment from a prior step in the work process, and in getting ready for another. Equally important, training for specialization is more efficient from the organization's perspective. It's easier and less costly to find and train workers to do specific and repetitive tasks. This is especially true of highly sophisticated and complex operations. For example, could Cessna produce one Citation jet a year if one person had to build the entire plane alone? Not likely! Finally, work specialization increases efficiency and productivity by encouraging the creation of special inventions and machinery.

For much of the first half of the twentieth century, managers viewed work specialization as an unending source of increased productivity. And they were probably right. Because specialization was not widely practiced, its introduction almost always generated higher productivity. But by the 1960s, there arose increasing evidence that a good thing can be carried too far. The point had been reached in some jobs at which the human diseconomies from specialization—which surfaced as boredom, fatigue, stress, low productivity, poor quality, increased absenteeism, and high turnover—more than offset the economic advantages (see Exhibit 14-2). In such cases, productivity could be increased by enlarging, rather than narrowing, the scope of job activities. In addition, a number of companies found that by giving employees a variety of activities to do, allowing them to do a whole and complete job, and putting them into teams with interchangeable skills, they often achieved significantly higher output, with increased employee satisfaction.

Most managers today see work specialization as neither obsolete nor an unending source of increased productivity. Rather, managers recognize the economies it provides in certain types of jobs and the problems it creates when it's carried too far. You'll find, for example, high work specialization being used by McDonald's to efficiently make and sell hamburgers and fries and by medical specialists in most health maintenance organizations. On the other hand, companies such as Saturn Corporation have had success by broadening the scope of jobs and reducing specialization.

Departmentalization

Once you've divided jobs up through work specialization, you need to group these jobs together so that common tasks can be coordinated. The basis by which jobs are grouped together is called **departmentalization**.

One of the most popular ways to group activities is by *functions* performed. A manufacturing manager might organize a plant by separating engineering, accounting, manufacturing, personnel, and supply specialists into different departments. Of course,

EXHIBIT 14-2   Economies and Diseconomies of Work Specialization

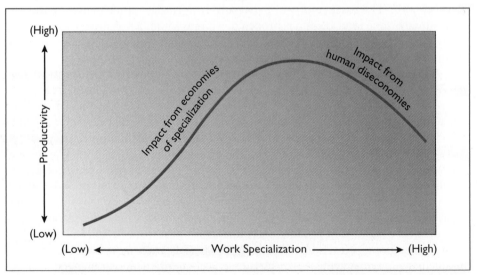

departmentalization by function can be used in all types of organizations. Only the functions change to reflect the organization's objectives and activities. A hospital might have departments devoted to research, patient care, accounting, and so forth. A professional football franchise might have departments entitled Player Personnel, Ticket Sales, and Travel and Accommodations. The major advantage to this type of grouping is obtaining efficiencies from putting like specialists together. Functional departmentalization seeks to achieve economies of scale by placing people with common skills and orientations into common units.

Jobs can also be departmentalized by the type of *product* the organization produces. Procter & Gamble, for instance, is organized along these lines. Each major product—such as Tide, Pampers, Charmin, and Pringles—is placed under the authority of an executive who has complete global responsibility for that product. The major advantage to this type of grouping is increased accountability for product performance since all activities related to a specific product are under the direction of a single manager. If an organization's activities were service related rather than product related, each service would be autonomously grouped.

Another way to departmentalize is on the basis of *geography*, or territory. The sales function, for instance, may have western, southern, midwestern, and eastern regions. Each of these regions is, in effect, a department organized around geography. If an organization's customers are scattered over a large geographic area and have similar needs based on their location, then this form of departmentalization can be valuable.

Process departmentalization can be used for processing customers as well as products. If you've ever been to a state motor vehicle office to get a driver's license, you probably went through several departments before receiving your license. In one state, applicants must go through three steps, each handled by a separate department: (1) validation by motor vehicles division, (2) processing by the licensing department, and (3) payment collection by the treasury department.

A final category of departmentalization is to use the particular type of *customer* the organization seeks to reach. Microsoft, for instance, is organized around four customer markets: consumers, large corporations, software developers, and small businesses. The assumption underlying customer departmentalization is that customers in each department have a common set of problems and needs that can best be met by having specialists for each.

Large organizations may use all of the forms of departmentalization that we've described. A major Japanese electronics firm, for instance, organizes each of its divisions along functional lines and its manufacturing units around processes; it departmentalizes sales around seven geographic regions and divides each sales region into four customer groupings. Across organizations of all sizes, one strong trend has developed over the past decade. Rigid, functional departmentalization is increasingly complemented by teams that cross over traditional departmental lines. As tasks have become more complex and more diverse skills are needed to accomplish those tasks, management has turned to cross-functional teams.

—As tasks have become more complex and more diverse skills have been needed to accomplish those tasks, management has turned to cross-functional teams.

Chain of Command

Thirty-five years ago, the chain-of-command concept was a basic cornerstone in the design of organizations. As you'll see, it has far less importance today.[2] But contemporary managers should still consider its implications when they decide how best to structure their organizations. The **chain of command** is an unbroken line of authority that extends from the top of the organization to the lowest echelon and clarifies who reports to whom. It answers questions for employees such as "To whom do I go if I have a problem?" and "To whom am I responsible?"

You can't discuss the chain of command without discussing two complementary concepts: *authority* and *unity of command.* **Authority** refers to the rights inherent in a managerial position to give orders and expect the orders to be obeyed. To facilitate coordination, each managerial position is given a place in the chain of command, and each manager is given a degree of authority in order to meet his or her responsibilities. The **unity-of-command** principle helps preserve the concept of an unbroken line of authority. It states that a person should have one and only one superior to whom that person is directly responsible. If the unity of command is broken, an employee might have to cope with conflicting demands or priorities from several superiors.

Times change, and so do the basic tenets of organizational design. The concepts of chain of command, authority, and unity of command have substantially less relevance today because of advancements in information technology and the trend toward empowering employees. For instance, a low-level employee today can access information in seconds that 35 years ago was available only to top managers. Similarly, networked computers increasingly allow employees anywhere in an organization to communicate with anyone else without going through formal channels. Moreover, the concepts of authority and maintaining the chain of command are increasingly less relevant as operating employees are being empowered to make decisions that previously were reserved for management. Add to this the popularity of self-managed and cross-functional teams and the creation of new structural designs that include multiple bosses, and the unity-of-command concept takes on less relevance. There are, of course, still many organizations that find they can be most productive by enforcing the chain of command; there just seem to be fewer of them today.

Span of Control

How many employees can a manager efficiently and effectively direct? This question of **span of control** is important because, to a large degree, it determines the number of levels and managers an organization has. All things being equal, the wider or larger the span, the more efficient the organization. An example can illustrate the validity of this statement.

Assume that we have two organizations, each of which has approximately 4,100 operative-level employees. As Exhibit 14-3 illustrates, if one has a uniform span of four and the other a span of eight, the wider span would have two fewer levels and approximately 800 fewer managers. If the average manager made $50,000 a year, the wider span would save $40 million a year in management salaries! Obviously, wider spans are more efficient in terms of cost. However, at some point, wider spans reduce effectiveness. That is, when the span becomes too large, employee performance suffers because supervisors no longer have the time to provide the necessary leadership and support.

Narrow, or small, spans have their advocates. By keeping the span of control to five or six employees, a manager can maintain close control.[3] But narrow spans have three major drawbacks. First, as already described, they're expensive because they add

EXHIBIT 14-3   Contrasting Spans of Control

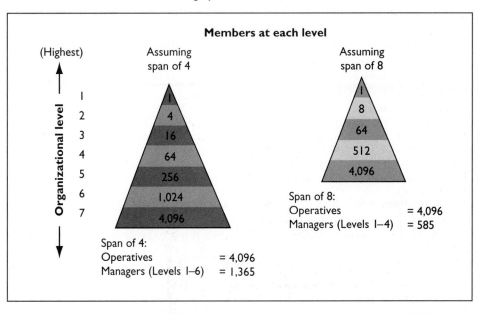

Members at each level

(Highest)   Assuming span of 4   Assuming span of 8

Organizational level

Level	Span of 4	Span of 8
1	1	1
2	4	8
3	16	64
4	64	512
5	256	4,096
6	1,024	
7	4,096	

Span of 4:
Operatives = 4,096
Managers (Levels 1–6) = 1,365

Span of 8:
Operatives = 4,096
Managers (Levels 1–4) = 585

levels of management. Second, they make vertical communication in the organization more complex. The added levels of hierarchy slow down decision making and tend to isolate upper management. Third, narrow spans of control encourage overly tight supervision and discourage employee autonomy.

The trend in recent years has been toward wider spans of control.[4] They're consistent with recent efforts by companies to reduce costs, cut overhead, speed up decision making, increase flexibility, get closer to customers, and empower employees. However, to ensure that performance doesn't suffer because of these wider spans, organizations have been investing heavily in employee training. Managers recognize that they can handle a wider span when employees know their jobs inside and out or can turn to their coworkers when they have questions.

Centralization and Decentralization

In some organizations, top managers make all the decisions. Lower-level managers merely carry out top management's directives. At the other extreme, there are organizations in which decision making is pushed down to the managers who are closest to the action. The former organizations are highly centralized; the latter are decentralized.

The term **centralization** refers to the degree to which decision making is concentrated at a single point in the organization. The concept includes only formal authority—that is, the rights inherent in one's position. Typically, it's said that if top management makes the organization's key decisions with little or no input from lower-level personnel, then the organization is centralized. In contrast, the more that lower-level personnel provide input or are actually given the discretion to make decisions, the more decentralization there is. An organization characterized by centralization is an inherently different structural animal from one that is decentralized.

In a decentralized organization, action can be taken more quickly to solve problems, more people provide input into decisions, and employees are less likely to feel alienated from those who make the decisions that affect their work lives.

Consistent with recent management efforts to make organizations more flexible and responsive, there has been a marked trend toward decentralizing decision making. In large companies, lower-level managers are closer to "the action" and typically have more detailed knowledge about problems than do top managers. For instance, big retailers such as Sears and JCPenney have given their store managers considerably more discretion in choosing what merchandise to stock. This allows those stores to compete more effectively against local merchants.

Formalization

Formalization refers to the degree to which jobs within the organization are standardized. If a job is highly formalized, then the job incumbent has a minimum amount of discretion over what is to be done, when it is to be done, and how it is to be done. Employees can be expected always to handle the same input in exactly the same way, resulting in a consistent and uniform output. There are explicit job descriptions, many organizational rules, and clearly defined procedures covering work processes in organizations in which there is high formalization. Where formalization is low, job behaviors are relatively nonprogrammed, and employees have a great deal of freedom to exercise discretion in their work. Because an individual's discretion on the job is inversely related to the amount of behavior in that job that is preprogrammed by the organization, the greater the standardization, the less input the employee has into how the work is to be done. Not only does standardization eliminate the possibility of employees engaging in alternative behaviors, it even removes the need for employees to consider alternatives.

The degree of formalization can vary widely between organizations and within organizations. Certain jobs, for instance, are well known to have little formalization. College book travelers—the representatives of publishers who call on professors to inform them of their company's new publications—have a great deal of freedom in their jobs.

—The simple structure has a low degree of departmentalization, wide spans of control, authority centralized in a single person, and little formalization.

They have no standard sales "spiel," and the extent of rules and procedures governing their behavior may be little more than the requirement that they submit a weekly sales report and some suggestions on what to emphasize for the various new titles. At the other extreme, there are clerical and editorial positions in the same publishing houses for which employees are required to be at their desks by 8:00 A.M. or be docked a half-hour's pay and, once at that desk, to follow a set of precise procedures dictated by management.

COMMON ORGANIZATIONAL DESIGNS

We now turn to describing three of the more common organizational designs found in use: the *simple structure*, the *bureaucracy*, and the *matrix structure*.

The Simple Structure

What do a small retail store, an electronics firm run by a hard-driving entrepreneur, and an airline in the midst of a company-wide pilot's strike have in common? They probably all use the **simple structure**.

The simple structure is said to be characterized most by what it is not rather than by what it is. The simple structure is not elaborate.[5] It has a low degree of departmentalization, wide spans of control, authority centralized in a single person, and little formalization. The simple structure is a "flat" organization; it usually has only two or three vertical levels, a loose body of employees, and one individual in whom the decision-making authority is centralized.

The strength of the simple structure lies in its simplicity. It's fast, flexible, and inexpensive to maintain, and accountability is clear. One major weakness is its use in large organizations. It becomes increasingly inadequate as an organization grows because its low formalization and high centralization tend to create information overload at the top. As size increases, decision making typically becomes slower and can eventually come to a standstill as the single executive tries to continue making all the decisions. This often proves to be the undoing of many small businesses. When an organization begins to employ 50 or 100 people, it's very difficult for the owner-manager to make all the choices. If the structure isn't changed and made more elaborate, the firm often loses momentum and can eventually fail. The simple structure's other weakness is it's riskiness—everything depends on one person. One heart attack can literally destroy the organization's information and decision-making center.

The Bureaucracy

Standardization! That's the key concept that underlies all bureaucracies. Take a look at the bank where you keep your checking account; the department store where you buy your clothes; or the government offices that collect your taxes, enforce health regulations, or provide local fire protection. They all rely on standardized work processes for coordination and control.

The **bureaucracy** is characterized by highly routine operating tasks achieved through specialization, very formalized rules and regulations, tasks that are grouped into functional departments, centralized authority, narrow spans of control, and decision making that follows the chain of command. *Bureaucracy* is a dirty word in many people's minds. However, it does have its advantages. The primary strength of bureaucracy lies in its ability to perform standardized activities in a highly efficient manner. Putting like specialties together in functional departments results in economies of scale, minimal duplication of personnel and equipment, and employees who have the opportunity to talk "the same language" among their peers. Furthermore, bureaucracies can get by nicely with less talented—and, hence, less costly—middle- and lower-level managers. The pervasiveness of rules and regulations substitutes for managerial discretion. Standardized operations, coupled with high formalization, allow decision making to be centralized. There is little need, therefore, for innovative and experienced decision makers below the level of senior executives.

One of the major weaknesses of a bureaucracy is illustrated in the following dialogue among four executives in one company: "Ya know, nothing happens in this place until we *produce* something," said the production executive. "Wrong," commented the research and development manager. "Nothing happens until we *design* something!" "What are you talking about?" asked the marketing executive. "Nothing happens here until we *sell* something!" Finally, the exasperated accounting manager responded, "It doesn't matter what you produce, design, or sell. No one knows what happens until we *tally up the results*!" This conversation points to the fact that specialization creates subunit conflicts. Functional unit goals can override the overall goals of the organization.

The other major weakness of a bureaucracy is something we've all experienced at one time or another when dealing with people who work in these organizations: obsessive concern with following the rules. When cases arise that don't precisely fit the rules, there is no room for modification. The bureaucracy is efficient only as long as employees confront problems that they have previously encountered and for which programmed decision rules have already been established.

The Matrix Structure

Another popular organizational design option is the **matrix structure**. You'll find it is used in advertising agencies, aerospace firms, research and development laboratories, construction companies, hospitals, government agencies, universities, management consulting firms, and entertainment companies.[6] Essentially, the matrix combines two forms of departmentalization: functional and product departmentalization.

The strength of functional departmentalization lies in putting like specialists together, which minimizes the number necessary while allowing the pooling and sharing of specialized resources across products. Its major disadvantage is the difficulty of coordinating the tasks of diverse functional specialists so that their activities are completed on time and on budget. Product departmentalization, on the other hand, has exactly the opposite benefits and disadvantages. It facilitates coordination among specialties to achieve on-time completion and to meet budget targets. Furthermore, it provides clear responsibility for all activities related to a product, but with duplication of activities and costs. The matrix attempts to gain the strengths of each, while avoiding their weaknesses.

The most obvious structural characteristic of the matrix is that it breaks the unity-of-command concept. Employees in the matrix have two bosses—their functional department managers and their product managers. Therefore, the matrix has a dual chain of command.

Exhibit 14-4 shows the matrix form as used in a college of business administration. The academic departments of accounting, decision and information systems, marketing, and so forth are functional units. In addition, specific programs (that is, products) are overlaid on the functions. In this way, members in a matrix structure have a dual assignment—to their functional department and to their product groups. For instance, a professor of accounting who is teaching an undergraduate course may report to the director of undergraduate programs as well as to the chairperson of the accounting department.

The strength of the matrix lies in its ability to facilitate coordination when the organization has a multiplicity of complex and interdependent activities. As an organization gets larger, its information-processing capacity can become overloaded. In a bureaucracy, complexity results in increased formalization. The direct and frequent contact between different specialties in the matrix can create better communication and more flexibility. Information permeates the organization and quickly reaches the people who need to take account of it. Furthermore, the matrix reduces "bureaupathologies"; the dual lines of authority reduce the tendencies of departmental members to become so busy protecting their little worlds that the organization's overall goals become secondary.

There is another advantage to the matrix: It facilitates the efficient allocation of specialists. When individuals with highly specialized skills are lodged in one functional department or product group, their talents are monopolized and underused. The matrix

EXHIBIT 14-4   Matrix Structure for a College of Business Administration

Programs / Academic departments	Undergraduate	Master's	Ph.D.	Research	Executive development	Community service
Accounting						
Finance						
Decision and information systems						
Management						
Marketing						

achieves the advantages of economies of scale by providing the organization with both the best resources and an effective way of ensuring their efficient deployment.

The major disadvantages of the matrix lie in the confusion it creates, its propensity to foster power struggles, and the stress it places on individuals.[7] When you dispense with the unity-of-command concept, ambiguity is significantly increased, and ambiguity often leads to conflict. For example, it's frequently unclear who reports to whom, and it is not unusual for product managers to fight over getting the best specialists assigned to their products. Confusion and ambiguity also create the seeds of power struggles. Bureaucracy reduces the potential for power grabs by defining the rules of the game. When those rules are "up for grabs," power struggles between functional and product managers result. For individuals who desire security and absence from ambiguity, this work climate can produce stress. Reporting to more than one boss introduces role conflict, and unclear expectations introduce role ambiguity. The comfort of bureaucracy's predictability is absent, replaced by insecurity and stress.

NEW DESIGN OPTIONS

Over the past decade or two, senior managers in a number of organizations have been working to develop new structural options that can better help their firms to compete effectively. In this section, we'll describe two such structural designs: the *virtual organization* and the *boundaryless organization*.

The Virtual Organization

Why own when you can rent? This question captures the essence of the **virtual organization** (also sometimes called the *network*, or *modular*, organization), typically a small, core organization that outsources major business functions.[8] In structural terms, the virtual organization is highly centralized, with little or no departmentalization.

Ancle Hsu and David Ji run a virtual organization. Their firm, California-based Apex Digital, is one of the world's largest producers of DVD players, yet the company neither owns a factory nor employs an engineer. They contract everything out to firms in China. With minimal investment, Apex has grown from nothing to annual sales of over $500 million in just 3 years. Similarly, Paul Newman's food products company, Newman's Own, sells over $120 million every year yet employs only nineteen people. This is possible because it outsources almost everything—manufacturing, procurement, shipping, and quality control.

Almost all large organizations have increased their outsourcing. Boeing, for example, assembles all of its planes in the Seattle area, but outsources the production of many of its components. Other companies may outsource their entire information systems to organizations like EDS or IBM. Still others, such as AT&T, Dell, and Time Warner, outsource entire operations—such as customer service or technical support—to other (often overseas) organizations.

What's going on here? A quest for maximum flexibility. These virtual organizations have created networks of relationships that allow them to contract out manufacturing, distribution, marketing, or any other business function for which management feels that others can do better or more cheaply. The virtual organization stands in sharp contrast to the typical bureaucracy that has many vertical levels of management and where control is sought through ownership. In such organizations, research and development are done in-house, production occurs in company-owned plants, and sales and marketing are performed by the company's own employees. To support all this, management has to employ extra staff, including accountants, human resource specialists, and lawyers. The virtual organization, however, outsources many of these functions and concentrates on what it does best. For most U.S. firms, that means focusing on design or marketing.

Exhibit 14-5 shows a virtual organization in which management outsources all of the primary functions of the business. The core of the organization is a small group of executives whose job is to oversee directly any activities that are done in-house and to coordinate relationships with the other organizations that manufacture, distribute, and perform other crucial functions for the virtual organization. The dotted lines in Exhibit 14-5 represent the relationships typically maintained under contracts. In

EXHIBIT 14-5   A Virtual Organization

essence, managers in virtual structures spend most of their time coordinating and controlling external relations, typically by way of computer-network links.

The major advantage to the virtual organization is its flexibility. For instance, it allows individuals with an innovative idea and little money, such as Ancle Hsu and David Ji, to successfully compete against the likes of Sony, Hitachi, and Sharp Electronics. The primary drawback to this structure is the reduction in management's control over key parts of its business.

The Boundaryless Organization

General Electric's former chairman, Jack Welch, coined the term **boundaryless organization** to describe his idea of what he wanted GE to become. Welch wanted to turn his company into a "family grocery store."[9] That is, in spite of its monstrous size (2007 revenues were $173 billion), he wanted to eliminate *vertical* and *horizontal* boundaries within GE and break down *external* barriers between the company and its customers and suppliers. The boundaryless organization seeks to eliminate the chain of command, have limitless spans of control, and replace departments with empowered teams. This structure relies so heavily on information technology that some have turned to calling this a *T-form* (or technology-based) organization.[10] Although GE has not yet achieved this boundaryless state—and probably never will—it has made significant progress toward that end. So have other companies, such as Hewlett-Packard, AT&T, Motorola, and 3M. Let's take a look at what a boundaryless organization would look like and what some firms are doing to try to make it a reality.[11]

By removing vertical boundaries, management flattens the hierarchy. Status and rank are minimized. Cross-hierarchical teams (which include top executives, middle managers, supervisors, and operative employees), participative decision-making practices, and the use of 360-degree performance appraisals (in which peers and others above and below the employee evaluate performance) are examples of what GE is doing to break down vertical boundaries. At Oticon A/S, a $160-million-per-year Danish hearing aid manufacturer, all traces of hierarchy have disappeared. Everyone works at uniform mobile workstations and project teams, not functions or departments, coordinate work.

Functional departments create horizontal boundaries, which stifle interaction between functions, product lines, and units. The way to reduce these barriers is to replace functional departments with cross-functional teams and to organize activities around processes. For instance, Xerox now develops new products through multidisciplinary teams that work in a single process instead of around narrow functional tasks. Similarly, some AT&T units are now creating annual budgets based not on functions or departments but on processes such as the maintenance of a worldwide telecommunications network. Another way management can cut through horizontal barriers is to use lateral transfers, rotating people into and out of different functional areas. This approach turns specialists into generalists.

WHY DO STRUCTURES DIFFER?

In the previous sections, we described a variety of organizational designs ranging from the highly structured and standardized bureaucracy to the loose and amorphous boundaryless organization. The other designs we discussed tend to exist somewhere between these two extremes.

Exhibit 14-6 reconceptualizes our previous discussions by presenting two extreme models of organizational design. One extreme we'll call the **mechanistic model**. It's generally synonymous with the bureaucracy in that it has extensive departmentalization, high formalization, a limited information network (mostly downward communication), and little participation by low-level members in decision making. At the other extreme is the **organic model**. This model looks a lot like the boundaryless organization. It's flat, uses cross-hierarchical and cross-functional teams, has low formalization, possesses a comprehensive information network (using lateral and upward communication as well as downward), and involves high participation in decision making.[12]

With these two models in mind, we're now prepared to address a couple of questions: Why are some organizations structured along more mechanistic lines, whereas others follow organic characteristics? What are the forces that influence the design that is chosen? There are four major forces that determine an organization's structure: strategy, organization size, technology, and the environment.[13] Let's review each of these.

Strategy

An organization's structure is meant to help management achieve its objectives. Because objectives are derived from the organization's overall strategy, it's only logical that strategy and structure should be closely linked. More specifically, structure should follow strategy. If management makes a significant change in its organization's strategy, the structure will need to be modified to accommodate and support this change.[14] Most current strategy frameworks focus on three strategy

EXHIBIT 14-6   Mechanistic Versus Organic Models

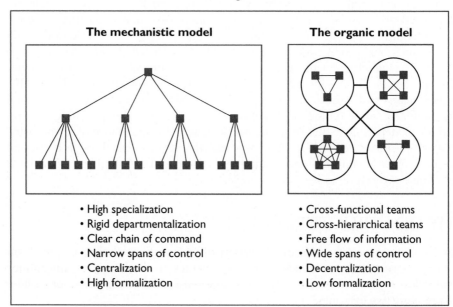

The mechanistic model	The organic model
• High specialization	• Cross-functional teams
• Rigid departmentalization	• Cross-hierarchical teams
• Clear chain of command	• Free flow of information
• Narrow spans of control	• Wide spans of control
• Centralization	• Decentralization
• High formalization	• Low formalization

dimensions—innovation, cost minimization, and imitation—and the structural design that works best with each.[15]

To what degree does an organization introduce major new products or services? An **innovation strategy** does not mean a strategy merely for simple or cosmetic changes from previous offerings but rather one for meaningful and unique innovations (e.g., Apple). An organization that is pursuing a **cost-minimization strategy** tightly controls costs, refrains from incurring unnecessary innovation or marketing expenses, and cuts prices in selling a basic product (e.g., Wal-Mart). Finally, organizations following an **imitation strategy** try to capitalize on the best of both of the previous strategies. They seek to minimize risk and maximize opportunity for profit. Their strategy is to move into new products or new markets only after viability has been proven by innovators. They take the successful ideas of innovators and copy them (e.g., Caterpillar).

Organization Size

There is considerable evidence to support the idea that an organization's size significantly affects its structure.[16] For instance, large organizations—those that typically employ 2,000 or more people—tend to have more specialization, more departmentalization, more vertical levels, and more rules and regulations than do small organizations. However, the relationship isn't linear. Rather, size affects structure at a decreasing rate. The impact of size becomes less important as an organization expands. Why is this? Essentially, once an organization has around 2,000 employees, it's already fairly mechanistic. An additional 500 employees will not have much impact. On the other hand, adding 500 employees to an organization that has only 300 members is likely to result in a significant shift toward a more mechanistic structure.

Technology

The term **technology** refers to how an organization transfers its inputs into outputs. Every organization has at least one technology for converting financial, human, and physical resources into products or services. The Ford Motor Co., for instance, predominantly uses an assembly-line process to make its products. On the other hand, colleges may use a number of instruction technologies—the ever-popular formal lecture method, the case-analysis method, the experiential exercise method, the programmed learning method, and so forth.

What is the relationship between technology and structure? We find that organizations operating with routine, stable technologies tend to have taller and more departmentalized structures. Heavy manufacturing (e.g., John Deere, Boeing, GM), therefore, tends to be more hierarchical than organizations facing ever-changing technologies (e.g., Google, eBay).

Environment

An organization's **environment** is composed of institutions or forces outside the organization that potentially affect the organization's performance. These typically include suppliers, customers, competitors, government regulatory agencies, public pressure groups, and the like.

Why should an organization's structure be affected by its environment? Because of environmental uncertainty. Some organizations face relatively static environments—few forces in their environment are changing. There are, for example, no new competitors, no new technological breakthroughs by current competitors, or little activity by public pressure groups to influence the organization. Other organizations face very dynamic environments—rapidly changing government regulations affecting their business, new competitors, difficulties in acquiring raw materials, continually changing product preferences by customers, and so on. Static environments create significantly less uncertainty for managers than do dynamic ones. And because uncertainty is a threat to an organization's effectiveness, management will try to minimize it. One way to reduce environmental uncertainty is through adjustments in the organization's structure.[17] Essentially, the more dynamic and uncertain the environment, the greater the need for flexibility. Hence, the organic structure will lead to higher organizational effectiveness. Conversely, in stable and predictable environments, the mechanistic form will be the structure of choice.

ORGANIZATIONAL DESIGNS AND EMPLOYEE BEHAVIOR

We opened this chapter by implying that an organization's structure can have significant effects on its members. In this section, we want to assess directly those effects.

A review of the evidence linking organizational structures to employee performance and satisfaction leads to a pretty clear conclusion—you can't generalize! Not everyone prefers the freedom and flexibility of organic structures. Some people are most productive and satisfied when work tasks are standardized and ambiguity is minimized—that is, in mechanistic structures. So any discussion of the effect of organizational design on employee behavior has to address individual differences. To illustrate this point, let's consider employee preferences for work specialization, span of control, and centralization.[18]

The evidence generally indicates that work specialization contributes to higher employee productivity but at the price of reduced job satisfaction. However, this statement ignores individual differences and the type of job tasks people do. As we noted previously, work specialization is not an unending source of higher productivity. Problems start to surface, and productivity begins to suffer, when the human diseconomies of doing repetitive and narrow tasks overtake the economies of specialization. As the workforce has become more highly educated and desirous of jobs that are intrinsically rewarding, the point at which productivity begins to decline seems to be reached more quickly than in decades past.

—*Globalization, strategic alliances, customer-organization links, and telecommuting are all examples of practices that reduce external boundaries.*

Although more people today are undoubtedly turned off by overly specialized jobs than were their parents or grandparents, it would be naive to ignore the reality that there is still a segment of the workforce that prefers the routine and repetitiveness of highly specialized jobs. Some individuals want work that makes minimal intellectual demands and provides the security of routine. For these people, high work specialization is a source of job satisfaction. The empirical question, of course, is whether this represents 2 percent of the workforce or 52 percent. Given that there is some self-selection operating in the choice of careers, we might conclude that negative behavioral outcomes from high specialization are most likely to surface in professional jobs occupied by individuals with high needs for personal growth and diversity.

A review of the research indicates that it is probably safe to say there is no evidence to support a relationship between *span of control* and employee performance. Although it is intuitively attractive to argue that large spans might lead to higher employee performance because they provide more distant supervision and more opportunity for personal initiative, the research fails to support this notion. At this point it's impossible to state that any particular span of control is best for producing high performance or high satisfaction among employees. Again, the reason is probably individual differences. That is, some people like to be left alone, while others prefer the security of a boss who is quickly available at all times. Consistent with several of the contingency theories of leadership discussed in Chapter 11, we would expect factors such as employees' experiences and abilities and the degree of structure in their tasks to explain when wide or narrow spans of control are likely to contribute to their performance and job satisfaction. However, there is some evidence indicating that a manager's job satisfaction increases as the number of employees supervised increases.

We find fairly strong evidence linking *centralization* and job satisfaction. In general, organizations that are less centralized have a greater amount of autonomy. And the evidence suggests that autonomy is positively related to job satisfaction. But, again, individual differences surface. Although one employee may value her freedom, another may find autonomous environments frustratingly ambiguous.

Our conclusion: To maximize employee performance and satisfaction, individual differences, such as experience, personality, and the work task, should be taken into account. As we'll note shortly, culture needs to be taken into consideration, too.

One obvious insight needs to be made before we leave this topic: People don't select employers randomly. There is substantial evidence that individuals are attracted to, selected by, and stay with organizations that suit their personal characteristics.[19] Job candidates who prefer predictability, for instance, are likely to seek out and take employment in mechanistic structures, and those who want autonomy are more likely to end up in an organic structure. So the effect of structure on employee behavior is undoubtedly reduced when the selection process facilitates proper matching of individual characteristics with organizational characteristics.

GLOBAL IMPLICATIONS

When we think about how culture influences how organizations are structured, several questions come to mind. First, does culture really matter to organizational structure? Second, do employees in different countries vary in their perceptions of different types of organizational structures? Finally, how do cultural considerations fit with our discussion of the boundaryless organization? Let's tackle each of these questions in turn.

Culture and Organizational Structure   Does culture really affect organizational structure? The answer might seem obvious—yes!—but there are reasons culture may not matter as much as you think. The U.S. model of business has been very influential, so much so that the organizational structures in other countries may mirror those of U.S. organizations. Moreover, U.S. structures themselves have been influenced by structures in other countries (especially Japan, Great Britain, and Germany). However, cultural concerns still might be important. Bureaucratic structures still dominate in many parts of Europe and Asia. Moreover, one management expert argues that U.S. management often places too much emphasis on individual leadership, which may be jarring in countries where decision making is more decentralized.[20]

Culture and Employee Structure Preferences   Although there isn't a great deal of research out there, it does suggest that national culture influences the preference for organizational structure, so it, too, needs to be considered.[21] For instance, organizations that operate with people from high power distance cultures, such as those found in Greece, France, and most of Latin America, find employees much more accepting of mechanistic structures than where employees come from low power distance countries. So you need to consider cultural differences along with individual differences when making predictions on how structure will affect employee performance and satisfaction.

Culture and the Boundaryless Organization   When fully operational, the boundaryless organization also breaks down barriers created by geography. Most large U.S. companies today see themselves as global corporations, and may well do as much business overseas as in the United States (Coca-Cola, for example). As a result, many companies struggle with the problem of how to incorporate geographic regions into their structure. The boundaryless organization provides one solution to this problem because geography is considered more of a tactical, logistical issue than a structural issue. In short, the goal of the boundaryless organization is to break down cultural barriers.

One way to break down barriers is through strategic alliances. Firms such as NEC Corp., Boeing, and Apple Computer each have strategic alliances or joint partnerships with dozens of companies. These alliances blur the distinction between one organization and another as employees work on joint projects. And some companies are allowing customers to perform functions that previously were completed by management. For instance, some AT&T units are receiving bonuses based on customer evaluations of the teams that serve them. Finally, telecommuting is blurring organizational boundaries. The security analyst with Merrill Lynch who performs his job from his ranch in Montana or the software designer who works for a San Francisco company but completes her job in Boulder, Colorado, are just two examples of the millions of workers who work outside the physical boundaries of their employers' premises.

IMPLICATIONS FOR MANAGERS

An organization's internal structure contributes to explaining and predicting employee behavior. That is, in addition to individual and group factors, the structural relationships in which people work have an important bearing on their attitudes and behavior.

What's the basis for the argument that structure has an effect on both attitudes and behavior? Because an organization's structure reduces ambiguity and clarifies relationships, it shapes employees' attitudes and facilitates and motivates them to higher levels of performance.

Of course, structure also constrains employees, to the extent that it limits and controls what they do. For example, an organization gives employees little autonomy when it is structured around high levels of formalization and specialization, strict adherence to the chain of command, limited delegation of authority, and narrow spans of control. Controls in such organizations are tight, and behavior will tend to vary within a narrow range. In contrast, an organization structured around limited specialization, low formalization, wide spans of control, and the like provides employees greater freedom and, thus, will be characterized by greater behavioral diversity.

CHAPTER 15

Organizational Culture

1. Define *organizational culture* and describe its common characteristics.
2. Compare the functional and dysfunctional effects of organizational culture on employees and the organization.
3. Explain the factors that create and sustain an organization's culture.
4. Show how culture is transmitted to employees.
5. Demonstrate how an ethical culture and a positive culture can be created.
6. Show how national culture may affect the way organizational culture is transported to a different country.

Just as individuals have personalities, so, too, do organizations. In Chapter 2, we found that individuals have relatively enduring and stable traits that help us predict their attitudes and behaviors. In this chapter, we propose that organizations, like people, can be characterized as, for example, rigid, friendly, warm, innovative, or conservative. These traits, in turn, can then be used to predict attitudes and behaviors of the people within these organizations.

The culture of any organization, although it may be hard to measure precisely, nevertheless exists and is generally recognized by its employees. We call this variable *organizational culture*. Just as tribal cultures have totems and taboos that dictate how each member will act toward fellow members and outsiders, organizations have cultures that govern how members behave. In this chapter, we'll discuss just what organizational culture is, how it affects employee attitudes and behavior, where it comes from, and whether it can be managed.

WHAT IS ORGANIZATIONAL CULTURE?

A number of years back, an executive was asked what he thought *organizational culture* meant. He gave essentially the same answer that a Supreme Court justice once gave in attempting to define pornography: "I can't define it, but I know it when I see it." This executive's approach to defining organizational culture isn't acceptable for our purposes. We need a basic definition to provide a point of departure for our quest to better understand the phenomenon. In this section, we propose a specific definition and review several peripheral issues that revolve around this definition.

> —Organizational culture is concerned with how employees perceive the characteristics of an organization's culture, not with whether or not they like them. An organization's culture develops over many years and is rooted in deeply held values to which employees are strongly committed.

A Definition of *Organizational Culture*

There seems to be wide agreement that **organizational culture** refers to a system of shared meaning held by members that distinguishes the organization from other organizations.[1] This system of shared meaning is, on closer examination, a set of key characteristics that the organization values. The research suggests that there are seven primary characteristics that, in aggregate, capture the essence of an organization's culture:[2]

1. *Innovation and risk taking.* The degree to which employees are encouraged to be innovative and take risks.
2. *Attention to detail.* The degree to which employees are expected to exhibit precision, analysis, and attention to detail.
3. *Outcome orientation.* The degree to which management focuses on results or outcomes rather than on the techniques and processes used to achieve those outcomes.
4. *People orientation.* The degree to which management decisions take into consideration the effect of outcomes on people within the organization.
5. *Team orientation.* The degree to which work activities are organized around teams rather than individuals.
6. *Aggressiveness.* The degree to which people are aggressive and competitive rather than easygoing.
7. *Stability.* The degree to which organizational activities emphasize maintaining the status quo in contrast to growth.

Each of these characteristics exists on a continuum from low to high. Appraising the organization on these seven characteristics, then, gives a composite picture of the organization's culture. This picture becomes the basis for feelings of shared understanding that members have about the organization, how things are done in it, and the way members are supposed to behave.

Culture Is a Descriptive Term

Organizational culture is concerned with how employees perceive the characteristics of an organization's culture, not with whether they like them; that is, it's a descriptive term. This is important because it differentiates this concept from job satisfaction.

Research on organizational culture has sought to measure how employees see their organization: Does it encourage teamwork? Does it reward innovation? Does it stifle initiative? In contrast, job satisfaction seeks to measure affective responses to the work environment. It's concerned with how employees feel about the organization's expectations, reward practices, and the like. Although the two terms undoubtedly have overlapping characteristics, keep in mind that the term *organizational culture* is descriptive, whereas *job satisfaction* is evaluative.

Do Organizations Have Uniform Cultures?

Organizational culture represents a common perception held by the organization's members. This was made explicit when we defined culture as a system of *shared* meaning. We should expect, therefore, that individuals with different backgrounds or at different levels in the organization will tend to describe the organization's culture in similar terms.[3]

Acknowledgment that organizational culture has common properties does not mean, however, that there cannot be subcultures within any given culture. Most large organizations have a dominant culture and numerous sets of subcultures. A **dominant culture** expresses the core values that are shared by a majority of the organization's members. When talking about an organization's culture, we are referring to its dominant culture. It is this macro view of culture that gives an organization its distinct personality. **Subcultures** tend to develop in large organizations to reflect common problems, situations, or experiences that members face. These subcultures are likely to be defined by department designations and geographical separation. The purchasing department, for example, can have a subculture that is uniquely shared by members of that department. It will include the **core values** of the dominant culture plus additional values unique to members of the purchasing department. Similarly, an office or unit of the organization that is physically separated from the organization's main operations may take on a different personality. Again, the core values are essentially retained, but they are modified to reflect the separated unit's distinct situation.

Strong Versus Weak Cultures

It has become increasingly popular to differentiate between strong and weak cultures.[4] The argument here is that strong cultures have a greater impact on employee behavior and are more directly related to reduced turnover.

In a **strong culture**, the organization's core values are both intensely held and widely shared. The more members accept the core values and the greater their commitment to those values, the stronger the culture. Consistent with this definition, a strong culture will have a great influence on the behavior of its members because the high degree of sharedness and intensity creates an internal climate of high behavioral control. For example, Seattle-based Nordstrom has developed one of the strongest service cultures in the retailing industry. Nordstrom employees know in no uncertain terms what is expected of them, and these expectations go a long way in shaping their behavior.

One specific result of a strong culture should be lower employee turnover. A strong culture demonstrates high agreement among members about what the organization stands for. Such unanimity of purpose builds cohesiveness, loyalty, and organizational commitment. These qualities, in turn, lessen employees' propensity to leave the organization.[5]

Culture Versus Formalization

A strong organizational culture increases behavioral consistency. In this sense, we should recognize that a strong culture can act as a substitute for formalization.

In the previous chapter, we discussed how formalization's rules and regulations act to regulate employee behavior. High formalization in an organization creates predictability, orderliness, and consistency. Our point here is that a strong culture achieves the same end without the need for written documentation. Therefore, we should view formalization and culture as two different roads to a common destination. The stronger an organization's culture, the less management needs to be concerned with developing formal rules and regulations to guide employee behavior. Those guides will be internalized in employees when they accept the organization's culture.

WHAT DO CULTURES DO?

We've alluded to the impact of organizational culture on behavior. We've also explicitly argued that a strong culture should be associated with reduced turnover. In this section, we will more carefully review the functions that culture performs and assess whether culture can be a liability for an organization.

Culture's Functions

Culture performs a number of functions within an organization. First, it has a boundary-defining role; that is, it creates distinctions between one organization and others. Second, it conveys a sense of identity for organization members. Third, culture facilitates the generation of commitment to something larger than one's individual self interest. Fourth, it enhances the stability of the social system. Culture is the social glue that helps hold the organization together by providing appropriate standards for what employees should say and do. Finally, culture serves as a sense-making and control mechanism that guides and shapes the attitudes and behavior of employees. It is this last function that is of particular interest to us.[6] Culture defines the rules of the game.

The role of culture in influencing employee behavior appears to be increasingly important in today's workplace. As organizations have widened spans of control, flattened structures, introduced teams, reduced formalization, and empowered employees, the *shared meaning* provided by a strong culture ensures that everyone is pointed in the same direction.

As we show later in this chapter, who receives a job offer to join the organization, who is appraised as a high performer, and who gets a promotion are strongly influenced by the individual–organization "fit"—that is, whether the applicant's or employee's attitudes and behavior are compatible with the culture. It's not a coincidence that employees at Disney theme parks appear to be almost universally attractive, clean, and wholesome looking, with bright smiles. That's the image Disney seeks. The company selects employees who will maintain that image. And once on the job, a strong culture, supported by formal rules and regulations, ensures that Disney theme-park employees will act in a relatively uniform and predictable way.

Culture as a Liability

We are treating culture in a nonjudgmental manner. We haven't said that it's good or bad, only that it exists. Many of its functions, as outlined, are valuable for both the organization and the employee. Culture enhances organizational commitment and increases the consistency of employee behavior. These are clearly benefits to an organization. From an employee's standpoint, culture is valuable because it reduces ambiguity. It tells employees how things are done and what's important. But we shouldn't ignore the potentially dysfunctional aspects of culture, especially a strong one, on an organization's effectiveness.

Barriers to Change   Culture is a liability when the shared values are not in agreement with those that will further the organization's effectiveness. This is most likely to occur when an organization's environment is dynamic.[7] When an environment is undergoing rapid change, an organization's entrenched culture may no longer be appropriate. So consistency of behavior is an asset to an organization when it faces a stable environment. It may, however, burden the organization and make it difficult to respond to changes in the environment. This helps to explain the challenges that executives at organizations like Mitsubishi, Eastman Kodak, Boeing, and the U.S. Federal Bureau of Investigation have had in recent years in adapting to upheavals in their environment.[8] These organizations have strong cultures that worked well for them in the past. But these strong cultures become barriers to change when "business as usual" is no longer effective.

Barriers to Diversity   Hiring new employees who, because of race, age, gender, disability, or other differences, are not like the majority of the organization's members creates a paradox.[9] Management wants new employees to accept the organization's core cultural values. Otherwise, these employees are unlikely to fit in or be accepted. At the same time, management wants to openly acknowledge and demonstrate support for the differences that these employees bring to the workplace.

Strong cultures put considerable pressure on employees to conform. They limit the range of values and styles that are acceptable. In some instances, such as the widely publicized Texaco case (which was settled on behalf of 1,400 employees for $176 million) in which senior managers made disparaging remarks about minorities, a strong culture that condones prejudice can even undermine formal corporate diversity policies.[10] Organizations seek out and hire diverse individuals because of the alternative strengths these people bring to the workplace. Yet these diverse behaviors and strengths are likely to diminish in strong cultures as people attempt to fit in. Strong cultures, therefore, can be liabilities when they effectively eliminate the unique strengths that people of different backgrounds bring to the organization. Moreover, strong cultures can also be liabilities when they support institutional bias or become insensitive to people who are different.

Barriers to Acquisitions and Mergers   Historically, the key factors that management looked at in making acquisition or merger decisions were related to financial advantages or product synergy. In recent years, cultural compatibility has become the primary concern.[11] Although a favorable financial statement or product line may be the initial attraction of an acquisition candidate, whether the acquisition actually works seems to have more to do with how well the two organizations' cultures match up.

Many acquisitions fail shortly after their consummation. A survey by consulting firm A.T. Kearney revealed that 58 percent of mergers failed to reach the value goals set by top managers.[12] The primary cause of failure is conflicting organizational cultures. As one expert commented, "Mergers have an unusually high failure rate, and it's always because of people issues." For instance, the 2001 $183 billion merger between America Online (AOL) and Time Warner was the largest in corporate history. The merger has been a disaster—only 2 years later, the stock had fallen an astounding 90 percent. Culture clash is commonly argued to be one of the causes of AOL Time Warner's problems. As one expert noted, "In some ways the merger of AOL and Time Warner was like the marriage of a teenager to a middle-aged banker. The cultures were vastly different. There were open collars and jeans at AOL. Time Warner was more buttoned-down."[13]

CREATING AND SUSTAINING CULTURE

An organization's culture doesn't pop out of thin air. Once established, it rarely fades away. What forces influence the creation of a culture? What reinforces and sustains these forces once they're in place? We answer both of these questions in this section.

How a Culture Begins

An organization's current customs, traditions, and general way of doing things are largely due to what it has done before and the degree of success it has had with those endeavors. This leads us to the ultimate source of an organization's culture: its founders.

The founders of an organization traditionally have a major impact on that organization's early culture. They have a vision of what the organization should be. They are unconstrained by previous customs or ideologies. The small size that typically characterizes new organizations further facilitates the founders' imposition of their vision on all organizational members. Culture creation occurs in three ways.[14] First, founders hire and keep only employees who think and feel the same way they do. Second, they indoctrinate and socialize these employees to their way of thinking and feeling. And finally, the founders' own behavior acts as a role model that encourages employees to identify with them and thereby internalize their beliefs, values, and assumptions. When the organization succeeds, the founders' vision is seen as a primary determinant of that success. At this point, the founders' entire personality becomes embedded in the culture of the organization.

Keeping a Culture Alive

Once a culture is in place, there are practices within the organization that act to maintain it by giving employees a set of similar experiences.[15] For example, many of the human resource practices we discuss in the next chapter reinforce the organization's culture. The selection process, performance evaluation criteria, training and development activities, and promotion procedures ensure that those hired fit in with the culture, reward those who support it, and penalize (and even expel) those who challenge it. Three forces play a particularly important part in sustaining a culture: selection practices, the actions of top management, and socialization methods. Let's take a closer look at each.

Selection The explicit goal of the selection process is to identify and hire individuals who have the knowledge, skills, and abilities to perform the jobs within the organization successfully. Typically, more than one candidate will be identified who meets any given job's requirements. When that point is reached, it would be naïve to ignore the fact that the final decision as to who is hired will be significantly influenced by the decision maker's judgment of how well the candidates will fit into the organization. This attempt to ensure a proper match, whether purposely or inadvertently, results in the hiring of people who have values essentially consistent with those of the organization, or at least a good portion of those values.[16] In addition, the selection process provides information to applicants about the organization. Candidates learn about the organization, and, if they perceive a conflict between their values and those of the organization, they can self-select themselves out of the applicant pool. Selection, therefore, becomes a two-way street, allowing employers or applicants to abrogate a marriage if there appears to be a mismatch. In this way, the selection process sustains an organization's culture by selecting out those individuals who might attack or undermine its core values.

Top Management   The actions of top management also have a major impact on the organization's culture.[17] Through what they say and how they behave, senior executives establish norms that filter down through the organization as to whether risk taking is desirable; how much freedom managers should give their employees; what is appropriate dress; what actions will pay off in terms of pay raises, promotions, and other rewards; and the like.

Socialization   No matter how good a job the organization does in recruiting and selection, new employees are not fully indoctrinated in the organization's culture. Because they are unfamiliar with the organization's culture, new employees are potentially likely to disturb the beliefs and customs that are in place. The organization will, therefore, want to help new employees adapt to its culture. This adaptation process is called **socialization**.

As we discuss socialization, keep in mind that the most critical socialization stage is at the time of entry into the organization. This is when the organization seeks to mold the outsider into an employee "in good standing." Employees who fail to learn the essential or pivotal role behaviors risk being labeled "nonconformists" or "rebels," which often leads to expulsion. But the organization will be socializing every employee, though maybe not as explicitly, throughout his or her entire career in the organization. This further contributes to sustaining the culture.

Socialization can be conceptualized as a process made up of three stages: prearrival, encounter, and metamorphosis.[18] The first stage encompasses all the learning that occurs before a new member joins the organization. In the second stage, the new employee sees what the organization is really like and confronts the possibility that expectations and reality may diverge. In the third stage, the relatively long-lasting changes take place. The new employee masters the skills required for the job, successfully performs the new roles, and makes the adjustments to the work group's values and norms. This three-stage process has an impact on the new employee's work productivity, commitment to the organization's objectives, and eventual decision to stay with the organization. Exhibit 15-1 depicts this process.

The **prearrival stage** explicitly recognizes that each individual arrives with a set of values, attitudes, and expectations. These cover both the work to be done and the organization. For instance, in many jobs, particularly professional work, new members will have undergone a considerable degree of prior socialization in training and in school. One major purpose of a business school, for example, is to socialize

EXHIBIT 15-1   A Socialization Model

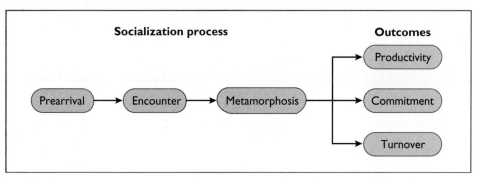

business students to the attitudes and behaviors that business firms want. If business executives believe that successful employees value the profit ethic, are loyal, will work hard, and desire to achieve, they can hire individuals out of business schools who have been premolded in this pattern. Moreover, most people in business realize that no matter how well they think they can socialize newcomers, the most important predictor of newcomers' future behavior is their past behavior. Research shows that what people know before joining the organization, and how proactive their personality is, are critical predictors of how well they adjust to a new culture.[19]

One way to capitalize on the importance of prehire characteristics in socialization is to select employees with the "right stuff" and to use the selection process to inform prospective employees about the organization as a whole. In addition, as noted previously, the selection process also acts to ensure the inclusion of the "right type"—those who will fit in. "Indeed, the ability of the individual to present the appropriate face during the selection process determines his ability to move into the organization in the first place. Thus, success depends on the degree to which the aspiring member has correctly anticipated the expectations and desires of those in the organization in charge of selection."[20]

On entry into the organization, the new member enters the **encounter stage**. Here the individual confronts the possible dichotomy between expectations—about the job, the coworkers, the boss, and the organization in general—and reality. If expectations prove to have been more or less accurate, the encounter stage merely provides a reaffirmation of the perceptions gained earlier. However, this is often not the case. Where expectations and reality differ, the new employee must undergo socialization that will detach her from previous assumptions and replace them with another set that the organization deems desirable. At the extreme, a new member may become totally disillusioned with the actualities of the job and resign. Proper selection should significantly reduce the probability of the latter occurrence. Also, an employee's network of friends and coworkers can play a critical role in helping them "learn the ropes." Newcomers are more committed to the organization when their friendship networks are large and diverse. Thus, organizations can help newcomers socialize by encouraging friendship ties in organizations.[21]

Finally, the new member must work out any problems discovered during the encounter stage. This may mean going through changes—hence, we call this the **metamorphosis stage**. The options presented in Exhibit 15-2 are alternatives

EXHIBIT 15-2   Entry Socialization Options

Formal vs. Informal The more a new employee is segregated from the ongoing work setting and differentiated in some way to make explicit his or her newcomer's role, the more formal socialization is. Specific orientation and training programs are examples. Informal socialization puts the new employee directly into the job, with little or no special attention.

Individual vs. Collective   New members can be socialized individually. This describes how it's done in many professional offices. They can also be grouped together and processed through an identical set of experiences, as in military boot camp.

Fixed vs. variable This refers to the time schedule in which newcomers make the transition from outsider to insider. A fixed schedule establishes standardized stages of transition. This characterizes rotational training programs. It also includes probationary periods, such as the 8- to 10-year "associate" status used by accounting and law firms before deciding on whether or not a candidate is made a partner. Variable schedules give no advance notice of their transition timetable. Variable schedules describe the typical promotion system, in which one is not advanced to the next stage until one is "ready."

Serial vs. Random Serial socialization is characterized by the use of role models who train and encourage the newcomer. Apprenticeship and mentoring programs are examples. In random socialization, role models are deliberately withheld. New employees are left on their own to figure things out.

Investiture vs. Divestiture Investiture socialization assumes that the newcomer's qualities and qualifications are the necessary ingredients for job success, so these qualities and qualifications are confirmed and supported. Divestiture socialization tries to strip away certain characteristics of the recruit. Fraternity and sorority "pledges" go through divestiture socialization to shape them into the proper role.

Source: Based on J. VanMaanen, "People Processing: Strategies of Organizational Socialization," *Organizational Dynamics,* Summer 1978, pp. 19-36; and E. H. Schein, "Organizational Culture," *American Psychologist,* February 1990, p. 116.

designed to bring about the desired metamorphosis. Note, for example, that the more management relies on socialization programs that are formal, collective, fixed, serial, and emphasize divestiture, the greater the likelihood that newcomers' differences and perspectives will be stripped away and replaced by standardized and predictable behaviors. Careful selection by management of newcomers' socialization experiences can—at the extreme—create conformists who maintain traditions and customs, or inventive and creative individualists who consider no organizational practice sacred.

We can say that metamorphosis and the entry socialization process is complete when new members have become comfortable with the organization and their job. They have internalized the norms of the organization and their work group, and understand and accept those norms. New members then feel accepted by their peers as trusted and valued individuals. They are self-confident that they have the competence to complete the job successfully. They understand the system—not only their own tasks but the rules, procedures, and informally accepted practices as well. Finally, they know how they will be evaluated; that is, what criteria will be used to measure and appraise their work. They know what is expected of them and what constitutes a job "well done." As Exhibit 15-1 shows, successful metamorphosis should have a positive impact on new employees' productivity and their commitment to the organization and reduce their propensity to leave the organization.

Formal vs. Informal   The more a new employee is segregated from the ongoing work setting and differentiated in some way to make explicit his or her newcomer's role, the more formal socialization is. Specific orientation and training programs are examples. Informal socialization puts the new employee directly into the job, with little or no special attention.

Individual vs. Collective New members can be socialized individually. This describes how it's done in many professional offices. They can also be grouped together and processed through an identical set of experiences, as in military boot camp.

Fixed vs. Variable This refers to the time schedule in which newcomers make the transition from outsider to insider. A fixed schedule establishes standardized stages of transition. This characterizes rotational training programs. It also includes probationary periods, such as the 8- to 10-year "associate" status used by accounting and law firms before deciding on whether or not a candidate is made a partner. Variable schedules give no advance notice of their transition timetable. Variable schedules describe the typical promotion system, in which one is not advanced to the next stage until one is "ready."

Serial vs. Random Serial socialization is characterized by the use of role models who train and encourage the newcomer. Apprenticeship and mentoring programs are examples. In random socialization, role models are deliberately withheld. New employees are left on their own to figure things out.

Investiture vs. Divestiture Investiture socialization assumes that the newcomer's qualities and qualifications are the necessary ingredients for job success, so these qualities and qualifications are confirmed and supported. Divestiture socialization tries to strip away certain characteristics of the recruit. Fraternity and sorority "pledges" go through divestiture socialization to shape them into the proper role.

Summary: How Cultures Form

Exhibit 15-3 summarizes how an organization's culture is established and sustained. The original culture is derived from the founder's philosophy. This, in turn, strongly influences the criteria used in hiring. The actions of the current top management set the general climate of what is and is not acceptable behavior. How employees are socialized will depend both on the degree of success achieved in matching new employees' values to those of the organization's in the selection process and on top management's preference for socialization methods.

EXHIBIT 15-3   How Organization Cultures Form

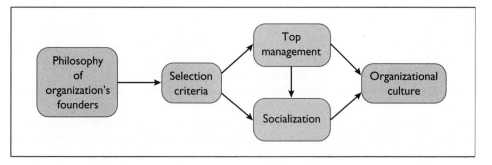

HOW EMPLOYEES LEARN CULTURE

Culture is transmitted to employees in a number of forms, the most potent being stories, rituals, material symbols, and language.

Stories

During the days when Henry Ford II was chairman of the Ford Motor Co., you would have been hard-pressed to find a manager who hadn't heard the story about Mr. Ford reminding his executives, when they were too arrogant, that "it's my name that's on the building." The message was clear: Henry Ford II ran the company.

Stories such as this circulate through many organizations, typically containing a narrative of events about the organization's founders, rule breaking, rags-to-riches successes, reductions in the workforce, relocation of employees, reactions to past mistakes, and organizational coping.[22] These stories anchor the present in the past and provide explanations and legitimacy for current practices.

Rituals

Rituals are repetitive sequences of activities that express and reinforce the key values of the organization—what goals are most important, which people are important, and which people are expendable.[23] One of the better-known corporate rituals is Wal-Mart's company chant. Begun by the company's founder, Sam Walton, as a way to motivate and unite his workforce, "Gimme a W, gimme an A, gimme an L, gimme a squiggle, give me an M, A, R, T!" has become a company ritual that bonds Wal-Mart workers and reinforces Sam Walton's belief in the importance of his employees to the company's success.[24]

Material Symbols

The headquarters of Alcoa doesn't look like your typical head-office operation. There are few individual offices, even for senior executives. It is essentially made up of cubicles, common areas, and meeting rooms. This informal corporate headquarters conveys to employees that Alcoa values openness, equality, creativity, and flexibility. Some corporations provide their top executives with chauffeur-driven limousines and, when traveling by air, unlimited use of the corporate jet. Others may not get to ride in limousines or private jets, but they might still get a car and air transportation paid for by the company. Only the car is a Chevrolet (with no driver), and the jet seat is in the economy section of a commercial airliner.

Language

Many organizations and units within organizations use language as a way to identify members of a culture or subculture. By learning this language, members attest to their acceptance of the culture and, in so doing, help to preserve it.

Organizations, over time, often develop unique terms to describe equipment, offices, key personnel, suppliers, customers, or products that relate to its business. New employees are frequently overwhelmed with acronyms and jargon that, after 6 months on the job, have become fully part of their language. Upon assimilation, this terminology acts as a common denominator to unite members of a given culture or subculture.

CREATING AN ETHICAL ORGANIZATIONAL CULTURE

The content and strength of a culture influence an organization's ethical climate and the ethical behavior of its members.[25] An organizational culture most likely to shape high ethical standards is one that's high in risk tolerance, low to moderate in aggressiveness, and focuses on means as well as outcomes. Managers in such a culture are supported for taking risks and innovating, are discouraged from engaging in unbridled competition, and will pay attention to *how* goals are achieved as well as to *what* goals are achieved.

A strong organizational culture will exert more influence on employees than a weak one. If the culture is strong and supports high ethical standards, it should have a very powerful and positive influence on employee behavior. Johnson & Johnson, for example, has a strong culture that has long stressed corporate obligations to customers, employees, the community, and shareholders, in that order. When poisoned Tylenol (a Johnson & Johnson product) was found on store shelves, employees at Johnson & Johnson across the United States independently pulled the product from these stores before management had even issued a statement concerning the tampering. No one had to tell these individuals what was morally right; they knew what Johnson & Johnson would expect them to do. On the other hand, a strong culture that encourages pushing the limits can be a powerful force in shaping unethical behavior. For instance, Enron's aggressive culture, with unrelenting pressure on executives to rapidly expand earnings, encouraged ethical corner-cutting and eventually contributed to the company's collapse.[26]

What can management do to create a more ethical culture? We suggest a combination of the following practices:

- *Be a visible role model.* Employees will look to the behavior of top management as a benchmark for defining appropriate behavior. When senior management is seen as taking the ethical high road, it provides a positive message for all employees.

- *Communicate ethical expectations.* Ethical ambiguities can be minimized by creating and disseminating an organizational code of ethics. It should state the organization's primary values and the ethical rules that employees are expected to follow.

- *Provide ethical training.* Set up seminars, workshops, and similar ethical training programs. Use these training sessions to reinforce the organization's standards of conduct, to clarify what practices are and are not permissible, and to address possible ethical dilemmas.

- *Visibly reward ethical acts and punish unethical ones.* Performance appraisals of managers should include a point-by-point evaluation of how his or her decisions measure up against the organization's code of ethics. Appraisals must include the means taken to achieve goals as well as the ends themselves. People who act ethically should be visibly rewarded for their behavior. Just as importantly, unethical acts should be conspicuously punished.

> —It is possible to form ethical cultures and positive organizational cultures, but the means by which such cultures are attained are quite different.

- *Provide protective mechanisms.* The organization needs to provide formal mechanisms so that employees can discuss ethical dilemmas and report unethical behavior without fear of reprimand. This might include creation of ethical counselors, ombudsmen, or ethical officers.

CREATING A POSITIVE ORGANIZATIONAL CULTURE

It's often difficult to separate management fads from lasting changes in management thinking, especially early in the development of trends or fads. In this book, we try to keep current while staying away from fads. There is one early trend, though, that we think is here to stay: creating a positive organizational culture.

At first blush, creating a positive culture may sound hopelessly naïve, or like a Michael Scott–like scheme from the TV show *The Office*. The one thing that makes us believe this trend is here to stay is that there are signs that management practice and OB research are converging.

A **positive organizational culture** is defined as a culture that emphasizes building on employee strengths, rewards more than it punishes, and emphasizes individual vitality and growth.[27] Let's consider each of these areas.

Building on Employee Strengths A lot of OB, and management practice, is concerned with how to fix employee problems. Although a positive organizational culture does not ignore problems, it does emphasize showing workers how they can capitalize on their strengths. As management guru Peter Drucker said, "Most Americans do not know what their strengths are. When you ask them, they look at you with a blank stare, or they respond in terms of subject knowledge, which is the wrong answer." Can you name your strengths? Wouldn't it be better to be in an organizational culture that helped you discover those, and learn ways to make the most of them?

Rewarding More Than Punishing There is, of course, a time and place for discipline, but there is also a time and place for rewards. Although most organizations are sufficiently focused on extrinsic rewards like pay and promotions, they often forget about the power of smaller (and cheaper) rewards like praise. Creating a positive organizational culture means that managers "catch employees doing something right." Part of creating a positive culture is articulating praise. Many managers withhold praise either because they're afraid employees will coast, or because they think praise is not valued. Failing to praise can become a "silent killer" like escalating blood pressure. Because employees generally don't ask for praise, managers usually don't realize the costs of failing to do it.

Emphasizing Vitality and Growth A positive organizational culture emphasizes not only organizational effectiveness, but individuals' growth as well. No organization will get the best out of employees if the employees see themselves as mere tools or parts of the organization. A positive culture recognizes that employees' career aspirations are important, and shows an interest not only in what the employee does to contribute to organizational effectiveness, but what the organization can do to help employees' advance their own career goals. The figure is even higher in some industries, such as banking, manufacturing, communications, and utilities. Although it may take more creativity to encourage employee growth in some types of industries, it can happen in the fast-paced food service industry.

Limits of Positive Culture Is a positive culture a panacea? Cynics (or should we say realists?) may be skeptical about the benefits of positive organizational culture. To be sure, even though some companies such as GE, Xerox, Boeing, and 3M have embraced aspects of a positive organizational culture, it is a new enough area that there is some uncertainty about how and when it works best. Moreover, any OB scholar or manager needs to make sure he is objective about the benefits—and risks—of cultivating a positive organizational culture.

—Organizational culture and national culture are not the same thing, though to some degree, an organization's culture reflects the dominant values of its host country.

Not all cultures value being positive as much as the U.S. culture, and, even within U.S. culture, there surely are limits to how far we should go to preserve a positive culture. For example, Admiral, a British insurance company, has established a Ministry of Fun in its call centers to organize such events as poem writings, foosball, conker competitions (a British game involving chestnuts), and fancy dress days. When does the pursuit of a positive culture start to seem coercive or even Orwellian? As one critic notes, "Promoting a social orthodoxy of positiveness focuses on a particular constellation of desirable states and traits but, in so doing, can stigmatize those who fail to fit the template."[28]

Our point is that there may be benefits to establishing a positive culture, but an organization also needs to be careful to be objective, and not pursue it past the point of effectiveness.

GLOBAL IMPLICATIONS

We considered global cultural values (collectivism–individualism, power distance, and so on) in Chapter 2. Here our focus is a bit narrower: How is organizational culture affected by a global context? Organizational cultures are so powerful that they often transcend national boundaries. But that doesn't mean that organizations should, or could, be blissfully ignorant of local culture.

This is becoming a bigger issue. In 2007, half of GE's revenue came from outside the United States. GE even moved the headquarters of its health care division to the United Kingdom, and the number of non-U.S. citizens among GE's top 500 managers has tripled since 2001. GE is hardly alone. Large and small organizations alike are often heavily dependent on foreign product markets, foreign labor markets, or both.

As we noted in Chapter 2, national cultures differ. Organizational cultures often reflect national culture. For example, the culture at AirAsia, a Malaysian-based airline, emphasizes informal dress so as not to create status differences. The carrier has lots of parties, participative management, and no private offices. This organizational culture reflects Malaysia's relatively collectivistic culture. However, the culture of US Airways does not reflect the same degree of informality. If US Airways were to set up operations in Malaysia, or merge with AirAsia, it would need to take these cultural differences into account. So when an organization opens up operations in another country, it ignores the local culture at its own risk.

One of the primary things U.S. managers can do is to be culturally sensitive. The United States is a dominant force in business and in culture, and with that influence comes a reputation. "We are broadly seen throughout the world as arrogant people, totally self-absorbed and loud," says one U.S. executive. Companies such as American Airlines, Lowe's, Novell, ExxonMobil, and Microsoft have implemented training programs to sensitize their managers to cultural differences. Some ways in which U.S. managers can be culturally sensitive include talking in a low tone of voice, speaking slowly, listening more, and avoiding discussions of religion and politics.

U.S. employees are not the only ones who need to be culturally sensitive. For example, three times a week, employees at the Canadian unit of Japanese video game maker Koei begin each day standing next to their desks, facing their boss, and saying in unison, "Good morning." That is followed by employees delivering short speeches on topics that range from corporate principles to 3D game engines. Koei also has employees punch a time clock. And Koei asks women to serve tea to top executive guests. Although these practices are consistent with Koei's culture, they do not fit Canadian culture very well. "It's kind of like school," says one Canadian employee.[29]

IMPLICATIONS FOR MANAGERS

With little doubt, culture has a strong influence on employee behavior. But what can management do to design a culture that molds employees in the way management wants?

When an organization is just being established, management has a great deal of influence. No traditions have been established and the organization is small. Subcultures, if any, are few. Everyone knows the founder and is directly touched by his or her vision of the organization. Not surprisingly, under these conditions management has the opportunity to create a culture that will best facilitate the achievement of the organization's goals. However, when the organization is well established, so too is its dominant culture. Given that this culture is made up of relatively stable and permanent characteristics, it becomes very resistant to change. The culture took time to form, and once established it tends to become entrenched. Strong cultures are particularly resistant to change because employees become so committed to them. So, if a given culture, over time, becomes a handicap to management and inappropriate to an organization, management may be able to do little to change it, especially in the short run. Under the most favorable conditions, cultural changes must be measured in years, not weeks or months. The favorable conditions that increase the probability that cultural change can be successfully implemented are the existence of a dramatic crisis, a turnover in the organization's top leadership, an organization that is both young and small, and a dominant culture that is weak.

Organizational Change

1. Identify forces that act as stimulants to change.
2. List the sources for resistance to change.
3. Compare the three main approaches to managing organizational change.
4. Describe the causes and consequences of work stress.
5. Describe the characteristics of a learning organization.
6. Explain global differences in organizational change and stress.

This chapter is about change. We describe environmental forces that require managers to implement comprehensive change programs. We also consider why people and organizations often resist change and how this resistance can be overcome. We review various processes for managing organizational change. We also discuss contemporary change issues for today's managers.

FORCES FOR CHANGE

No company today is in a particularly stable environment. Even traditionally stable industries such as energy and utilities have witnessed—and will continue to experience—turbulent change. Companies that occupy a dominant market share in their industries must change, sometimes radically. While Microsoft continues to struggle with its controversial new operating system—Vista—it also is trying to outflank smaller companies such as Google that are increasingly offering free, Web-based software packages. How well Microsoft performs is not simply a function of managing one change but a matter of how well it can manage both short-term and long-term changes.

We will discuss six environmental factors that act as forces for change. In a number of places in this book, we've discussed the *changing nature of the workforce.* For instance, almost every organization is adjusting to a multicultural environment. Demographic changes, immigration, and outsourcing also have transformed the nature of the workforce.

Technology is changing jobs and organizations. Just about the time an organization adapts to one technological change, other technological challenges and opportunities come to the forefront. It is not hard to imagine the very idea of an office becoming an antiquated concept in the near future. We'll have more to say about technology later in this chapter.

Economic shocks have continued to impose changes on organizations. In recent years, for instance, new dot-com businesses have been created, turned tens of thousands of investors into overnight millionaires, then crashed, and others arose in their wake. And record low interest rates first stimulated a rapid rise in home values, helped sustain consumer spending, and benefited many industries, especially construction and banking. But when the bubble burst, businesses in these same industries suffered.

Competition is changing. The global economy means that competitors are as likely to come from across the ocean as from across town. Heightened competition means that successful organizations will be the ones that can change in response to the competition. They'll be fast on their feet, capable of developing new products rapidly, and getting them to market quickly. They'll rely on short production runs, short product cycles, and an ongoing stream of new products. In other words, they'll be flexible. They will require an equally flexible and responsive workforce that can adapt to rapidly and even radically changing conditions.

Social trends don't remain static. For instance, in contrast to just 15 years ago, people are meeting and sharing information in Internet chat rooms, baby boomers have begun to retire, and consumers are increasingly doing their shopping at "big-box" retailers and online. A company like Liz Claiborne needs to continually adjust its product and marketing strategies to be sensitive to changing social trends, as it did when it sold off brands (like Ellen Tracy), de-emphasized large department stores like Macy's as vendors, and streamlined its operations and cut staff.

Throughout this book we have argued strongly for the importance of seeing OB in a global context. Business schools have been preaching a global perspective since the early 1980s, but no one—not even the strongest proponents of globalization—could have imagined how *world politics* would change in recent years. In the past few years, the governments in many of the world's biggest economies have changed, including, of course, the United States, as well as France, Germany, Italy, Great Britain, Mexico, Argentina, and Japan. These turbulent political times often pose special challenges for organizations that operate or do business in these nations.

RESISTANCE TO CHANGE

—One of the most well-documented findings from studies of individual and organizational behavior is that organizations and their members resist change.

One of the best well-documented findings from studies of individual and organizational behavior is that organizations and their members resist change. One recent study showed that even when employees are shown data that suggests they need to change, they latch onto whatever data they can find that suggests they are okay and don't need to change. Our egos are fragile, and we often see change as threatening.[1]

EXHIBIT 16-1 Sources of Resistance to Change

Individual Sources

Habit—To cope with life's complexities, we rely on habits or programmed responses. But when confronted with change, this tendency to respond in our accustomed ways becomes a source of resistance.

Security—People with a high need for security are likely to resist change because it threatens feelings of safety.

Economic factors—Changes in job tasks or established work routines can arouse economic fears if people are concerned that they won't be able to perform the new tasks or routines to their previous standards, especially when pay is closely tied to productivity.

Fear of the unknown—Change substitutes ambiguity and uncertainty for the unknown.

Selective information processing—Individuals are guilty of selectively processing information in order to keep their perceptions intact. They hear what they want to hear and they ignore information that challenges the world they've created.

Organizational Sources

Structural inertia—Organizations have built-in mechanisms—like their selection processes and formalized regulations—to produce stability. When an organization is confronted with change, this structural inertia acts as a counterbalance to sustain stability.

Limited focus of change—Organizations are made up of a number of interdependent subsystems. One can't be changed without affecting the others. So limited changes in subsystems tend to be nullified by the larger system.

Group inertia—Even if individuals want to change their behavior, group norms may act as a constraint.

Threat to expertise—Changes in organizational patterns may threaten the expertise of specialized groups.

Threat to established power relationships—Any redistribution of decision-making authority can threaten long-established power relationships within the organization.

Threat to established resource allocations—Groups in the organization that control sizable resources often see change as a threat. They tend to be content with the way things are.

Exhibit 16-1 summarizes major forces for resistance to change, categorized by individual and organizational sources. Individual sources of resistance reside in basic human characteristics such as perceptions, personalities, and needs. Organizational sources reside in the structural makeup of organizations themselves.

Before we move on to ways to overcome resistance to change, it's important to note that not all change is good. Research has shown that sometimes an emphasis on making speedy decisions can lead to bad decisions. Sometimes the line between resisting needed change and falling into a "speed trap" is a fine one indeed. What's more, sometimes in the "fog of change," those who are initiating change fail to realize the full magnitude of the effects they are causing or to estimate their true costs to the organization. Thus, although the perspective generally taken is that rapid, transformational change is good, this is not always the case. Some organizations, such as Baring Brothers Bank in the United Kingdom, have collapsed for this reason.[2]

Change Agents

Before discussing how to overcome resistance to change, it's important to ask, Who in organizations is responsible for managing change activities? The answer is *change agents*.[3] Change agents can be managers or nonmanagers, current employees of the organization, newly hired employees, or outside consultants. Whether change agents are insiders or outsiders often depends on the magnitude of the change.

For major change efforts, internal management will hire the services of outside consultants to provide advice and assistance with major change efforts. Because they are from the outside, these individuals can offer an objective perspective often unavailable to insiders. Outside consultants, however, are disadvantaged because they usually have an inadequate understanding of the organization's history, culture, operating procedures, and personnel. Outside consultants also may be prone to initiating more drastic changes—which can be a benefit or a disadvantage—because they don't have to live with the repercussions after the change is implemented. In contrast, internal staff specialists or managers, when acting as change agents, may be more thoughtful (and possibly more cautious) because they have to live with the consequences of their actions.

Overcoming Resistance to Change

Seven tactics have been suggested for use by change agents in dealing with resistance to change.[4] Let's review them briefly.

1. *Education and Communication* Resistance can be reduced through communication with employees to help them see the logic of a change. Communication can reduce resistance because it fights the effects of misinformation and poor communication: If employees receive the full facts and get any misunderstandings cleared up, resistance should subside. Communication also can be helpful in "selling" the need for change. Indeed, research shows that the way the need for change is sold matters—change is more likely when the necessity of changing is packaged properly.[5]

2. *Participation* It's difficult for individuals to resist a change decision in which they participated. Prior to making a change, those opposed can be brought into the decision process. Assuming that the participants have the expertise to make a meaningful contribution, their involvement can reduce resistance, garner commitment, and increase the quality of the change decision.

3. *Building Emotional Commitment* Research on middle managers has shown that when managers or employees have low emotional commitment to change, they favor the status quo and resist it.[6] So firing up employees can also help them emotionally commit to the change rather than embracing the status quo.

4. *Implementing Changes Fairly* Try as managers might to have employees see change positively, most workers tend to react negatively. But one way organizations can minimize the negative impact of change, even when employees frame it as a negative, is to makes sure the change is implemented fairly. As we learned in Chapter 5, procedural fairness becomes especially important when employees perceive an outcome as negative; thus, when implementing changes, it's crucial that organizations bend over backwards to make sure employees see that the changes are being implemented consistently and fairly.[7]

5. *Cooptation* Cooptation seeks to "buy off" the leaders of a resistance group by giving them a key role in the change decision. The leaders' advice is sought, not to seek a better decision, but to get their endorsement. Both manipulation and cooptation are relatively inexpensive and easy ways to gain the support of adversaries, but the tactics can backfire if the targets become aware that they are being tricked or used. Once discovered, the change agent's credibility may drop to zero.

6. *Selecting People Who Accept Change* Research suggests that the ability to easily accept and adapt to change is related to personality—some people simply have more positive attitudes about change than others.[8] It appears that people who adjust best to change are those who are open to experience, take a positive attitude toward themselves, are willing to take risks, and are flexible in their behavior. Another study found that selecting people based on a resistance-to-change scale worked well in winnowing out those who tended to react emotionally to change or to be rigid.[9]

7. *Coercion* Last on the list of tactics is coercion; that is, the application of direct threats or force on the resisters. If corporate management really is determined to close a manufacturing plant if employees don't acquiesce to a pay cut, then coercion would be the label attached to its change tactic. Other examples of coercion are threats of transfer, loss of promotions, negative performance evaluations, and a poor letter of recommendation. The advantages and drawbacks of coercion are approximately the same as those mentioned for cooptation.

APPROACHES TO MANAGING ORGANIZATIONAL CHANGE

Now we turn to several approaches to managing change: Lewin's classic three-step model of the change process, Kotter's eight-step plan, and organizational development.

Lewin's Three-Step Model

Kurt Lewin argued that successful change in organizations should follow three steps: **unfreezing** the status quo, **movement** to a desired end state, and **refreezing** the new change to make it permanent.[10] (See Exhibit 16-2.)

The status quo can be considered an equilibrium state. To move from this equilibrium—to overcome the pressures of both individual resistance and group conformity—unfreezing is necessary. It can be achieved in one of three ways. (See Exhibit 16-3.) First, the **driving forces**, which direct behavior away from the status quo, can be increased. Second, the **restraining forces**, which hinder movement from the existing equilibrium, can be decreased. A third alternative is to combine the first two approaches. Companies that have been successful in the past are likely to encounter restraining forces because people question the need for change.[11] Similarly, research shows that companies with strong cultures excel at incremental change but are overcome by restraining forces against radical change.[12]

Research on organizational change has shown that, to be effective, change has to happen quickly.[13] Organizations that build up to change do poorly than those that get to and through the movement stage quickly.

Once the change has been implemented, if it is to be successful, the new situation needs to be refrozen so that it can be sustained over time. Unless this last step is

EXHIBIT 16-2   Lewin's Three-Step Change Model

EXHIBIT 16-3 Unfreezing the Status Quo

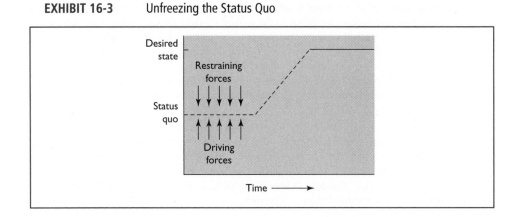

taken, there is a very high chance that the change will be short-lived and that employees will attempt to revert to the previous equilibrium state. The objective of refreezing, then, is to stabilize the new situation by balancing the driving and restraining forces.

Kotter's Eight-Step Plan for Implementing Change

John Kotter of the Harvard Business School built on Lewin's three-step model to create a more detailed approach for implementing change.[14] Kotter began by listing common failures that managers make when trying to initiate change. These included the inability to create a sense of urgency about the need for change, failure to create a coalition for managing the change process, the absence of a vision for change and to effectively communicate that vision, not removing obstacles that could impede the achievement of the vision, failure to provide short-term and achievable goals, the tendency to declare victory too soon, and not anchoring the changes into the organization's culture.

Kotter then established eight sequential steps, listed in Exhibit 16-4, to overcome these problems.

Notice how Exhibit 16-4 builds on Lewin's model. Kotter's first four steps essentially extrapolate on the "unfreezing" stage, steps 5 through 7 represent "movement,"

EXHIBIT 16-4 Kotter's Eight-Step Plan for Implementing Change

1. Establish a sense of urgency by creating a compelling reason for why change is needed.
2. Form a coalition with enough power to lead the change.
3. Create a new vision to direct the change and strategies for achieving the vision.
4. Communicate the vision throughout the organization.
5. Empower others to act on the vision by removing barriers to change and encouraging risk taking and creative problem solving.
6. Plan for, create, and reward short-term "wins" that move the organization toward the new vision.
7. Consolidate improvements, reassess changes, and make necessary adjustments in the new programs.
8. Reinforce the changes by demonstrating the relationship between new behaviors and organizational success.

Source: Based on J. P. Kotter, *Leading Change* (Boston: Harvard Business School Press, 1996).

and the final step works on "refreezing." So Kotter's contribution lies in providing managers and change agents with a more detailed guide for successfully implementing change.

Organizational Development

No discussion of managing change would be complete without including organizational development. **Organizational development (OD)** is not an easily defined single concept. Rather, it's a term used to encompass a collection of change interventions built on humanistic-democratic values that seek to improve organizational effectiveness and employee well-being.[15]

The OD paradigm values human and organizational growth, collaborative and participative processes, and a spirit of inquiry.[16] The change agent may be directive in OD; however, there is a strong emphasis on collaboration. The following briefly identifies the underlying values in most OD efforts:

1. *Respect for people.* Individuals are perceived as being responsible, conscientious, and caring. They should be treated with dignity and respect.
2. *Trust and support.* An effective and healthy organization is characterized by trust, authenticity, openness, and a supportive climate.
3. *Power equalization.* Effective organizations de-emphasize hierarchical authority and control.
4. *Confrontation.* Problems shouldn't be swept under the rug. They should be openly confronted.
5. *Participation.* The more that people who will be affected by a change are involved in the decisions surrounding that change, the more they will be committed to implementing those decisions.

What are some of the OD techniques or interventions for bringing about change? Here, we present four interventions that change agents might consider using.

1. *Sensitivity Training* It can go by a variety of names—**sensitivity training**, laboratory training, encounter groups, or T-groups (training groups)—but all refer to a method of changing behavior through unstructured group interaction.[17] Members are brought together in a free and open environment in which participants discuss themselves and their interactive processes, loosely directed by a professional behavioral scientist. The professional creates the opportunity for participants to express their ideas, beliefs, and attitudes about change, and does not accept—in fact, overtly rejects—any leadership role.
2. *Survey Feedback* One tool for assessing attitudes held by organizational members, identifying discrepancies among member perceptions, and solving these differences is the **survey feedback** approach.[18] A questionnaire, usually completed by all members in the organization or unit, typically asks members for their perceptions and attitudes on a broad range of topics, including, of course, the issues involved with the organizational change(s). The data from this questionnaire are tabulated with data pertaining to an individual's specific "family" and to the entire organization and then distributed to employees. These data then become the springboard for identifying problems and clarifying issues that may be creating resistance to change. Generally, results are shared with employees, which often helps acceptance of change, and provides ideas for how to address areas of concern and resistance.

3. *Process Consultation* No organization operates perfectly. Managers often sense that their unit's performance can be improved, but they're unable to identify what can be improved and how it can be improved. The purpose of **process consultation (PC)** is for an outside consultant to assist a client, usually a manager, "to perceive, understand, and act upon the "change event" with which the manager must deal.[19] PC is similar to sensitivity training in its assumption that acceptance of change can be improved by dealing with interpersonal problems and in its emphasis on involvement. But PC is more task-directed than sensitivity training. Consultants in PC are there to "give the client 'insight' into the situation."[20] They do not magically resolve resistance to change. Rather, the consultant is a guide or coach who advises on the process to help the client find his or her change management solutions.

4. *Appreciative Inquiry* Most OD approaches are problem-centered. They identify a problem or set of problems, and then look for a solution. **Appreciative inquiry (AI)** accentuates the positive.[21] Rather than looking for problems to fix, this approach seeks to identify the unique qualities and special strengths of an organization, which can then be built on to improve acceptance of change. That is, it focuses on an organization's successes rather than on its problems. Advocates of AI argue that problem-solving approaches always ask people to look backward at yesterday's failures, to focus on shortcomings, and rarely result in new visions. Instead of creating a climate for positive change, OD techniques such as survey feedback and process consultation end up placing blame and generating defensiveness. AI proponents claim it makes more sense to refine and enhance what the organization is already doing well. This allows the organization to change by playing to its strengths and competitive advantages.

The AI process essentially consists of four steps, often played out in a large-group meeting over a 2- or 3-day time period and overseen by a trained change agent. The first step is *discovery*. The idea is to find out what people think are the strengths of the organization. For instance, employees are asked to recount times they felt the organization worked best or when they specifically felt most satisfied with their jobs. The second step is *dreaming*. The information from the discovery phase is used to speculate on possible futures for the organization. For instance, people are asked to envision the organization in 5 years and to describe what's different. The third step is *design*. Based on the dream articulation, participants focus on finding a common vision of how the organization will look and agree on its unique qualities. The fourth stage seeks to define the organization's *destiny*. In this final step, participants discuss how the organization is going to fulfill its dream. This typically includes the writing of action plans and development of implementation strategies.

CREATING A CULTURE FOR CHANGE

We've considered how organizations can adapt to change. Recently, some OB scholars have focused on a more proactive approach to change—how organizations can embrace change by transforming their cultures. In this section we will review how a culture of innovation can be created.

Stimulating a Culture of Innovation

How can an organization become more innovative? An excellent model is W. L. Gore, the $1.4-billion-per-year company best known as the maker of Gore-Tex fabric.[22]

Gore has developed a reputation as one of America's most innovative companies by developing a stream of diverse products—including guitar strings, dental floss, medical devices, and fuel cells.

—There are various approaches that can be used to manage organizational change and for developing a culture for change; it is unlikely one approach is always best in every situation.

What's the secret of Gore's success? What can other organizations do to duplicate its track record for innovation? Although there is no guaranteed formula, certain characteristics surface again and again when researchers study innovative organizations. We've grouped them into structural, cultural, and human resource categories. Our message to change agents is that they should consider introducing these characteristics into their organization if they want to create an innovative climate. Before we look at these characteristics, however, let's clarify what we mean by innovation.

Definition of *Innovation* We said change refers to making things different. **Innovation** is a more specialized kind of change. Innovation is a new idea applied to initiating or improving a product, process, or service.[23] All innovations involve change, but not all changes necessarily involve new ideas or lead to significant improvements. Innovations in organizations can range from small incremental improvements, such as Nabisco's extension of the Oreo product line to include double-stuffed cookies and chocolate-covered Oreos, up to radical breakthroughs, such as Toyota's battery-powered Prius.

Sources of Innovation *Structural variables* have been the most studied potential source of innovation.[24] A comprehensive review of the structure–innovation relationship leads to the following conclusions.[25] First, organic structures positively influence innovation. Because they're lower in vertical differentiation, formalization, and centralization, organic organizations facilitate the flexibility, adaptation, and cross-fertilization that make the adoption of innovations easier. Second, long tenure in management is associated with innovation. Managerial tenure apparently provides legitimacy and knowledge of how to accomplish tasks and obtain desired outcomes. Third, innovation is nurtured when there are slack resources. Having an abundance of resources allows an organization to afford to purchase innovations, bear the cost of instituting innovations, and absorb failures. Finally, interunit communication is high in innovative organizations.[26] These organizations utilize committees, task forces, cross-functional teams, and other mechanisms that facilitate interaction across departmental lines.

Innovative organizations tend to have similar *cultures*. They encourage experimentation, reward both successes and failures, and celebrate mistakes. Unfortunately, in too many organizations, people are rewarded for the absence of failures rather than for the presence of successes. Such cultures extinguish risk taking and innovation. People will suggest and try new ideas only when they feel such behaviors do not exact penalties. Managers in innovative organizations recognize that failures are a natural by-product of venturing into the unknown. When Barry Bonds set the Major League Baseball record for home runs (73), he also had more strikeouts (93). And he is remembered (and paid $20 million per year) for the former, not the latter.

Within the *human resources* category, we find that innovative organizations actively promote the training and development of their members so that they keep current, offer high job security so employees don't fear getting fired for making mistakes, and encourage individuals to become champions of change. Once a new idea is developed, **idea champions** actively and enthusiastically promote the idea, build support, overcome resistance, and ensure that the innovation is implemented.[27] The evidence indicates that idea champions have common personality characteristics: extremely high self-confidence, persistence, energy, and a tendency to take risks. Idea champions also display characteristics associated with transformational leadership. They inspire and energize others with their vision of the potential of an innovation and through their strong personal conviction in their mission. They are also good at gaining the commitment of others to support their mission. In addition, idea champions have jobs that provide considerable decision-making discretion. This autonomy helps them introduce and implement innovations in organizations.[28]

CONTEMPORARY ISSUES IN ORGANIZATIONAL CHANGE

Next, let's address four contemporary change issues. First, how are changes in *technology in the workplace* affecting the work lives of employees? Second, since change is stressful to most, how do I reduce *work stress* among my work staff? Third, how do managers go about *creating a learning organization*, one that continually learns and adapts? Finally, as part of our **Global Implications** section in each chapter, here we ask: *Is managing change culture bound?*

Technology in the Workplace

As we noted at the beginning of this chapter, recent advances in technology are changing the workplace and affecting the work lives of employees. There are two specific issues related to process technology and work: *continuous improvement processes* and *process reengineering*.

Continuous Improvement Processes   The search for continuous improvement recognizes that *good isn't good enough* and that even excellent performance can, and should, be improved upon. For instance, a 99.9 percent error-free performance sounds like a high standard of excellence. However, it doesn't sound so great when you realize that this standard would result in the United States Postal Service losing 2,000 pieces of mail an hour or two plane crashes a day at O'Hare Airport in Chicago![29] Quality management programs seek to achieve continuous process improvements so that variability is constantly reduced. When you eliminate variations, you increase the uniformity of the product or service. Increasing uniformity, in turn, results in lower costs and higher quality.

As tens of thousands of organizations introduce continuous process improvement, how will employees be affected? They will no longer be able to rest on their previous accomplishments and successes. So, some people may experience increased stress from a work climate that no longer accepts complacency with the status quo. A race with no finish line can never be won—and that's a situation that creates constant tension. This tension may be positive for the organization (remember *functional conflict* from Chapter 13), but the pressures from an unrelenting search for process improvements can create stress in some employees.

Process Reengineering   The term *reengineering* comes from the process of taking apart an electronic product and designing a better version. As applied to organizations, process reengineering means that management should start with a clean sheet of paper—rethinking and redesigning those processes by which the organization creates value and does work, ridding itself of operations that have become antiquated.[30] The three key elements of process reengineering include:

- Identifying an organization's distinctive competencies
- Assessing core processes
- Reorganizing horizontally by process

An organization's distinctive competencies define what it is that the organization does better than its competition. And, identifying distinctive competencies is so important because it guides decisions regarding what activities are crucial to the organization's success. Dell, for instance, differentiates itself from its competitors by emphasizing high-quality hardware, comprehensive service and technical support, and low prices.

Management also needs to assess the core processes that clearly add value to the organization's distinctive competencies—the processes that transform materials, capital, information, and labor into products and services that the customer values. When the organization is viewed as a series of processes, ranging from strategic planning to after-sales customer support, management can determine to what degree each process adds value. This process–value analysis typically uncovers many activities that add little or nothing of value and whose only justification is "We've always done it this way."

Process reengineering requires management to reorganize around horizontal processes. This means using cross-functional and self-managed teams, focusing on processes rather than functions, and cutting out unnecessary levels of middle management.

Process reengineering has been popular since the early 1990s. One of the main consequences has been that many people—especially support staff and middle managers—have lost their jobs. Those employees who keep their jobs after process reengineering have typically found that their jobs are no longer the same. These new jobs typically require a wider range of skills, including more interaction with customers and suppliers, greater challenge, increased responsibilities, and higher pay. However, the 3- to 5-year period it takes to implement process reengineering is usually tough on employees. They suffer from uncertainty and anxiety associated with taking on new tasks and having to discard long-established work practices and formal social networks.

Work Stress

Most of us are aware that employee stress is an increasing problem in organizations. Friends tell us they're stressed out from greater workloads and having to work longer hours because of downsizing at their company. Though organizational change is not the cause of all stress in organizations, it certainly is one of the main culprits. Not only can change be *directly* stressful to individuals—as we've noted earlier, most of us love our routines and do not embrace change—it also can be *indirectly* stressful because it leads to other events such as shifting responsibilities, increased workload, downsizing, changes in product lines and customers, and new rules and regulations to which one must acclimate.[31]

Regardless of its specific source, **stress** is a dynamic condition in which an individual is confronted with an opportunity, demand, or resource related to what the individual desires and for which the outcome is perceived to be both uncertain and important.[32] This is a complicated definition. Let's look at its components more closely.

Like change, stress is not necessarily bad in and of itself. Although stress is typically discussed in a negative context, it also has a positive value.[33] It's an opportunity when it offers potential gain. Consider, for example, the superior performance that an athlete or stage performer gives in crucial situations. Such individuals often use stress positively to rise to the occasion and perform at or near their maximum. Similarly, many professionals see the pressures of heavy workloads and deadlines as positive challenges that enhance the quality of their work and the satisfaction they get from their jobs.

In short, some stress can be good, and some can be bad. Recently, researchers have argued that *challenge stress*, or stress associated with challenges in the work environment (such as having lots of projects, assignments, and responsibilities), operates quite differently from *hindrance stress*, or stress that keeps you from reaching your goals (red tape, office politics, and confusion over job responsibilities). Although research on challenge and hindrance stress is just starting to accumulate, early evidence suggests that challenge stress has many fewer negative implications than hindrance stress.[34]

More typically, stress is associated with **demands** and **resources**. Demands are responsibilities, pressures, obligations, and even uncertainties that individuals face in the workplace. Resources are matters within an individual's control that can be used to resolve demands. This demands–resources model has received increasing support in literature.[35]

For example, when taking a test at school or undergoing your annual performance review at work, you feel stress because you confront opportunities and performance pressures. A good performance review may lead to a promotion, greater responsibilities, and a higher salary, but a poor review may prevent you from getting the promotion. An extremely poor review might even result in your being fired. In such a situation, to the extent you can apply resources to the demands—such as being prepared, placing the exam or review in perspective, or obtaining social support—you will feel less stress.

> —*Change is often stressful to individuals, but, like change, researchers are beginning to accept that not all stress is harmful.*

Managing Stress   Not all stress is dysfunctional. Moreover, realistically, as with change, stress can never be totally eliminated from a person's life, either off the job or on. As we review stress-reduction techniques, keep in mind that our concern is with reducing the part of stress that is dysfunctional.

In terms of organizational factors, any attempt to lower stress levels has to begin with employee *selection*. Management needs to make sure that an employee's abilities match the requirements of the job. When employees are in over their heads, their stress levels will typically be high. An objective job preview during the selection process will also lessen stress by reducing ambiguity. Improved *organizational communications* will keep ambiguity-induced stress to a minimum. Similarly, a *goal-setting* program will clarify job responsibilities and provide clear performance objectives. *Job redesign* is another way to reduce stress. If stress can be traced directly to boredom or work overload, jobs should be redesigned to increase challenge or reduce the work-load. Redesigns that increase opportunities for employees to participate in decisions and to gain social support have also been found to lessen stress.

Stress that arises from an employee's personal life creates two problems. First, it's difficult for the manager to control directly. Second, there are ethical considerations. Specifically, does the manager have any right to intrude—even in the most subtle ways—in the employee's personal life? If a manager believes it is ethical to do so and the employee is receptive, the manager can consider a few approaches. Employee *counseling* can provide stress relief. Employees often want to talk to someone about their problems; and the organization—through its managers, in-house personnel coun-selors, or free or low-cost outside professional help—can meet that need. For employ-ees whose personal lives suffer from a lack of planning and organization that, in turn, creates stress, the offering of a *time management* program may prove beneficial in help-ing them sort their priorities. Still another approach is organizationally sponsored *physical activity* programs. Some large corporations employ physical fitness specialists who provide employees with exercise advice, teach relaxation techniques, and show individual employees physical activities they can use to keep their stress levels down.

Creating a Learning Organization

Our final topic in contemporary change is issues in creating a learning organization. The *learning organization* has recently developed a groundswell of interest from managers and organization theorists looking for new ways to successfully respond to a world of interdependence and change.[36]

What's a Learning Organization?   A **learning organization** is an organization that has developed the continuous capacity to adapt and change. Just as individuals learn, so too do organizations. "All organizations learn, whether they consciously choose to or not—it is a fundamental requirement for their sustained existence."[37] However, some organizations just do it better than others.

Most organizations engage in what has been called **single-loop learning**.[38] When errors are detected, the correction process relies on past routines and present policies. In contrast, learning organizations use **double-loop learning**. When an error is detected, it's corrected in ways that involve the modification of the organization's objectives, policies, and standard routines. Double-loop learning challenges deeply rooted assumptions and norms within an organization. In this way, it provides opportunities for radically different solutions to problems and dramatic jumps in improvement.

Exhibit 16-5 summarizes the five basic characteristics of a learning organization, in which people put aside their old ways of thinking, learn to be open with each other, understand how their organizations really work, form a plan or vision that everyone can agree on, and then work together to achieve that vision.[39]

Proponents of the learning organization envision it as a remedy for three funda-mental problems inherent in traditional organizations: fragmentation, competition, and reactiveness.[40]

1. *Fragmentation* based on specialization creates "walls" and "chimneys" that separate different functions into independent and often warring fiefdoms.

EXHIBIT 16-5 Characteristics of a Learning Organization

1. There exists a shared vision which everyone agrees on.
2. People discard their old ways of thinking and the standard routines they use for solving problems or doing their jobs.
3. Members think of all organizational processes, activities, functions, and interactions with the environment as part of a system of interrelationships.
4. People openly communicate with each other (across vertical and horizontal boundaries) without fear of criticism or punishment.
5. People sublimate their personal self-interests and fragmented departmental interests to work together to achieve the organization's shared vision.

Source: Based on P. M. Senge, *The Fifth Discipline* (New York: Doubleday, 1990).

2. An overemphasis on *competition* often undermines collaboration. Members of the management team compete with one another to show who is right, who knows more, or who is more persuasive. Divisions compete with one another when they ought to cooperate and share knowledge. Team project leaders compete to show who is the best manager.

3. *Reactiveness* misdirects management's attention to problem solving rather than creation. The problem solver tries to make something go away, whereas a creator tries to bring something new into being. An emphasis on reactiveness pushes out innovation and continuous improvement and, in its place, encourages people to run around "putting out fires."

It may help to better understand what a learning organization is if you think of it as an *ideal* model that builds on a number of previous OB concepts. No company has successfully achieved all the characteristics described in Exhibit 16-5. As such, you should think of a learning organization as an ideal to strive toward rather than a realistic description of structured activity. Note, too, how learning organizations draw on previously described OB concepts, such as quality management, organizational culture, the boundaryless organization, functional conflict, and transformational leadership. For instance, the learning organization adopts quality management's commitment to continuous improvement. Learning organizations are also characterized by a specific culture that values risk taking, openness, and growth. It seeks boundarylessness through breaking down barriers created by hierarchical levels and fragmented departmentalization. A learning organization supports the importance of disagreements, constructive criticism, and other forms of functional conflict. And, transformational leadership is needed in a learning organization to implement the shared vision.

Managing Learning   How do you change an organization to make it into a continual learner? What can managers do to make their firms learning organizations?

- *Establish a strategy* Management needs to make explicit its commitment to change, innovation, and continuous improvement.
- *Redesign the organization's structure* The formal structure can be a serious impediment to learning. By flattening the structure, eliminating or combining departments, and increasing the use of cross-functional teams, interdependence is reinforced and interpersonal boundaries are reduced.
- *Reshape the organization's culture* As we noted previously, learning organizations are characterized by risk taking, openness, and growth. Management sets the tone for

the organization's culture both by what it says (strategy) and what it does (behavior). Managers need to demonstrate by their actions that taking risks and admitting failures are desirable traits. That means rewarding people who take chances and make mistakes. And, management needs to encourage functional conflict. "The key to unlocking real openness at work," says one expert on learning organizations, "is to teach people to give up having to be in agreement. We think agreement is so important. Who cares? You have to bring paradoxes, conflicts, and dilemmas out in the open, so collectively we can be more intelligent than we can be individually."[41]

GLOBAL IMPLICATIONS

Is Managing Change Culture Bound?

A number of change issues we've discussed in this chapter are culture bound. To illustrate, let's briefly look at five questions: (1) Do people believe change is possible? (2) If it's possible, how long will it take to bring about? (3) Is resistance to change greater in some cultures than in others? (4) Does culture influence how change efforts will be implemented? (5) Do successful idea champions do things differently in different cultures?

Do people believe change is possible? Remember that cultures vary in terms of beliefs about their ability to control their environment. In cultures in which people believe that they can dominate their environment, individuals will take a proactive view of change. This, for example, would describe the United States and Canada. In many other countries, such as Iran and Saudi Arabia, people see themselves as subjugated to their environment and thus will tend to take a passive approach toward change.

If change is possible, how long will it take to bring about? A culture's time orientation can help us answer this question. Societies that focus on the long term, such as Japan, will demonstrate considerable patience while waiting for positive outcomes from change efforts. In societies with a short-term focus, such as the United States and Canada, people expect quick improvements and will seek change programs that promise fast results.

Is resistance to change greater in some cultures than in others? Resistance to change will be influenced by a society's reliance on tradition. Italians, as an example, focus on the past, whereas U.S. adults emphasize the present. Italians, therefore, should generally be more resistant to change efforts than their U.S. counterparts.

Does culture influence how change efforts will be implemented? Power distance can help with this issue. In high power distance cultures, such as Spain or Thailand, change efforts will tend to be autocratically implemented by top management. In contrast, low power distance cultures value democratic methods. We'd predict, therefore, a greater use of participation in countries such as Denmark and the Netherlands.

Finally, do successful idea champions do things differently in different cultures? Yes.[42] People in collectivist cultures prefer appeals for cross-functional support for innovation efforts; people in high power distance cultures prefer champions to work closely with those in authority to approve innovative activities before work is begun; and the higher the uncertainty avoidance of a society, the more champions should work within the organization's rules and procedures to develop the innovation. These findings suggest that effective managers will alter their organization's championing strategies to reflect cultural values. So, for instance, although idea champions in Russia might succeed by ignoring budgetary limitations and working around confining procedures, champions in Austria, Denmark, Germany, or other cultures high in uncertainty avoidance will be more effective by closely following budgets and procedures.

Stress

In considering global differences in stress, there are three questions to answer: (1) Do the causes of stress vary across countries? (2) Do the outcomes of stress vary across cultures? and (3) Do the factors that lessen the effects of stress vary by culture? Let's deal with each of these questions in turn.

First, research suggests that the job conditions that cause stress show some differences across cultures. One study of U.S. and Chinese employees revealed that whereas U.S. employees were stressed by a lack of control, Chinese employees were stressed by job evaluations and lack of training. Although job conditions that lead to stress may differ across countries, it doesn't appear that personality effects on stress are different across cultures. One study of employees in Hungary, Italy, the United Kingdom, Israel, and the United States found that Type A personality traits (see Chapter 2) predicted stress equally well across countries.[43]

Second, evidence tends to suggest that stressors are associated with perceived stress and strains among employees in different countries. In other words, stress is equally bad for employees of all cultures.[44]

Third, although not all factors that reduce stress have been compared across cultures, research does suggest that, whereas the demand to work long hours leads to stress, this stress can be reduced by the resource of social support such as having friends or family to talk to. A recent study found this to be true of workers in a diverse set of countries (Australia, Canada, England, New Zealand, the United States, China, Taiwan, Argentina, Brazil, Colombia, Ecuador, Mexico, Peru, and Uruguay).[45]

IMPLICATIONS FOR MANAGERS

The need for change encompasses almost all the concepts within organizational behavior. Think about attitudes, perceptions, teams, leadership, motivation, organizational design, and the like. It's impossible to think about these concepts without inquiring about change.

If environments were perfectly static, if employees' skills and abilities were always up to date and incapable of deteriorating, and if tomorrow were always exactly the same as today, organizational change would have little or no relevance to managers. But, the real world is turbulent, requiring organizations and their members to undergo dynamic change in order to perform at competitive levels.

In the past, managers could treat change as an occasional disturbance in their otherwise peaceful and predictable world. Such a world no longer exists for most managers. Today's managers are increasingly finding that the world is one of constant and chaotic change. In this world, managers must continually act as change agents.

Epilogue

The end of a book typically has the same meaning to an author that it has to the reader: It generates feelings of both accomplishment and relief. As both of us rejoice at having completed our tour of the essential concepts in organizational behavior, this is a good time to examine where we've been and what it all means.

The underlying theme of this book has been that the behavior of people at work is not a random phenomenon. Employees are complex entities, but their attitudes and behavior can nevertheless be explained and predicted with a reasonable degree of accuracy. Our approach has been to look at organizational behavior at three levels: the individual, the group, and the organization system.

We started with the individual and reviewed the major psychological contributions to understanding why individuals act as they do. We found that many of the individual differences among employees can be systematically labeled and categorized, and therefore generalizations can be made. For example, we know that individuals with a conventional type of personality are better matched to certain jobs in corporate management than are people with investigative personalities. So placing people into jobs that are compatible with their personality types should result in higher-performing and more satisfied employees.

Next, our analysis moved to the group level. We argued that the understanding of group behavior is more complex than merely multiplying what we know about individuals by the number of members in the group, because people act differently in a group than when they are alone. We demonstrated how roles, norms, leadership styles, power relationships, and other similar group factors affect the behavior of employees.

Finally, we overlaid system-wide variables on our knowledge of individual and group behavior to further improve our understanding of organizational behavior. Major emphasis was given to showing how an organization's structure, design, and culture affect both the attitudes and the behavior of employees.

It may be tempting to criticize the stress this book placed on theoretical concepts, but as noted psychologist Kurt Lewin is purported to have said, "There is nothing so practical as a good theory." Of course, it's also true that there is nothing so impractical as a good theory that leads nowhere. To avoid presenting theories that lead nowhere, this book included a wealth of examples and illustrations. And we regularly stopped to inquire about the implications of theory for the practice of management. The result has been the presentation of numerous concepts that, individually, offer some insights into behavior, but which, when taken together, provide a complex system to help you explain, predict, and control organizational behavior.

Endnotes

CHAPTER 1

1. Cited in R. Alsop, "Playing Well with Others." *Wall Street Journal*, September 9, 2002, pp. R11, R14.

2. I. S. Fulmer, B. Gerhart, and K. S. Scott, "Are the 100 Best Better? An Empirical Investigation of the Relationship Between Being a 'Great Place to Work' and Firm Performance," *Personnel Psychology*, Winter 2003, pp. 965–993.

3. See, for instance, C. Heath and S. B. Sitkin, "Big-B Versus Big-O: What Is *Organizational* About Organizational Behavior?" *Journal of Organizational Behavior*, February 2001, pp. 43–58. For a review of what one eminent researcher believes *should* be included in organizational behavior, based on survey data, see J. B. Miner, "The Rated Importance, Scientific Validity, and Practical Usefulness of Organizational Behavior Theories: A Quantitative Review," *Academy of Management Learning & Education*, September 2003, pp. 250–268.

4. D. M. Rousseau and S. McCarthy, "Educating Managers from an Evidence-Based Perspective," *Academy of Management Learning & Education* 6, no. 1 (2007), pp. 84–101.

5. See M. E. A. Jayne and R. L. Dipboye, "Leveraging Diversity to Improve Business Performance: Research Findings and Recommendations for Organizations," *Human Resource Management*, Winter 2004, pp. 409–424.

6. See, for instance, M. K. Brady and J. J. Cronin Jr., "Customer Orientation: Effects on Customer Service Perceptions and Outcome Behaviors," *Journal of Service Research*, February 2001, pp. 241–51; and M. Workman and W. Bommer, "Redesigning Computer Call Center Work: A Longitudinal Field Experiment," *Journal of Organizational Behavior*, May 2004, pp. 317–337.

7. See, for instance, J. M. Brett and L. K. Stroh, "Working 61 Plus Hours a Week: Why Do Managers Do It?" *Journal of Applied Psychology*, February 2003, pp. 67–78.

8. J. Merritt, "For MBAs, Soul-Searching 101," *BusinessWeek*, September 16, 2002, pp. 64–66; and S. Greenhouse, "The Mood at Work: Anger and Anxiety," *New York Times*, October 29, 2002, p. E1.

9. F. Luthans and C. M. Youssef, "Emerging Positive Organizational Behavior," *Journal of Management*, June 2007, pp. 321–349; and J. E. Dutton and S. Sonenshein, "Positive Organizational Scholarship," in C. Cooper and J. Barling (eds.), *Encyclopedia of Positive Psychology* (Thousand Oaks, CA: Sage, 2007).

10. L. M. Roberts, G. Spreitzer, J. Dutton, R. Quinn, E. Heaphy, and B. Barker, "How to Play to Your Strengths," *Harvard Business Review*, January 2005, pp. 1–6; and L. M. Roberts, J. E. Dutton,

G. M. Spreitzer, E. D. Heaphy, and R. E. Quinn, "Composing the Reflected Best-Self Portrait: Becoming Extraordinary in Work Organizations," *Academy of Management Review* 30, no. 4 (2005), pp. 712–736.

CHAPTER 2

1. G. W. Allport, *Personality: A Psychological Interpretation* (New York: Holt, Rinehart & Winston, 1937), p. 48.

2. K. I. van der Zee, J. N. Zaal, and J. Piekstra, "Validation of the Multicultural Personality Questionnaire in the Context of Personnel Selection," *European Journal of Personality* 17 (2003), pp. S77–S100.

3. T. A. Judge, C. A. Higgins, C. J. Thoresen, and M. R. Barrick, "The Big Five Personality Traits, General Mental Ability, and Career Success Across the Life Span," *Personnel Psychology* 52, no. 3 (1999), pp. 621–652.

4. See S. Pinker, *The Blank Slate: The Modern Denial of Human Nature* (New York: Viking, 2002).

5. See T. J. Bouchard, Jr., and J. C. Loehlin, "Genes, Evolution, and Personality," *Behavior Genetics*, May 2001, pp. 243–273.

6. S. Srivastava, O. P. John, and S. D. Gosling, "Development of Personality in Early and Middle Adulthood: Set Like Plaster or Persistent Change?" *Journal of Personality and Social Psychology*, May 2003, pp. 1041–1053.

7. See, for instance, G. W. Allport and H. S. Odbert, "Trait Names, A Psycholexical Study," *Psychological Monographs*, no. 47 (1936); and R. B. Cattell, "Personality Pinned Down," *Psychology Today*, July 1973, pp. 40–46.

8. R. B. Kennedy and D. A. Kennedy, "Using the Myers-Briggs Type Indicator in Career Counseling," *Journal of Employment Counseling*, March 2004, pp. 38–44.

9. See, for instance, D. J. Pittenger, "Cautionary Comments Regarding the Myers-Briggs Type Indicator," *Consulting Psychology Journal: Practice and Research*, Summer 2005, pp. 210–221; L. Bess and R. J. Harvey, "Bimodal Score Distributions and the Myers-Briggs Type Indicator: Fact or Artifact?" *Journal of Personality Assessment*, February 2002, pp. 176–186; and R. C. Arnau, B. A. Green, D. H. Rosen, D. H. Gleaves, and J. G. Melancon, "Are Jungian Preferences Really Categorical? An Empirical Investigation Using Taxometric Analysis," *Personality & Individual Differences*, January 2003, pp. 233–251.

10. See, for example, M. R. Barrick and M. K. Mount, "Yes, Personality Matters: Moving on to More Important Matters," *Human Performance* 18, no. 4 (2005), pp. 359–372.

11. See M. R. Barrick and M. K. Mount, "Select on Conscientiousness and Emotional Stability," in E. A. Locke (ed.), *Handbook of Principles of Organizational Behavior* (Malden, MA: Blackwell, 2004), pp. 15–28.

12. M. K. Mount, M. R. Barrick, and J. P. Strauss, "Validity of Observer Ratings of the Big Five Personality Factors," *Journal of Applied Psychology*, April 1994, p. 272; and M. R. Barrick, M. K. Mount, and T. A. Judge, "The FFM Personality Dimensions and Job Performance: Meta-analysis of Meta-analyses," *International Journal of Selection and Assessment* 9 (2001), pp. 9–30.

13. M. Tamir and M. D. Robinson, "Knowing Good from Bad: The Paradox of Neuroticism, Negative Affect, and Evaluative Processing," *Journal of Personality & Social Psychology* 87, no. 6 (2004), pp. 913–925.

14. R. J. Foti and M. A. Hauenstein, "Pattern and Variable Approaches in Leadership Emergence and Effectiveness," *Journal of Applied Psychology*, March 2007, pp. 347–355.

15. L. I. Spirling and R. Persaud, "Extraversion as a Risk Factor," *Journal of the American Academy of Child & Adolescent Psychiatry* 42, no. 2 (2003), p. 130.

16. J. A. LePine, J. A. Colquitt, and A. Erez, "Adaptability to Changing Task Contexts: Effects of General Cognitive Ability, Conscientiousness, and Openness to Experience," *Personnel Psychology* 53 (2000), pp. 563–595.

17. B. Laursen, L. Pulkkinen, and R. Adams, "The Antecedents and Correlates of Agreeableness in Adulthood," *Developmental Psychology* 38, no. 4 (2002), pp. 591–603.

18. B. Barry and R. A. Friedman, "Bargainer Characteristics in Distributive and Integrative Negotiation," *Journal of Personality and Social Psychology*, February 1998, pp. 345–359.

19. T. Bogg and B. W. Roberts, "Conscientiousness and Health-Related Behaviors: A Meta-Analysis of the Leading Behavioral Contributors to Mortality," *Psychological Bulletin* 130, no. 6 (2004), pp. 887–919.

20. S. Lee and H. J. Klein, "Relationships Between Conscientiousness, Self-Efficacy, Self-Deception, and Learning over Time," *Journal of Applied Psychology* 87, no. 6 (2002), pp. 1175–1182; and G. J. Feist, "A Meta-analysis of Personality in Scientific and Artistic Creativity," *Personality and Social Psychology Review* 2, no. 4 (1998), pp. 290–309.

21. A. Erez and T. A. Judge, "Relationship of Core Self-Evaluations to Goal Setting, Motivation, and Performance," *Journal of Applied Psychology* 86, no. 6 (2001), pp. 1270–1279.

22. U. Malmendier and G. Tate, "CEO Overconfidence and Corporate Investment," *Journal of Finance* 60, no. 6 (December 2005), pp. 2661–2700.

23. R. Sandomir, "Star Struck," *New York Times*, January 12, 2007, pp. C10, C14.

24. See M. Snyder, *Public Appearances/Private Realities: The Psychology of Self-Monitoring* (New York: W. H. Freeman, 1987); and S. W. Gangestad and M. Snyder, "Self-Monitoring: Appraisal and Reappraisal," *Psychological Bulletin*, July 2000, pp. 530–555.

25. Snyder, *Public Appearances/Private Realities*.

26. D. V. Day, D. J. Shleicher, A. L. Unckless, and N. J. Hiller, "Self-Monitoring Personality at Work: A Meta-analytic Investigation of Construct Validity," *Journal of Applied Psychology*, April 2002, pp. 390–401.

27. M. Kilduff and D. V. Day, "Do Chameleons Get Ahead? The Effects of Self-Monitoring on Managerial Careers," *Academy of Management Journal*, August 1994, pp. 1047–1060; and A. Mehra, M. Kilduff, and D. J. Brass, "The Social Networks of High and Low Self-Monitors: Implications for Workplace Performance," *Administrative Science Quarterly*, March 2001, pp. 121–146.

28. M. Friedman and R. H. Rosenman, *Type A Behavior and Your Heart* (New York: Alfred A. Knopf, 1974), p. 84.

29. Ibid., pp. 84–85.

30. S. E. Seibert, M. L. Kraimer, and J. M. Crant, "What Do Proactive People Do? A Longitudinal Model Linking Proactive Personality and Career Success," *Personnel Psychology*, Winter 2001, p. 850.

31. T. S. Bateman and J. M. Crant, "The Proactive Component of Organizational Behavior: A Measure and Correlates," *Journal of Organizational Behavior*, March 1993, pp. 103–118.

32. J. D. Kammeyer-Mueller and C. R. Wanberg, "Unwrapping the Organizational Entry Process: Disentangling Multiple Antecedents and Their Pathways to Adjustment," *Journal of Applied Psychology* 88, no. 5 (2003), pp. 779–794.

33. M. Rokeach, *The Nature of Human Values* (New York: The Free Press, 1973), p. 5.

34. M. Rokeach and S. J. Ball-Rokeach, "Stability and Change in American Value Priorities, 1968–1981," *American Psychologist* 44, no. 5 (1989), pp. 775–784; and B. M. Meglino and E. C. Ravlin, "Individual Values in Organizations: Concepts, Controversies, and Research," *Journal of Management* 24, no. 3 (1998), p. 355.

35. Rokeach, *The Nature of Human Values*, p. 6.

36. J. M. Munson and B. Z. Posner, "The Factorial Validity of a Modified Rokeach Value Survey for Four Diverse Samples," *Educational and Psychological Measurement*, Winter 1980, pp. 1073–1079; and W. C. Frederick and J. Weber, "The Values of Corporate Managers and Their Critics: An Empirical Description and Normative Implications," in W. C. Frederick and L. E. Preston (eds.), *Business Ethics: Research Issues and Empirical Studies* (Greenwich, CT: JAI Press, 1990), pp. 123–144.

37. Frederick and Weber, "The Values of Corporate Managers and Their Critics," pp. 123–144.

38. See, for example, J. Levitz, "Pitching 401(k)s to Generation Y Is a Tough Sell," *Wall Street Journal*, September 27, 2006, pp. B1, B2.

39. K. W. Smola and C. D. Sutton, "Generational Differences: Revisiting Generational Work Values for the New Millennium," *Journal of Organizational Behavior* 23 (2002), pp. 363–382.

40. N. A. Hira, "You Raised Them, Now Manage Them," *Fortune*, May 28, 2007, pp. 38–46; R. R. Hastings, "Surveys Shed Light on Generation Y Career Goals," *SHRM Online*, March 2007, www.shrm.org; and S. Jayson, "The 'Millennials' Come of Age," *USA Today*, June 29, 2006, pp. 1D, 2D.

41. J. L. Holland, *Making Vocational Choices: A Theory of Vocational Personalities and Work Environments* (Odessa, FL: Psychological Assessment Resources, 1997).

42. See, for example, J. L. Holland, "Exploring Careers with a Typology: What We Have Learned and Some New Directions," *American Psychologist*, April 1996, pp. 397–406.

43. See A. L. Kristof, "Person–Organization Fit: An Integrative Review of Its Conceptualizations, Measurement, and Implications," *Personnel Psychology*, Spring 1996, pp. 1–49; and B. Schneider, D. B. Smith, S. Taylor, and J. Fleenor, "Personality and Organizations: A Test of the Homogeneity of Personality Hypothesis," *Journal of Applied Psychology*, June 1998, pp. 462–470.

44. Based on T. A. Judge and D. M. Cable, "Applicant Personality, Organizational Culture, and Organization Attraction," *Personnel Psychology*, Summer 1997, pp. 359–394.

45. M. L. Verquer, T. A. Beehr, and S. E. Wagner, "A Meta-analysis of Relations Between Person–Organization Fit and Work Attitudes," *Journal of Vocational Behavior* 63, no. 3 (2003), pp. 473–489.

46. See, for instance, R. R. McCrae and P. T. Costa, Jr., "Personality Trait Structure as a Human Universal," *American Psychologist*, May 1997, pp. 509–516; and R. R. McCrae, P. T. Costa, Jr., T. A. Martin, V. E. Oryol, A. A. Rukavishnikov, I. G. Senin, M. Hrebickova, and T. Urbanek, "Consensual Validation of Personality Traits Across Cultures," *Journal of Research in Personality* 38, no. 2 (2004), pp. 179–201.

47. A. T. Church and M. S. Katigbak, "Trait Psychology in the Philippines," *American Behavioral Scientist*, September 2000, pp. 73–94.

48. J. F. Salgado, "The Five Factor Model of Personality and Job Performance in the European Community," *Journal of Applied Psychology*, February 1997, pp. 30–43.

49. G. Hofstede, *Culture's Consequences: International Differences in Work-Related Values* (Beverly Hills, CA: Sage, 1980); and G. Hofstede and M. F. Peterson, "National Values and Organizational Practices," in N. M. Ashkanasy, C. M. Wilderom, and M. F. Peterson (eds.), *Handbook of Organizational Culture and Climate* (Thousand Oaks, CA: Sage, 2000), pp. 401–416.

50. M. H. Bond, "Reclaiming the Individual from Hofstede's Ecological Analysis—A 20-Year Odyssey: Comment on Oyserman et al. (2002)." *Psychological Bulletin* 128, no. 1 (2002), pp. 73–77; and G. Hofstede, "The Pitfalls of Cross-National Survey Research: A Reply to the Article by Spector et al. on the Psychometric Properties of the Hofstede Values Survey Module 1994," *Applied Psychology: An International Review* 51, no. 1 (2002), pp. 170–178.

51. M. Javidan and R. J. House, "Cultural Acumen for the Global Manager: Lessons from Project GLOBE," *Organizational Dynamics* 29, no. 4 (2001), pp. 289–305; and R. J. House, P. J. Hanges, M. Javidan, and P. W. Dorfman (eds.), *Leadership, Culture, and Organizations: The GLOBE Study of 62 Societies* (Thousand Oaks, CA: Sage, 2004).

52. P. C. Early, "Leading Cultural Research in the Future: A Matter of Paradigms and Taste," *Journal of International Business Studies*, September 2006, pp. 922–931.

53. L. A. Witt, "The Interactive Effects of Extraversion and Conscientiousness on Performance," *Journal of Management* 28, no. 6 (2002), p. 836.

54. R. P. Tett and D. D. Burnett, "A Personality Trait–Based Interactionist Model of Job Performance," *Journal of Applied Psychology*, June 2003, pp. 500–517.

CHAPTER 3

1. H. H. Kelley, "Attribution in Social Interaction," in E. Jones et al. (eds.), *Attribution: Perceiving the Causes of Behavior* (Morristown, NJ: General Learning Press, 1972).

2. See A. G. Miller and T. Lawson, "The Effect of an Informational Option on the Fundamental Attribution Error," *Personality and Social Psychology Bulletin*, June 1989, pp. 194–204.

3. See, for instance, M. Goerke, J. Moller, S. Schulz-Hardt, U. Napiersky, and D. Frey, "'It's not My Fault—but Only I Can Change It': Counterfactual and Prefactual Thoughts of Managers," *Journal of Applied Psychology*, April 2004, pp. 279–292.

4. P. Burrows, "HP's Carly Fiorina: The Boss" *BusinessWeek*, August 2, 1999; J. D. Markman, "Lessons of Carly Fiorina's Fall," *TheStreet.com*, February 10, 2005; and C. Edwards, "Where Fiorina Went Wrong," *BusinessWeek*, February 9, 2005.

5. J. L. Hilton and W. von Hippel, "Stereotypes," in J. T. Spence, J. M. Darley, and D. J. Foss (eds.), *Annual Review of Psychology*, vol. 47 (Palo Alto, CA: Annual Reviews, 1996), pp. 237–271.

6. See, for example, G. N. Powell, "The Good Manager: Business Students' Stereotypes of Japanese Managers Versus Stereotypes of American Managers," *Group & Organizational Management*, March 1992, pp. 44–56; W. C. K. Chiu, A. W. Chan, E. Snape, and T. Redman, "Age Stereotypes and Discriminatory Attitudes Towards Older Workers: An East–West Comparison," *Human Relations*, May 2001, pp. 629–661; C. Ostroff and L. E. Atwater, "Does Whom You Work with Matter? Effects of Referent Group Gender and Age Composition on Managers' Compensation," *Journal of Applied Psychology*, August 2003, pp. 725–740; and M. E. Heilman, A. S. Wallen, D. Fuchs, and M. M. Tamkins, "Penalties for Success: Reactions to Women Who Succeed at Male Gender-Typed Tasks," *Journal of Applied Psychology*, June 2004, pp. 416–427.

7. J. L. Eberhardt, P. G. Davies, V. J. Purdic-Vaughns, and S. L. Johnson, "Looking Deathworthy: Perceived Stereotypicality of Black Defendants Predicts Capital-Sentencing Outcomes," *Psychological Science* 17, no. 5 (2006), pp. 383–386.

8. See H. A. Simon, "Rationality in Psychology and Economics," *Journal of Business*, October 1986, pp. 209–224; and E. Shafir and R. A. LeBoeuf, "Rationality," in S. T. Fiske, D. L. Schacter, and C. Zahn-Waxler (eds.), *Annual Review of Psychology*, vol. 53 (Palo Alto, CA: Annual Reviews, 2002), pp. 491–517.

9. M. Bazerman, *Judgment in Managerial Decision Making*, 3rd ed. (New York: Wiley, 1994), p. 5.

10. J. E. Russo, K. A. Carlson, and M. G. Meloy, "Choosing an Inferior Alternative," *Psychological Science* 17, no. 10 (2006), pp. 899–904.

11. D. Kahneman, "Maps of Bounded Rationality: Psychology for Behavioral Economics," *The American Economic Review* 93, no. 5 (2003), pp. 1449–1475; and J. Zhang, C. K. Hsee, and Z. Xiao, "The Majority Rule in Individual Decision Making," *Organizational Behavior and Human Decision Processes* 99 (2006), pp. 102–111.

12. See H. A. Simon, *Administrative Behavior*, 4th ed. (New York: The Free Press, 1997); and M. Augier, "Simon Says: Bounded Rationality Matters," *Journal of Management Inquiry*, September 2001, pp. 268–275.

13. See T. Gilovich, D. Griffin, and D. Kahneman, *Heuristics and Biases: The Psychology of Intuitive Judgment* (New York: Cambridge University Press, 2002).

14. E. Dane and M. G. Pratt, "Exploring Intuition and Its Role in Managerial Decision Making," *Academy of Management Review* 32, no. 1 (2007), pp. 33–54.

15. See, for instance, Burke and Miller, "Taking the Mystery Out of Intuitive Decision Making," *Academy of Management Executive* 13, no. 4 (October 1999), pp. 91–99.

16. S. P. Robbins, *Decide & Conquer: Making Winning Decisions and Taking Control of Your Life* (Upper Saddle River, NJ: Financial Times/Prentice Hall, 2004), p. 13.

17. S. Plous, *The Psychology of Judgment and Decision Making* (New York: McGraw-Hill, 1993), p. 217.

18. B. Fischhoff, P. Slovic, and S. Lichtenstein, "Knowing with Certainty: The Appropriateness of Extreme Confidence," *Journal of Experimental Psychology: Human Perception and Performance*, November 1977, pp. 552–564.

19. Kruger and Dunning, "Unskilled and Unaware of It: How Difficulties in Recognizing One's Own Incompetence Lead to Inflated Self-Assessments," *Journal of Personality and Social Psychology* 77, no. 6 (1999), pp. 1121–1134.

20. See, for instance, A. Tversky and D. Kahneman, "Judgment Under Uncertainty: Heuristics and Biases," *Science*, September 1974, pp. 1124–1131.

21. See A. Tversky and D. Kahneman, "Availability: A Heuristic for Judging Frequency and Probability," in D. Kahneman, P. Slovic, and A. Tversky (eds.), *Judgment Under Uncertainty: Heuristics and Biases* (Cambridge, UK: Cambridge University Press, 1982), pp. 163–178; and B. J. Bushman and G. L. Wells, "Narrative Impressions of Literature: The Availability Bias and the Corrective Properties of Meta-analytic Approaches," *Personality and Social Psychology Bulletin*, September 2001, pp. 1123–1130.

22. See B. M. Staw, "The Escalation of Commitment to a Course of Action," *Academy of Management Review*, October 1981, pp. 577–587; K. Fai, E. Wong, M. Yik, and J. Y. Y. Kwong, "Understanding the Emotional Aspects of Escalation of Commitment: The Role of Negative Affect," *Journal of Applied Psychology* 91, no. 2 (2006), pp. 282–297; H. Moon, "Looking Forward and Looking Back: Integrating Completion and Sunk-Cost Effects Within an Escalation-of-Commitment Progress Decision," *Journal of Applied Psychology*, February 2001, pp. 104–113; and A. Zardkoohi, "Do Real Options Lead to Escalation of Commitment? Comment," *Academy of Management Review*, January 2004, pp. 111–119.

23. B. M. Staw, "Knee-Deep in the Big Muddy: A Study of Escalating Commitment to a Chosen Course of Action," *Organizational Behavior and Human Performance* 16 (1976), pp. 27–44.

24. K. F. E. Wong and J. Y. Y. Kwong, "The Role of Anticipated Regret in Escalation of Commitment," *Journal of Applied Psychology* 92, no. 2 (2007), pp. 545–554.

25. R. L. Guilbault, F. B. Bryant, J. H. Brockway, and E. J. Posavac, "A Meta-analysis of Research on Hindsight Bias," *Basic and Applied Social Psychology*, September 2004, pp. 103–117; and L. Werth, F. Strack, and J. Foerster, "Certainty and Uncertainty: The Two Faces of the Hindsight Bias," *Organizational Behavior and Human Decision Processes*, March 2002, pp. 323–341.

26. M. Gladwell, "Connecting the Dots," *The New Yorker*, March 10, 2003.

27. A. Wildavsky, *The Politics of the Budgetary Process* (Boston: Little, Brown, 1964).

28. G. F. Cavanagh, D. J. Moberg, and M. Valasquez, "The Ethics of Organizational Politics," *Academy of Management Journal*, June 1981, pp. 363–374.

29. See, for example, T. Machan, ed., *Commerce and Morality* (Totowa, NJ: Rowman and Littlefield, 1988).

30. T. M. Amabile, "A Model of Creativity and Innovation in Organizations," in B. M. Staw and L. L. Cummings (eds.), *Research in Organizational Behavior*, vol. 10 (Greenwich, CT: JAI Press, 1988), p. 126; and J. E. Perry-Smith and C. E. Shalley, "The Social Side of Creativity: A Static and Dynamic Social Network Perspective," *Academy of Management Review*, January 2003, pp. 89–106.

31. R. Florida, "A Search for Jobs in Some of the Wrong Places," *USA Today*, February 13, 2006, p. 11A; and R. Alsop, "Schools Find Fun a Worthy Teacher to Foster Creativity," *Wall Street Journal*, September 12, 2006, p. B8.

32. G. J. Feist and F. X. Barron, "Predicting Creativity from Early to Late Adulthood: Intellect, Potential, and Personality," *Journal of Research in Personality*, April 2003, pp. 62–88.

33. This section is based on T. M. Amabile, "Motivating Creativity in Organizations: On Doing What You Love and Loving What You Do," *California Management Review* 40, no. 1 (Fall 1997), pp. 39–58.

34. A. M. Isen, "Positive Affect," in T. Dalgleish and M. J. Power (eds.), *Handbook of Cognition and Emotion* (New York: Wiley, 1999), pp. 521–539.

35. J. Zhou, "When the Presence of Creative Coworkers Is Related to Creativity: Role of Supervisor Close Monitoring, Developmental Feedback, and Creative Personality," *Journal of Applied Psychology* 88, no. 3 (June 2003), pp. 413–422.

36. J. E. Perry-Smith, "Social yet Creative: The Role of Social Relationships in Facilitating Individual Creativity," *Academy of Management Journal* 49, no. 1 (2006), pp. 85–101.

37. W. J. J. Gordon, *Synectics* (New York: Harper & Row, 1961).

38. See T. M. Amabile, *KEYS: Assessing the Climate for Creativity* (Greensboro, NC: Center for Creative Leadership, 1995); N. Madjar, G. R. Oldham, and M. G. Pratt, "There's No Place Like Home? The Contributions of Work and Nonwork Creativity Support to Employees' Creative Performance," *Academy of Management Journal*, August 2002, pp. 757–767; and C. E. Shalley, J. Zhou, and G. R. Oldham, "The Effects of Personal and Contextual Characteristics on Creativity: Where Should We Go from Here?" *Journal of Management*, November 2004, pp. 933–958.

39. See, for instance, G. R. Semin, "A Gloss on Attribution Theory," *British Journal of Social and Clinical Psychology*,

November 1980, pp. 291–230; M. W. Morris and K. Peng, "Culture and Cause: American and Chinese Attributions for Social and Physical Events," *Journal of Personality and Social Psychology*, December 1994, pp. 949–971; and D. S. Krull, M. H.-M. Loy, J. Lin, C.-F. Wang, S. Chen, and X. Zhao, "The Fundamental Attribution Error: Correspondence Bias in Individualistic and Collectivist Cultures," *Personality & Social Psychology Bulletin*, October 1999, pp. 1208–1219.

40. S. Nam, "Cultural and Managerial Attributions for Group Performance," unpublished doctoral dissertation; University of Oregon. Cited in R. M. Steers, S. J. Bischoff, and L. H. Higgins, "Cross-Cultural Management Research," *Journal of Management Inquiry*, December 1992, pp. 325–326.

41. M. J. Gelfand, M. Erez, and Z. Aycan, "Cross-Cultural Organizational Behavior," *Annual Review of Psychology*, January 2007, pp. 479–514; and A. S. Tsui, S. S. Nifadkar, and A. Y. Ou, "Cross-National, Cross-Cultural Organizational Behavior Research: Advances, Gaps, and Recommendations," *Journal of Management*, June 2007, pp. 426–478.

42. N. J. Adler, *International Dimensions of Organizational Behavior*, 4th ed. (Cincinnati, OH: SouthWestern Publishing, 2002), pp. 182–189.

43. T. Jackson, "Cultural Values and Management Ethics: A 10-Nation Study," *Human Relations*, October 2001, pp. 1267–1302; see also J. B. Cullen, K. P. Parboteeah, and M. Hoegl, "Cross-National Differences in Managers' Willingness to Justify Ethically Suspect Behaviors: A Test of Institutional Anomie Theory," *Academy of Management Journal*, June 2004, pp. 411–421.

44. W. Chow Hou, "To Bribe or Not to Bribe?" *Asia, Inc.*, October 1996, p. 104.

45. P. Digh, "Shades of Gray in the Global Marketplace," *HRMagazine*, April 1997, p. 91.

CHAPTER 4

1. S. J. Breckler, "Empirical Validation of Affect, Behavior, and Cognition as Distinct Components of Attitude," *Journal of Personality and Social Psychology*, May 1984, pp. 1191–1205; and S. L. Crites, Jr., L. R. Fabrigar, and R. E. Petty, "Measuring the Affective and Cognitive Properties of Attitudes: Conceptual and Methodological Issues," *Personality and Social Psychology Bulletin*, December 1994, pp. 619–634.

2. A. W. Wicker, "Attitude Versus Action: The Relationship of Verbal and Overt Behavioral Responses to Attitude Objects," *Journal of Social Issues*, Autumn 1969, pp. 41–78.

3. L. Festinger, *A Theory of Cognitive Dissonance* (Stanford, CA: Stanford University Press, 1957).

4. See, for instance, I. R. Newby-Clark, I. McGregor, and M. P. Zanna, "Thinking and Caring About Cognitive Consistency: When and for Whom Does Attitudinal Ambivalence Feel Uncomfortable?" *Journal of Personality & Social Psychology*, February 2002, pp. 157–166.

5. See, for instance, J. Nocera, "If It's Good for Philip Morris, Can It also Be Good for Public Health?" *New York Times*, June 18, 2006.

6. See L. R. Glasman and D. Albarracín, "Forming Attitudes That Predict Future Behavior: A Meta-analysis of the Attitude–Behavior Relation," *Psychological Bulletin*, September 2006, pp. 778–822.

7. D. A. Harrison, D. A. Newman, and P. L. Roth, "How Important Are Job Attitudes? Meta-analytic Comparisons of Integrative Behavioral Outcomes and Time Sequences," *Academy of Management Journal* 49, no. 2 (2006), pp. 305–325.

8. P. P. Brooke, Jr., D. W. Russell, and J. L. Price, "Discriminant Validation of Measures of Job Satisfaction, Job Involvement, and Organizational Commitment," *Journal of Applied Psychology*, May 1988, pp. 139–145.

9. See, for example, J. M. Diefendorff, D. J. Brown, and A. M. Kamin, "Examining the Roles of Job Involvement and Work Centrality in Predicting Organizational Citizenship Behaviors and Job Performance," *Journal of Organizational Behavior*, February 2002, pp. 93–108.

10. A. Ergeneli, G. Saglam, and S. Metin, "Psychological Empowerment and Its Relationship to Trust in Immediate Managers," *Journal of Business Research*, January 2007, pp. 41–49.

11. B. J. Avolio, W. Zhu, W. Koh, and P. Bhatia, "Transformational Leadership and Organizational Commitment: Mediating Role of Psychological Empowerment and Moderating Role of Structural Distance," *Journal of Organizational Behavior* 25, no. 8 (2004), pp. 951–968.

12. G. J. Blau, "Job Involvement and Organizational Commitment as Interactive Predictors of Tardiness and Absenteeism," *Journal of Management*, Winter 1986, pp. 577–584.

13. J. P. Meyer, N. J. Allen, and C. A. Smith, "Commitment to Organizations and Occupations: Extension and Test of a Three-Component Conceptualization," *Journal of Applied Psychology* 78, no. 4 (1993), pp. 538–551.

14. M. Riketta, "Attitudinal Organizational Commitment and Job Performance: A Meta-analysis," *Journal of Organizational Behavior*, March 2002, pp. 257–266.

15. T. A. Wright and D. G. Bonett, "The Moderating Effects of Employee Tenure on the Relation Between Organizational Commitment and Job Performance: A Meta-analysis," *Journal of Applied Psychology*, December 2002, pp. 1183–1190.

16. See, for instance, T. Simons and Q. Roberson, "Why Managers Should Care About Fairness: The Effects of Aggregate Justice Perceptions on Organizational Outcomes," *Journal of Applied Psychology* 88, no. 3 (2003), pp. 432–443.

17. R. B. Dunham, J. A. Grube, and M. B. Castañeda, "Organizational Commitment: The Utility of an Integrative Definition," *Journal of Applied Psychology* 79, no. 3 (1994), pp. 370–380.

18. D. M. Rousseau, "Organizational Behavior in the New Organizational Era," in J. T. Spence, J. M. Darley, and D. J. Foss (eds.), *Annual Review of Psychology*, vol. 48 (Palo Alto, CA: Annual Reviews, 1997), p. 523.

19. E. Snape and T. Redman, "An Evaluation of a Three-Component Model of Occupational Commitment: Dimensionality and Consequences Among United Kingdom Human Resource Management Specialists," *Journal of Applied Psychology* 88, no. 1 (2003), pp. 152–159.

20. L. Rhoades, R. Eisenberger, and S. Armeli, "Affective Commitment to the Organization: The Contribution of

Perceived Organizational Support," *Journal of Applied Psychology* 86, no. 5 (2001), pp. 825–836.

21. Z. X. Chen, S. Aryee, and C. Lee, "Test of a Mediation Model of Perceived Organizational Support," *Journal of Vocational Behavior*, June 2005, pp. 457–470.

22. J. K. Harter, F. L. Schmidt, and T. L. Hayes, "Business-Unit-Level Relationship Between Employee Satisfaction, Employee Engagement, and Business Outcomes: A Meta-analysis," *Journal of Applied Psychology* 87, no. 2 (2002), pp. 268–279.

23. N. R. Lockwood, *Leveraging Employee Engagement for Competitive Advantage* (Alexandria, VA: Society for Human Resource Management, 2007); and R. J. Vance, *Employee Engagement and Commitment* (Alexandria, VA: Society for Human Resource Management, 2006).

24. R. L. Payne and D. Morrison, "The Differential Effects of Negative Affectivity on Measures of Well-Being Versus Job Satisfaction and Organizational Commitment," *Anxiety, Stress & Coping: An International Journal* 15, no. 3 (2002), pp. 231–244.

25. See E. Spector, *Job Satisfaction: Application, Assessment, Causes, and Consequences* (Thousand Oaks, CA: Sage, 1997), p. 3.

26. J. Wanous, A. E. Reichers, and M. J. Hudy, "Overall Job Satisfaction: How Good Are Single-Item Measures?" *Journal of Applied Psychology*, April 1997, pp. 247–252.

27. K. Bowman, "Attitudes About Work, Chores, and Leisure in America," *AEI Opinion Studies*, August 25, 2003.

28. J. Barling, E. K. Kelloway, and R. D. Iverson, "High-Quality Work, Job Satisfaction, and Occupational Injuries," *Journal of Applied Psychology* 88, no. 2 (2003), pp. 276–283.

29. E. Diener, E. Sandvik, L. Seidlitz, and M. Diener, "The Relationship Between Income and Subjective Well-Being: Relative or Absolute?" *Social Indicators Research* 28 (1993), pp. 195–223.

30. E. Diener and M. E. P. Seligman, "Beyond Money: Toward an Economy of Well-Being," *Psychological Science in the Public Interest* 5, no. 1 (2004), pp. 1–31; and A. Grant, "Money=Happiness? That's Rich: Here's the Science Behind the Axiom," *The* (South Mississippi) *Sun Herald*, January 8, 2005.

31. See J. Zhou and J. M. George, "When Job Dissatisfaction Leads to Creativity: Encouraging the Expression of Voice," *Academy of Management Journal*, August 2001, pp. 682–696; and A. Davis-Blake, J. P. Broschak, and E. George, "Happy Together? How Using Nonstandard Workers Affects Exit, Voice, and Loyalty Among Standard Employees," *Academy of Management Journal* 46, no. 4 (2003), pp. 475–485.

32. R. B. Freeman, "Job Satisfaction as an Economic Variable," *American Economic Review*, January 1978, pp. 135–141.

33. T. A. Judge, C. J. Thoresen, J. E. Bono, and G. K. Patton, "The Job Satisfaction–Job Performance Relationship: A Qualitative and Quantitative Review," *Psychological Bulletin*, May 2001, pp. 376–407.

34. C. Ostroff, "The Relationship Between Satisfaction, Attitudes, and Performance: An Organizational Level Analysis," *Journal of Applied Psychology*, December 1992, pp. 963–974.

35. B. J. Hoffman, C. A. Blair, J. P. Maeriac, and D. J. Woehr, "Expanding the Criterion Domain? A Quantitative Review of the OCB Literature," *Journal of Applied Psychology* 92, no. 2

(2007), pp. 555–566; and J. A. LePine, A. Erez, and D. E. Johnson, "The Nature and Dimensionality of Organizational Citizenship Behavior: A Critical Review and Meta-analysis," *Journal of Applied Psychology*, February 2002, pp. 52–65.

36. M. A. Konovsky and D. W. Organ, "Dispositional and Contextual Determinants of Organizational Citizenship Behavior," *Journal of Organizational Behavior*, May 1996, pp. 253–266.

37. See, for instance, B. Schneider and D. E. Bowen, "Employee and Customer Perceptions of Service in Banks: Replication and Extension," *Journal of Applied Psychology*, August 1985, pp. 423–433; and J. Griffith, "Do Satisfied Employees Satisfy Customers? Support-Services Staff Morale and Satisfaction Among Public School Administrators, Students, and Parents," *Journal of Applied Social Psychology*, August 2001, pp. 1627–1658.

38. E. A. Locke, "The Nature and Causes of Job Satisfaction," in M. D. Dunnette (ed.), *Handbook of Industrial and Organizational Psychology* (Chicago: Rand McNally, 1976), p. 1331; and K. D. Scott and G. S. Taylor, "An Examination of Conflicting Findings on the Relationship between Job Satisfaction and Absenteeism: A Meta-analysis," *Academy of Management Journal*, September 1985, pp. 599–612.

39. F. J. Smith, "Work Attitudes as Predictors of Attendance on a Specific Day," *Journal of Applied Psychology*, February 1977, pp. 16–19.

40. W. Hom and R. W. Griffeth, *Employee Turnover* (Cincinnati, OH: South-Western Publishing, 1995); R. W. Griffeth, P. W. Hom, and S. Gaertner, "A Meta-analysis of Antecedents and Correlates of Employee Turnover: Update, Moderator Tests, and Research Implications for the Next Millennium," *Journal of Management* 26, no. 3 (2000), p. 479; and G. Johns, "The Psychology of Lateness, Absenteeism, and Turnover," in N. Anderson, D. Ones, H. Sinangil and C. Viswesvarian (eds.), *Handbook of Industrial, Work and Organizational Psychology* (London: Sage, 2001), p. 237.

41. See, for example, C. L. Hulin, M. Roznowski, and D. Hachiya, "Alternative Opportunities and Withdrawal Decisions: Empirical and Theoretical Discrepancies and an Integration," *Psychological Bulletin*, July 1985, pp. 233–250; and J. M. Carsten and P. E. Spector, "Unemployment, Job Satisfaction, and Employee Turnover: A Meta-analytic Test of the Muchinsky Model," *Journal of Applied Psychology*, August 1987, pp. 374–381.

42. D. G. Spencer and R. M. Steers, "Performance as a Moderator of the Job Satisfaction–Turnover Relationship," *Journal of Applied Psychology*, August 1981, pp. 511–514.

43. K. A. Hanisch, C. L. Hulin, and M. Roznowski, "The Importance of Individuals' Repertoires of Behaviors: The Scientific Appropriateness of Studying Multiple Behaviors and General Attitudes," *Journal of Organizational Behavior* 19, no. 5 (1998), pp. 463–480.

44. K. Holland, "Inside the Minds of Your Employees," *New York Times* (January 28, 2007), p. B1; "Study Sees Link Between Morale and Stock Price," *Workforce Management* (February 27, 2006), p. 15; and "The Workplace as a Solar System," *New York Times* (October 28, 2006), p. B5.

45. M. J. Gelfand, M. Erez, and Z. Aycan, "Cross-Cultural Organizational Behavior," *Annual Review of Psychology* 58 (2007), pp. 479–514; and A. S. Tsui, S. S. Nifadkar, and A. Y. Ou,

"Cross-National, Cross-Cultural Organizational Behavior Research: Advances, Gaps, and Recommendations," *Journal of Management*, June 2007, pp. 426–478.

46. M. Benz and B. S. Frey, "The Value of Autonomy: Evidence from the Self-Employed in 23 Countries," working paper 173, Institute for Empirical Research in Economics, University of Zurich, November 2003 (http://ssrn.com/abstract=475140); and P. Warr, *Work, Happiness, and Unhappiness* (Mahwah, NJ: Laurence Erlbaum, 2007).

47. Harrison, Newman, and Roth, "How Important Are Job Attitudes?" pp. 320–321.

CHAPTER 5

1. Cited in D. Jones, "Firms Spend Billions to Fire Up Workers—With Little Luck," *USA Today*, May 10, 2001, p. 1A.

2. "Wasted Time at Work Costs Employers Billions," *IPMA-HR Bulletin*, August 11, 2006, pp. 1–7.

3. See, for instance, T. R. Mitchell, "Matching Motivational Strategies with Organizational Contexts," in L. L. Cummings and B. M. Staw (eds.), *Research in Organizational Behavior*, vol. 19 (Greenwich, CT: JAI Press, 1997), pp. 60–62.

4. A. Maslow, *Motivation and Personality* (New York: Harper & Row, 1954).

5. See, for example, E. E. Lawler III and J. L. Suttle, "A Causal Correlation Test of the Need Hierarchy Concept," *Organizational Behavior and Human Performance*, April 1972, pp. 265–287; A. K. Korman, J. H. Greenhaus, and I. J. Badin, "Personnel Attitudes and Motivation," in M. R. Rosenzweig and L. W. Porter (eds.), *Annual Review of Psychology* (Palo Alto, CA: Annual Reviews, 1977), pp. 178–179; and J. Rauschenberger, N. Schmitt, and J. E. Hunter, "A Test of the Need Hierarchy Concept by a Markov Model of Change in Need Strength," *Administrative Science Quarterly*, December 1980, pp. 654–670.

6. M. A. Wahba and L. G. Bridwell, "Maslow Reconsidered: A Review of Research on the Need Hierarchy Theory," *Organizational Behavior and Human Performance*, April 1976, pp. 212–240.

7. D. McGregor, *The Human Side of Enterprise* (New York: McGraw-Hill, 1960). For an updated analysis of Theory X and Theory Y constructs, see R. J. Summers and S. F. Cronshaw, "A Study of McGregor's Theory X, Theory Y and the Influence of Theory X, Theory Y Assumptions on Causal Attributions for Instances of Worker Poor Performance," in S. L. McShane (ed.), Organizational Behavior, *ASAC 1988 Conference Proceedings*, vol. 9, Part 5, Halifax, Nova Scotia, 1988, pp. 115–123.

8. F. Herzberg, B. Mausner, and B. Snyderman, *The Motivation to Work* (New York: Wiley, 1959).

9. R. J. House and L. A. Wigdor, "Herzberg's Dual-Factor Theory of Job Satisfaction and Motivations: A Review of the Evidence and Criticism," *Personnel Psychology*, Winter 1967, pp. 369–389; D. P. Schwab and L. L. Cummings, "Theories of Performance and Satisfaction: A Review," *Industrial Relations*, October 1970, pp. 403–430; and J. Phillipchuk and J. Whittaker, "An Inquiry into the Continuing Relevance of Herzberg's Motivation Theory," *Engineering Management Journal* 8 (1996), pp. 15–20.

10. D. C. McClelland, *The Achieving Society* (New York: Van Nostrand Reinhold, 1961); J. W. Atkinson and J. O. Raynor, *Motivation and Achievement* (Washington, DC: Winston, 1974); D. C. McClelland, *Power: The Inner Experience* (New York: Irvington, 1975); and M. J. Stahl, *Managerial and Technical Motivation: Assessing Needs for Achievement, Power, and Affiliation* (New York: Praeger, 1986).

11. D. C. McClelland and D. G. Winter, *Motivating Economic Achievement* (New York: The Free Press, 1969); and J. B. Miner, N. R. Smith, and J. S. Bracker, "Role of Entrepreneurial Task Motivation in the Growth of Technologically Innovative Firms: Interpretations from Follow-up Data," *Journal of Applied Psychology*, October 1994, pp. 627–630.

12. D. C. McClelland, *Power*; D. C. McClelland and D. H. Burnham, "Power Is the Great Motivator," *Harvard Business Review*, March–April 1976, pp. 100–110; and R. E. Boyatzis, "The Need for Close Relationships and the Manager's Job," in D. A. Kolb, I. M. Rubin, and J. M. McIntyre, *Organizational Psychology: Readings on Human Behavior in Organizations*, 4th ed. (Upper Saddle River, NJ: Prentice Hall, 1984), pp. 81–86.

13. J. B. Miner, *Studies in Management Education* (New York: Springer, 1965).

14. E. L. Deci, *Intrinsic Motivation* (New York: Plenum, 1975); J. Cameron and W. D. Pierce, "Reinforcement, Reward, and Intrinsic Motivation: A Meta-analysis," *Review of Educational Research*, Fall 1994, pp. 363–423; S. Tang and V. C. Hall, "The Overjustification Effect: A Meta-analysis," *Applied Cognitive Psychology*, October 1995, pp. 365–404; E. L. Deci, R. Koestner, and R. M. Ryan, "A Meta-analytic Review of Experiments Examining the Effects of Extrinsic Rewards on Intrinsic Motivation," *Psychological Bulletin* 125, no. 6 (1999), pp. 627–668; and N. Houlfort, R. Koestner, M. Joussemet, A. Nantel-Vivier, and N. Lekes, "The Impact of Performance-Contingent Rewards on Perceived Autonomy and Competence," *Motivation & Emotion* 26, no. 4 (2002), pp. 279–295.

15. G. R. Salancik, "Interaction Effects of Performance and Money on Self-Perception of Intrinsic Motivation," *Organizational Behavior and Human Performance*, June 1975, pp. 339–351; and F. Luthans, M. Martinko, and T. Kess, "An Analysis of the Impact of Contingency Monetary Rewards on Intrinsic Motivation," *Proceedings of the Nineteenth Annual Midwest Academy of Management*, St. Louis, Missouri, 1976, pp. 209–221.

16. Deci, Koestner, and Ryan, "A Meta-analytic Review of Experiments Examining the Effects of Extrinsic Rewards on Intrinsic Motivation," pp. 627–668.

17. E. A. Locke, "Toward a Theory of Task Motivation and Incentives," *Organizational Behavior and Human Performance*, May 1968, pp. 157–189.

18. See M. E. Tubbs, "Goal Setting: A Meta-analytic Examination of the Empirical Evidence," *Journal of Applied Psychology*, August 1986, pp. 474–483; E. A. Locke and G. P. Latham, "Building a Practically Useful Theory of Goal Setting and Task Motivation," *American Psychologist*, September 2002, pp. 705–717; and E. A. Locke and G. P. Latham, "New Directions in Goal-Setting Theory," *Current Directions in Psychological Science* 15, no. 5 (2006), pp. 265–268.

19. J. M. Ivancevich and J. T. McMahon, "The Effects of Goal Setting, External Feedback, and Self-Generated Feedback on Outcome Variables: A Field Experiment," *Academy of*

Management Journal, June 1982, pp. 359–372; and E. A. Locke, "Motivation through Conscious Goal Setting," *Applied and Preventive Psychology* 5 (1996), pp. 117–124.

20. See, for example, G. P. Latham, M. Erez, and E. A. Locke, "Resolving Scientific Disputes by the Joint Design of Crucial Experiments by the Antagonists: Application to the Erez-Latham Dispute Regarding Participation in Goal Setting," *Journal of Applied Psychology*, November 1988, pp. 753–772; and S. G. Harkins and M. D. Lowe, "The Effects of Self-Set Goals on Task Performance," *Journal of Applied Social Psychology*, January 2000, pp. 1–40.

21. See R. E. Wood, A. J. Mento, and E. A. Locke, "Task Complexity as a Moderator of Goal Effects: A Meta-analysis," *Journal of Applied Psychology*, August 1987, pp. 416–425; R. Kanfer and P. L. Ackerman, "Motivation and Cognitive Abilities: An Integrative/Aptitude-Treatment Interaction Approach to Skill Acquisition," *Journal of Applied Psychology* (monograph), vol. 74 (1989), pp. 657–690; and T. R. Mitchell and W. S. Silver, "Individual and Group Goals When Workers Are Interdependent: Effects on Task Strategies and Performance," *Journal of Applied Psychology*, April 1990, pp. 185–193.

22. "KEYGroup Survey Finds Nearly Half of All Employees Have No Set Performance Goals," *IPMA-HR Bulletin*, March 10, 2006, p. 1; S. Hamm, "SAP Dangles a Big, Fat Carrot," *BusinessWeek*, May 22, 2006, pp. 67–68; and "P&G CEO Wields High Expectations but No Whip," *USA Today*, February 19, 2007, p. 3B.

23. See, for instance, S. J. Carroll and H. L. Tosi, *Management by Objectives: Applications and Research* (New York: Macmillan, 1973); and R. Rodgers and J. E. Hunter, "Impact of Management by Objectives on Organizational Productivity," *Journal of Applied Psychology*, April 1991, pp. 322–336.

24. A. Bandura and D. Cervone, "Differential Engagement in Self-Reactive Influences in Cognitively-Based Motivation," *Organizational Behavior and Human Decision Processes*, August 1986, pp. 92–113.

25. A. Bandura, *Self-Efficacy: The Exercise of Control* (New York: Freeman, 1997).

26. T. A. Judge, C. L. Jackson, J. C. Shaw, B. Scott, and B. L. Rich, "Self-Efficacy and Work-Related Performance: The Integral Role of Individual Differences," *Journal of Applied Psychology* 92, no. 1 (2007), pp. 107–127.

27. Ibid.

28. J. S. Adams, "Inequity in Social Exchanges," in L. Berkowitz (ed.), *Advances in Experimental Social Psychology* (New York: Academic Press, 1965), pp. 267–300.

29. C. Ostroff and L. E. Atwater, "Does Whom You Work with Matter? Effects of Referent Group Gender and Age Composition on Managers' Compensation," *Journal of Applied Psychology* 88, no. 4 (2003), pp. 725–740.

30. See, for example, R. C. Huseman, J. D. Hatfield, and E. W. Miles, "A New Perspective on Equity Theory: The Equity Sensitivity Construct," *Academy of Management Journal*, April 1987, pp. 222–234; K. S. Sauley and A. G. Bedeian, "Equity Sensitivity: Construction of a Measure and Examination of Its Psychometric Properties," *Journal of Management* 26, no. 5 (2000), pp. 885–910; and J. A. Colquitt, "Does the Justice of

One Interact with the Justice of Many? Reactions to Procedural Justice in Teams," *Journal of Applied Psychology* 89, no. 4 (2004), pp. 633–646.

31. J. Greenberg and S. Ornstein, "High Status Job Title as Compensation for Underpayment: A Test of Equity Theory," *Journal of Applied Psychology*, May 1983, pp. 285–297; and J. Greenberg, "Equity and Workplace Status: A Field Experiment," *Journal of Applied Psychology*, November 1988, pp. 606–613.

32. See, for instance, J. Greenberg, *The Quest for Justice on the Job* (Thousand Oaks, CA: Sage, 1996); R. Cropanzano and J. Greenberg, "Progress in Organizational Justice: Tunneling through the Maze," in C. L. Cooper and I. T. Robertson (eds.), *International Review of Industrial and Organizational Psychology*, vol. 12 (New York: Wiley, 1997); J. A. Colquitt, D. E. Conlon, M. J. Wesson, C. O. L. H. Porter, and K. Y. Ng, "Justice at the Millennium: A Meta-Analytic Review of the 25 Years of Organizational Justice Research," *Journal of Applied Psychology*, June 2001, pp. 425–445; T. Simons and Q. Roberson, "Why Managers Should Care About Fairness: The Effects of Aggregate Justice Perceptions on Organizational Outcomes," *Journal of Applied Psychology*, June 2003, pp. 432–443; and G. P. Latham and C. C. Pinder, "Work Motivation Theory and Research at the Dawn of the Twenty-First Century," *Annual Review of Psychology* 56 (2005), pp. 485–516.

33. "Americans Feel They Pay Fair Share of Taxes, Says Poll," *NewsTarget.com*, May 2, 2005, www.newstarget.com/007297.html.

34. G. S. Leventhal, "What Should Be Done with Equity Theory? New Approaches to the Study of Fairness in Social Relationships," in K. Gergen, M. Greenberg, and R. Willis (eds.), *Social Exchange: Advances in Theory and Research* (New York: Plenum, 1980), pp. 27–55.

35. J. C. Shaw, E. Wild, and J. A. Colquitt, "To Justify or Excuse? A Meta-Analytic Review of the Effects of Explanations," *Journal of Applied Psychology* 88, no. 3 (2003), pp. 444–458.

36. R. Cropanzano, C. A. Prehar, and P. Y. Chen, "Using Social Exchange Theory to Distinguish Procedural from Interactional Justice," *Group & Organization Management* 27, no. 3 (2002), pp. 324–351; and S. G. Roch and L. R. Shanock, "Organizational Justice in an Exchange Framework: Clarifying Organizational Justice Dimensions," *Journal of Management*, April 2006, pp. 299–322.

37. Colquitt, Conlon, Wesson, Porter, and Ng, "Justice at the Millennium," pp. 425–445.

38. J. Reb, B. M. Goldman, L. J. Kray, and R. Cropanzano, "Different Wrongs, Different Remedies? Reactions to Organizational Remedies After Procedural and Interactional Injustice," *Personnel Psychology* 59 (2006), pp. 31–64; and "Northwest Airlines Flight Cancellations Mount as Labor Woes Continue," *Aero-News.net*, June 26, 2007, www.aero-news.net.

39. For criticism, see T. R. Mitchell, "Expectancy Models of Job Satisfaction, Occupational Preference and Effort: A Theoretical, Methodological and Empirical Appraisal," *Psychological Bulletin*, November 1974, pp. 1053–1077; and W. Van Eerde and H. Thierry, "Vroom's Expectancy Models and Work-Related Criteria: A Meta-analysis," *Journal of Applied Psychology*, October

1996, pp. 575–586. For support, see L. W. Porter and E. E. Lawler III, *Managerial Attitudes and Performance* (Homewood, IL: Irwin, 1968); and J. J. Donovan, "Work Motivation," in N. Anderson et al. (eds.), *Handbook of Industrial, Work & Organizational Psychology*, vol. 2 (Thousand Oaks, CA: Sage, 2001), pp. 56–59.

40. P. M. Muchinsky, "A Comparison of Within- and Across-Subjects Analyses of the Expectancy-Valence Model for Predicting Effort," *Academy of Management Journal*, March 1977, pp. 154–158; and C. W. Kennedy, J. A. Fossum, and B. J. White, "An Empirical Comparison of Within-Subjects and Between-Subjects Expectancy Theory Models," *Organizational Behavior and Human Decision Process*, August 1983, pp. 124–143.

41. R. J. House, H. J. Shapiro, and M. A. Wahba, "Expectancy Theory as a Predictor of Work Behavior and Attitudes: A Re-evaluation of Empirical Evidence," *Decision Sciences*, January 1974, pp. 481–506.

42. N. J. Adler, *International Dimensions of Organizational Behavior*, 4th ed. (Cincinnati, OH: South-Western Publishing, 2002), p. 174.

43. G. Hofstede, "Motivation, Leadership, and Organization: Do American Theories Apply Abroad?" *Organizational Dynamics*, Summer 1980, p. 55.

44. Ibid.

45. J. K. Giacobbe-Miller, D. J. Miller, and V. I. Victorov, "A Comparison of Russian and U.S. Pay Allocation Decisions, Distributive Justice Judgments, and Productivity Under Different Payment Conditions," *Personnel Psychology*, Spring 1998, pp. 137–163.

46. S. L. Mueller and L. D. Clarke, "Political-Economic Context and Sensitivity to Equity: Differences Between the United States and the Transition Economies of Central and Eastern Europe," *Academy of Management Journal*, June 1998, pp. 319–329.

47. I. Harpaz, "The Importance of Work Goals: An International Perspective," *Journal of International Business Studies*, First Quarter 1990, pp. 75–93.

48. G. E. Popp, H. J. Davis, and T. T. Herbert, "An International Study of Intrinsic Motivation Composition," *Management International Review*, January 1986, pp. 28–35.

CHAPTER 6

1. J. R. Hackman and G. R. Oldham, "Motivation Through the Design of Work: Test of a Theory," *Organizational Behavior and Human Performance*, August 1976, pp. 250–279; and J. R. Hackman and G. R. Oldham, *Work Redesign* (Reading, MA: Addison-Wesley, 1980).

2. See "Job Characteristics Theory of Work Redesign," in J. B. Miner, *Theories of Organizational Behavior* (Hinsdale, IL: Dryden Press, 1980), pp. 231–266; B. T. Loher, R. A. Noe, N. L. Moeller, and M. P. Fitzgerald, "A Meta-analysis of the Relation of Job Characteristics to Job Satisfaction," *Journal of Applied Psychology*, May 1985, pp. 280–289; Y. Fried and G. R. Ferris, "The Validity of the Job Characteristics Model: A Review and Meta-analysis," *Personnel Psychology*, Summer 1987, pp. 287–322; and S. J. Behson, E. R. Eddy, and S. J. Lorenzet, "The

Importance of the Critical Psychological States in the Job Characteristics Model: A Meta-analytic and Structural Equations Modeling Examination," *Current Research in Social Psychology*, May 2000, pp. 170–189.

3. T. A. Judge, S. K. Parker, A. E. Colbert, D. Heller, and R. Ilies, "Job Satisfaction: A Cross-Cultural Review," in N. Anderson, D. S. Ones (eds.), *Handbook of Industrial, Work and Organizational Psychology*, vol. 2 (Thousand Oaks, CA: Sage Publications, 2002), pp. 25–52.

4. C. A. O'Reilly and D. F. Caldwell, "Informational Influence as a Determinant of Perceived Task Characteristics and Job Satisfaction," *Journal of Applied Psychology*, April 1979, pp. 157–165.

5. See, for instance, data on job enlargement described in M. A. Campion and C. L. McClelland, "Follow-up and Extension of the Interdisciplinary Costs and Benefits of Enlarged Jobs," *Journal of Applied Psychology*, June 1993, pp. 339–351.

6. Hackman and Oldham, *Work Redesign*.

7. See, for example, Hackman and Oldham, *Work Redesign*; Miner, *Theories of Organizational Behavior*, pp. 231–266; and R. W. Griffin, "Effects of Work Redesign on Employee percep-tions, Attitudes, and Behaviors: A Long-Term Investigation," *Academy of Management Journal* 34, no. 2 (1991), pp. 425–435.

8. F. P. Morgeson, M. D. Johnson, M. A. Campion, G. J. Medsker, and T. V. Mumford, "Understanding Reactions to Job Redesign: A Quasi-Experimental Investigation of the Moderating Effects of Organizational Contact on Perceptions of Performance Behavior," *Personnel Psychology* 39 (2006), pp. 333–363.

9. From the National Study of the Changing Workforce, cited in S. Shellenbarger, "Number of Women Managers Rise," *Wall Street Journal*, September 30, 2003, p. D2.

10. Cited in "Flextime Gains in Popularity in Germany," *Manpower Argus*, September 2000, p. 4.

11. See, for example, D. A. Ralston and M. F. Flanagan, "The Effect of Flextime on Absenteeism and Turnover for Male and Female Employees," *Journal of Vocational Behavior*, April 1985, pp. 206–217; and B. B. Baltes, T. E. Briggs, J. W. Huff, J. A. Wright, and G. A. Neuman, "Flexible and Compressed Workweek Schedules: A Meta-analysis of Their Effects on Work-Related Criteria," *Journal of Applied Psychology* 84, no. 4 (1999), pp. 496–513.

12. Ibid., p. 54.

13. C. Dawson, "Japan: Work-Sharing Will Prolong the Pain," *BusinessWeek*, December 24, 2001, p. 46.

14. See, for example, E. J. Hill, M. Ferris, and V. Martinson, "Does It Matter Where You Work? A Comparison of How Three Work Venues (Traditional Office, Virtual Office, and Home Office) Influence Aspects of Work and Personal/Family Life," *Journal of Vocational Behavior* 63, no. 2 (2003), pp. 220–241.

15. N. B. Kurland and D. E. Bailey, "Telework: The Advantages and Challenges of Working Here, There, Anywhere, and Anytime," *Organizational Dynamics*, Autumn 1999, pp. 53–68; and Wells, "Making Telecommuting Work," *HR Magazine* 46 (October 2001), p. 34.

16. U. Huws, "Wired in the Country," *People Management*, November 1999, pp. 46–47.

17. Cited in R. W. Judy and C. D'Amico, *Workforce 2020* (Indianapolis: Hudson Institute, 1997), p. 58.

18. See, for example, the increasing body of literature on empowerment, such as W. A. Randolph, "Re-Thinking Empowerment: Why Is It So Hard to Achieve?" *Organizational Dynamics*, 29, no. 2 (2000), pp. 94–107; and S. E. Seibert, S. R. Silver, and W. A. Randolph, "Taking Empowerment to the Next Level: A Multiple-Level Model of Empowerment, Performance, and Satisfaction," *Academy of Management Journal* 47, no. 3 (2004), pp. 332–349.

19. F. Heller, E. Pusic, G. Strauss, and B. Wilpert, *Organizational Participation: Myth and Reality* (Oxford, UK: Oxford University Press, 1998).

20. See, for instance, K. L. Miller and P. R. Monge, "Participation, Satisfaction, and Productivity: A Meta-analytic Review," *Academy of Management Journal*, December 1986, pp. 727–753; E. A. Locke, M. Alavi, and J. A. Wagner III, "Participation in Decision Making: An Information Exchange Perspective," in G. R. Ferris (ed.), *Research in Personnel and Human Resource Management*, vol. 15 (Greenwich, CT: JAI Press, 1997), pp. 293–331; and J. A. Wagner III and J. A. LePine, "Effects of Participation on Performance and Satisfaction: Additional Meta-analytic Evidence," *Psychological Reports*, June 1999, pp. 719–725.

21. Cotton, *Employee Involvement*, (Newbury Park, CA: Sage 1993), p. 114.

22. See, for example, M. Gilman and P. Marginson, "Negotiating European Works Council: Contours of Constrained Choice," *Industrial Relations Journal*, March 2002, pp. 36–51; and B. Keller, "The European Company Statute: Employee Involvement—And Beyond," *Industrial Relations Journal*, December 2002, pp. 424–445.

23. Cotton, *Employee Involvement*, pp. 129–130, 139–140.

24. Ibid., p. 140.

25. E. White, "Opportunity Knocks, and It Pays a Lot Better," *Wall Street Journal*, November 13, 2006, p. B3.

26. P. S. Goodman and P. P. Pan, "Chinese Workers Pay for Wal-Mart's Low Prices," *Washington Post*, February 8, 2004, p. A1.

27. L. Wiener, "Paycheck Plus," *U.S. News & World Report*, February 24/March 3, 2003, p. 58.

28. Cited in "Pay Programs: Few Employees See the Pay-for-Performance Connection," *Compensation & Benefits Report*, June 2003, p. 1.

29. B. Wysocki, Jr., "Chilling Reality Awaits Even the Employed," *Wall Street Journal*, November 5, 2001, p. A1.

30. "Tensions of a New Pay Plan," *New York Times*, May 17, 1992, p. F5.

31. See, for instance, D.-O. Kim, "Determinants of the Survival of Gainsharing Programs," *Industrial & Labor Relations Review*, October 1999, pp. 21–42; and M. R. Dixon, L. J. Hayes, and J. Stack, "Changing Conceptions of Employee Compensation," *Journal of Organizational Behavior Management* 23, no. 2–3 (2003), pp. 95–116.

32. Employment Policy Foundation, *U.S. Wage and Productivity Growth Attainable Through Gainsharing*, Accessed May 10, 2000 at http://www.epf.org.

33. "The Employee Ownership 100," *National Center for Employee Ownership*, Accessed July 2003, www.nceo.org.

34. See data in D. Stamps, "A Piece of the Action," *Training*, March 1996, p. 66.

35. C. G. Hanson and W. D. Bell, *Profit Sharing and Profitability: How Profit Sharing Promotes Business Success* (London: Kogan Page, 1987); and D. D'Art and T. Turner, "Profit Sharing, Firm Performance, and Union Influence in Selected European Countries," *Personnel Review* 33, no. 3 (2004), pp. 335–350.

36. T. M. Welbourne and L. R. Gomez-Mejia, "Gainsharing: A Critical Review and a Future Research Agenda," *Journal of Management* 21, no. 3 (1995), pp. 559–609.

37. C. B. Cadsby, F. Song, and F. Tapon, "Sorting and Incentive Effects of Pay for Performance: An Experimental Investigation," *Academy of Management Journal* 50, no. 2 (2007), pp. 387–405.

38. See, for instance, M. W. Barringer and G. T. Milkovich, "A Theoretical Exploration of the Adoption and Design of Flexible Benefit Plans: A Case of Human Resource Innovation," *Academy of Management Review*, April 1998, pp. 305–324; and N. D. Cole and D. H. Flint, "Perceptions of Distributive and Procedural Justice in Employee Benefits: Flexible Versus Traditional Benefit Plans," *Journal of Managerial Psychology* 19, no. 1 (2004), pp. 19–40.

39. D. A. DeCenzo and S. P. Robbins, *Human Resource Management*, 7th ed. (New York: Wiley, 2002), pp. 346–348.

40. S. E. Markham, K. D. Scott, and G. H. McKee, "Recognizing Good Attendance: A Longitudinal, Quasi-Experimental Field Study," *Personnel Psychology*, Autumn 2002, p. 641; and S. J. Peterson and F. Luthans, "The Impact of Financial and Nonfinancial Incentives on Business Unit Outcomes over Time," *Journal of Applied Psychology* 91, no. 1 (2006), pp. 156–165.

41. D. Drickhamer, "Best Plant Winners: Nichols Foods Ltd.," *IndustryWeek*, October 1, 2001, pp. 17–19.

42. M. Littman, "Best Bosses Tell All," *Working Woman*, October 2000, p. 54.

43. Cited in S. Caudron, "The Top 20 Ways to Motivate Employees," *IndustryWeek*, April 3, 1995, pp. 15–16. See also B. Nelson, "Try Praise," *INC.*, September 1996, p. 115.

44. Cited in K. J. Dunham, "Amid Shrinking Workplace Morale, Employers Turn to Recognition," *Wall Street Journal*, November 19, 2002, p. B8.

45. Ibid.

46. B. M. Meglino and A. M. Korsgaard, "The Role of Other Orientation in Reactions to Job Characteristics," *Journal of Management*, February 2007, pp. 57–83.

47. M. F. Peterson and S. A. Ruiz-Quintanilla, "Cultural Socialization as a Source of Intrinsic Work Motivation," *Group & Organization Management*, June 2003, pp. 188–216.

48. P. Peters and L. den Dulk, "Cross Cultural Differences in Managers' Support for Home-Based Telework: A Theoretical Elaboration," *International Journal of Cross Cultural Management*, December 2003, pp. 329–346.

49. S. C. L. Fong and M. A. Shaffer, "The Dimensionality and Determinants of Pay Satisfaction: A Cross-Cultural Investigation of a Group Incentive Plan," *International Journal of Human Resource Management*, June 2003, pp. 559–580.

50. Brown, "Everybody Loves Flex.," *Canadian HR Reporter* (November 2002), p. 1.

51. E. Unsworth, "U.K. Employers Find Flex Benefits Helpful: Survey," *Business Insurance*, May 21, 2001, pp. 19–20.

52. See, for instance, A. Sagie and Z. Aycan, "A Cross-Cultural Analysis of Participative Decision-Making in Organizations," *Human Relations*, April 2003, pp. 453–473; and J. Brockner, "Unpacking Country Effects: On the Need to Operationalize the Psychological Determinants of Cross-National Differences," in R. M. Kramer and B. M. Staw (eds.), *Research in Organizational Behavior*, vol. 25 (Oxford, UK: Elsevier, 2003), pp. 336–340.

53. C. Robert, T. M. Probst, J. J. Martocchio, R. Drasgow, and J. J. Lawler, "Empowerment and Continuous Improvement in the United States, Mexico, Poland, and India: Predicting Fit on the Basis of the Dimensions of Power Distance and Individualism," *Journal of Applied Psychology*, October 2000, pp. 643–658.

CHAPTER 7

1. See, for instance, C. D. Fisher and N. M. Ashkanasy, "The Emerging Role of Emotions in Work Life: An Introduction," *Journal of Organizational Behavior*, Special Issue 2000, pp. 123–129; and N. M. Ashkanasy, C. E. J. Hartel, and C. S. Daus, "Diversity and Emotion: The New Frontiers in Organizational Behavior Research," *Journal of Management* 28, no. 3 (2002), pp. 307–338.

2. H. M. Weiss and R. Cropanzano, "Affective Events Theory: A Theoretical Discussion of the Structure, Causes and Consequences of Affective Experiences at Work," in B. M. Staw and L. L. Cummings (eds.), *Research in Organizational Behavior*, vol. 18 (Greenwich, CT: JAI Press, 1996), pp. 17–19.

3. N. H. Frijda, "Moods, Emotion Episodes and Emotions," in M. Lewis and J. M. Haviland (eds.), *Handbook of Emotions* (New York: Guilford Press, 1993), p. 381.

4. See P. Ekman and R. J. Davidson (eds.), *The Nature of Emotions*. (Oxford, England: Oxford University Press, 1994).

5. Weiss and Cropanzano, "Affective Events Theory," pp. 20–22.

6. Cited in R. D. Woodworth, *Experimental Psychology* (New York: Holt, 1938).

7. J. T. Cacioppo and W. L. Gardner, "Emotion," in *Annual Review of Psychology*, vol. 50 (Palo Alto, CA: Annual Reviews, 1999), pp. 191–214.

8. A. R. Damasio, *Descartes' Error: Emotion, Reason, and the Human Brain* (New York: Quill, 1994).

9. L. Cosmides and J. Tooby, "Evolutionary Psychology and the Emotions," in M. Lewis and J. M. Haviland-Jones (eds.), *Handbook of Emotions*, 2nd ed. (New York: Guilford Press, 2000), pp. 91–115.

10. D. M. Buss, "Cognitive Biases and Emotional Wisdom in the Evolution of Conflict Between the Sexes," *Current Directions in Psychological Science* 10, no. 6 (December 2001), pp. 219–223.

11. K. Hundley, "An Unspoken Problem: Two-Thirds of Female Lawyers Say They Have Experienced or Seen Harassment at Work. But Few Want to Talk About It," *St. Petersburg* (Florida) *Times*, April 25, 2004, www.sptimes.com/2005/04/24/Business/An_unspoken_problem.shtml.

12. K. N. Laland and G. R. Brown, *Sense and Nonsense: Evolutionary Perspectives on Human Behaviour* (Oxford, UK: Oxford University Press, 2002).

13. D. Watson, *Mood and Temperament* (New York: Guilford Press, 2000).

14. Ibid.

15. Ibid., p. 100.

16. Ibid., p. 73.

17. J. A. Fuller, J. M. Stanton, G. G. Fisher, C. Spitzmüller, S. S. Russell, and P. C. Smith, "A Lengthy Look at the Daily Grind: Time Series Analysis of Events, Mood, Stress, and Satisfaction," *Journal of Applied Psychology* 88, no. 6 (December 2003), pp. 1019–1033.

18. See "Monday Blahs," May 16, 2005, www.ashidome.com/blogger/housearrest.asp?c=809&m=5&y=2005.

19. A. M. Isen, "Positive Affect as a Source of Human Strength," in L. G. Aspinwall and U. Staudinger (eds.), *The Psychology of Human Strengths* (Washington, DC: American Psychological Association, 2003), pp. 179–195.

20. Watson, *Mood and Temperament* (2000).

21. *Sleep in America Poll* (Washington, DC: National Sleep Foundation, 2005).

22. M. Lavidor, A. Weller, and H. Babkoff, "How Sleep Is Related to Fatigue," *British Journal of Health Psychology* 8 (2003), pp. 95–105; and J. J. Pilcher and E. Ott, "The Relationships Between Sleep and Measures of Health and Well-Being in College Students: A Repeated Measures Approach," *Behavioral Medicine* 23 (1998), pp. 170–178.

23. B. A. Scott and T. A. Judge, "Tired and Cranky? The Effects of Sleep Quality on Employee Emotions and Job Satisfaction," working paper, Department of Management, University of Florida, 2005.

24. P. R. Giacobbi, H. A. Hausenblas, and N. Frye, "A Naturalistic Assessment of the Relationship Between Personality, Daily Life Events, Leisure-Time Exercise, and Mood," *Psychology of Sport & Exercise* 6, no. 1 (January 2005), pp. 67–81.

25. L. L. Carstensen, M. Pasupathi, M. Ulrich, and J. R. Nesselroade, "Emotional Experience in Everyday Life Across the Adult Life Span," *Journal of Personality and Social Psychology* 79, no. 4 (2000), pp. 644–655.

26. N. James, "Emotional Labour: Skill and Work in the Social Regulations of Feelings," *Sociological Review*, February 1989, pp. 15–42; and A. Hochschild, *The Second Shift* (New York: Viking, 1989).

27. A. Rafaeli, "When Clerks Meet Customers: A Test of Variables Related to Emotional Expression on the Job," *Journal of Applied Psychology*, June 1989, pp. 385–393; and LaFrance and Banaji, "Toward a Reconsideration of the Gender–Emotion Relationship." in M. Clark (ed.), *Emotion and Social Behavior* (Thousand Oaks, CA: Sage, 1992), pp. 178–201.

28. See J. A. Morris and D. C. Feldman, "Managing Emotions in the Workplace," *Journal of Managerial Issues* 9, no. 3 (1997), pp. 257–274; and S. M. Kruml and D. Geddes, "Catching Fire Without Burning Out: Is There an Ideal Way to Perform Emotion Labor?" in N. M. Ashkansay, C. E. J. Hartel, and W. J. Zerbe, *Emotions in the Workplace* (New York: Quorum Books, 2000), pp. 177–188.

29. A. Grandey, "Emotion Regulation in the Workplace: A New Way to Conceptualize Emotional Labor," *Journal of Occupational Health Psychology* 5, no. 1 (2000), pp. 95–110; and R. Cropanzano, D. E. Rupp, and Z. S. Byrne, "The Relationship of Emotional Exhaustion to Work Attitudes, Job Performance, and Organizational Citizenship Behavior," *Journal of Applied Psychology*, February 2003, pp. 160–169.

30. A. R. Hochschild, "Emotion Work, Feeling Rules, and Social Structure," *American Journal of Sociology*, November 1979, pp. 551–575; W.-C. Tsai, "Determinants and Consequences of Employee Displayed Positive Emotions," *Journal of Management* 27, no. 4 (2001), pp. 497–512; and J. M. Diefendorff and E. M. Richard, "Antecedents and Consequences of Emotional Display Rule Perceptions," *Journal of Applied Psychology*, April 2003, pp. 284–294.

31. B. M. DePaulo, "Nonverbal Behavior and Self-Presentation," *Psychological Bulletin*, March 1992, pp. 203–243.

32. C. S. Hunt, "Although I Might Be Laughing Loud and Hearty, Deep Inside I'm Blue: Individual Perceptions Regarding Feeling and Displaying Emotions at Work," paper presented at the Academy of Management Conference, Cincinnati, August 1996, p. 3.

33. A. A. Grandey, "When 'the Show Must Go On': Surface Acting and Deep Acting as Determinants of Emotional Exhaustion and Peer-Rated Service Delivery," *Academy of Management Journal*, February 2003, pp. 86–96; and A. A. Grandey, D. N. Dickter, and H. Sin, "The Customer Is Not Always Right: Customer Aggression and Emotion Regulation of Service Employees," *Journal of Organizational Behavior* 25, no. 3 (May 2004), pp. 397–418.

34. Based on D. R. Caruso, J. D. Mayer, and P. Salovey, "Emotional Intelligence and Emotional Leadership," in R. E. Riggio, S. E. Murphy, and F. J. Pirozzolo (eds.), *Multiple Intelligences and Leadership* (Mahwah, NJ: Lawrence Erlbaum, 2002), p. 70.

35. This section is based on Daniel Goleman, *Emotional Intelligence* (New York: Bantam, 1995); P. Salovey and D. Grewal, "The Science of Emotional Intelligence," *Current Directions in Psychological Science* 14, no. 6 (2005), pp. 281–285; D. Geddes and R. R. Callister, "Crossing the Line(s): A Dual Threshold Model of Anger in Organizations," *Academy of Management Review* 32, no. 3 (2007), pp. 721–746; and J. Ciarrochi, J. P. Forgas, and J. D. Mayer (eds.), *Emotional Intelligence in Everyday Life* (Philadelphia: Psychology Press, 2001).

36. F. I. Greenstein, *The Presidential Difference: Leadership Style from FDR to Clinton* (Princeton, NJ: Princeton University Press, 2001).

37. C. Cherniss, "The Business Case for Emotional Intelligence," *Consortium for Research on Emotional Intelligence in Organizations*, 1999, www.eiconsortium.org/research/business_case_for_ei.pdf.

38. K. S. Law, C. Wong, and L. J. Song, "The Construct and Criterion Validity of Emotional Intelligence and Its Potential Utility for Management Studies," *Journal of Applied Psychology* 89, no. 3 (2004), pp. 483–496.

39. H. A. Elfenbein and N. Ambady, "Predicting Workplace Outcomes from the Ability to Eavesdrop on Feelings," *Journal of Applied Psychology* 87, no. 5 (October 2002), pp. 963–971.

40. D. L. Van Rooy and C. Viswesvaran, "Emotional Intelligence: A Meta-analytic Investigation of Predictive Validity and Nomological Net," *Journal of Vocational Behavior* 65, no. 1 (August 2004), pp. 71–95.

41. R. Bar-On, D. Tranel, N. L. Denburg, and A. Bechara, "Exploring the Neurological Substrate of Emotional and Social Intelligence," *Brain* 126, no. 8 (August 2003), pp. 1790–1800.

42. E. A. Locke, "Why Emotional Intelligence Is an Invalid Concept," *Journal of Organizational Behavior* 26, no. 4 (June 2005), pp. 425–431.

43. J. M. Conte, "A Review and Critique of Emotional Intelligence Measures," *Journal of Organizational Behavior* 26, no. 4 (June 2005), pp. 433–440; and M. Davies, L. Stankov, and R. D. Roberts, "Emotional Intelligence: In Search of an Elusive Construct," *Journal of Personality and Social Psychology* 75, no. 4 (1998), pp. 989–1015.

44. T. Decker, "Is Emotional Intelligence a Viable Concept?" *Academy of Management Review* 28, no. 2 (April 2003), pp. 433–440; and Davies, Stankov, and Roberts, "Emotional Intelligence: In Search of an Elusive Construct."

45. F. J. Landy, "Some Historical and Scientific Issues Related to Research on Emotional Intelligence," *Journal of Organizational Behavior* 26, no. 4 (June 2005), pp. 411–424.

46. L. M. J. Spencer, D. C. McClelland, and S. Kelner, *Competency Assessment Methods: History and State of the Art* (Boston: Hay/McBer, 1997).

47. See A. M. Isen, "Positive Affect and Decision Making," in M. Lewis and J. M. Haviland-Jones (eds.), *Handbook of Emotions*, 2nd ed. (New York: Guilford, 2000), pp. 261–277.

48. L. B. Alloy and L. Y. Abramson, "Judgement of Contingency in Depressed and Nondepressed Students: Sadder but Wiser?" *Journal of Experimental Psychology: General* 108 (1979), pp. 441–485.

49. N. Ambady and H. M. Gray, "On Being Sad and Mistaken: Mood Effects on the Accuracy of Thin-Slice Judgments," *Journal of Personality and Social Psychology* 83, no. 4 (2002), pp. 947–961.

50. A. M. Isen, "On the Relationship Between Affect and Creative Problem Solving," in S. W. Russ (ed.), *Affect, Creative Experience and Psychological Adjustment* (Philadelphia, PA: Brunner/Mazel, 1999), pp. 3–17; and S. Lyubomirsky, L. King, and E. Diener, "The Benefits of Frequent Positive Affect: Does Happiness Lead to Success?" *Psychological Bulletin* 131, no. 6 (2005), pp. 803–855.

51. S. Lyubomirsky, L. King, and E. Diener, "The Benefits of Frequent Positive Affect: Does Happiness Lead to Success?" *Psychological Bulletin* 131, no. 6 (2005), pp. 803–855.

52. N. Madjar, G. R. Oldham, and M. G. Pratt, "There's No Place Like Home? The Contributions of Work and Nonwork Creativity Support to Employees' Creative Performance," *Academy of Management Journal* 45, no. 4 (2002), pp. 757–767.

53. J. M. George and J. Zhou, "Understanding When Bad Moods Foster Creativity and Good Ones Don't: The Role of Context and Clarity of Feelings," *Journal of Applied Psychology* 87, no. 4 (August 2002), pp. 687–697.

54. L. L. Martin, "Mood as Input: A Configural View of Mood Effects," in L. L. Martin and G. L. Clore (eds.), *Theories of Mood*

and Cognition: A User's Guidebook (Mahwah, NJ: Lawrence Erlbaum, 2001), pp. 135–157.

55. A. Erez and A. M. Isen, "The Influence of Positive Affect on the Components of Expectancy Motivation," *Journal of Applied Psychology* 87, no. 6 (2002), pp. 1055–1067.

56. R. Ilies and T. A. Judge, "Goal Regulation Across Time: The Effect of Feedback and Affect," *Journal of Applied Psychology* 90, no. 3 (May 2005), pp. 453–467.

57. J. M. George, "Trait and State Affect," in K. R. Murphy (ed.), *Individual Differences and Behavior in Organizations* (San Francisco: Jossey-Bass, 1996), p. 162.

58. B. E. Ashforth and R. H. Humphrey, "Emotion in the Workplace: A Reappraisal," *Human Relations*, February 1995, p. 116.

59. N. Reynolds, "Whiz-Kids Gamble on TV Channel for Poker,"*telegraph.co.uk*, April 16, 2005, www.telegraph.co.uk.

60. G. A. Van Kleef, C. K. W. De Dreu, and A. S. R. Manstead, "The Interpersonal Effects of Emotions in Negotiations: A Motivated Information Processing Approach," *Journal of Personality and Social Psychology* 87, no. 4 (2004), pp. 510–528; and G. A. Van Kleef, C. K. W. De Dreu, and A. S. R. Manstead, "The Interpersonal Effects of Anger and Happiness in Negotiations," *Journal of Personality and Social Psychology* 86, no. 1 (2004), pp. 57–76.

61. K. M. O'Connor and J. A. Arnold, "Distributive Spirals: Negotiation Impasses and the Moderating Role of Disputant Self-Efficacy," *Organizational Behavior and Human Decision Processes* 84, no. 1 (2001), pp. 148–176.

62. B. Shiv, G. Loewenstein, A. Bechara, H. Damasio, and A. R. Damasio, "Investment Behavior and the Negative Side of Emotion," *Psychological Science* 16, no. 6 (2005), pp. 435–439.

63. W.-C. Tsai and Y.-M. Huang, "Mechanisms Linking Employee Affective Delivery and Customer Behavioral Intentions," *Journal of Applied Psychology*, October 2002, pp. 1001–1008.

64. Grandey, "When 'the Show Must Go On.'"

65. See P. B. Barker and A. A. Grandey, "Service with a Smile and Encounter Satisfaction: Emotional Contagion and Appraisal Mechanisms," *Academy of Management Journal* 49, no. 6 (2006), pp. 1229–1238; and S. D. Pugh, "Service with a Smile: Emotional Contagion in the Service Encounter," *Academy of Management Journal*, October 2001, pp. 1018–1027.

66. D. E. Rupp and S. Spencer, "When Customers Lash Out: The Effects of Customer Interactional Injustice on Emotional Labor and the Mediating Role of Emotions," *Journal of Applied Psychology* 91, no. 4 (2006), pp. 971–978; and Tsai and Huang, "Mechanisms Linking Employee Affective Delivery and Customer Behavioral Intentions."

67. R. Rau, "Job Strain or Healthy Work: A Question of Task Design," *Journal of Occupational Health Psychology* 9, no. 4 (October 2004), pp. 322–338; and R. Rau and A. Triemer, "Overtime in Relation to Blood Pressure and Mood During Work, Leisure, and Night Time," *Social Indicators Research* 67, no. 1–2 (June 2004), pp. 51–73.

68. T. A. Judge and R. Ilies, "Affect and Job Satisfaction: A Study of Their Relationship at Work and at Home," *Journal of Applied Psychology* 89 (2004), pp. 661–673.

69. See R. J. Bennett and S. L. Robinson, "Development of a Measure of Workplace Deviance," *Journal of Applied Psychology*, June 2000, pp. 349–360. See also P. R. Sackett and C. J. DeVore, "Counterproductive Behaviors at Work," in N. Anderson, D. S. Ones, H. K. Sinangil, and C. Viswesvaran (eds.), *Handbook of Industrial, Work & Organizational Psychology*, vol. 1 (Thousand Oaks, CA: Sage, 2001), pp. 145–164.

70. A. G. Bedeian, "Workplace Envy," *Organizational Dynamics*, Spring 1995, p. 50; and Ben-Ze'ev, *The Subtlety of Emotions*, (Cambridge, MA: MIT Press, 2000), pp. 281–326.

71. K. Lee and N. J. Allen, "Organizational Citizenship Behavior and Workplace Deviance: The Role of Affect and Cognition," *Journal of Applied Psychology* 87, no. 1 (2002), pp. 131–142; and T. A. Judge, B. A. Scott, and R. Ilies, "Hostility, Job Attitudes, and Workplace Deviance: Test of a Multilevel Model," *Journal of Applied Psychology* 91, no. 1 (2006) 126–138.

72. T. Sy, S. Côté, and R. Saavedra, "The Contagious Leader: Impact of the Leader's Mood on the Mood of Group Members, Group Affective Tone, and Group Processes," *Journal of Applied Psychology* 90, no. 2 (2005), pp. 295–305.

73. P. Totterdell, "Catching Moods and Hitting Runs: Mood Linkage and Subjective Performance in Professional Sports Teams," *Journal of Applied Psychology* 85, no. 6 (2000), pp. 848–859.

74. M. Eid and E. Diener, "Norms for Experiencing Emotions in Different Cultures: Inter- and International Differences," *Journal of Personality & Social Psychology* 81, no. 5 (2001), pp. 869–885.

75. S. Oishi, E. Diener, and C. Napa Scollon, "Cross-Situational Consistency of Affective Experiences Across Cultures," *Journal of Personality & Social Psychology* 86, no. 3 (2004), pp. 460–472.

76. Eid and Diener, "Norms for Experiencing Emotions in Different Cultures."

77. Ibid.

78. Ashforth and Humphrey, "Emotion in the Workplace," p. 104; B. Plasait, "Accueil des Touristes Dans les Grands Centres de Transit Paris," *Rapport du Bernard Plasait*, October 4, 2004, www.tourisme.gouv.fr/fr/navd/presse/dossiers/att00005767/dp_plasait.pdf; B. Mesquita, "Emotions in Collectivist and Individualist Contexts," *Journal of Personality and Social Psychology* 80, no. 1 (2001), pp. 68–74; and D. Rubin, "Grumpy German Shoppers Distrust the Wal-Mart Style," *Seattle Times*, December 30, 2001, p. A15.

79. H. A. Elfenbein and N. Ambady, "When Familiarity Breeds Accuracy: Cultural Exposure and Facial Emotional Recognition," *Journal of Personality and Social Psychology* 85, no. 2 (2003), pp. 276–290.

80. R. I. Levy, *Tahitians: Mind and Experience in the Society Islands* (Chicago: University of Chicago Press, 1973).

81. B. Mesquita and N. H. Frijda, "Cultural Variations in Emotions: A Review," *Psychological Bulletin*, September 1992, pp. 179–204; and B. Mesquita, "Emotions in Collectivist and Individualist Contexts," *Journal of Personality and Social Psychology*, January 2001, pp. 68–74.

82. D. Matsumoto, "Cross-Cultural Psychology in the 21st Century," http://teachpsych.lemoyne.edu/teachpsych/faces/script/Ch05.htm.

83. S. Nelton, "Emotions in the Workplace," *Nation's Business*, February 1996, p. 25.

CHAPTER 8

1. L. R. Sayles, "Work Group Behavior and the Larger Organization," in C. Arensburg, et al. (eds.), *Research in Industrial Relations* (New York: Harper & Row, 1957), pp. 131–145.

2. J. F. McGrew, J. G. Bilotta, and J. M. Deeney, "Software Team Formation and Decay: Extending the Standard Model for Small Groups," *Small Group Research* 30, no. 2 (1999), pp. 209–234.

3. B. W. Tuckman, "Developmental Sequences in Small Groups," *Psychological Bulletin*, June 1965, pp. 384–399; B. W. Tuckman and M. C. Jensen, "Stages of Small-Group Development Revisited," *Group and Organizational Studies*, December 1977, pp. 419–427; M. F. Maples, "Group Development: Extending Tuckman's Theory," *Journal for Specialists in Group Work*, Fall 1988, pp. 17–23; and K. Vroman and J. Kovacich, "Computer-Mediated Interdisciplinary Teams: Theory and Reality," *Journal of Interprofessional Care* 16, no. 2 (2002), pp. 159–170.

4. J. F. George and L. M. Jessup, "Groups over Time: What Are We Really Studying?" *International Journal of Human-Computer Studies* 47, no. 3 (1997), pp. 497–511.

5. P. G. Zimbardo, C. Haney, W. C. Banks, and D. Jaffe, "The Mind Is a Formidable Jailer: A Pirandellian Prison," *New York Times*, April 8, 1973, pp. 38–60; and C. Haney and P. G. Zimbardo, "Social Roles and Role-Playing: Observations from the Stanford Prison Study," *Behavioral and Social Science Teacher*, January 1973, pp. 25–45.

6. C. A. Kiesler and S. B. Kiesler, *Conformity* (Reading, MA: Addison-Wesley, 1969).

7. Ibid., p. 27.

8. S. E. Asch, "Effects of Group Pressure upon the Modification and Distortion of Judgments," in H. Guetzkow (ed.), *Groups, Leadership and Men* (Pittsburgh: Carnegie Press, 1951), pp. 177–190; and S. E. Asch, "Studies of Independence and Conformity: A Minority of One Against a Unanimous Majority," *Psychological Monographs: General and Applied* 70, no. 9 (1956), pp. 1–70.

9. R. Bond and P. B. Smith, "Culture and Conformity: A Meta-analysis of Studies Using Asch's (1952, 1956) Line Judgment Task," *Psychological Bulletin*, January 1996, pp. 111–137.

10. See S. L. Robinson and R. J. Bennett, "A Typology of Deviant Workplace Behaviors: A Multidimensional Scaling Study," *Academy of Management Journal*, April 1995, pp. 555–572; S. L. Robinson and A. M. O'Leary-Kelly, "Monkey See, Monkey Do: The Influence of Work Groups on the Antisocial Behavior of Employees," *Academy of Management Journal*, December 1998, pp. 658–672; and R. J. Bennett and S. L. Robinson, "The Past, Present, and Future of Workplace Deviance," in J. Greenberg (ed.), *Organizational Behavior: The State of the Science*, 2nd ed. (Mahwah, NJ: Erlbaum, 2003), pp. 237–271.

11. C. M. Pearson, L. M. Andersson, and C. L. Porath, "Assessing and Attacking Workplace Civility," *Organizational Dynamics* 29, no. 2 (2000), p. 130; see also C. Pearson, L. M. Andersson, and C. L. Porath, "Workplace Incivility," in S. Fox and P. E. Spector (eds.), *Counterproductive Work Behavior: Investigations of Actors and Targets* (Washington, DC American Psychological Association, 2005), pp. 177–200.

12. Robinson and O'Leary-Kelly, "Monkey See, Monkey Do."

13. A. Erez, H. Elms, and E. Fong, "Lying, Cheating, Stealing: It Happens More in Groups," paper presented at the European Business Ethics Network Annual Conference, Budapest, Hungary, August 30, 2003.

14. See R. S. Feldman, *Social Psychology*, 3rd ed. (Upper Saddle River, NJ: Prentice Hall, 2001), pp. 464–465.

15. O. J. Harvey and C. Consalvi, "Status and Conformity to Pressures in Informal Groups," *Journal of Abnormal and Social Psychology*, Spring 1960, pp. 182–187.

16. See J. M. Levine and R. L. Moreland, "Progress in Small Group Research," in J. T. Spence, J. M. Darley, and D. J. Foss (eds.), *Annual Review of Psychology*, vol. 41 (Palo Alto, CA: Annual Reviews, 1990), pp. 585–634; S. D. Silver, B. P. Cohen, and J. H. Crutchfield, "Status Differentiation and Information Exchange in Face-to-Face and Computer-Mediated Idea Generation," *Social Psychology Quarterly*, 1994, pp. 108–123; and J. M. Twenge, "Changes in Women's Assertiveness in Response to Status and Roles: A Cross-Temporal Meta-analysis, 1931–1993," *Journal of Personality and Social Psychology*, July 2001, pp. 133–145.

17. E. J. Thomas and C. F. Fink, "Effects of Group Size," *Psychological Bulletin*, July 1963, pp. 371–384; A. P. Hare, *Handbook of Small Group Research* (New York: The Free Press, 1976); and M. E. Shaw, *Group Dynamics: The Psychology of Small Group Behavior*, 3rd ed. (New York: McGraw-Hill, 1981).

18. G. H. Seijts and G. P. Latham, "The Effects of Goal Setting and Group Size on Performance in a Social Dilemma," *Canadian Journal of Behavioural Science* 32, no. 2 (2000), pp. 104–116.

19. Shaw, *Group Dynamics: The Psychology of Small Group Behavior*.

20. See, for instance, D. R. Comer, "A Model of Social Loafing in Real Work Groups," *Human Relations*, June 1995, pp. 647–667; S. M. Murphy, S. J. Wayne, R. C. Liden, and B. Erdogan, "Understanding Social Loafing: The Role of Justice Perceptions and Exchange Relationships," *Human Relations*, January 2003, pp. 61–84; and R. C. Liden, S. J. Wayne, R. A. Jaworski, and N. Bennett, "Social Loafing: A Field Investigation," *Journal of Management*, April 2004, pp. 285–304.

21. W. Moede, "Die Richtlinien der Leistungs-Psychologie," *Industrielle Psychotechnik* 4 (1927), pp. 193–207. See also D. A. Kravitz and B. Martin, "Ringelmann Rediscovered: The Original Article," *Journal of Personality and Social Psychology*, May 1986, pp. 936–941.

22. See, for example, J. A. Shepperd, "Productivity Loss in Performance Groups: A Motivation Analysis," *Psychological Bulletin*, January 1993, pp. 67–81; and S. J. Karau and K. D. Williams, "Social Loafing: A Meta-analytic Review and Theoretical Integration," *Journal of Personality and Social Psychology*, October 1993, pp. 681–706.

23. A. Gunnthorsdottir and A. Rapoport, "Embedding Social Dilemmas in Intergroup Competition Reduces Free-Riding," *Organizational Behavior and Human Decision Processes* 101 (2006), pp. 184–199.

24. For some of the controversy surrounding the definition of cohesion, see J. Keyton and J. Springston, "Redefining Cohesiveness in Groups," *Small Group Research*, May 1990, pp. 234–254.

25. B. Mullen and C. Cooper, "The Relation Between Group Cohesiveness and Performance: An Integration," *Psychological*

Bulletin, March 1994, pp. 210–227; P. M. Podsakoff, S. B. MacKenzie, and M. Ahearne, "Moderating Effects of Goal Acceptance on the Relationship Between Group Cohesiveness and Productivity," *Journal of Applied Psychology*, December 1997, pp. 974–983; and D. J. Beal, R. R. Cohen, M. J. Burke, and C. L. McLendon, "Cohesion and Performance in Groups: A Meta-analytic Clarification of Construct Relations," *Journal of Applied Psychology*, December 2003, pp. 989–1004.

26. Ibid.

27. Based on J. L. Gibson, J. M. Ivancevich, and J. H. Donnelly, Jr., *Organizations*, 8th ed. (Burr Ridge, IL: Irwin, 1994), p. 323.

28. N. Foote, E. Matson, L. Weiss, and E. Wenger, "Leveraging Group Knowledge for High-Performance Decision-Making," *Organizational Dynamics* 31, no. 2 (2002), pp. 280–295.

29. See N. R. F. Maier, "Assets and Liabilities in Group Problem Solving: The Need for an Integrative Function," *Psychological Review*, April 1967, pp. 239–249; G. W. Hill, "Group Versus Individual Performance: Are N+1 Heads Better Than One?" *Psychological Bulletin*, May 1982, pp. 517–539; A. E. Schwartz and J. Levin, "Better Group Decision Making," *Supervisory Management*, June 1990, p. 4; and R. F. Martell and M. R. Borg, "A Comparison of the Behavioral Rating Accuracy of Groups and Individuals," *Journal of Applied Psychology*, February 1993, pp. 43–50.

30. D. Gigone and R. Hastie, "Proper Analysis of the Accuracy of Group Judgments," *Psychological Bulletin*, January 1997, pp. 149–167; and B. L. Bonner, S. D. Sillito, and M. R. Baumann, "Collective Estimation: Accuracy, Expertise, and Extroversion as Sources of Intra-Group Influence," *Organizational Behavior and Human Decision Processes* 103 (2007), pp. 121–133.

31. See, for example, W. C. Swap and Associates, *Group Decision Making* (Newbury Park, CA: Sage, 1984).

32. I. L. Janis, *Groupthink* (Boston: Houghton Mifflin, 1982); W. Park, "A Review of Research on Groupthink," *Journal of Behavioral Decision Making*, July 1990, pp. 229–245; J. N. Choi and M. U. Kim, "The Organizational Application of Groupthink and Its Limits in Organizations," *Journal of Applied Psychology*, April 1999, pp. 297–306; and W. W. Park, "A Comprehensive Empirical Investigation of the Relationships Among Variables of the Groupthink Model," *Journal of Organizational Behavior*, December 2000, pp. 873–887.

33. Janis, *Groupthink*.

34. Ibid.

35. G. Moorhead, R. Ference, and C. P. Neck, "Group Decision Fiascos Continue: Space Shuttle Challenger and a Revised Groupthink Framework," *Human Relations*, May 1991, pp. 539–550; E. J. Chisson, *The Hubble Wars* (New York: HarperPerennial, 1994); and C. Covault, "*Columbia* Revelations Alarming E-Mails Speak for Themselves. But Administrator O'Keefe Is More Concerned About Board Findings on NASA Decision-Making," *Aviation Week & Space Technology*, March 3, 2003, p. 26.

36. J. Eaton, "Management Communication: The Threat of Groupthink," *Corporate Communication* 6, no. 4 (2001), pp. 183–192.

37. See N. R. F. Maier, *Principles of Human Relations* (New York: Wiley, 1952); I. L. Janis, *Groupthink: Psychological Studies of Policy Decisions and Fiascoes*, 2nd ed. (Boston: Houghton Mifflin, 1982); C. R. Leana, "A Partial Test of Janis' Groupthink Model: Effects

of Group Cohesiveness and Leader Behavior on Defective Decision Making," *Journal of Management*, Spring 1985, pp. 5–17; and N. Richardson Ahlfinger and J. K. Esser, "Testing the Groupthink Model: Effects of Promotional Leadership and Conformity Predisposition," *Social Behavior & Personality* 29, no. 1 (2001), pp. 31–41.

38. See D. J. Isenberg, "Group Polarization: A Critical Review and Meta-Analysis," *Journal of Personality and Social Psychology*, December 1986, pp. 1141–1151; J. L. Hale and F. J. Boster, "Comparing Effect Coded Models of Choice Shifts," *Communication Research Reports*, April 1988, pp. 180–186; and P. W. Paese, M. Bieser, and M. E. Tubbs, "Framing Effects and Choice Shifts in Group Decision Making," *Organizational Behavior and Human Decision Processes*, October 1993, pp. 149–165.

39. R. D. Clark III, "Group-Induced Shift Toward Risk: A Critical Appraisal," *Psychological Bulletin*, October 1971, pp. 251–270.

40. A. F. Osborn, *Applied Imagination: Principles and Procedures of Creative Thinking*, 3rd ed. (New York: Scribner, 1963). See also T. Rickards, "Brainstorming Revisited: A Question of Context," *International Journal of Management Reviews*, March 1999, pp. 91–110; and R. P. McGlynn, D. McGurk, V. S. Effland, N. L. Johll, and D. J. Harding, "Brainstorming and Task Performance in Groups Constrained by Evidence," *Organizational Behavior and Human Decision Processes*, January 2004, pp. 75–87.

41. N. L. Kerr and R. S. Tindale, "Group Performance and Decision-Making," *Annual Review of Psychology* 55 (2004), pp. 623–655.

42. See A. L. Delbecq, A. H. Van deVen, and D. H. Gustafson, *Group Techniques for Program Planning: A Guide to Nominal and Delphi Processes* (Glenview, IL: Scott, Foresman, 1975); and P. B. Paulus and H.-C. Yang, "Idea Generation in Groups: A Basis for Creativity in Organizations," *Organizational Behavior and Human Decision Processing*, May 2000, pp. 76–87.

43. C. Faure, "Beyond Brainstorming: Effects of Different Group Procedures on Selection of Ideas and Satisfaction with the Process," *Journal of Creative Behavior* 38 (2004), pp. 13–34.

44. This section is based on P. R. Harris and R. T. Moran, *Managing Cultural Differences*, 5th ed. (Houston: Gulf Publishing, 1999).

45. D. S. Staples and L. Zhao, "The Effects of Cultural Diversity in Virtual Teams Versus Face-to-Face Teams," *Group Decision and Negotiation*, July 2006, pp. 389–406.

46. K. W. Phillips and D. L. Loyd, "When Surface and Deep-Level Diversity Collide: The Effects on Dissenting Group Members," *Organizational Behavior and Human Decision Processes* 99 (2006), pp. 143–160; and S. R. Sommers, "On Racial Diversity and Group Decision Making: Identifying Multiple Effects of Racial Composition on Jury Deliberations," *Journal of Personality and Social Psychology*, April 2006, pp. 597–612.

CHAPTER 9

1. Cited in C. Joinson, "Teams at Work," *HR Magazine*, May 1999, p. 30; and P. Strozniak, "Teams at Work," *Industry Week*, September 18, 2000, p. 47.

2. This section is based on J. R. Katzenbach and D. K. Smith, *The Wisdom of Teams* (Cambridge, MA: Harvard University Press,

1993), pp. 21, 45, 85; and D. C. Kinlaw, *Developing Superior Work Teams* (Lexington, MA: Lexington Books, 1991), pp. 3–21.

3. G. Bodinson and R. Bunch, "AQP's National Team Excellence Award: Its Purpose, Value and Process," *Journal for Quality and Participation*, Spring 2003, pp. 37–42.

4. See, for instance, R. A. Cook and J. L. Goff, "Coming of Age with Self-Managed Teams: Dealing with a Problem Employee," *Journal of Business and Psychology*, Spring 2002, pp. 485–496; and C. W. Langfred, "Too Much of a Good Thing? Negative Effects of High Trust and Individual Autonomy in Self-Managing Teams," *Academy of Management Journal*, June 2004, pp. 385–399.

5. Bodinson and Bunch, "AQP's National Team Excellence Award."

6. See, for example, C. B. Gibson and S. G. Cohen (eds.), *Virtual Teams That Work* (San Francisco: Jossey-Bass, 2003); and L. L. Martins, L. L. Gilson, and M. T. Maynard, "Virtual Teams: What Do We Know and Where Do We Go from Here?" *Journal of Management*, November 2004, pp. 805–835.

7. A. Malhotra, A. Majchrzak, and B. Rosen, "Leading Virtual Teams," *Academy of Management Perspectives*, February 2007, pp. 60–70.

8. This model is based on M. A. Campion, E. M. Papper, and G. J. Medsker, "Relations Between Work Team Characteristics and Effectiveness: A Replication and Extension," *Personnel Psychology*, Summer 1996, pp. 429–452; L. Thompson, *Making the Team* (Upper Saddle River, NJ: Prentice Hall, 2000), pp. 18–33; and J. R. Hackman, *Leading Teams: Setting the Stage for Great Performance* (Boston: Harvard Business School Press, 2002).

9. Hyatt and Ruddy, "An Examination of the Relationship Between Work Group Characteristics and Performance: Once More Into the Breech," *Personnel Psychology* 50 (October 1, 1997), p. 577.

10. P. Balkundi and D. A. Harrison, "Ties, Leaders, and Time in Teams: Strong Inference About Network Structure's Effects on Team Viability and Performance," *Academy of Management Journal* 49, no. 1 (2006), pp. 49–68; G. Chen, B. L. Kirkman, R. Kanfer, D. Allen, and B. Rosen, "A Multilevel Study of Leadership, Empowerment, and Performance in Teams," *Journal of Applied Psychology* 92, no. 2 (2007), pp. 331–346; L. A. DeChurch and M. A. Marks, "Leadership in Multiteam Systems," *Journal of Applied Psychology* 91, no. 2 (2006), pp. 311–329; A. Srivastava, K. M. Bartol, and E. A. Locke, "Empowering Leadership in Management Teams: Effects on Knowledge Sharing, Efficacy, and Performance," *Academy of Management Journal* 49, no. 6 (2006), pp. 1239–1251; and J. E. Mathieu, K. K. Gilson, and T. M. Ruddy, "Empowerment and Team Effectiveness: An Empirical Test of an Integrated Model," *Journal of Applied Psychology* 91, no. 1 (2006), pp. 97–108.

11. K. T. Dirks, "Trust in Leadership and Team Performance: Evidence from NCAA Basketball," *Journal of Applied Psychology*, December 2000, pp. 1004–1012.

12. See L. N. McClurg, "Team Rewards: How Far Have We Come?" *Human Resource Management*, Spring 2001, pp. 73–86.

13. R. R. Hirschfeld, M. H. Jordan, H. S. Feild, W. F. Giles, and A. A. Armenakis, "Becoming Team Players: Team Members' Mastery of Teamwork Knowledge as a Predictor of Team Task Proficiency and Observed Teamwork Effectiveness," *Journal of Applied Psychology* 91, no. 2 (2006), pp. 467–474.

14. H. Moon, J. R. Hollenbeck, and S. E. Humphrey, "Asymmetric Adaptability: Dynamic Team Structures as One-Way Streets," *Academy of Management Journal* 47, no. 5 (October 2004), pp. 681–695; A. P. J. Ellis, J. R. Hollenbeck, and D. R. Ilgen, "Team Learning: Collectively Connecting the Dots," *Journal of Applied Psychology* 88, no. 5 (October 2003), pp. 821–835; and C. L. Jackson and J. A. LePine, "Peer Responses to a Team's Weakest Link: A Test and Extension of LePine and Van Dyne's Model," *Journal of Applied Psychology* 88, no. 3 (June 2003), pp. 459–475.

15. S. T. Bell, "Deep-Level Composition Variables as Predictors of Team Performance: A Meta-analysis," *Journal of Applied Psychology* 92, no. 3 (2007), pp. 595–615; and M. R. Barrick, G. L. Stewart, M. J. Neubert, and M. K. Mount, "Relating Member Ability and Personality to Work-Team Processes and Team Effectiveness," *Journal of Applied Psychology*, June 1998, pp. 377–391.

16. Ellis, Hollenbeck, and Ilgen, "Team Learning"; C. O. L. H. Porter, J. R. Hollenbeck, and D. R. Ilgen, "Backing Up Behaviors in Teams: The Role of Personality and Legitimacy of Need," *Journal of Applied Psychology* 88, no. 3 (June 2003), pp. 391–403; A. Colquitt, J. R. Hollenbeck, and D. R. Ilgen, "Computer-Assisted Communication and Team Decision-Making Performance: The Moderating Effect of Openness to Experience," *Journal of Applied Psychology* 87, no. 2 (April 2002), pp. 402–410; J. A. LePine, J. R. Hollenbeck, D. R. Ilgen, and J. Hedlund, "The Effects of Individual Differences on the Performance of Hierarchical Decision Making Teams: Much More Than G," *Journal of Applied Psychology* 82 (1997), pp. 803–811; Jackson and LePine, "Peer Responses to a Team's Weakest Link"; and J. LePine, "Team Adaptation and Postchange Performance: Effects of Team Composition in Terms of Member's Cognitive Ability and Personality," *Journal of Applied Psychology* 88, no. 1 (2003), pp. 27–39.

17. Barrick, Stewart, Neubert, and Mount, "Relating Member Ability and Personality to Work-Team Processes and Team Effectiveness," p. 388; and S. E. Humphrey, J. R. Hollenbeck, C. J. Meyer, and D. R. Ilgen, "Trait Configurations in Self-Managed Teams: A Conceptual Examination of the Use of Seeding for Maximizing and Minimizing Trait Variance in Teams," *Journal of Applied Psychology* 92, no. 3 (2007), pp. 885–892.

18. E. Mannix and M. A. Neale, "What Differences Make a Difference: The Promise and Reality of Diverse Teams in Organizations," *Psychological Science in the Public Interest*, October 2005, pp. 31–55.

19. G. S. Van Der Vegt, J. S. Bunderson, and A. Oosterhof, "Expertness Diversity and Interpersonal Helping in Teams: Why Those Who Need the Most Help End Up Getting the Least," *Academy of Management Journal* 49, no. 5 (2006), pp. 877–893.

20. J. Katzenbach, "What Makes Teams Work?" *Fast Company*, November 2000, p. 110.

21. The evidence in this section is described in Thompson, *Making the Team*, pp. 65–67. See also L. A. Curral, R. H. Forrester, and J. F. Dawson, "It's What You Do and the Way That You Do It: Team Task, Team Size, and Innovation-Related Group Processes," *European Journal of Work & Organizational Psychology* 10, no. 2 (June 2001), pp. 187–204; and R. C. Liden, S. J. Wayne, and R. A. Jaworski, "Social Loafing: A Field Investigation," *Journal of Management* 30, no. 2 (2004), pp. 285–304.

22. "Is Your Team Too Big? Too Small? What's the Right Number?" *Knowledge@Wharton*, June 14, 2006, pp. 1–5.

23. Hyatt and Ruddy, "An Examination of the Relationship Between Work Group Characteristics and Performance"; and S. A. Kiffin-Peterson and J. L. Cordery, "Trust, Individualism, and Job Characteristics of Employee Preference for Teamwork," *International Journal of Human Resource Management*, February 2003, pp. 93–116.

24. R. Wageman, "Critical Success Factors for Creating Superb Self-Managing Teams," *Organizational Dynamics*, Summer 1997, p. 55.

25. Campion, Papper, and Medsker, "Relations Between Work Team Characteristics and Effectiveness," p. 430; and D. C. Man and S. S. K. Lam, "The Effects of Job Complexity and Autonomy on Cohesiveness in Collectivist and Individualist Work Groups: A Cross-Cultural Analysis," *Journal of Organizational Behavior*, December 2003, pp. 979–1001.

26. I. D. Steiner, *Group Processes and Productivity* (New York: Academic Press, 1972).

27. K. Hess, *Creating the High-Performance Team* (New York: Wiley, 1987).

28. J. E. Mathieu and W. Schulze, "The Influence of Team Knowledge and Formal Plans on Episodic Team Process— Performance Relationships," *Academy of Management Journal* 49, no. 3 (2006), pp. 605–619.

29. A. Gurtner, F. Tschan, N. K. Semmer, and C. Nagele, "Getting Groups to Develop Good Strategies: Effects of Reflexivity Interventions on Team Process, Team Performance, and Shared Mental Models," *Organizational Behavior and Human Decision Processes* 102 (2007), pp. 127–142; M. C. Schippers, D. N. Den Hartog, and P. L. Koopman, "Reflexivity in Teams: A Measure and Correlates," *Applied Psychology: An International Review* 56, no. 2 (2007), pp. 189–211; and C. S. Burke, K. C. Stagl, E. Salas, L. Pierce, and D. Kendall, "Understanding Team Adaptation: A Conceptual Analysis and Model," *Journal of Applied Psychology* 91, no. 6 (2006), pp. 1189–1207.

30. E. Weldon and L. R. Weingart, "Group Goals and Group Performance," *British Journal of Social Psychology*, Spring 1993, pp. 307–334.

31. K. Tasa, S. Taggar, and G. H. Seijts, "The Development of Collective Efficacy in Teams: A Multilevel and Longitudinal Perspective," *Journal of Applied Psychology* 92, no. 1 (2007), pp. 17–27; and C. B. Gibson, "The Efficacy Advantage: Factors Related to the Formation of Group Efficacy," *Journal of Applied Social Psychology*, October 2003, pp. 2153–2086.

32. A. P. J. Ellis, "System Breakdown: The Role of Mental Models and Transactive Memory on the Relationships Between Acute Stress and Team Performance," *Academy of Management Journal* 49, no. 3 (2006), pp. 576–589.

33. S. W. J. Kozlowski and D. R. Ilgen, "Enhancing the Effectiveness of Work Groups and Teams," *Psychological Science in the Public Interest*, December 2006, pp. 77–124; and B. D. Edwards, E. A. Day, W. Arthur, Jr., and S. T. Bell, "Relationships Among Team Ability Composition, Team Mental Models, and Team Performance," *Journal of Applied Psychology* 91, no. 3 (2006), pp. 727–736.

34. K. A. Jehn, "A Qualitative Analysis of Conflict Types and Dimensions in Organizational Groups," *Administrative Science Quarterly*, September 1997, pp. 530–557. See also R. S. Peterson and K. J. Behfar, "The Dynamic Relationship Between Performance Feedback, Trust, and Conflict in Groups: A Longitudinal Study," *Organizational Behavior and Human Decision Processes*, September–November 2003, pp. 102–112.

35. K. H. Price, D. A. Harrison, and J. H. Gavin, "Withholding Inputs in Team Contexts: Member Composition, Interaction Processes, Evaluation Structure, and Social Loafing," *Journal of Applied Psychology* 91, no. 6 (2006), pp. 1375–1384.

36. See, for instance, B. L. Kirkman and D. L. Shapiro, "The Impact of Cultural Values on Employee Resistance to Teams: Toward a Model of Globalized Self-Managing Work Team Effectiveness," *Academy of Management Review*, July 1997, pp. 730–757; and B. L. Kirkman, C. B. Gibson, and D. L. Shapiro, "'Exporting' Teams: Enhancing the Implementation and Effectiveness of Work Teams in Global Affiliates," *Organizational Dynamics* 30, no. 1 (2001), pp. 12–29.

37. G. Hertel, U. Konradt, and K. Voss, "Competencies for Virtual Teamwork: Development and Validation of a Web-Based Selection Tool for Members of Distributed Teams," *European Journal of Work and Organizational Psychology* 15, no. 4 (2006), pp. 477–504.

38. "Teaming Up for Success," *Training*, January 1994, p. s41.

39. J. S. DeMatteo, L. T. Eby, and E. Sundstrom, "Team-Based Rewards: Current Empirical Evidence and Directions for Future Research," in B. M. Staw and L. L. Cummings (eds.), *Research in Organizational Behavior*, vol. 20, pp. 141–183.

40. B. Geber, "The Bugaboo of Team Pay," *Training*, August 1995, pp. 27, 34.

41. C. E. Naquin and R. O. Tynan, "The Team Halo Effect: Why Teams Are Not Blamed for Their Failures," *Journal of Applied Psychology*, April 2003, pp. 332–340.

42. A. B. Drexler and R. Forrester, "Teamwork—Not Necessarily the Answer," *HR Magazine*, January 1998, pp. 55–58. See also R. Saavedra, P. C. Earley, and L. Van Dyne, "Complex Interdependence in Task-Performing Groups," *Journal of Applied Psychology*, February 1993, pp. 61–72; and K. A. Jehn, G. B. Northcraft, and M. A. Neale, "Why Differences Make a Difference: A Field Study of Diversity, Conflict, and Performance in Workgroups," *Administrative Science Quarterly*, December 1999, pp. 741–763.

43. "Watson Wyatt's Global Work Studies." *WatsonWyatt.com*, www.watsonwyatt.com/research/featured/workstudy.asp

44. C. Nicholls, H. Lane, and M. Brehm Brechu, "Taking Self-Managed Teams to Mexico," *Academy of Management Executive* 13, no. 3, pp. 15–27.

45. W. E. Watson, K. Kumar, and L. K. Michaelsen, "Cultural Diversity's Impact on Interaction Process and Performance: Comparing Homogeneous and Diverse Task Groups," *Academy of Management Journal*, June 1993, pp. 590–602; and S. Mohammed and L. C. Angell, "Surface- and Deep-Level Diversity in Work-groups: Examining the Moderating Effects of Team Orientation and Team Process on Relationship Conflict," *Journal of Organizational Behavior*, December 2004, pp. 1015–1039.

46. Watson, Kumar, and Michaelsen, "Cultural Diversity's Impact on Interaction Process and Performance: Comparing Homogeneous and Diverse Task Groups."

CHAPTER 10

1. D. K. Berlo, *The Process of Communication* (New York: Holt, Rinehart & Winston, 1960), pp. 30–32.

2. J. Langan-Fox, "Communication in Organizations: Speed, Diversity, Networks, and Influence on Organizational Effectiveness, Human Health, and Relationships," in N. Anderson, D. S. Ones, H. K. Sinangil, and C. Viswesvaran (eds.), *Handbook of Industrial, Work and Organizational Psychology*, vol. 2 (Thousand Oaks, CA: Sage, 2001), p. 190.

3. R. L. Simpson, "Vertical and Horizontal Communication in Formal Organizations," *Administrative Science Quarterly*, September 1959, pp. 188–196; B. Harriman, "Up and Down the Communications Ladder," *Harvard Business Review*, September–October 1974, pp. 143–151; A. G. Walker and J. W. Smither, "A Five-Year Study of Upward Feedback: What Managers Do with Their Results Matter," *Personnel Psychology*, Summer 1999, pp. 393–424; and J. W. Smither and A. G. Walker, "Are the Characteristics of Narrative Comments Related to Improvement in Multirater Feedback Ratings Over Time?" *Journal of Applied Psychology* 89, no. 3 (June 2004), pp. 575–581.

4. P. Dvorak, "How Understanding the 'Why' of Decisions Matters," *Wall Street Journal* (March 19, 2007), p. B3.

5. E. Nichols, "Hyper-Speed Managers," *HRMagazine*, April 2007, pp. 107–110.

6. L. Dulye, "Get Out of Your Office," *HRMagazine*, July 2006, pp. 99–101.

7. L. S. Rashotte, "What Does That Smile Mean? The Meaning of Nonverbal Behaviors in Social Interaction," *Social Psychology Quarterly*, March 2002, pp. 92–102.

8. N. M. Henley, "Body Politics Revisited: What Do We Know Today?" in P. J. Kalbfleisch and M. J. Cody (eds.), *Gender, Power, and Communication in Human Relationships* (Hillsdale, NJ: Erlbaum, 1995), pp. 27–61.

9. Cited in "Heard It Through the Grapevine," *Forbes*, February 10, 1997, p. 22.

10. See, for instance, J. W. Newstrom, R. E. Monczka, and W. E. Reif, "Perceptions of the Grapevine: Its Value and Influence," *Journal of Business Communication*, Spring 1974, pp. 12–20; and S. J. Modic, "Grapevine Rated Most Believable," *IndustryWeek*, May 15, 1989, p. 14.

11. K. Davis, cited in R. Rowan, "Where Did That Rumor Come From?" *Fortune*, August 13, 1979, p. 134.

12. R. L. Rosnow and G. A. Fine, *Rumor and Gossip: The Social Psychology of Hearsay* (New York: Elsevier, 1976).

13. J. K. Bosson, A. B. Johnson, K. Niederhoffer, and W. B. Swann, Jr., "Interpersonal Chemistry Through Negativity: Bonding by Sharing Negative Attitudes About Others," *Personal Relationships* 13 (2006), pp. 135–150.

14. D. Brady, "*!#?@ the E-mail. Can We Talk?" *BusinessWeek*, December 4, 2006, p. 109.

15. E. Binney, "Is E-mail the New Pink Slip?" *HRMagazine*, November 2006, pp. 32–33; and R. L. Rundle, "Critical Case: How an Email Rant Jolted a Big HMO," *Wall Street Journal*, April 24, 2007, pp. A1, A16.

16. "Some Email Recipients Say 'Enough Already'," *Gainesville* (Florida) *Sun*, June 3, 2007, p. 1G.

17. D. Goleman, "Flame First, Think Later: New Clues to E-mail Misbehavior," *New York Times*, February 20, 2007, p. D5; and E. Krell, "The Unintended Word," *HRMagazine*, August 2006, pp. 50–54.

18. R. Zeidner, "Keeping E-mail in Check," *HRMagazine*, June 2007, pp. 70–74; "E-mail May Be Hazardous to Your Career," *Fortune*, May 14, 2007, p. 24; and "More Firms Fire Employees for E-mail Violations," *Gainesville* (Florida) *Sun*, June 6, 2006, p. B1.

19. Cited in C. Y. Chen, "The IM Invasion," *Fortune*, May 26, 2003, pp. 135–138.

20. C. Hymowitz, "Have Advice, Will Travel," *Wall Street Journal*, June 5, 2006, pp. B1, B3.

21. "Survey Finds Mixed Reviews on Checking E-mail During Meetings," *IPMA-HR Bulletin*, April 27, 2007, p. 1.

22. D. Lidsky, "It's Not Just Who You Know," *Fast Company*, May 2007, p. 56.

23. A. Bahney, "Interns? No Bloggers Need Apply," *New York Times*, May 25, 2006, pp. 1–2; "Bosses Battle Risk by Firing E-mail, IM & Blog Violators," *IPMA-HR Bulletin*, January 12, 2007, pp. 1–2; G. Krants, "Blogging with a Vendetta," *Workforce Week* 8, no. 25 (June 10, 2007), www.workforce.com/section/quick_takes/49486_3.html; D. Jones, "Sun CEO Sees Competitive Advantage in Blogging," *USA Today*, June 26, 2006, p. 7B; and B. Leonard, "Blogs Can Present New Challenges to Employers," *SHRM Online*, March 13, 2006, pp. 1–2.

24. P. R. Carlile, "Transferring, Translating, and Transforming: An Integrative Framework for Managing Knowledge Across Boundaries," *Organization Science* 15, no. 5 (September–October 2004), pp. 555–568; and S. Thurm, "Companies Struggle to Pass on Knowledge That Workers Acquire," *Wall Street Journal*, January 23, 2006, p. B1.

25. B. Fryer, "Get Smart," *INC*, September 15, 1999, p. 63.

26. "At Many Companies, Hunt for Leakers Expands Arsenal of Monitoring Tactics," *Wall Street Journal*, September 11, 2006, pp. B1, B3; and B. J. Alge, G. A. Ballinger, S. Tangirala, and J. L. Oakley, "Information Privacy in Organizations: Empowering Creative and Extrarole Performance," *Journal of Applied Psychology* 91, no. 1 (2006), pp. 221–232.

27. J. Sandberg, "The Jargon Jumble," *Wall Street Journal*, October 24, 2006, p. B1.

28. J. C. McCroskey, J. A. Daly, and G. Sorenson, "Personality Correlates of Communication Apprehension," *Human Communication Research*, Spring 1976, pp. 376–380.

29. See, for instance, B. H. Spitzberg and M. L. Hecht, "A Competent Model of Relational Competence," *Human Communication Research*, Summer 1984, pp. 575–599; and S. K. Opt and D. A. Loffredo, "Rethinking Communication Apprehension: A Myers-Briggs Perspective," *Journal of Psychology*, September 2000, pp. 556–570.

30. R. E. Axtell, *Gestures: The Do's and Taboos of Body Language Around the World* (New York: Wiley, 1991); "Effective Communication: A Leading Indicator of Financial Performance," Watson Wyatt 2006, www.watsonwyatt.com; and A. Markels, "Turning the Tide at P&G," *U.S. News & World Report*, October 30, 2006, p. 69.

31. See M. Munter, "Cross-Cultural Communication for Managers," *Business Horizons*, May–June 1993, pp. 75–76.

32. N. Adler, *International Dimensions of Organizational Behavior*, 4th ed. (Cincinnati, OH: South-Western Publishing, 2002), p. 94.

33. See, for example. R. S. Schuler, "A Role Perception Transactional Process Model for Organizational Communication-Outcome Relationships," *Organizational Behavior and Human Performance*, April 1979, pp. 268–291.

34. J. P. Walsh, S. J. Ashford, and T. E. Hill, "Feedback Obstruction: The Influence of the Information Environment on Employee Turnover Intentions," *Human Relations*, January 1985, pp. 23–46.

CHAPTER 11

1. J. P. Kotter, "What Leaders Really Do," *Harvard Business Review*, May–June 1990, pp. 103–111.

2. J. G. Geier, "A Trait Approach to the Study of Leadership in Small Groups," *Journal of Communication*, December 1967, pp. 316–323.

3. S. A. Kirkpatrick and E. A. Locke, "Leadership: Do Traits Matter?" *Academy of Management Executive*, May 1991, pp. 48–60.

4. See T. A. Judge, J. E. Bono, R. Ilies, and M. W. Gerhardt, "Personality and Leadership: A Qualitative and Quantitative Review," *Journal of Applied Psychology*, August 2002, pp. 765–780.

5. Judge, Bono, Ilies, and Gerhardt, "Personality and Leadership."

6. D. R. Ames and F. J. Flynn, "What Breaks a Leader: The Curvilinear Relation Between Assertiveness and Leadership," *Journal of Personality and Social Psychology* 92, no. 2 (2007), pp. 307–324.

7. D. Goleman, "What Makes a Leader?" *Harvard Business Review*, November–December 1998, pp. 93–102.

8. R. M. Stogdill and A. E. Coons (eds.), *Leader Behavior: Its Description and Measurement*, Research Monograph no. 88 (Columbus: Ohio State University, Bureau of Business Research, 1951); and T. A. Judge, R. F. Piccolo, and R. Ilies, "The Forgotten Ones? The Validity of Consideration and Initiating Structure in Leadership Research," *Journal of Applied Psychology*, February 2004, pp. 36–51.

9. D. Akst, "The Rewards of Recognizing a Job Well Done," *Wall Street Journal*, January 31, 2007, p. D9.

10. G. Yukl, and D. D. Van Fleet, "Theory and Research on Leadership in Organizations," in M. D. Dunnette and L. M. Hough (eds.), *Handbook of Industrial and Organizational Psychology*, vol. 2 (Palo Alto, CA: Consulting Psychologists Press, 1992), pp. 147–197.

11. R. R. Blake and J. S. Mouton, *The Managerial Grid* (Houston: Gulf, 1964).

12. F. E. Fiedler, *A Theory of Leadership Effectiveness* (New York: McGraw-Hill, 1967).

13. L. H. Peters, D. D. Hartke, and J. T. Pohlmann, "Fiedler's Contingency Theory of Leadership: An Application of the Meta-Analysis Procedures of Schmidt and Hunter," *Psychological Bulletin*, March 1985, pp. 274–285.

14. D. Duchon, S. G. Green, and T. D. Taber, "Vertical Dyad Linkage: A Longitudinal Assessment of Antecedents, Measures, and Consequences," *Journal of Applied Psychology*, February 1986, pp. 56–60.

15. O. Janssen and N. W. Van Yperen, "Employees' Goal Orientations, the Quality of Leader-Member Exchange, and the Outcomes of Job Performance and Job Satisfaction," *Academy of Management Journal*, 47(3), June 2004, pp. 368–384.

16. K. M. Kacmar, L. A. Witt, and S. Zivnuska, "The Interactive Effect of Leader-Member Exchange and Communication Frequency on Performance Ratings," *Journal of Applied Psychology*, 88(4), August 2003, pp. 764–772.

17. See C. R. Gerstner and D. V. Day, "Meta-Analytic Review of Leader-Member Exchange Theory: Correlates and Construct Issues," *Journal of Applied Psychology*, December 1997, pp. 827–844.

18. D. Eden, "Leadership and Expectations: Pygmalion Effects and Other Self-Fulfilling Prophecies in Organizations," *Leadership Quarterly*, Winter 1992, pp. 278–279.

19. J. A. Conger and R. N. Kanungo, "Behavioral Dimensions of Charismatic Leadership," in J. A. Conger, R. N. Kanungo, and Associates (eds.), *Charismatic Leadership* (San Francisco: Jossey-Bass, 1988), p. 79.

20. J. A. Conger and R. N. Kanungo, *Charismatic Leadership in Organizations* (Thousand Oaks, CA: Sage, 1998).

21. See J. A. Conger and R. N. Kanungo, "Training Charismatic Leadership: A Risky and Critical Task," *Charismatic Leadership* (San Francisco: Jossey-Bass, 1988), pp. 309–323; and M. Frese, S. Beimel, and S. Schoenborn, "Action Training for Charismatic Leadership: Two Evaluations of Studies of a Commercial Training Module on Inspirational Communication of a Vision," *Personnel Psychology*, Autumn 2003, pp. 671–697.

22. R. J. Richardson and S. K. Thayer, *The Charisma Factor: How to Develop Your Natural Leadership Ability* (Upper Saddle River, NJ: Prentice Hall, 1993).

23. J. M. Howell and P. J. Frost, "A Laboratory Study of Charismatic Leadership," *Organizational Behavior and Human Decision Processes*, April 1989, pp. 243–269. See also Frese, Beimel, and Schoenborn, "Action Training for Charismatic Leadership."

24. B. Shamir, R. J. House, and M. B. Arthur, "The Motivational Effects of Charismatic Leadership: A Self-Concept Theory," *Organization Science*, November 1993, pp. 577–594.

25. B. Kark, R. Gan, and B. Shamir, "The Two Faces of Transformational Leadership: Empowerment and Dependency," *Journal of Applied Psychology*, April 2003, pp. 246–255.

26. S. A. Kirkpatrick and E. A. Locke, "Direct and Indirect Effects of Three Core Charismatic Leadership Components on Performance and Attitudes," *Journal of Applied Psychology*, February 1996, pp. 36–51.

27. A. H. B. de Hoogh, D. N. den Hartog, P. L. Koopman, H. Thierry, P. T. van den Berg, and J. G. van der Weide, "Charismatic Leadership, Environmental Dynamism, and Performance," *European Journal of Work & Organizational Psychology*, December 2004, pp. 447–471; S. Harvey, M. Martin, and D. Stout, "Instructor's Transformational Leadership: University Student Attitudes and Ratings," *Psychological Reports*, April 2003, pp. 395–402; and D. A. Waldman, M. Javidan, and P. Varella, "Charismatic Leadership at the Strategic Level: A New Application of Upper Echelons Theory," *Leadership Quarterly*, June 2004, pp. 355–380.

28. Robert J. House and Ram N. Aditya, "The Social Scientific Study of Leadership," *Journal of Management* 23, no. 3 (1997), p. 441.

29. M. G. Ehrhart and K. J. Klein, "Predicting Followers' Preferences for Charismatic Leadership: The Influence of Follower Values and Personality," *Leadership Quarterly*, Summer 2001, pp. 153–179.

30. H. L. Tosi, V. Misangyi, A. Fanelli, D. A. Waldman, and F. J. Yammarino, "CEO Charisma, Compensation, and Firm Performance," *Leadership Quarterly*, June 2004, pp. 405–420.

31. See, for instance, R. Khurana, *Searching for a Corporate Savior: The Irrational Quest for Charismatic CEOs* (Princeton, NJ: Princeton University Press, 2002); and J. A. Raelin, "The Myth of Charismatic Leaders," *Training & Development*, March 2003, pp. 47–54.

32. See, for instance, B. M. Bass, B. J. Avolio, D. I. Jung, and Y. Berson, "Predicting Unit Performance by Assessing Transformational and Transactional Leadership," *Journal of Applied Psychology*, April 2003, pp. 207–218.

33. D. I. Jung, C. Chow, and A. Wu, "The Role of Transformational Leadership in Enhancing Organizational Innovation: Hypotheses and Some Preliminary Findings," *Leadership Quarterly*, August–October 2003, pp. 525–544; and S. J. Shin and J. Zhou, "Transformational Leadership, Conservation, and Creativity: Evidence from Korea," *Academy of Management Journal*, December 2003, pp. 703–714.

34. J. E. Bono and T. A. Judge, "Self-Concordance at Work: Toward Understanding the Motivational Effects of Transformational Leaders," *Academy of Management Journal*, October 2003, pp. 554–571; Y. Berson and B. J. Avolio, "Transformational Leadership and the Dissemination of Organizational Goals: A Case Study of a Telecommunication Firm," *Leadership Quarterly*, October 2004, pp. 625–646; and S. Shinn, "21st-Century Engineer," *BizEd*, January/February, 2005, pp. 18–23.

35. J. R. Baum, E. A. Locke, and S. A. Kirkpatrick, "A Longitudinal Study of the Relation of Vision and Vision Communication to Venture Growth in Entrepreneurial Firms," *Journal of Applied Psychology*, February 2000, pp. 43–54.

36. R. T. Keller, "Transformational Leadership, Initiating Structure, and Substitutes for Leadership: A Longitudinal Study of Research and Development Project Team Performance," *Journal of Applied Psychology* 91, no. 1 (2006), pp. 202–210.

37. Judge and Piccolo, "Transformational and Transactional Leadership."

38. H. Hetland, G. M. Sandal, and T. B. Johnsen, "Burnout in the Information Technology Sector: Does Leadership Matter?" *European Journal of Work and Organizational Psychology* 16, no. 1 (2007), pp. 58–75; and K. B. Lowe, K. G. Kroeck, and N. Sivasubramaniam, "Effectiveness Correlates of Transformational and Transactional Leadership: A Meta-Analytic Review of the MLQ Literature," *Leadership Quarterly*, Fall 1996, pp. 385–425.

39. See, for instance, J. Barling, T. Weber, and E. K. Kelloway, "Effects of Transformational Leadership Training on Attitudinal and Financial Outcomes: A Field Experiment," *Journal of Applied Psychology*, December 1996, pp. 827–832.

40. R. J. House and P. M. Podsakoff, "Leadership Effectiveness: Past Perspectives and Future Directions for Research," in J. Greenberg (ed.), *Organizational Behavior: The State of the Science* (Hillsdale, NJ: Erlbaum, 1994), pp. 45–82; and B. M. Bass, *Leadership and Performance Beyond Expectations* (New York: The Free Press, 1985).

41. B. J. Avolio and B. M. Bass, "Transformational Leadership, Charisma and Beyond," working paper, School of management, State University of New York, Binghamton, 1985, p. 14.

42. See B. J. Avolio, W. L. Gardner, F. O. Walumbwa, F. Luthans, and D. R. May, "Unlocking the Mask: A Look at the Process by Which Authentic Impact Follower Attitudes and Behaviors," *Leadership Quarterly*, December 2004, pp. 801–823; and M. M. Novicevic, M. G. Harvey, M. R. Buckley, J. A. Brown-Radford, and R. Evans, "Authentic Leadership: A Historical Perspective," *Journal of Leadership and Organizational Behavior* 13, no. 1 (2006), pp. 64–76.

43. A. Carter, "Lighting a Fire Under Campbell," *BusinessWeek*, December 4, 2006, pp. 96–101.

44. R. Ilies, F. P. Morgeson, and J. D. Nahrgang, "Authentic Leadership and Eudaemonic Wellbeing: Understanding Leader-Follower Outcomes," *Leadership Quarterly* 16 (2005), pp. 373–394.

45. This section is based on E. P. Hollander, "Ethical Challenges in the Leader–Follower Relationship," *Business Ethics Quarterly*, January 1995, pp. 55–65; and L. K. Treviño, M. Brown, and L. P. Hartman, "A Qualitative Investigation of Perceived Executive Ethical Leadership: Perceptions from Inside and Outside the Executive Suite," *Human Relations*, January 2003, pp. 5–37.

46. J. L. Lunsford, "Piloting Boeing's New Course," *Wall Street Journal*, June 13, 2006, pp. B1, B3.

47. M. E. Brown and L. K. Treviño, "Socialized Charismatic Leadership, Values Congruence, and Deviance in Work Groups," *Journal of Applied Psychology* 91, no. 4 (2006), pp. 954–962.

48. Comment by Jim Collins and cited in J. Useem, "Conquering Vertical Limits," *Fortune*, February 19, 2001, p. 94.

49. See, for instance, J. R. Meindl, "The Romance of Leadership as a Follower-Centric Theory: A Social Constructionist Approach," *Leadership Quarterly*, Fall 1995, pp. 329–341.

50. R. G. Lord, C. L. DeVader, and G. M. Alliger, "A Meta-analysis of the Relation Between Personality Traits and Leadership Perceptions: An Application of Validity Generalization Procedures," *Journal of Applied Psychology*, August 1986, pp. 402–410.

51. J. R. Meindl, S. B. Ehrlich, and J. M. Dukerich, "The Romance of Leadership," *Administrative Science Quarterly*, March 1985, pp. 78–102.

52. B. R. Agle, N. J. Nagarajan, J. A. Sonnenfeld, and D. Srinivasan, "Does CEO Charisma Matter?" *Academy of Management Journal* 49, no. 1 (2006), pp. 161–174.

53. S. Kerr and J. M. Jermier, "Substitutes for Leadership: Their Meaning and Measurement," *Organizational Behavior and Human Performance*, December 1978, pp. 375–403; and E. de Vries Reinout, R. A. Roe, and T. C. B. Taillieu, "Need for Leadership as a Moderator of the Relationships Between Leadership and Individual Outcomes," *Leadership Quarterly*, April 2002, pp. 121–138.

54. S. D. Dionne, F. J. Yammarino, L. E. Atwater, and L. R. James, "Neutralizing Substitutes for Leadership Theory: Leadership Effects and Common-Source Bias," *Journal of Applied Psychology*, 87 (2002), pp. 454–464.

55. See, for instance, P. Dvorak, "M.B.A. Programs Hone 'Soft Skills,'" *Wall Street Journal*, February 12, 2007, p. B3.

56. J. Weber, "The Leadership Factor," *BusinessWeek*, June 12, 2006, pp. 60–64.

57. See, for instance, Barling, Weber, and Kelloway, "Effects of Transformational Leadership Training on Attitudinal and Financial Outcomes."

58. M. Sashkin, "The Visionary Leader," in J. A. Conger, R. N. Kanungo et al. (eds.), *Charismatic Leadership* (San Francisco: Jossey-Bass, 1988), p. 150.

59. D. V. Day, "Leadership Development: A Review in Context," *Leadership Quarterly*, Winter 2000, pp. 590–593.

60. Howell and Frost, "A Laboratory Study of Charismatic Leadership."

61. A. J. Towler, "Effects of Charismatic Influence Training on Attitudes, Behavior, and Performance," *Personnel Psychology*, Summer 2003, pp. 363–381; and Barling, Weber, and Kelloway, "Effects of Transformational Leadership Training on Attitudinal and Financial Outcomes."

62. M. Javidan, P. W. Dorfman, M. S. de Luque, and R. J. House, "In the Eye of the Beholder: Cross Cultural Lessons in Leadership from Project GLOBE," *Academy of Management Perspectives*, February 2006, pp. 67–90.

CHAPTER 12

1. Based on B. M. Bass, *Bass & Stogdill's Handbook of Leadership*, 3rd ed. (New York: The Free Press, 1990).

2. J. R. P. French, Jr., and B. Raven, "The Bases of Social Power," in D. Cartwright (ed.), *Studies in Social Power* (Ann Arbor, MI: University of Michigan, Institute for Social Research, 1959), pp. 150–167; and B. J. Raven, "The Bases of Power: Origins and Recent Developments," *Journal of Social Issues*, Winter 1993, pp. 227–251.

3. P. M. Podsakoff and C. A. Schriesheim, "Field Studies of French and Raven's Bases of Power: Critique, Reanalysis, and Suggestions for Future Research," *Psychological Bulletin*, May 1985, pp. 387–411; and P. P. Carson, K. D. Carson, and C. W. Roe, "Social Power Bases: A Meta-Analytic Examination of Interrelationships and Outcomes," *Journal of Applied Social Psychology* 23, no. 14 (1993), pp. 1150–1169.

4. See, for example, D. Kipnis and S. M. Schmidt, "Upward-Influence Styles: Relationship with Performance Evaluations, Salary, and Stress," *Administrative Science Quarterly*, December 1988, pp. 528–542; and G. Yukl and J. B. Tracey, "Consequences of Influence Tactics Used with Subordinates, Peers, and the Boss," *Journal of Applied Psychology*, August 1992, pp. 525–535.

5. G. Yukl, *Leadership in Organizations*, 5th ed. (Upper Saddle River, NJ: Prentice Hall, 2002), pp. 141–174; and C. A. Higgins, T. A. Judge, and G. R. Ferris, "Influence Tactics and Work Outcomes: A Meta-analysis," *Journal of Organizational Behavior*, March 2003, pp. 89–106.

6. G. R. Ferris, D. C. Treadway, R. W. Kolokinsky, W. A. Hochwarter, C. J. Kacmar, and D. D. Frink, "Development and Validation of the Political Skill Inventory," *Journal of Management*, February 2005, pp. 126–152.

7. D. Farrell and J. C. Petersen, "Patterns of Political Behavior in Organizations," *Academy of Management Review*, July 1982, p. 405.

8. J. Pfeffer, *Power in Organizations* (Marshfield, MA: Pitman, 1981).

9. A. Drory and T. Romm, "The Definition of Organizational Politics A Review," *Human Relations* (November 1990), pp. 1133–1154.

10. See, for example, G. R. Ferris, G. S. Russ, and P. M. Fandt, "Politics in Organizations," in R. A. Giacalone and P. Rosenfeld (eds.), *Impression Management in the Organization* (Hillsdale, NJ: Lawrence Erlbaum, 1989), pp. 155–156; and W. E. O'Connor and T. G. Morrison, "A Comparison of Situational and Dispositional Predictors of Perceptions of Organizational Politics," *Journal of Psychology*, May 2001, pp. 301–312.

11. Farrell and Petersen, "Patterns of Political Behavior in Organizations," p. 408.

12. See, for example, P. M. Fandt and G. R. Ferris, "The Management of Information and Impressions: When Employees Behave Opportunistically," *Organizational Behavior and Human Decision Processes*, February 1990, pp. 140–158; Ferris, Russ, and Fandt, "Politics in Organizations," p. 147; and J. M. L. Poon, "Situational Antecedents and Outcomes of Organizational Politics Perceptions," *Journal of Managerial Psychology* 18, no. 2 (2003), pp. 138–155.

13. Ferris, Russ, and Fandt, "Politics in Organizations"; and K. M. Kacmar, D. P. Bozeman, D. S. Carlson, and W. P. Anthony, "An Examination of the Perceptions of Organizational Politics Model: Replication and Extension," *Human Relations*, March 1999, pp. 383–416.

14. W. A. Hochwarter, C. Kiewitz, S. L. Castro, P. L. Perrewe, and G. R. Ferris, "Positive Affectivity and Collective Efficacy as Moderators of the Relationship Between Perceived Politics and Job Satisfaction," *Journal of Applied Social Psychology*, May 2003, pp. 1009–1035; and C. C. Rosen, P. E. Levy, and R. J. Hall, "Placing Perceptions of Politics in the Context of Feedback Environment, Employee Attitudes, and Job Performance," *Journal of Applied Psychology* 91, no. 1 (2006), pp. 211–230.

15. G. R. Ferris, D. D. Frink, M. C. Galang, J. Zhou, K. M. Kacmar, and J. L. Howard, "Perceptions of Organizational Politics: Prediction, Stress-Related Implications, and Outcomes," *Human Relations*, February 1996, pp. 233–266.

16. C. Kiewitz, W. A. Hochwarter, G. R. Ferris, and S. L. Castro, "The Role of Psychological Climate in Neutralizing the Effects of Organizational Politics on Work Outcomes," *Journal of Applied Social Psychology*, June 2002, pp. 1189–1207.

17. S. Aryee, Z. Chen, and P. S. Budhwar, "Exchange Fairness and Employee Performance: An Examination of the Relationship Between Organizational Politics and Procedural Justice," *Organizational Behavior & Human Decision Processes*, May 2004, pp. 1–14.

18. Kacmar, Bozeman, Carlson, and Anthony, "An Examination of the Perceptions of Organizational Politics Model," p. 389.

19. M. Valle and P. L. Perrewe, "Do Politics Perceptions Relate to Political Behaviors? Tests of an Implicit Assumption and Expanded Model," *Human Relations*, March 2000, pp. 359–386.

20. See, for instance, B. R. Schlenker, *Impression Management: The Self-Concept, Social Identity, and Interpersonal Relations* (Monterey, CA: Brooks/Cole, 1980); and S. Zivnuska, K. M. Kacmar, L. A. Witt, D. S. Carlson, and V. K. Bratton, "Interactive Effects of Impression Management and Organizational Politics on Job Performance," *Journal of Organizational Behavior*, August 2004, pp. 627–640.

21. M. Snyder and J. Copeland, "Self-monitoring Processes in Organizational Settings," in Giacalone and Rosenfeld (eds.), *Impression Management in the Organization* (Hillsdale, NJ: Lawrence Erlbaum, 1989), p. 11; and W. H. Turnley and M. C. Bolino, "Achieved Desired Images While Avoiding Undesired Images: Exploring the Role of Self-Monitoring in Impression Management," *Journal of Applied Psychology*, April 2001, pp. 351–360.

22. M. R. Leary and R. W. Kowalski, "Impression Management: A Literature Review and Two-Component Model," *Psychological Bulletin* (January 1990)," p. 40.

23. C. K. Stevens and A. L. Kristof, "Making the Right Impression: A Field Study of Applicant Impression Management During Job Interviews," *Journal of Applied Psychology* 80 (1995), pp. 587–606; and L. A. McFarland, A. M. Ryan, and \S. D. Kriska, "Impression Management Use and Effectiveness Across Assessment Methods," *Journal of Management* 29, no. 5 (2003), pp. 641–661.

24. D. C. Gilmore and G. R. Ferris, "The Effects of Applicant Impression Management Tactics on Interviewer Judgments." *Journal of Management* (December 1989), pp. 557-564.

25. Stevens and Kristof, "Making the Right Impression: A Field Study of Applicant Impression Management During Job Interviews."

26. C. A. Higgins, T. A. Judge, and G. R. Ferris, "Influence Tactics and Work Outcomes: A Meta-Analysis," *Journal of Organizational Behavior*, March 2003, pp. 89–106.

27. Ibid.

28. J. D. Westphal and I. Stern, "Flattery Will Get You Everywhere (Especially if You Are a Male Caucasian): How Ingratiation, Boardroom Behavior, and Demographic Minority Status Affect Additional Board Appointments of U.S. Companies," *Academy of Management Journal* 50, no. 2 (2007), pp. 267–288.

29. O. J. Ladebo, "Perceptions of Organisational Politics: Examination of the Situational Antecedent and Consequences Among Nigeria's Extension Personnel," *Applied Psychology: An International Review* 55, no. 2 (2006), pp. 255–281.

30. P. P. Fu and G. Yukl, "Perceived Effectiveness of Influence Tactics in the United States and China," *Leadership Quarterly*, Summer 2000, pp. 251–266; O. Branzei, "Cultural Explanations of Individual Preferences for Influence Tactics in Cross-Cultural Encounters," *International Journal of Cross Cultural Management*, August 2002, pp. 203–218; G. Yukl, P. P. Fu, and R. McDonald, "Cross-Cultural Differences in Perceived Effectiveness of Influence Tactics for Initiating or Resisting Change," *Applied Psychology: An International Review*, January 2003, pp. 66–82; and P. P. Fu, T. K. Peng, J. C. Kennedy, and G. Yukl, "Examining the Preferences of Influence Tactics in Chinese Societies: A Comparison of Chinese Managers in Hong Kong, Taiwan, and Mainland China," *Organizational Dynamics* 33, no. 1 (2004), pp. 32–46.

31. Fu and Yukl, "Perceived Effectiveness of Influence Tactics in the United States and China."

32. S. J. Heine, "Making Sense of East Asian Self-Enhancement," *Journal of Cross-Cultural Psychology*, September 2003, pp. 596–602.

33. J. L. T. Leong, M. H. Bond, and P. P. Fu, "Perceived Effectiveness of Influence Strategies in the United States and Three Chinese Societies," *International Journal of Cross Cultural Management*, May 2006, pp. 101–120.

CHAPTER 13

1. K. W. Thomas, "Conflict and Negotiation Processes in Organizations," in M. D. Dunnette and L. M. Hough (eds.), *Handbook of Industrial and Organizational Psychology*, 2nd ed., vol. 3 (Palo Alto, CA: Consulting Psychologists Press, 1992), pp. 651–717.

2. For a comprehensive review of the interactionist approach, see C. De Dreu and E. Van de Vliert (eds.), *Using Conflict in Organizations* (London: Sage, 1997).

3. See K. A. Jehn, "A Multimethod Examination of the Benefits and Detriments of Intragroup Conflict," *Administrative Science Quarterly*, June 1995, pp. 256–282; K. A. Jehn, "A Qualitative Analysis of Conflict Types and Dimensions in Organizational Groups," *Administrative Science Quarterly*, September 1997, pp. 530–557; K. A. Jehn and E. A. Mannix, "The Dynamic Nature of Conflict: A Longitudinal Study of Intragroup Conflict and Group Performance," *Academy of Management Journal*, April 2001, pp. 238–251; and C. K. W. De Dreu and L. R. Weingart, "Task Versus Relationship Conflict, Team Performance, and Team Member Satisfaction: A Meta-Analysis," *Journal of Applied Psychology*, August 2003, pp. 741–749.

4. J. Yang and K. W. Mossholder, "Decoupling Task and Relationship Conflict: The Role of Intragroup Emotional Processing," *Journal of Organizational Behavior* 25, no. 5 (August 2004), pp. 589–605.

5. "Survey Shows Managers Have Their Hands Full Resolving Staff Personality Conflicts," *IPMA-HR Bulletin*, November 3, 2006.

6. R. S. Peterson and K. J. Behfar, "The Dynamic Relationship Between Performance Feedback, Trust, and Conflict in Groups: A Longitudinal Study," *Organizational Behavior & Human Decision Processes*, September–November 2003, pp. 102–112.

7. Jehn, "A Multimethod Examination of the Benefits and Detriments of Intragroup Conflict."

8. L. R. Pondy, "Organizational Conflict: Concepts and Models," *Administrative Science Quarterly*, September 1967, p. 302.

9. A. M. Isen, A. A. Labroo, and P. Durlach, "An Influence of Product and Brand Name on Positive Affect: Implicit and Explicit Measures," *Motivation & Emotion*, March 2004, pp. 43–63.

10. See, for instance, K. A. Jehn, "Enhancing Effectiveness: An Investigation of Advantages and Disadvantages of Value-Based Intragroup Conflict," *International Journal of Conflict Management*, July 1994, pp. 223–238; R. L. Priem, D. A. Harrison, and N. K. Muir, "Structured Conflict and Consensus Outcomes in Group Decision Making," *Journal of Management* 21, no. 4 (1995), pp. 691–710; and K. A. Jehn and E. A. Mannix, "The Dynamic Nature of Conflict: A Longitudinal Study of Intragroup Conflict and Group Performance," *Academy of Management Journal*, April 2001, pp. 238–251.

11. J. Hall and M. S. Williams, "A Comparison of Decision-Making Performances in Established and Ad-hoc Groups," *Journal of Personality and Social Psychology*, February 1966, p. 217.

12. R. L. Hoffman, "Homogeneity of Member Personality and Its Effect on Group Problem-Solving," *Journal of Abnormal and Social Psychology*, January 1959, pp. 27–32; R. L. Hoffman and N. R. F. Maier, "Quality and Acceptance of Problem Solutions by Members of Homogeneous and Heterogeneous Groups," *Journal of Abnormal and Social Psychology*, March 1961, pp. 401–407; and P. Pitcher and A. D. Smith, "Top Management Team Heterogeneity: Personality, Power, and Proxies," *Organization Science*, January–February 2001, pp. 1–18.

13. For example, see J. A. Wall, Jr., and R. R. Callister, "Conflict and Its Management," *Journal of Management* 21, no. 3 (June 1, 1995), pp. 523–526 for evidence supporting the argument that conflict is almost uniformly dysfunctional; see also P. J. Hinds and D. E. Bailey, "Out of Sight, Out of Sync: Understanding Conflict in Distributed Teams," *Organization Science*, November–December 2003, pp. 615–632.

14. M. Geyelin and E. Felsenthal, "Irreconcilable Differences Force Shea & Gould Closure," *Wall Street Journal*, January 31, 1994, p. B1.

15. This section is based on F. Sommerfield, "Paying the Troops to Buck the System," *Business Month*, May 1990, pp. 77–79; S. Wetlaufer, "Common Sense and Conflict," *Harvard Business Review*, January–February 2000, pp. 114–124; and G. A. Okhuysen and K. M. Eisenhardt, "Excel Through Group Process," in E. A. Locke (ed.), *Handbook of Principles of Organizational Behavior* (Malden, MA: Blackwell, 2004), pp. 216–218.

16. J. A. Wall, Jr., *Negotiation: Theory and Practice* (Glenview, IL: Scott, Foresman, 1985).

17. R. E. Walton and R. B. McKersie, *A Behavioral Theory of Labor Negotiations: An Analysis of a Social Interaction System* (New York: McGraw-Hill, 1965).

18. J. C. Magee, A. D. Galinsky, and D. H. Gruenfeld, "Power, Propensity to Negotiate, and Moving First in Competitive Interactions," *Personality and Social Psychology Bulletin*, February 2007, pp. 200–212.

19. H. R. Bowles, L. Babcock, and L. Lei, "Social Incentives for Gender Differences in the Propensity to Initiative Negotiations: Sometimes It Does Hurt to Ask," *Organizational Behavior and Human Decision Processes* 103 (2007), pp. 84–103.

20. J. R. Curhan, H. A. Elfenbein, and H. Xu, "What Do People Value When They Negotiate? Mapping the Domain of Subjective Value in Negotiation," *Journal of Personality and Social Psychology* 91, no. 3 (2006), pp. 493–512.

21. C. E. Naquin, "The Agony of Opportunity in Negotiation: Number of Negotiable Issues, Counterfactual Thinking, and Feelings of Satisfaction," *Organizational Behavior & Human Decision Processes*, May 2003, pp. 97–107.

22. C. K. W. De Dreu, L. R. Weingart, and S. Kwon, "Influence of Social Motives on Integrative Negotiation: A Meta-analytic Review and Test of Two Theories," *Journal of Personality & Social Psychology*, May 2000, pp. 889–905.

23. This model is based on R. J. Lewicki, "Bargaining and Negotiation," *Exchange: The Organizational Behavior Teaching Journal* 6, no. 2 (1981), pp. 39–40.

24. M. H. Bazerman and M. A. Neale, *Negotiating Rationally* (New York: The Free Press, 1992), pp. 67–68.

25. J. A. Wall, Jr., and M. W. Blum, "Negotiations," *Journal of Management*, June 1991, pp. 278–282.

26. B. Barry and R. A. Friedman, "Bargainer Characteristics in Distributive and Integrative Negotiation," *Journal of Personality & Social Psychology*, February 1998, pp. 345–359.

27. S. Kopelman, A. S. Rosette, and L. Thompson, "The Three Faces of Eve: Strategic Displays of Positive, Negative, and Neutral Emotions in Negotiations," *Organizational Behavior and Human Decision Processes* 99 (2006), pp. 81–101; and J. M. Brett, M. Olekalns, R. Friedman, N. Goates, C. Anderson, and C. C. Lisco, "Sticks and Stones: Language, Face, and Online Dispute Resolution," *Academy of Management Journal* 50, no. 1 (2007), pp. 85–99.

28. C. Watson and L. R. Hoffman, "Managers as Negotiators: A Test of Power Versus Gender as Predictors of Feelings, Behavior, and Outcomes," *Leadership Quarterly*, Spring 1996, pp. 63–85.

29. A. E. Walters, A. F. Stuhlmacher, and L. L. Meyer, "Gender and Negotiator Competitiveness: A Meta-analysis," *Organizational Behavior and Human Decision Processes*, October 1998, pp. 1–29; and A. F. Stuhlmacher and A. E. Walters, "Gender Differences in Negotiation Outcome: A Meta-analysis," *Personnel Psychology*, Autumn 1999, pp. 653–677.

30. Stuhlmacher and Walters, "Gender Differences in Negotiation Outcome," p. 655.

31. Bowles, Babcock, and Lei, "Social Incentives for Gender Differences in the Propensity to Initiative Negotiations."

32. L. J. Kray, A. D. Galinsky, and L. Thompson, "Reversing the Gender Gap in Negotiations: An Exploration of Stereotype Regeneration," *Organizational Behavior & Human Decision Processes*, March 2002, pp. 386–409.

33. C. K. Stevens, A. G. Bavetta, and M. E. Gist, "Gender Differences in the Acquisition of Salary Negotiation Skills: The Role of Goals, Self-Efficacy, and Perceived Control," *Journal of Applied Psychology* 78, no. 5 (October 1993), pp. 723–735.

34. M. J. Gelfand, M. Higgins, L. H. Nishii, J. L. Raver, A. Dominguez, F. Murakami, S. Yamaguchi, and M. Toyama, "Culture and Egocentric Perceptions of Fairness in Conflict and Negotiation," *Journal of Applied Psychology*, October 2002,

pp. 833–845; Z. Ma, "Chinese Conflict Management Styles and Negotiation Behaviours: An Empirical Test," *International Journal of Cross Cultural Management*, April 2007, pp. 101–119.

35. Gelfand et al., "Culture and Egocentric Perceptions of Fairness in Conflict and Negotiation," pp. 833–845; and X. Lin and S. J. Miller, "Negotiation Approaches: Direct and Indirect Effect of National Culture," *International Marketing Review* 20, no. 3 (2003), pp. 286–303.

36. W. L. Adair, T. Okumura, and J. M. Brett, "Negotiation Behavior When Cultures Collide: The United States and Japan," *Journal of Applied Psychology*, June 2001, pp. 371–385; and W. L. Adair, L. Weingart, and J. Brett, "The Timing and Function of Offers in U.S. and Japanese Negotiations," *Journal of Applied Psychology* 92, no. 4 (2007), pp. 1056–1068.

37. E. S. Glenn, D. Witmeyer, and K. A. Stevenson, "Cultural Styles of Persuasion," *Journal of Intercultural Relations*, Fall 1977, pp. 52–66.

38. J. Graham, "The Influence of Culture on Business Negotiations," *Journal of International Business Studies*, Spring 1985, pp. 81–96.

39. K. W. Thomas, "Toward Multidimensional Values in Teaching: The Example of Conflict Behaviors," *Academy of Management Review*, July 1977, p. 487.

40. Based on R. Fisher and W. Ury, *Getting to Yes: Negotiating Agreement Without Giving In* (Boston: Houghton Mifflin, 1981); Wall and Blum, "Negotiations," pp. 295–96; and Bazerman and Neale, *Negotiating Rationally*.

CHAPTER 14

1. See, for instance, R. L. Daft, *Organization Theory and Design*, 8th ed. (Cincinnati, OH: South-Western Publishing, 2004).

2. C. Hymowitz, "Managers Suddenly Have to Answer to a Crowd of Bosses," *Wall Street Journal*, August 12, 2003, p. B1.

3. See, for instance, J. H. Gittell, "Supervisory Span, Relational Coordination, and Flight Departure Performance: A Reassessment of Postbureaucracy Theory," *Organization Science*, July–August 2001, pp. 468–483.

4. J. Child and R. G. McGrath, "Organizations Unfettered: Organizational Form in an Information-Intensive Economy," *Academy of Management Journal*, December 2001, pp. 1135–1148.

5. H. Mintzberg, *Structure in Fives: Designing Effective Organizations* (Upper Saddle River, NJ: Prentice Hall, 1983), p. 157.

6. L. R. Burns and D. R. Wholey, "Adoption and Abandonment of Matrix Management Programs: Effects of Organizational Characteristics and Interorganizational Networks," *Academy of Management Journal*, February 1993, pp. 106–138.

7. See, for instance, T. Sy and S. Cote, "Emotional Intelligence: A Key Ability to Succeed in the Matrix Organization," *Journal of Management Development* 23, no. 5 (2004), pp. 437–455.

8. See, for instance, R. E. Miles and C. C. Snow, "The New Network Firm: A Spherical Structure Built on Human Investment Philosophy," *Organizational Dynamics*, Spring 1995, pp. 5–18; J. Gertner, "Newman's Own: Two Friends and a Canoe Paddle," *New York Times*, November 16, 2003, p. 4BU; and Y. Shin,

"A Person-Environment Fit Model for Virtual Organizations," *Journal of Management*, October 2004, pp. 725–743.

9. "GE: Just Your Average Everyday $60 Billion Family Grocery Store," *IndustryWeek*, May 2, 1994, pp. 13–18.

10. H. C. Lucas Jr., *The T-Form Organization: Using Technology to Design Organizations for the 21st Century* (San Francisco: Jossey-Bass, 1996).

11. This section is based on D. D. Davis, "Form, Function and Strategy in Boundaryless Organizations," in A. Howard (ed.), *The Changing Nature of Work* (San Francisco: Jossey-Bass, 1995), pp. 112–138; and R. Ashkenas, D. Ulrich, T. Jick, and S. Kerr, *The Boundaryless Organization: Breaking the Chains of Organizational Structure*, revised and updated (San Francisco: Jossey-Bass, 2002).

12. T. Burns and G. M. Stalker, *The Management of Innovation* (London: Tavistock, 1961); and J. A. Courtright, G. T. Fairhurst, and L. E. Rogers, "Interaction Patterns in Organic and Mechanistic Systems," *Academy of Management Journal*, December 1989, pp. 773–802.

13. This analysis is referred to as a contingency approach to organization design. See, for instance, J. M. Pennings, "Structural Contingency Theory: A Reappraisal," in B. M. Staw and L. L. Cummings (eds.), *Research in Organizational Behavior*, vol. 14 (Greenwich, CT: JAI Press, 1992), pp. 267–309.

14. The strategy–structure thesis was originally proposed in A. D. Chandler, Jr., *Strategy and Structure: Chapters in the History of the Industrial Enterprise* (Cambridge, MA: MIT Press, 1962). For an updated analysis, see T. L. Amburgey and T. Dacin, "As the Left Foot Follows the Right? The Dynamics of Strategic and Structural Change," *Academy of Management Journal*, December 1994, pp. 1427–1452.

15. See R. E. Miles and C. C. Snow, *Organizational Strategy, Structure, and Process* (New York: McGraw-Hill, 1978); and I. C. Harris and T. W. Ruefli, "The Strategy/Structure Debate: An Examination of the Performance Implications," *Journal of Management Studies*, June 2000, pp. 587–603.

16. See, for instance, P. M. Blau and R. A. Schoenherr, *The Structure of Organizations* (New York: Basic Books, 1971); and A. C. Bluedorn, "Pilgrim's Progress: Trends and Convergence in Research on Organizational Size and Environments," *Journal of Management*, Summer 1993, pp. 163–192.

17. See F. E. Emery and E. Trist, "The Causal Texture of Organizational Environments," *Human Relations*, February 1965, pp. 21–32; P. Lawrence and J. W. Lorsch, *Organization and Environment: Managing Differentiation and Integration* (Boston: Harvard Business School, Division of Research, 1967); and M. Arndt and B. Bigelow, "Presenting Structural Innovation in an Institutional Environment: Hospitals' Use of Impression Management," *Administrative Science Quarterly*, September 2000, pp. 494–522.

18. See, for instance, L. W. Porter and E. E. Lawler III, "Properties of Organization Structure in Relation to Job Attitudes and Job Behavior," *Psychological Bulletin*, July 1965, pp. 23–51.

19. See, for instance, B. Schneider, H. W. Goldstein, and D. B. Smith, "The ASA Framework: An Update," *Personnel Psychology* 48, no. 4 (1995), pp. 747–773.

20. P. Dvorak, "Making U.S. Management Ideas Work Elsewhere," *Wall Street Journal*, May 22, 2006, p. B3.

21. See, for example, P. R. Harris and R. T. Moran, *Managing Cultural Differences*, 5th ed. (Houston: Gulf Publishing, 1999).

CHAPTER 15

1. See, for example, H. S. Becker, "Culture: A Sociological View," *Yale Review*, Summer 1982, pp. 513–527; and E. H. Schein, *Organizational Culture and Leadership* (San Francisco: Jossey-Bass, 1985), p. 168.

2. This seven-item description is based on C. A. O'Reilly III, J. Chatman, and D. F. Caldwell, "People and Organizational Culture: A Profile Comparison Approach to Assessing Person-Organization Fit," *Academy of Management Journal*, September 1991, pp. 487–516; and J. A. Chatman and K. A. Jehn, "Assessing the Relationship between Industry Characteristics and Organizational Culture: How Different Can You Be?" *Academy of Management Journal*, June 1994, pp. 522–553.

3. The view that there will be consistency among perceptions of organizational culture has been called the "integration" perspective. For a review of this perspective and conflicting approaches, see D. Meyerson and J. Martin, "Cultural Change: An Integration of Three Different Views," *Journal of Management Studies*, November 1987, pp. 623–647; and P. J. Frost, L. F. Moore, M. R. Louis, C. C. Lundberg, and J. Martin (eds.), *Reframing Organizational Culture* (Newbury Park, CA: Sage, 1991).

4. See, for example, J. B. Sorensen, "The Strength of Corporate Culture and the Reliability of Firm Performance," *Administrative Science Quarterly*, March 2002, pp. 70–91.

5. C. Vandenberghe, "Organizational Culture, Person-Culture Fit, and Turnover: A Replication in the Health Care Industry," *Journal of Organizational Behavior*, March 1999, pp. 175–184.

6. See C. A. O'Reilly and J. A. Chatman, "Culture as Social Control: Corporations, Cults, and Commitment," in B. M. Staw and L. L. Cummings (eds.), *Research in Organizational Behavior*, vol. 18 (Greenwich, CT: JAI Press, 1996), pp. 157–200. See also M. Pinae Cunha, "The 'Best Place to Be': Managing Control and Employee Loyalty in a Knowledge-Intensive Company," *Journal of Applied Behavioral Science*, December 2002, pp. 481–495.

7. Sorensen, "The Strength of Corporate Culture and the Reliability of Firm Performance."

8. See, for instance, P. L. Moore, "She's Here to Fix the Xerox," *BusinessWeek*, August 6, 2001, pp. 47–48; and C. Ragavan, "FBI Inc.," *U.S. News & World Report*, June 18, 2001, pp. 15–21.

9. See C. Lindsay, "Paradoxes of Organizational Diversity: Living Within the Paradoxes," in L. R. Jauch and J. L. Wall (eds.), *Proceedings of the 50th Academy of Management Conference* (San Francisco, 1990), pp. 374–378.

10. K. Labich, "No More Crude at Texaco," *Fortune*, September 6, 1999, pp. 205–212; and "Rooting Out Racism," *BusinessWeek*, January 10, 2000, p. 66.

11. A. F. Buono and J. L. Bowditch, *The Human Side of Mergers and Acquisitions: Managing Collisions Between People, Cultures, and Organizations* (San Francisco: Jossey-Bass, 1989); S. Cartwright and C. L. Cooper, "The Role of Culture Compatibility in Successful Organizational Marriages," *Academy of Management Executive*, May 1993, pp. 57–70; E. Krell, "Merging Corporate Cultures," *Training*, May 2001, pp. 68–78; and R. A. Weber and C. F. Camerer, "Cultural Conflict and Merger Failure: An Experimental Approach," *Management Science*, April 2003, pp. 400–412.

12. P. Gumbel, "Return of the Urge to Merge," *Time Europe Magazine*, July 13, 2003, www. time. com/ time/ europe/ magazine/ article/ 0,13005,901030721-464418,00. html.

13. T. A. Lambert, L. T. Eby, and M. P. Reeves, "Predictors of Networking Intensity and Network Quality Among White-Collar Job Seekers," *Journal of Career Development*, June 2006, pp. 351–365; and J. A. Thompson, "Proactive Personality and Job Performance: A Social Capital Perspective," *Journal of Applied Psychology*, September 2005, pp. 1011–1017.

14. E. H. Schein, "Leadership and Organizational Culture," in F. Hesselbein, M. Goldsmith, and R. Beckhard (eds.), *The Leader of the Future* (San Francisco: Jossey-Bass, 1996), pp. 61–62.

15. See, for example, J. R. Harrison and G. R. Carroll, "Keeping the Faith: A Model of Cultural Transmission in Formal Organizations," *Administrative Science Quarterly*, December 1991, pp. 552–582; see also G. George, R. G. Sleeth, and M. A. Siders, "Organizational Culture: Leader Roles, Behaviors, and Reinforcement Mechanisms," *Journal of Business & Psychology*, Summer 1999, pp. 545–560.

16. B. Schneider, H. W. Goldstein, and D. B. Smith, "The ASA Framework: An Update," *Personnel Psychology*, Winter 1995, pp. 747–773; A. L. Kristof, "Person–Organization Fit: An Integrative Review of Its Conceptualizations, Measurement, and Implications," *Personnel Psychology*, Spring 1996, pp. 1–49.

17. D. C. Hambrick and P. A. Mason, "Upper Echelons: The Organization as a Reflection of Its Top Managers," *Academy of Management Review*, April 1984, pp. 193–206.

18. J. Van Maanen and E. H. Schein, "Career Development," in J. R. Hackman and J. L. Suttle (eds.), *Improving Life at Work* (Santa Monica, CA: Goodyear, 1977), pp. 58–62.

19. G. Chen and R. J. Klimoski, "The Impact of Expectations on Newcomer Performance in Teams as Mediated by Work Characteristics, Social Exchanges, and Empowerment," *Academy of Management Journal* 46 (2003), pp. 591–607; C. R. Wanberg and J. D. Kammeyer-Mueller, "Predictors and Outcomes of Proactivity in the Socialization Process," *Journal of Applied Psychology* 85 (2000), pp. 373–385; J. D. Kammeyer-Mueller and C. R. Wanberg, "Unwrapping the Organizational Entry Process: Disentangling Multiple Antecedents and Their Pathways to Adjustment," *Journal of Applied Psychology* 88 (2003), pp. 779–794; and E. W. Morrison, "Longitudinal Study of the Effects of Information Seeking on Newcomer Socialization," *Journal of Applied Psychology* 78 (2003), pp. 173–183.

20. G. Chen and R. J. Klimoski, "The Impact of Expectations on Newcomer Performance in Teams as Mediated by Work Characteristics, Social Exchanges, and Empowerment," *Academy of Management Journal* 46 (2003), pp. 591–607; C. R. Wanberg and J. D. Kammeyer-Mueller, "Predictors and Outcomes of Proactivity in the Socialization Process," *Journal of Applied Psychology* 85 (2000), pp. 373–385; J. D. Kammeyer-Mueller and C. R. Wanberg, "Unwrapping the Organizational Entry Process:

Disentangling Multiple Antecedents and Their Pathways to Adjustment," *Journal of Applied Psychology* 88 (2003), pp. 779–794; and E. W. Morrison, "Longitudinal Study of the Effects of Information Seeking on Newcomer Socialization," *Journal of Applied Psychology* 78 (2003), pp. 173–183. See K. Kamoche, "Rhetoric, Ritualism, and Totemism in Human Resource Management," *Human Relations*, April 1995, pp. 367–385.

21. V. Matthews, "Starting Every Day with a Shout and a Song," *Financial Times*, May 2, 2001, p. 11; and M. Gimein, "Sam Walton Made Us a Promise," *Fortune*, March 18, 2002, pp. 121–130.

22. See B. Victor and J. B. Cullen, "The Organizational Bases of Ethical Work Climates," *Administrative Science Quarterly*, March 1988, pp. 101–125; and R. L. Dufresne, "An Action Learning Perspective on Effective Implementation of Academic Honor Codes," *Group & Organization Management*, April 2004, pp. 201–218.

23. J. A. Byrne, "The Environment Was Ripe for Abuse," *BusinessWeek*, February 25, 2002, pp. 118–120; and A. Raghavan, K. Kranhold, and A. Barrionuevo, "How Enron Bosses Created a Culture of Pushing Limits," *Wall Street Journal*, August 26, 2002, p. A1.

24. D. L. Nelson and C. L. Cooper (eds.), *Positive Organizational Behavior* (London: Sage, 2007); K. S. Cameron, J. E. Dutton, and R. E. Quinn (eds.), *Positive Organizational Scholarship: Foundations of a New Discipline* (San Francisco: Berrett-Koehler, 2003); and F. Luthans and C. M. Youssef, "Emerging Positive Organizational Behavior," *Journal of Management*, June 2007, pp. 321–349.

25. S. Fineman, "On Being Positive: Concerns and Counterpoints," *Academy of Management Review* 31, no. 2 (2006), pp. 270–291.

26. P. Dvorak, "A Firm's Culture Can Get Lost in Translation," *Wall Street Journal*, April 3, 2006, pp. B1, B3; K. Kranhold, "The Immelt Era, Five Years Old, Transforms GE," *Wall Street Journal*, September 11, 2006, pp. B1, B3; and S. McCartney, "Teaching Americans How to Behave Abroad," *Wall Street Journal*, April 11, 2006, pp. D1, D4.

CHAPTER 16

1. P. G. Audia and S. Brion, "Reluctant to Change: Self-Enhancing Responses to Diverging Performance Measures," *Organizational Behavior and Human Decision Processes* 102 (2007), pp. 255–269.

2. M. T. Hannan, L. Pólos, and G. R. Carroll, "The Fog of Change: Opacity and Asperity in Organizations," *Administrative Science Quarterly*, September 2003. pp. 399–432.

3. See K. H. Hammonds, "Practical Radicals," *Fast Company*, September 2000, pp. 162–174; and P. C. Judge, "Change Agents," *Fast Company*, November 2000, pp. 216–226.

4. J. P. Kotter and L. A. Schlesinger, "Choosing Strategies for Change," *Harvard Business Review*, March–April 1979, pp. 106–114.

5. J. E. Dutton, S. J. Ashford, R. M. O'Neill, and K. A. Lawrence, "Moves That Matter: Issue Selling and Organizational Change," *Academy of Management Journal*, August 2001, pp. 716–736.

6. D. M. Herold, D. B. Fedor, and S. D. Caldwell, "Beyond Change Management: A Multilevel Investigation of Contextual and Personal Influences on Employees' Commitment to Change," *Journal of Applied Psychology* 92, no. 4 (2007), pp. 942–951; and G. B. Cunningham, "The Relationships Among Commitment to Change, Coping with Change, and Turnover Intentions," *European Journal of Work and Organizational Psychology* 15, no. 1 (2006), pp. 29–45.

7. D. B. Fedor, S. Caldwell, and D. M. Herold, "The Effects of Organizational Changes on Employee Commitment: A Multilevel Investigation," *Personnel Psychology* 59 (2006), pp. 1–29.

8. S. Oreg, "Personality, Context, and Resistance to Organizational Change," *European Journal of Work and Organizational Psychology* 15, no. 1 (2006), pp. 73–101.

9. J. A. LePine, J. A. Colquitt, and A. Erez, "Adaptability to Changing Task Contexts: Effects of General Cognitive Ability, Conscientiousness, and Openness to Experience," *Personnel Psychology*, Fall, 2000, pp. 563–593; and T. A. Judge, C. J. Thoresen, V. Pucik, and T. M. Welbourne, "Managerial Coping with Organizational Change: A Dispositional Perspective," *Journal of Applied Psychology*, February 1999, pp. 107–122.

10. K. Lewin, *Field Theory in Social Science* (New York: Harper & Row, 1951).

11. P. G. Audia, E. A. Locke, and K. G. Smith, "The Paradox of Success: An Archival and a Laboratory Study of Strategic Persistence Following Radical Environmental Change," *Academy of Management Journal*, October 2000, pp. 837–853.

12. J. B. Sorensen, "The Strength of Corporate Culture and the Reliability of Firm Performance," *Administrative Science Quarterly*, March 2002, pp. 70–91.

13. J. Amis, T. Slack, and C. R. Hinings, "The Pace, Sequence, and Linearity of Radical Change," *Academy of Management Journal*, February 2004, pp. 15–39; and E. Autio, H. J. Sapienza, and J. G. Almeida, "Effects of Age at Entry, Knowledge Intensity, and Imitability on International Growth," *Academy of Management Journal*, October 2000, pp. 909–924.

14. J. P. Kotter, "Leading Changes: Why Transformation Efforts Fail," *Harvard Business Review*, March–April 1995, pp. 59–67.

15. For a sampling of various OD definitions, see N. Nicholson (ed.), *Encyclopedic Dictionary of Organizational Behavior* (Malden, MA: Blackwell, 1998), pp. 359–361.

16. See, for instance, R. Lines, "Influence of Participation in Strategic Change: Resistance, Organizational Commitment and Change Goal Achievement," *Journal of Change Management*, September 2004, pp. 193–215.

17. S. Highhouse, "A History of the T-Group and Its Early Application in Management Development," *Group Dynamics: Theory, Research, & Practice*, December 2002, pp. 277–290.

18. J. E. Edwards and M. D. Thomas, "The Organizational Survey Process: General Steps and Practical Considerations," in P. Rosenfeld, J. E. Edwards, and M. D. Thomas (eds.), *Improving Organizational Surveys: New Directions, Methods, and Applications* (Newbury Park, CA: Sage, 1993), pp. 3–28.

19. E. H. Schein, *Process Consultation: Its Role in Organizational Development*, 2nd ed. (Reading, MA: Addison-Wesley, 1988), p. 9. See also E. H. Schein, *Process Consultation Revisited: Building Helpful Relationships* (Reading, MA: Addison-Wesley, 1999).

20. Schein, *Process Consultation*.

21. See, for example, R. Fry, F. Barrett, J. Seiling, and D. Whitney (eds.), *Appreciative Inquiry & Organizational Transformation: Reports from the Field* (Westport, CT: Quorum, 2002); J. K. Barge and C. Oliver, "Working with Appreciation in Managerial Practice," *Academy of Management Review*, January 2003, pp. 124–142; and D. van der Haar and D. M. Hosking, "Evaluating Appreciative Inquiry: A Relational Constructionist Perspective," *Human Relations*, August 2004, pp. 1017–1036.

22. D. Anfuso, "Core Values Shape W. L. Gore's Innovative Culture," *Workforce*, March 1999, pp. 48–51; and A. Harrington, "Who's Afraid of a New Product?" *Fortune*, November 10, 2003, pp. 189–192.

23. See, for instance, R. M. Kanter, "When a Thousand Flowers Bloom: Structural, Collective and Social Conditions for Innovation in Organizations," in B. M. Staw and L. L. Cummings (eds.), *Research in Organizational Behavior*, vol. 10 (Greenwich, CT: JAI Press, 1988), pp. 169–211.

24. F. Damanpour, "Organizational Innovation: A Meta-Analysis of Effects of Determinants and Moderators," *Academy of Management Journal*, September 1991, p. 557.

25. Ibid., pp. 555–590.

26. See P. R. Monge, M. D. Cozzens, and N. S. Contractor, "Communication and Motivational Predictors of the Dynamics of Organizational Innovation," *Organization Science*, May 1992, pp. 250–274.

27. J. M. Howell and C. A. Higgins, "Champions of Change," *Business Quarterly*, Spring 1990, pp. 31–32; and D. L. Day, "Raising Radicals: Different Processes for Championing Innovative Corporate Ventures," *Organization Science*, May 1994, pp. 148–172.

28. Howell and Higgins, "Champions of Change."

29. See, for example, H. S. Gitlow, *Quality Management Systems: A Practical Guide for Improvement* (Boca Raton, FL: CRC Press, 2001); and J. W. Cortada, *The Quality Yearbook 2001* (New York: McGraw-Hill, 2001).

30. M. Hammer and J. Champy, *Reengineering the Corporation: A Manifesto for Business Revolution* (New York: Harper-Business, 1993).

31. See K. Slobogin, "Many U.S. Employees Feel Overworked, Stressed, Study Says." Accessed May 16, 2001, at www.cnn.com; and S. Armour, "Rising Job Stress Could Affect Bottom Line," *USA Today*, July 29, 2003, p. 1B.

32. Adapted from R. S. Schuler, "Definition and Conceptualization of Stress in Organizations," *Organizational Behavior and Human Performance*, April 1980, p. 189. For an updated review of definitions, see C. L. Cooper, P. J. Dewe, and M. P. O'Driscoll, *Organizational Stress: A Review and Critique of Theory, Research, and Applications* (Thousand Oaks, CA: Sage, 2002).

33. See M. A. Cavanaugh, W. R. Boswell, M. V. Roehling, and J. W. Boudreau, "An Empirical Examination of Self-Reported Work Stress Among U.S. Managers," *Journal of Applied Psychology*, February 2000, pp. 65–74.

34. J. A. LePine, M. A. LePine, and C. L. Jackson, "Challenge and Hindrance Stress: Relationships with Exhaustion, Motivation to Learn, and Learning Performance," *Journal of Applied Psychology*, October 2004, pp. 883–891; and M. A. Cavanaugh, W. R. Boswell, M. V. Roehling, and J. W. Boudreau, "An Empirical Examination of Self-reported Work Stress Among U.S. Managers," *Journal of Applied Psychology*, February 2000, pp. 65–74.

35. E. Demerouti, A. B. Bakker, F. Nachreiner, and W. B. Schaufeli, "The Job Demands-Resources Model of Burnout," *Journal of Applied Psychology*, June 2001, pp. 499–512; N. W. Van Yperen and O. Janssen, "Fatigued and Dissatisfied or Fatigued but Satisfied? Goal Orientations and Responses to High Job Demands," *Academy of Management Journal*, December 2002, pp. 1,161–71; and N. W. Van Yperen and M. Hagedoorn, "Do High Job Demands Increase Intrinsic Motivation or Fatigue or Both? The Role of Job Control and Job Social Support," *Academy of Management Journal*, June 2003, pp. 339–348.

36. See, for example, the special edition on organizational learning in *Organizational Dynamics*, Autumn 1998; P. Senge, *The Dance of Change: The Challenges to Sustaining Momentum in Learning Organizations* (New York: Doubleday/Currency, 1999); A. M. Webber, "Will Companies Ever Learn?" *Fast Company*, October 2000, pp. 275–82; R. Snell, "Moral Foundations of the Learning Organization," *Human Relations*, March 2001, pp. 319–342; M. M. Brown and J. L. Brudney, "Learning Organizations in the Public Sector? A Study of Police Agencies Employing Information and Technology to Advance Knowledge," *Public Administration Review*, January/February 2003, pp. 30–43; and T. B. Lawrence, M. K. Mauws, B. Dyck, and R. F. Kleysen, "The Politics of Organizational Learning: Integrating Power into the 4I Framework," *Academy of Management Review*, January 2005, pp. 180–191.

37. D. H. Kim, "The Link Between Individual and Organizational Learning," *Sloan Management Review*, Fall 1993, p. 37.

38. C. Argyris and D. A. Schon, *Organizational Learning* (Reading, MA: Addison-Wesley, 1978).

39. B. Dumaine, "Mr. Learning Organization," *Fortune*, October 17, 1994, p. 148.

40. F. Kofman and P. M. Senge, "Communities of Commitment: The Heart of Learning Organizations," *Organizational Dynamics*, Autumn 1993, pp. 5–23.

41. Dumaine, "Mr. Learning Organization," p. 154.

42. See S. Shane, S. Venkataraman, and I. MacMillan, "Cultural Differences in Innovation Championing Strategies," *Journal of Management* 21, no. 5 (1995), pp. 931–952.

43. J. Chen, C. Silverthorne, and J. Hung, "Organization Communication, Job Stress, Organizational Commitment, and Job Performance of Accounting Professionals in Taiwan and America," *Leadership & Organization Development Journal* 27, no. 4 (2006), pp. 242–249; and C. Liu, P. E. Spector, and L. Shi, "Cross-National Job Stress: A Quantitative and Qualitative Study," *Journal of Organizational Behavior*, February 2007, pp. 209–239.

44. H. M. Addae and X. Wang, "Stress at Work: Linear and Curvilinear Effects of Psychological-, Job-, and Organization-Related Factors: An Exploratory Study of Trinidad and Tobago," *International Journal of Stress Management*, November 2006, pp. 476–493.

45. P. E. Spector et al., "A Cross-National Comparative Study of Work-Family Stressors, Working Hours, and Well-Being: China and Latin America Versus the Anglo World," *Personnel Psychology*, Spring 2004, pp. 119–142.

Glindex (Combined Glossary and Index)

Definitions are shown in *italics*.

H

Q

Quality and productivity, improving, 9

R

Radio Shack, 151
Rationality, myth of, 96
Rational persuasion, 184
Reagan, Ronald, 104–105, 167
Reference groups, 117
Referent power, 183
Reflexivity, 138
Regulations, formal, 41
Relationship conflict, 196
Representative participation, 87–88
Resistance point, 203
Resources, 134, 256
Rewarding employees
    bonuses, 90
    employee recognition programs, 92–93
    employee stock ownership plan (ESOP), 91
    external equity, 88
    flexible benefits, 91–92
    gainsharing, 91
    internal equity, 88
    intrinsic rewards, 92–93
    merit-based pay plans, 90
    pay structure, establishing a, 88
    piece-rate pay plans, 89
    profit-sharing plans, 90
    skill-based pay plans, 90
    variable-pay programs, 89–91
    work teams, 139–140
Reward systems, 41, 134
Rights, 41–42
Ringelmann, Max, 121
Risk aversion, 41
Rituals, 240
    repetitive sequences of activities that express and reinforce the key values of the organization
Roehm, Julie, 151
Rokeach, Milton, 23
Rokeach Value Survey (RVS), 23
Role conflict, 116
    when an individual finds that compliance with one role requirement may make it difficult to comply with another
Role expectations, 116
    the way others believe you should act in a given situation
Role identity, 115
    certain attitudes and actual behaviors are consistent with a role
Roles, 115
    a set of expected behavior patterns attributed to someone occupying a given position in a social unit
Roosevelt, Franklin, 104–105
Rules, 41
Rumors, 149–150

Russia
    change, attitude towards, 259–260
    job satisfaction, 60

S

Saban, Nick, 89
Safety needs, 63
SAP, 70
Satisfactory state of affairs, problem versus, 36
Satisfiers and dissatisfiers, comparison of, 65
Saturn Corp., 214
Scapegoating, 189
Schiller, Michael, 155
Schwartz, Jonathan, 152–153
Sears, Roebuck, 9, 58–59, 218
Selection
    change, 249
    emotions and moods and, 106
    leaders, 177
    organizational culture, 235–236
    stress, managing, 256
    team players, 139
Selective perception, 35, 154–155
    any characteristic that makes a person, object, or event stand out will increase the probability that it will be perceived
Self-actualization, 63
Self-actualization needs, 63
Self-efficacy theory, 71–73
Self-managed work teams, 131–132
    culture and, 141
    groups of employees who perform highly related or interdependent jobs and take on responsibilities of their former supervisors
Self-monitoring, 20–21
Self-promotion, 190, 191
Self-protection, 189
Self-serving bias, 35
Sender, 144
Sensitivity training, 251
Shared meaning, 233
Shea & Gould, 201
Short-term orientation, 28
Simple structure, 218–219
Singapore, 29
Singapore Airlines, 83
Situation, 33
Size
    group, 121–122
    organization, 225
Skill-based pay plans, 90
    sets pay levels on the basis of how many skills employees have or how many jobs they can do
Skilling, Jeff, 174
Skill variety, role of, 81
Sleep, 102–103
Sloan School of Management, 2
Smith Corona, 9
Social activities, 102
Social cognitive theory, 71–73